SMARTER GROWTH

SMARTER GROWTH
Market-Based Strategies for
Land-Use Planning in the 21st Century

Edited by Randall G. Holcombe
and Samuel R. Staley

Contributions in Economics and Economic History, Number 224

GREENWOOD PRESS
Westport, Connecticut • London

Library of Congress Cataloging-in-Publication Data

Smarter growth : market-based strategies for land-use planning in the 21st century /
edited by Randall G. Holcombe and Samuel R. Staley.
        p.   cm.—(Contributions in economics and economic history, ISSN 0084–9235 ; no.
    224)
    Includes bibliographical references and index.
    ISBN 0–313–31595–7 (alk. paper)
    1. Land use—United States—Planning.   2. Land use—Economic aspects—United
States.   3. Land use—Environmental aspects—United States.   4. City planning—United
States.   5. Cities and towns—United States—Growth—Management.   I. Holcombe,
Randall G.   II. Staley, Sam, 1961–   III. Series.
HD205.S6 2001
333.73′0973—dc21   00–061701

British Library Cataloguing in Publication Data is available.

Library of Congress Catalog Card Number: 00–061701
ISBN: 0–313–31595–7
ISSN: 0084–9235

First published in 2001

Greenwood Press, 88 Post Road West, Westport, CT 06881
An imprint of Greenwood Publishing Group, Inc.
www.greenwood.com

Printed in the United States of America

The paper used in this book complies with the
Permanent Paper Standard issued by the National
Information Standards Organization (Z39.48–1984).

10 9 8 7 6 5 4 3 2 1

Contents

Preface

This volume is based on a conference held in March 2000, at Florida State University in Tallahassee. The conference was sponsored by Florida State University's DeVoe L. Moore Center for the Study of Critical Issues in Economic Policy and Government. The DeVoe Moore Center was created to study the social, political, and economic impacts of state and local government policy.

At the transition from the twentieth to the twenty-first century, land-use planning and growth management have emerged as two of the most visible and controversial issues in state and local government policy. Until the 1970s, land-use planning was almost exclusively the province of local government, but toward the century's end, state governments became increasingly involved. As the twenty-first century begins, there are signs that the federal government is poised to increase its involvement, in part through environmental regulation, but also perhaps by more directly developing policies on optimal land use. Given these trends, these issues seemed ripe for exploration in an academic setting.

Land-use planning typically emphasizes the governmental regulations and restrictions limiting the ways that landowners can use and develop their property. The editors of this volume take a more market-oriented approach. Once the conference topic was determined, one of the volume's editors (Holcombe) at the DeVoe Moore Center contacted the other (Staley) about their cooperating to put together both the conference and the conference volume. The conference was developed from the beginning as a way to generate this volume, and our first step was to draw up an outline of topics that we wanted to cover. Next we contacted the chapter authors to try to interest them in addressing these topics in a book chapter. We deliberately looked for authors who share with us the market-oriented approach to land-use planning so that the volume would have a consistent theme. We felt that the ideas of those who want more government involvement in land-use planning were already well represented, especially in the public debate, and wanted to present an intellectual foundation for the idea that market mechanisms are in many cases superior to government planning in public policy regarding land use. This volume explains that point of view.

We are indebted to a number of individuals for helping us make this volume a reality. Obviously, the volume would not exist without the contributions of our authors, but we want to say a special word of thanks to them for meeting our deadlines, contributing productively to our conference, and adding their views to the policy debate. David Rasmussen, Director of the DeVoe Moore Center, helped at all stages to organize our conference, Harriet Crawford at the DeVoe Moore Center attended to many of the conference details and produced the final manuscript that we sent to the publisher, and Karen Wells modified and typeset the copyedited manuscript. The discussants at the conference, who offered critical comments and helped improve our chapters, were Jeff Bielling, Maria Cahill, Sam Cassela, Dale Eacker, Richard Feiock, and Tom Pierce. Finally, we offer our thanks to DeVoe Moore, who has taken an active interest in the center that bears his name.

Randall G. Holcombe
Samuel R. Staley

Chapter 1

Land-Use Planning:
An Overview of the Issues

RANDALL G. HOLCOMBE AND SAMUEL R. STALEY

The United States saw major changes in land-use patterns in the last half of the twentieth century, largely as a result of rising incomes, widespread automobile ownership, and the more decentralized living patterns that automobile ownership allows. One result has been improved living conditions in the form of larger houses and the movement toward single-family detached housing. As Americans have found better housing conditions in the suburbs, their migration also has resulted in longer travel distances, additional infrastructure costs, traffic congestion, the more rapid development of farmland and undeveloped areas, and the decline of inner cities. The public policy response to these effects of sprawling development has been to try to restrict private development in various ways and, increasingly, to use government mandates to control private land use. This volume critically examines both government land-use policies and the arguments that support them, and explores the market alternatives to government land-use planning. The contributors to this volume show that in many cases the problems of sprawling development have been misunderstood and overstated, and that land-use policy can be improved by using market mechanisms rather than through central planning by land-use bureaucracies. Moreover, these market-based mechanisms are more consistent with the underlying social, political, and economic institutional foundations of American culture.

PUBLIC CONCERN ABOUT SPRAWL

Land-use planning issues are becoming increasingly visible in the public policy arena. Up until the 1970s land-use issues were almost entirely the province of local government. Some states, most notably Oregon, Vermont, and Hawaii, went so far as to implement statewide growth management laws. Oregon's planning law has received national attention for its comprehensiveness and top-down nature. Supporters of government land-use planning hold it as a model for what states should be doing, while opponents argue that the results show why such planning is undesirable. In the 1980s and 1990s states became increasingly involved in land-use issues, and the issues related to urban sprawl became an ever-larger part of the public debate. By the mid-1990s, nineteen states had enacted statewide growth management laws or convened task forces to study the impacts on development on open space and farmland (Staley 1999). At the end of the decade, Vice President Al Gore brought land-use planning into the national arena with his promotion of "Smart Growth" to offset the negative effects of urban sprawl. In his January 1999 State of the Union Address, President Bill Clinton devoted 17 percent of his time to land use, land preservation, and urban development issues, more than any other single policy area except for foreign policy. At first glance, federalizing sprawl as a policy issue could generate significant political benefits for politicians, regardless of the merits of federal involvement, because such policies could generate political support. After all, most antisprawl measures pass at the local ballot box (P. Myers 1999; Staley 1999).

As the twenty-first century unfolds, the antisprawl movement seems to be facing rougher waters. While pressure to do something about growth has lifted urban sprawl's profile in the political consciousness, consensus on what to do about it has been elusive. The following examples show that citizens do not always favor antisprawl policies: Citizens in Berkeley, California, one of the nation's progressive hotspots, turned down a proposal to increase the city's density because residents feared it would change the character of their community; voters in Portland, Oregon, turned down additional bonding authority for the next leg in its ambitious light rail-transit program; and, voters in the California communities of San Ramon, Livingston, and Livermore turned down proposals that would have subjected new development to even more public scrutiny. In addition, increasing evidence suggests that politicizing land use decisions through mechanisms such as "ballot-box zoning" imposes significant costs on local communities in terms of growth (Staley 2001). Despite some cases in which specific antisprawl policies have met with political defeat, using government to combat the effects of sprawl remains politically popular.

While the emphasis in land-use planning primarily has been on ways that government can control private land-use decisions, these policies often have minimal direct effects on people who are already living in homes within the affected area. Even growth boundaries, one of the most popular policy tools in the conventional Smart Growth tool box (Staley, Edgens, and Mildner 1999), impose regulatory controls on future land uses, not on existing home owners and residents. Thus, landowners and developers often find themselves pitted against local residents who want to preserve the existing conditions in their area. One reason many antisprawl or Smart Growth policies have failed to garner broader support at the ballot box has been their focus on specific proposals that directly affect current residents.

Despite the apparent popularity of government restrictions on land use, a number of experts advocate a more market-based approach to land-use planning. This volume draws together the ideas of a number of scholars in this area. By drawing on these experts, this volume presents a market-oriented approach to land-use planning. We believe that this approach is more consistent with the general political and economic values and institutions that form America's complex system of state and local government. Indeed, the market-oriented approach is more likely to be successful at addressing the specific problems that Americans perceive as the most negative or problematic consequences of growth, including traffic congestion, infrastructure costs, and loss of open space.

Too often, when people perceive problems, they argue that the government should do something to remedy those problems. The resulting government action often cuts off the ability of the market to respond to problems, and government solutions often create new problems themselves. This volume looks at land-use planning in that spirit, and shows how market mechanisms can create sensible land-use decisions that enhance the quality of life. The contributors argue that market mechanisms often do a better job of land-use allocation than government planning. By collecting those arguments in one volume, we hope it will play a role in the debate on land-use planning in the twenty-first century.

THE ISSUES

Land-use planning issues could not have become a part of the political debate without the emergence of problems clearly visible to the general public. While one might construct a long list of issues that have created concern, only a few issues are highly visible and provide the foundation for political demands for smarter growth. The most visible issue is traffic congestion. In growing areas such as Austin; Atlanta; Washington, D.C.; the San Francisco Bay Area; or Southern California, people find themselves driving longer distances and stuck in traffic more often. Another important issue is an increased demand for environmental protection. People see development eating into farmland and undeveloped natural areas, and threatening species of plants and animals as well as whole ecosystems. A third concern is the desire to preserve local communities rather than let development rob them of their character and individuality. Every place starts to look the same as Wal-Marts and McDonalds displace local shops and restaurants. When examined in more detail, one finds that some of these issues are based on misconceptions about the effects of development patterns, and in many cases the solutions offered by Smart Growth advocates will make the underlying problems worse.

Chapter 2 examines land-use trends to show that concerns about development reducing farmland are misplaced. Developed areas in the United States consume less than 6 percent of the total land area, but most people do not realize how much of the nation is undeveloped because the majority live in the small percentage that is developed. In fact, three quarters of the American population live on less than 4 percent of the total land area (Staley 1999). Farmland is disappearing at a faster rate than land is being developed. Thus, the reduction in farm acreage is not due to development consuming it; rather, increasing agricultural productivity has meant that this "lost" farmland has, in fact, been left fallow or converted to forest, pasture, or park because less land is needed to produce the nation's food supply. Because of increasing agricultural productivity, the amount of farmland in the United States will continue to decline in the next several decades independent of development.

Because so much of the nation remains undeveloped, concern that development is consuming the natural environment is also misplaced. Of course, there are valuable environmental amenities that should be preserved, and these amenities should be set aside and put off limits to development. However, because so much of the nation remains undeveloped, there is little environmental gain to be had by pursuing policies intended to increase development density. Indeed, Kenneth Green argues in Chapter 5 that higher density development is likely to worsen the environment. Pollution levels are higher in more densely developed areas, and denser development reduces the ability of the natural environment to absorb pollutants. For example, in higher density development, storm water is less likely to be absorbed into the ground, and instead is channeled through storm drains along with pollutants washed from roads and rooftops. Americans support environmental preservation as a matter of public policy, as they should, but policies aimed at creating denser development patterns offer no significant environmental benefits. Despite concerns about the effects of urban sprawl on agriculture and the environment, there are no clear environmental benefits to the types of development pushed by Smart Growth advocates.

Robert Bruegmann (chapter 9) and Steven Hayward (chapter 13) provide insightful analyses of the impact of urban sprawl on local communities, on density, and on revitalizing cities. The general trend in cities everywhere is toward less density, for two related reasons. First, as people become wealthier, one of the things they want to buy with their increased wealth is more space. Cities like New York and Paris, often considered models for new urbanists, consistently saw reductions in their population densities throughout the twentieth century, and there is every reason to think that this trend will continue into the twenty-first century, both for big cities and in all developed areas. The second factor is the increased availability of private automobile transportation. The widespread availability of automobiles has meant that people do not have to live within walking distance of work or mass transit, giving them more locational freedom. People have chosen suburban living because land prices are lower, giving them the option to have more living space and their own yards. The land-use patterns criticized as urban sprawl have enabled people to have higher standards of living than ever before.

Automobile travel offers many advantages, including flexibility about when to travel and the ability to make deviations (such as stopping at a store on the way home from work) without advance planning. Shopping is more convenient because autos can carry more cargo than one can manage on mass transit or walking, and this in turn has enabled people to shop at supermarkets and discount stores that are farther from home. While many people lament the passing of the corner grocery and local shops, they have been replaced by larger chains because they are able to offer better prices and selections, further enhancing the overall standard of living. The demise of local shops and thriving downtowns are not solely the result of decentralized living patterns, however. Some problems with urban areas have been brought on by counterproductive policies that have produced high taxes and high crime rates, pushing productive citizens away. Many cities have pursued policies that have revitalized their downtowns, but this is best done by making those areas attractive destinations rather than by preventing development elsewhere.

Development patterns that Smart Growth advocates are trying to reverse are the result of the massive shift toward automobile travel in the second half of the twentieth century, and once all the issues are examined, it becomes apparent that transportation issues lie at the heart of the debate on urban sprawl. Land-use patterns have always revolved around transportation corridors, and up until about 1850 that primarily meant waterways. Cities grew on harbors and on navigable rivers. In the last half of the nineteenth century rail transportation became more important. Cities on major rail lines thrived, and major rail hubs became urban centers. In the last half of the twentieth century, roads became the key transportation corridors defining land-use patterns.

Nobody disputes the importance of transportation to issues of land-use planning, but how public policy should respond is more open to debate. Smart Growth advocates want to discourage automobile use and put resources into mass transit rather than roads, but the contributors to this volume question the wisdom of that approach. Mass transit makes up only about 5 percent of commuter trips nationwide at the beginning of the twenty-first century, and increasing wealth as well as lower population density even in the largest cities work against increasing its market share. Even if mass transit's market share doubled, it would still account for only 10 percent of commuters, so it would barely have an impact on traffic congestion and pollution levels.

A market-oriented approach to land-use planning needs to account for the fact that the twenty-first century will rely mainly on the automobile for transportation, and mass transit should be seen as a social program oriented mainly toward helping those who do not have access to automobile travel. For more effective land-use planning, policymakers should focus their attention more on the design of transportation corridors to accommodate automobile travel, and less on constraining what private landowners can do with their property. If transportation corridors are planned well in advance, then market incentives will produce efficient land-use patterns without government involvement (Siegan 1970, 1972). Commercial development will naturally gravitate toward major intersections and busy thoroughfares, while residential development will tend to be away from the busy corridors, but conveniently located to shopping and employment opportunities. Chapter 8 explains this idea in more detail and, given the importance of transportation issues to land-use planning, chapters 3, 4, and 12 also focus heavily on transportation issues.

Trends at the beginning of the twenty-first century reveal lower density development, even in the highest density cities, and increased reliance on the automobile for transportation. Smart Growth advocates hope to reverse these trends by using government policies to increase density and reduce automobile use. The prospects for success are not good, because market forces are working against them. Lower density living and travel by personal automobile are things that people want to buy to increase their standard of living, so the trends the Smart Growth advocates are trying to reverse are a consequence of rising incomes. If they succeed, the result will be a lower standard of living for people who are forced out of their cars and pushed into more crowded living conditions. The market approach to land-use planning recognizes these trends as manifestations of higher standards of living, and tries to accommodate them while minimizing their costs.

THE POLITICAL RESPONSE

It is one thing to identify problems, and another to find solutions to them. This is where Smart Growth solutions often diverge from the wishes of local residents and policymakers. Many Smart Growth advocates have mistakenly interpreted concern about the pace and pattern of growth as a public mandate for a particular type of growth. Indeed, the conventional Smart Growth movement often embraces an idealized urban form—small lots, high-density residential living, mixed uses, and mass transit-oriented—that is inconsistent with the real-world development of the modern American city. The twenty-first century city looks more like the low-density, automobile-oriented suburb of the Digital Age than the nineteenth century high-density, mixed-use city of the industrial era.

Advocates of more government control of land use and urban development often view the low-density character of the current urban form as both unsustainable and inconsistent with practical cities. Growth management policies are geared instead toward limiting low-density choices in order to reconstruct the nineteenth century inner-city neighborhood. Thus, urban growth boundaries are advocated as ways to limit large lot residential housing development. In Portland, Oregon, the nation's most comprehensive growth boundary (covering 3 counties and 24 cities) is helping to reduce lot sizes from more than 10,000 square feet to less than 8,000 square feet. Similarly, to reduce American dependence on the automobile, significant investments in mass transit are advocated, including record spending on light-rail systems in dozens of cities throughout the nation.

These responses, however, rarely achieve the goals of their advocates. The growth boundaries in Portland are contributing to rapidly rising housing costs that are pushing tens of thousands of housing units below thresholds of affordability (Staley, Edgens, and Mildner 1999). As housing demand is pushed inside the growth boundary, land costs are increasing dramatically and older housing renovations cost more than would be true without the boundary. Similarly, light rail systems have had virtually no impact on reducing congestion (Richmond 1999).

Meanwhile, conventional Smart Growth policies are dramatically changing the nature of local government in the United States. Florida's Growth Management Act (enacted in 1985) created a top-down planning system that gave the state's Department of Community Affairs much greater scope in shaping the form of local cities and counties. Indeed, one of the catch phrases of the state-level growth management movement is "consistency," the process of tying local land-use plans to specific state goals. The result is less local control and weakened home rule. Thus, power and authority over land development and urban planning are centralized at the state level. In most cases, this centralization of authority is justified on the grounds that continued urban sprawl has pervasive negative impacts that require government intervention.

On an academic level, more than thirty years of research has failed to find consistent negative impacts of low-density residential and commercial development on American communities and society. *The Costs of Sprawl-Revisited*, a survey of more than 475 studies on urban sprawl, identified more than 42 costs and benefits of sprawl in the scholarly and professional literature (Burchell et al. 1998, table 15, pp. 130-31). The researchers categorized each of these costs and benefits based on whether they found "general agreement," "some agreement," "no clear outcome," and "substantial disagreement" in the literature. Overall, the authors found "general agreement" on only six costs/benefits of sprawl: Costs included increased vehicle miles traveled (VMT), more auto trips, lost agricultural land, and lost environmentally fragile/sensitive lands; benefits included less congestion and the automobile as a more efficient transportation mode. "Some agreement" was found for fifteen costs and benefits, including the belief that sprawl had negative fiscal impacts on local communities, reduced the effectiveness of transit, and fostered spatial mismatch between low-income workers in inner cities and jobs in the suburbs. In addition, the literature found "some agreement" that low-density residential development was less costly for private developers, fostered greater economic well-being, and enhanced municipal diversity and choice. The authors found that "no clear outcome" could be gleaned from the literature on another eighteen costs/benefits. "Substantial disagreement" existed in the literature on two costs of sprawl—whether sprawl created more air pollution and whether it fostered suburban exclusion. In effect, the relative costs and benefits of low density, automobile-oriented development seem to be very local.

Given the disagreement in the scholarly literature and debate, consensus on political responses to the problems associated with sprawl become problematic.

Market-based approaches to planning provide a way out of this political and scholarly morass.

MARKET MECHANISMS

The theme of this volume is that market mechanisms can be employed in response to the land-use issues that were raised earlier in this chapter. Critics of this market approach will argue that the problems themselves were caused by the market mechanism, and the solution lies in controlling the market and insulating land-use decisions from market forces. This criticism misses the mark, for several reasons.

First, many features of late twentieth-century development that are labeled problems are really amenities that people want. While some argue about the wastefulness of single-family detached homes on large lots, the people who live in those homes prefer them to attached housing or apartment living, and want to have their own yards. If they did not, options remain almost everywhere for apartment living (and people who prefer that can choose it). As the nation has become wealthier, a lifestyle that was accessible to only a few of the highest-income Americans has now become accessible to the middle class, and even to poorer Americans.

Second, the market will not respond to problems before they become recognized (and the same is true of government). As suburban living became more desirable, and the increasing availability of automobiles made that option viable to more people, the market responded by producing suburbs. As traffic congestion has increased, and as people have lamented not having nearby shopping and work locations, private developers have responded by moving more toward mixed-use development. If people view living patterns as desirable, the market will provide those living patterns because there are financial incentives to do so. Thus, government land-use planning is often responding to issues that the market would respond to by itself, if left alone.

Third, many people have not recognized that some of the problems associated with urban sprawl are the result of poor government planning, and that better planning for roads and other infrastructure would create better private land-use decisions without government mandates. Private land-use decisions tend to be made in relation to infrastructure location, especially transportation corridors. When roads took over the central role as transportation corridors from rail lines, it meant some readjustment of land-use patterns—and sometimes major readjustment—as shippers and commuters altered their transportation mode choices. If developers know where major transportation corridors will be located, market incentives create efficient land-use patterns. Commercial activities are best located on major thoroughfares and at busy intersections. Because of the traffic, these locations are undesirable as residential locations. Land-use patterns will naturally evolve in an efficient manner if the infrastructure is planned well in advance. Thus, the solution is better planning for government resources, not increased government planning for how private individuals can use their property (see chapter 8).

Fourth, people operate under the tacit assumption that if there is agreement on a problem with land-use patterns, government planning can remedy the problem. When examined critically, this assumption fails for several reasons (see Holcombe 1995 and chapter 10). For one thing, many people might agree on a problem (the traffic is too heavy on certain roads), but there are many possible solutions and there will be less agreement on the appropriate way to deal with the problem. As a result, even though many people recognize the problem, few people would be satisfied with the solution that is implemented. Furthermore, government solutions are often political solutions that are hammered out by compromise, not imposed by omniscient planners. The political process is subject to problems, such as influence by special interests, that compromise everyone's idea of what would make an ideal plan.

In contrast to political solutions, market mechanisms provide the incentive to produce an outcome that maximizes the value of property. For example, many subdivisions include common areas with amenities such as swimming pools and tennis courts and provide local recreational opportunities. These amenities were built because developers believe they increase the price they can get for the homes they sell. Similarly, developers often make provisions for commercial areas located near residences for the same reason. Problems can arise when developers' actions impose costs on other residents, but these costs also can be controlled by using market mechanisms. For example, local governments have been accused of underpricing access to infrastructure such as sewer and water lines, thus creating incentives for sprawl; where this happens, charging full cost for such hookups and other public services is an obvious market mechanism that can be used to remedy the inefficiency.

THE MARKET ORDER

One of the great debates of the twentieth century was whether central economic planning was superior to a market economy for the allocation of economic resources. Reputable economists argued the merits of central planning as a superior method of allocating resources. Nobel laureate Paul Samuelson (1973, p. 883) argued in his best-selling introductory textbook that even though at that time the Soviet Union had a per capita income about half that of the United States, the superior Soviet economic system would grow faster. Samuelson predicted that the Soviet Union's per capita income would catch up to the United States perhaps as soon as 1990, and almost surely by 2010. By 1990, the Soviet Union had collapsed and the consensus of opinion was that market economies are superior to government-planned economies as a method of producing goods and services. However, in many areas, including land-use planning, people continue to argue that government planning is needed because, while the market system is good at producing goods and services, it often works against producing a high quality of life.

Advocates of government control argue that it is necessary for someone to coordinate the activities of many different landowners because the market mechanism provides no guarantees that the decisions made by some property owners will be in the public interest. Thus, government planning is needed to produce an orderly and efficient pattern of land use. However, the same characteristics that make market allocation of resources for the production of goods and services superior to government planning also apply to government planning of land use.

In the argument for central economic planning, one of the criticisms levied against the market was that, through central planning, the government could assure that everyone was working together to achieve mutually consistent goals. With markets, they said, people's activities would not necessarily be coordinated for the public good. The same arguments have been made for land-use planning.

In the case of the market economy, the answer to this criticism has been known for centuries. Adam Smith argued that in a market economy, individuals pursuing their own self interests are led by an "invisible hand" to do what is best for the whole society. People do what is best for everyone because the market system rewards activity that is valuable to others. That same argument applies to issues of land use. A related advantage is that market prices provide information to everyone about the value of alternative uses of resources (Hayek 1948). This is true whether one is considering the value of using milk to produce ice cream versus yogurt, or whether one is considering the value of using land to build townhouses versus single family detached homes.

The market economy works so well to allocate resources that people take it for granted. Imagine someone suddenly developing a craving for Cheerios. How could that person's desire be satisfied? Americans take it for granted that the person, at the spur of the moment, could go to a supermarket and buy some, without ordering the good ahead of time, and without doing any advance planning. Indeed, American consumers take this so much for granted that they become irritated if the good they want is not at the store when they want it. Consumers in the former Soviet Union often had to stand in long lines and had little choice in the goods that were available to them.

A reflection on the operation of the market economy shows that order can be produced without government planning. It is not that no one is planning; rather, everyone makes their own plans, and those plans are coordinated by market forces with the plans of everyone else (Hayek 1961). Land-use decisions can be coordinated by the invisible hand of the market in the same way.

In the twenty-first century, the efficient use of a parcel of land depends critically on its location relative to the transportation network. As noted earlier, commercial locations will be led to major intersections by market forces, and residential users will be led to locations convenient to the transportation network, but not directly on busy streets. Nobody wants a convenience store to locate next to their single family home, but market forces make this unlikely. People want their single family homes to be located on quiet streets, while retail locations are most profitable on highly traveled roads, thus leading to efficient land-use patterns. When conflicts arise, often it is because of changes in the transportation network.

Consider some simple examples. Someone may build a house on a rural road, only to find that as the area develops, traffic becomes heavier and the house is on a thoroughfare that has become a profitable commercial location. Meanwhile, in another area, a shopping center was developed but major thoroughfares developed away from the areas causing the shopping center to lose customers, perhaps to the point that it goes out of business and becomes a component of urban blight. In both cases, had the transportation network been planned well in advance, these problems could have been lessened or avoided. Of course, even if government plans out a transportation network, development patterns may not follow them if market forces lead development elsewhere, and shopping centers may become obsolete for reasons unrelated to the transportation network. However, the point is that optimal land-use patterns cannot be identified without reference to the transportation network, and government plans the roads. Planning in both the public and private sector will be more effective if governments plan future developments in the road network well in advance.

How can planners know now where future thoroughfares should be located? One must anticipate development patterns, to be sure, but the task is not as challenging as at first it appears once one realizes that future development patterns will be determined in large part by where the roads are. Thus, planners can determine land-use patterns just by planning roads, and without dictating to private landowners how they can use their property.

Sometimes the optimal use of a property changes, and again market forces work to enact the changes. Abandoned warehouses in many downtowns are redeveloped into apartments; meanwhile, houses on busy streets or in urban areas are converted into offices and other commercial locations. One of the important principles underlying the market approach to land-use planning is that market forces can create an orderly and efficient outcome without central planning. As with market economies, decentralized land-use planning tends to lead to better results than centralized planning. This does not mean there is nothing for planners to do. In a system where the transportation network is almost entirely owned by and controlled by the government, government planners must shape the government's own development. One conclusion of this study is that while the government does too much planning over how private landowners can use their property, it does not do enough to plan for its own infrastructure development.

CONCLUSION

This chapter gives an overview of the issues related to land-use planning at the beginning of the twenty-first century, and suggests how one can take a market-oriented approach to these issues. Many of the problems people perceive are real side effects of late twentieth-century development, while other issues, such as environmental and farmland concerns are perceived as problems even though on closer analysis there is little factual basis relating these concerns to development and sprawl. The real problems are traffic congestion, urban blight, unsightly rows of strip malls, and the transformation of neighborhoods in undesirable ways. While there is much agreement on people's perception of the problems, there is less agreement on the underlying causes, and even less agreement on the solutions. The authors in this volume make the case that when one understands the way that the invisible hand of the market works in land-use issues, the best solutions lie in the application of market forces rather than by increased government planning.

Chapter 2

An Overview of U.S. Urbanization and Land-Use Trends

SAMUEL R. STALEY

One of the key issues in the debate over urban sprawl and suburbanization has been the rate of land development. Headlines in local and national newspapers often depict the rate of development as reaching a "crisis point" (Staley 1999). Vice President Al Gore, for example, lamented the fact Americans have been building "horizontally" rather than "vertically," gobbling land at rates that eventually lead to suburban and cultural decline (Gore 1998). Gore's sentiment is often echoed by others who advocate additional restraints on low-density suburban development (e.g., Burchell, Shad, Listokin, et al. 1998; Rusk 1999).

The evidence conjured up to support the alarmist predictions of development vary from region to region. In the Central Valley of California and Midwestern states such as Iowa, Michigan, and Ohio, farmland loss is the target. In areas such as Southern California, Atlanta, and Boston, development is considered a primary cause of declining environmental quality, particularly air quality. The perception that land development is increasing at potentially unsustainable rates is a primary driver of public support for Smart Growth and regional planning initiatives. Advocates for traditional growth management create a sense of urgency by decrying the loss of open land to development at the rate of "ten acres an hour," "five acres an hour," and even "two acres an hour." Vice President Gore and others have repeatedly raised the specter of losing "fifty acres an hour" of prime farmland each year as the rallying cry for more comprehensive and centralized land-use planning at the local, regional, and state levels.

On the surface, critics of current land development trends seem to have a point. According to U.S. Department of Agriculture (USDA) data, land development rates between 1992 and 1997 nearly doubled from 1987–92 rates, increasing from an average annual rate of about 1.5 million acres to more than 3 million acres (Figure 2.1). These data, however, were recalled in March 2000 because of a computer programming error and may overestimate the true rate of land development (see the discussion below). Prior data suggested a moderation in rates of urbanization and development.

Figure 2.1
Average Annual Change in Developed Land in the United States

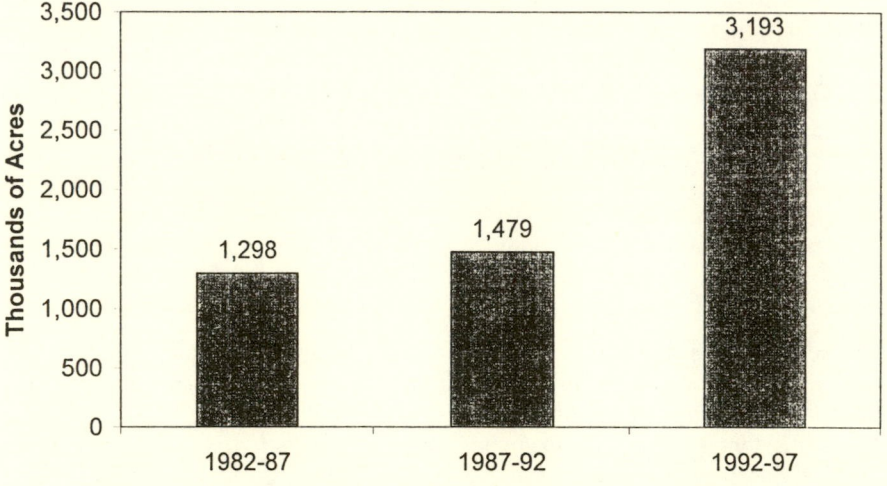

Source: U.S. Department of Agriculture, *Summary Report 1997 National Resources Inventory*. Washington, D.C.: National Resource Conservation Service, 1999.

Unfortunately, rhetoric about "vanishing farmland" and "rampant development" rarely conveys accurate information about real world land-use trends. An assessment of actual development trends as well as housing preferences is critical to understanding the magnitude and scope of the issue. A look at the data can help determine whether current rates of land development create a problem that should be the focus of public policy, and, if so, determining how public policy should be used to address their attendant problems.

This chapter explores land-use trends in the United States, drawing on existing research and the most recent data on urbanization from the USDA's National Resources Inventory (NRI) published by the Natural Resources Conservation Service prior to the March 2000 recall. The updated, corrected data were not used because they were not available when this volume went to press. The data, however, still help provide a context for assessing housing development trends and preferences and more fully understand future pressures on land markets and housing construction. In addition, this chapter provides a critique of the most recent NRI data, noting several inconsistencies in the uncorrected estimates that suggest these new estimates should be used with caution and skepticism.

HOW DEVELOPED IS THE U.S.?

Contrary to popular perception and rhetoric, most of the United States is rural, not developed. In fact, just 5.4 percent of the total surface area is developed (USDA 1999a). This is up 17.6 percent from 1992 levels, when 4.6 percent of the nation's land was developed according to the National Resources Inventory (NRI) (see Figure 2.2, and the discussion below on data reliability). It is

Figure 2.2
Percent of Land Developed in the U.S.

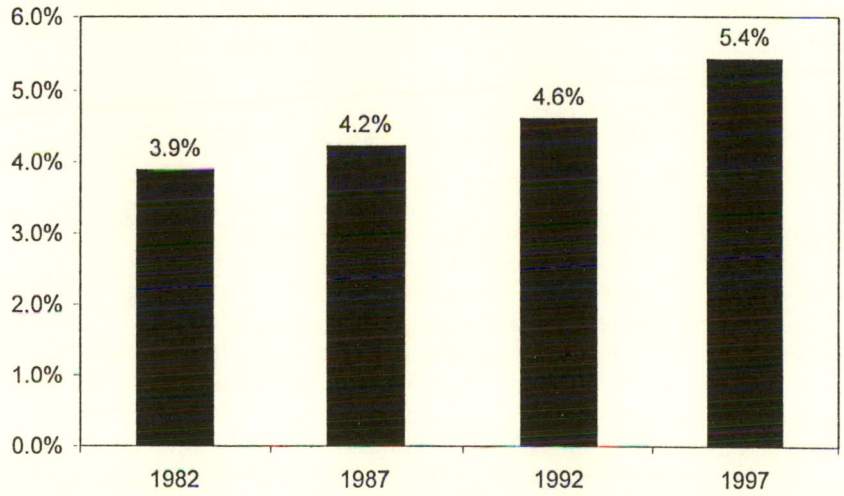

Source: U.S. Department of Agriculture, *Summary Report 1997 National Resources Inventory*. Washington, D.C.: National Conservation Service, 1999. (Uncorrected)

important to note that developed land refers to all land that is not in rural, open space, or recreational uses outside of cities, not only urbanized land. Developed land includes golf courses, parks, and other areas of open spaces of ten acres or less surrounded by open space. Urbanized land, in contrast, must meet additional criteria, including minimum density and contiguity requirements. Thus, not all developed land is urbanized. Nationally, urbanized land accounts for about quarters (75.2 percent) of the nation's developed land. The proportion varies from more than 90 percent in California to 55 percent or less in Arkansas, Kentucky, Maine, Mississippi, Montana, New Hampshire, North Carolina, South Carolina, Vermont, and West Virginia (Table 2.1).

Table 2.1
Most and Least Developed States: 1997

	Top 15 Most Developed		15 Least Developed States	
1.	New Jersey	35.5%	Arkansas	4.4%
2.	Massachusetts	29.0	Minnesota	4.4
3.	Connecticut	28.1	Maine	3.6
4.	Rhode Island	25.2	Colorado	2.6
5.	Maryland	16.4	Nebraska	2.6
6.	Delaware	15.5	North Dakota	2.5
7.	Pennsylvania	15.0	Arizona	2.3
8.	Florida	14.5	Oregon	2.1
9.	Ohio	14.4	South Dakota	2.1
10.	North Carolina	12.4	New Mexico	1.7
11.	South Carolina	11.7	Idaho	1.5
12.	Georgia	11.2	Utah	1.4
13.	New Hampshire	10.8	Wyoming	1.1
14.	New York	10.8	Montana	0.9
15.	Virginia	10.4	Nevada	0.6

Source: U.S. Department of Agriculture, Natural Resources Conservation Service, *Summary Report 1997 National Resources Inventory*, Washington, D.C., 1999.

States range widely across the nation with respect to their level of land development. New Jersey is the most developed, statistically: 35 percent of the state's land is developed. On the other hand, less than 3 percent of many southern and western states (i.e., Arizona, Colorado, Nevada, New Mexico, Wyoming, and others) are developed. Thus, contrary to popular perception, the nation and most states are not "running out of land." Vast tracts of land still exist in rural areas, and substantial portions of this land are in private and public protected wildlife areas and parks. In fact, the federal government owns more than 400 million acres, almost four times the amount currently developed nationwide. Some states, including many western states, have more than half of their land locked up in federal and state wildlife preserves. Indeed, almost one-third of New Jersey is currently protected through a network of state and federal parks that include the Pinelands National Reserve (the Pine Barrens). This suggests that concerns about the rate of development are primarily local and regional, not state or federal.

WHAT LAND IS URBANIZED?

Far more land is farmed than urbanized. More than 375 million acres nationwide are in cropland, land used to grow and harvest food. Another 403 million acres are held in rangeland, while pasture makes up 120 million acres. Forests consist of another 400 million acres. The data show that the federal government alone owns or controls as much land as is currently used as cropland, pasture, or forest, and about as much as the nation's range land.

A substantial amount of rhetoric about suburban sprawl stems from concerns over cropland loss (Staley 2000a). From 1992 to 1997, rural lands fell by 72.3 million acres according to the uncorrected NRI data, including a 45.9 million acre drop in cropland. However, during this same period, developed land increased by only 29.9 million acres, about two-thirds of the cropland loss, but less than half of all rural lands. Development is unlikely to have been the primary cause of cropland loss. Nationally, cropland varies significantly, depending on weather, the strength of export markets, and federal programs (USDA 1997). Moreover, development doesn't consume just cropland and farmland; land development also converts forest, range, and pasture that is often unused for agricultural purposes. Land uses tend to shift among several categories over time. While rural land fell by 72.3 million acres from 1982 to 1997, for example, 42.5 million acres were added to rural lands during the same period. More directly, only 12.2 percent of the decline in cropland can be attributed to land development during this period, (USDA 1999a, Table 5, p. 35) while 26 percent of the cropland loss was converted to pasture.

In terms of land development for urban uses, most land comes from forests. Between 1992 and 1997, according to NRI data, 6.4 million acres of forests were converted to developed land accounting for 39.9 percent of the increase. (USDA 1999a, Table 8, p. 38). Pasture and range land accounted for another 4.7 million acres, or 29.3 percent. Cropland accounted for a little more than one-quarter (26.6 percent) of the increase. From 1987 to 1992, cropland accounted for 28.7 percent of the increase in development land, while forests accounted for 40.7 percent, and pasture and range accounted for 33.8 percent.

Ohio State University agricultural economist Luther Tweeten (1998) found urbanization accounted for only 26 percent of the cropland loss from 1945 to 1992 after controlling for factors such as changing demographics, income, and industry profitability. While land in farms has declined steadily since the end of World War II, overall cropland levels have remained remarkably stable. In fact, cropland increased from 450.7 million acres in 1945 to 459.7 million in 1992 according to data from the U.S. Census of Agriculture. Meanwhile, agricultural productivity increased dramatically, rising by 47.9 percent from 1970 to 1993.

Thus, the nation's farms are boosting output on nearly the same amount of land. In fact, land is a declining factor in agricultural production. Two-thirds of agriculture's productivity is attributed to capital and technology and less than 18 percent to land (Tweeten 1989, p. 9). Clearly, urbanization does not appear to be threatening the nation's agricultural industry.

Within states, farmland loss is uneven. For example, the Michigan Farm Bureau identified 22 counties that had experienced farmland loss rates exceeding the state average between 1992 and 1997 (Staley 2000b). The counties were classified by the author according to whether they were "rural" (outside a census-defined metropolitan statistical area, or MSA), "central city" (inside an MSA with a central-urban center), and "suburban" (inside an MSA but outside the urban core). The average annual farmland loss from 1992 to 1997 for these counties exceeded the rate from 1982 to 1992 by 65.6 percent, an expected outcome given the counties used for the analysis. Ironically, farmland loss rates were the least severe in the central-city counties. Average annual loss rates were 28.7 percent higher than the previous decade. Farmland loss rates for central-city counties should have accelerated according to conventional wisdom since ongoing suburbanization should have significantly threatened existing farmland and the county's local business infrastructure should have shifted from serving agricultural needs to personal and other residential needs. Loss rates in the five rural counties averaged rates double the previous decade.

Interpreting these trends accurately, unfortunately, is problematic as an examination of individual county performance suggests. One-third of the counties experienced moderation in farmland loss rates. Four of the counties—Ingham (Lansing), Kalamazoo, Kent (Grand Rapids), and Washtenaw (Ann Arbor)—were central-city counties. Three counties—Macomb, Monroe, and Oakland—were already highly developed given their proximity to Detroit. Thus, generalizing about the experience of farmland loss from historical trends is difficult given the individual experiences of these counties.

Even if farmland loss rates were holding steady or increasing, trends in agricultural productivity suggest urbanization is not threatening the nation's (or world's) food supply. Food output is up 17.4 percent over 1980 levels and 47.9 percent over 1970 levels. This has contributed to the nation's agricultural exports. The United States continues to be a net exporter of food, selling 46.6 percent of its domestically produced rice, 31.4 percent of its wheat, 36.5 percent of its cotton, 33.6 percent of its soybeans, and 16.3 percent of its corn abroad (USDA 1998, p. 678).

More significantly, the relative price of food is falling. While food prices increased by 71 percent between 1980 and 1995, the Consumer Price Index for all items increased by 85 percent during the same period according to the U.S. Department of Labor. Thus, food became relatively cheaper when compared to other goods. Moreover, wages, salaries, and benefits increased by 154 percent, more than double the growth in food prices. If agricultural productivity and food supplies were threatened, prices would be increasing in relative and absolute terms. Indeed, one need look no further than the price of gasoline to see how responsive prices are to real and perceived shortages of key minerals and products.

Nevertheless, the recent development and urbanization trends from the 1997 NRI point to a dramatic increase in the rate of urbanization. In fact, given previous trends, the increase reflects a turnaround. Prior estimates and extrapolations from the USDA based on census data suggested urbanization would continue to increase by about 1 million acres per year (USDA 1999b). Moreover, based on estimates from the 1970s and early 1980s, urbanization rates appeared to be falling from 1.3 million acres per year between 1988 and 1987 and 800,000 acres per year for the period 1987 to 1992. The extended economic boom accounts for a substantial amount of increased land development, but the increases estimated by the 1997 NRI report are still dramatic, with rates of development more than double earlier periods.

NRI DATA RELIABILITY

The land-use trends just discussed were based on uncorrected NRI data. Several analysts, including this author, questioned the NRI data's accuracy and queried USDA officials directly about the accuracy of the estimates. This criticism may have contributed to a March 2000 reassessment and subsequent recall of the initial estimates. Many were skeptical that developed land could increase by 17.6 percent in just five years, an unprecedented expansion of land development (Cox and Utt 2000). Moreover, the magnitude of the expansion is dramatic given moderating farmland loss rates and urbanization trends based on census data.

To some extent, the rapid growth rate might be attributable to a downward revision in previous estimates of developed land. Developed land accounted for 92.4 million acres in the 1992 NRI report. In the 1997 report, the 1992 estimate was revised downward to 89.4 million acres. Overall, 2.9 million acres of developed land "disappeared." The effect, statistically, would be to boost the overall land development rate from 14.1 percent to 17.6 percent, an increase of almost 27 percent.

More troubling, perhaps, was that the 1997 revisions impacted states in different ways. Downward revisions reduced 1992 estimates of developed land in Michigan by 473,000 acres. Developed land fell by 466,000 in Texas; 368,000 acres in Minnesota; and 337,000 acres in Montana (see Table 2.2). While estimates in five states—Kansas, Idaho, New Mexico, Virginia, and Wyoming—were revised upward by 100,000 or more acres, two-thirds of the states found their estimates of developed land reduced. The net effect was a downward revision of almost 3 million acres between the 1992 and 1997 NRI reports. Individual state growth rates were impacted much more dramatically. In Michigan, where almost a half million developed acres "disappeared" statistically, the growth in developed land increased from 2.1 percent (using 1992 NRI estimates) to 17.2 percent using the 1997 NRI estimate (see Table 2.3), an eight-fold in-

crease. In Minnesota, under the 1992 estimate, developed land would have resulted in land being converted from developed to rural uses. Under the revised
estimates, Minnesota's land development rate was 15.2 percent.

Table 2.2
Estimates of Developed Land by State in 1992 and 1997

State	1992 NRI	1997 NRI	Differ- ence	State	1992	1997	Differ- ence
Alabama	2,046	1,965	-81	Nebraska	1,252	1,187	-65
Arizona	1,404	1,476	72	Nevada	394	374	-20
Arkansas	1,322	1,264	-59	N. Hampshire	563	534	-29
California	5,001	4,992	-8	New Jersey	1,588	1,566	-22
Colorado	1,694	1,585	-108	New Mexico	866	976	110
Connecticut	816	834	18	New York	3,005	2,881	-124
Delaware	205	203	-2	North Carolina	3,542	3,399	-143
Florida	4,645	4,503	-142	North Dakota	1,344	1,103	-242
Georgia	3,077	3,185	108	Ohio	3,558	3,275	-282
Hawaii	170	177	7	Oklahoma	1,875	1,772	-103
Idaho	587	690	103	Oregon	1,125	1,145	20
Illinois	3,094	2,969	-125	Pennsylvania	3,432	3,212	-220
Indiana	2,095	2,081	-13	Rhode Island	190	195	5
Iowa	1,779	1,700	-79	South Carolina	1,856	1,786	-71
Kansas	1,997	2,689	692	South Dakota	1,135	958	-177
Kentucky	1,653	1,601	-52	Tennessee	2,161	2,006	-155
Louisiana	1,764	1,520	-244	Texas	8,231	7,765	-466
Maine	697	579	-118	Utah	561	655	94
Maryland	1,095	1,068	-27	Vermont	324	320	-4
Massachusetts	1,309	1,268	-42	Virginia	2,183	2,338	155
Michigan	3,686	3,213	-473	Washington	1,851	1,864	13
Minnesota	2,418	2,050	-368	West Virginia	689	711	21
Mississippi	1,337	1,343	6	Wisconsin	2,357	2,260	-96
Missouri	2,336	2,342	6	Wyoming	541	663	122
Montana	1,096	759	-337				

Source: U.S. Department of Agriculture, Natural Resources Conservation Service, *National Resources Inventory* for 1992 and 1997.

Moreover, estimates of land development were dramatic in absolute terms
for many states. Pennsylvania, as the Pacific Research Institute's Steve Hayward
and others have pointed out, developed 1.1 million acres from 1992 to 1997,
more than 60 percent than the amount of land developed in California during the
same period (695,000 acres). California's population, however, grew 4.3 percent
to 32.2 million people while Pennsylvania's population growth was stagnant at
12 million people (see the discussion in Cox, Utt, and Husock 2000). The Commonwealth Foundation estimates that this rate of land development would have
required each new house to be built on 5.2 acre lots based on residential building
permit data from the Census Bureau (Mastrull 2000).

Table 2.3
Impact of Developed Land Revisions on Development Estimates in 20 States

	State	NRI Estimates of Developed Land					
		1997[1]	92 NRI[2]	97 NRI[3]	Difference[4]	92 NRI Growth[5]	97NRI Growth[6]
1	Michigan	3,764	3,686	3,213	-473	2.1%	17.2%
2	Texas	8,984	8,231	7,765	-466	9.1%	15.7%
3	Minnesota	2,361	2,418	2,050	-368	-2.3%	15.2%
4	Montana	881	1,096	759	-337	-19.6%	16.1%
5	Ohio	3,797	3,558	3,275	-282	6.7%	15.9%
6	Louisiana	1,693	1,764	1,520	-244	-4.0%	11.4%
7	N. Dakota	1,152	1,344	1,103	-242	-14.3%	4.5%
8	Pennsylvania	4,336	3,432	3,212	-220	26.3%	35.0%
9	S. Dakota	1,035	1,135	958	-177	-8.8%	8.0%
10	Tennessee	2,618	2,161	2,006	-155	21.2%	30.5%
11	N. Carolina	4,181	3,542	3,399	-143	18.0%	23.0%
12	Florida	5,449	4,645	4,503	-142	17.3%	21.0%
13	Illinois	3,262	3,094	2,969	-125	5.4%	9.9%
14	New York	3,373	3,005	2,881	-124	12.2%	17.1%
15	Maine	747	697	579	-118	7.2%	29.1%
16	Colorado	1,706	1,694	1,585	-108	0.7%	7.6%
17	Oklahoma	1,997	1,875	1,772	-103	6.5%	12.7%
18	Wisconsin	2,543	2,357	2,260	-96	7.9%	12.5%
19	Alabama	2,410	2,046	1,965	-81	17.8%	22.7%
20	Iowa	1,803	1,779	1,700	-79	1.4%	6.1%
	U.S.	105,369	92,352	89,403	-2,949	14.1%	17.6%

Notes   [1]Estimate of developed land in 1997
[2]Estimate of developed land for 1992 in 1992 NRI
[3]Estimate of developed land for 1992 in 1997 NRI
[4]Difference between 1992 and 1997 NRI
[5]Growth from 1992 to 1997 based on 1992 NRI estimate for 1992
[6]Growth from 1992 to 1997 based on 1997 NRI estimate for 1992
Source: U.S. Department of Agriculture, Natural Resources Conservation Service, *National Resources Inventory* for 1992 and 1997.

While USDA statisticians believe the March 2000 revisions will be minor, officials also admitted that they could not accurately predict the magnitude of error and they would affect every region of the nation (Mastrull 2000). "The revised statistical processing," the USDA announced on its web site (March 27, 2000), "is not expected to significantly change any previously announced finds. However, there will be minor revision in almost all the estimates contained in the 15 summary tables." More importantly, the source of the error appeared to be in the calculation of rural transportation uses, an error that would bias the results toward higher rates of land development (Mastrull 2000). Not surprisingly, until important questions are answered about the reclassification of land areas nationally and within states, analysts should be skeptical of the uncorrected 1997 NRI data.

HOUSING PREFERENCES AND TRENDS

Land-use trends aside, the debate over suburbanizaton often centers on the kind of housing that is emerging on the periphery of urban areas. Many opponents of so-called sprawl are also opposed to new development more generally. Proponents of Smart Growth, however, believe that current development patterns are wasteful because they consume more and more land. Few of the debates surrounding sprawl and Smart Growth, however, analyze consumer preferences for housing and land. In fact, current market trends may be reconciling traditional tensions between home and land ownership. Thus, reviewing current trends in housing is a critical first step toward understanding the role property markets play in determining land-use patterns.

The U.S. housing industry builds about 1.1 million homes annually, according to the National Association of Homebuilders (NAHB) (http://www.nahb.com). The amount of housing produced in any given year is heavily influenced by economic and business cycles. For example, about 1 million homes were built in 1989 and 1990, the years before the recession of the early 1990s. As the recession took hold, the number of homes completed dipped to 838,000 in 1991, then climbed to 964,000 in 1992, and then exceeded 1 million homes again after 1993 and the economy moved into a prolonged period of growth (see Figure 2.3). Over an 18-year period, almost 20 million homes were added to the nation's housing stock.

New home sales, however, are a relatively small component of total home sales. In 1998, more than 5.9 million homes were sold nationwide, but new homes constituted just 886,000 units, or 15.1 percent of the total. This proportion has been remarkably consistent since 1980. While 15.5 percent of home sales were new homes in 1980, and this figure increased to almost 19 percent in 1983, existing homes made up 85 percent or more of the total in every year from 1990 to 1995, with new homes only slightly exceeding 15 percent in 1996 and 1997.

More importantly, the kind of housing changed: New homes became bigger and used less land as shown in Figure 2.4. Overall, median house size has increased 25.4 percent since 1980, and 5 percent since 1990, growing from 1,596 to 1,890 square feet between 1980 and 1990, and then to 2,000 square feet by 1998. In addition, the proportion of homes over 2,400 square feet increased steadily from just 15 percent in 1980 to 31 percent in 1997. To accommodate this increase in size, U.S. homes were getting taller, not flatter. Less than one-third of the new homes built in 1980 were two stories. By the 1990s, almost half the new homes had two floors. New homes also have more amenities. While only one-quarter of the new homes in 1980 had 2½ baths or more, the proportion

Figure 2.3
Single-Family Homes Completed: 1980 to 1998

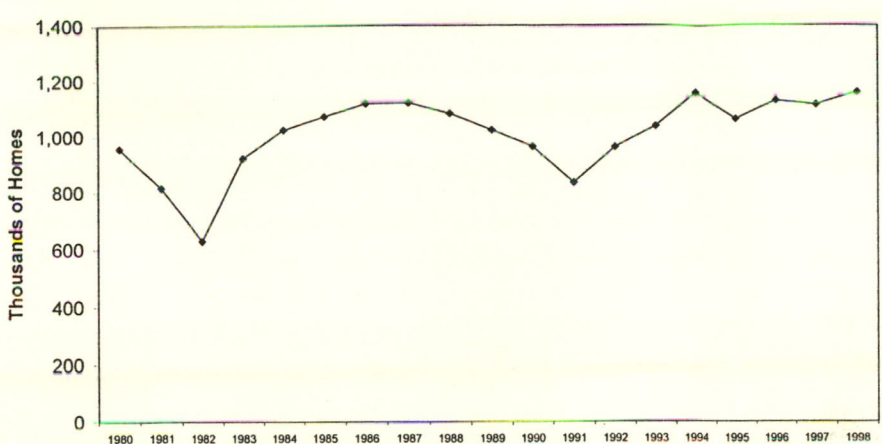

Source: National Association of Home Builders, http://www.nahb.com.

Figure 2.4
Median housing size: 1980 to 1998

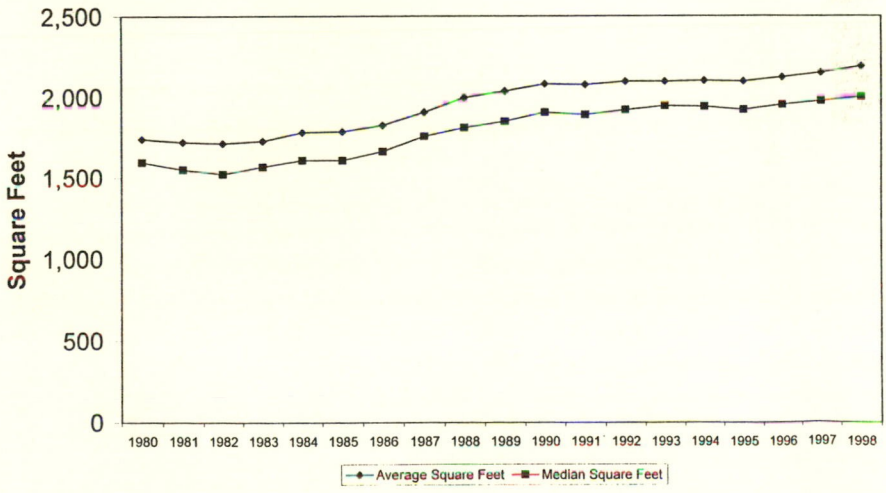

Source: National Association of Home Builders, http://www.nahb.com.

had climbed to 50 percent in 1997, and 52 percent in 1998. Clearly, Americans were building and buying larger homes with more of the qualities they wanted.

Meanwhile, the median lot size for new homes stabilized and has even fallen recently as illustrated in Figure 2.5. In 1980, the median lot size for a new home was 9,180 square feet, less than one-fifth of an acre. Median lot sizes increased throughout the 1980s, climbing to 10,000 square feet at its peak in 1990. Then lot sizes began to fall. By 1996, the median lot size for a new home had fallen to 9,100 square feet. Significantly, the average lot size was typically larger than the median lot size. This suggests that a substantial number of new homes were constructed on much larger lots. Nevertheless, average lot sizes paralleled the decline in the median lot size, falling from 14,680 square feet in 1990 (more than one-quarter of an acre) to 13,705 square feet in 1996.

Figure 2.5
Lot Size for New Single-Family Homes: 1980 to 1996

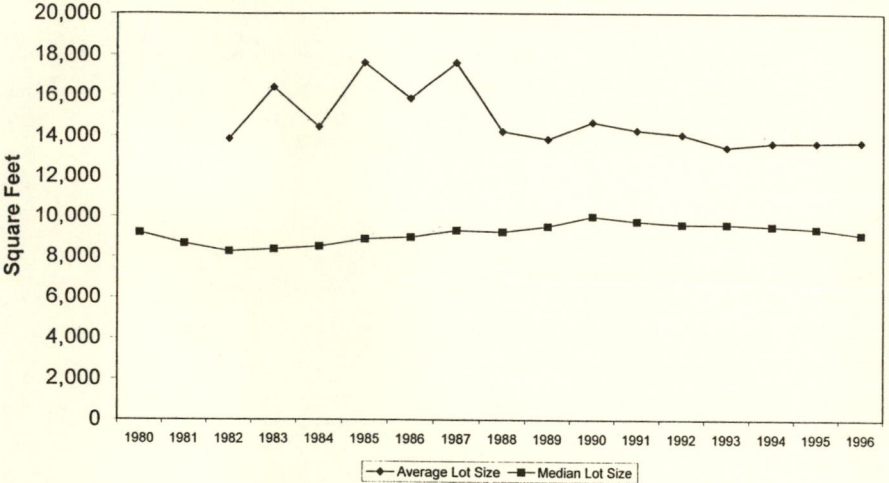

Source: National Association of Home Builders, http://www.nahb.com.

Similar trends were found for multifamily homes. While the number of multifamily buildings completed plummeted from, 546,000 in 1980 to 315,000 units in 1998, with fewer than 200,000 units completed in 1992-94, the size of the typical unit increased. In 1980, the median multifamily housing unit was 915 square feet. By 1998, the median size had climbed to 1,022 square feet. The share of new multifamily housing units over 1,200 square feet increased from 19.0 percent in 1980 to almost one third in 1997. The proportion of new multifamily housing units with two or more bathrooms increased from less than one third in 1980 to 49 percent in 1998.

Meanwhile, housing became cheaper. The National Association of Home Builders calculates an index (the Housing Opportunity Index, or HOI) to estimate how many households can afford the median home in a metropolitan area. In essence, the HOI reflects the proportion of a metropolitan area's households that could afford a home at the median home price in the area. Nationally, the HOI was 60, meaning that 60 percent of the households could afford the median price home. By 1998, the HOI had increased to 66.2. Thus, family incomes have kept pace with their ability to buy even larger homes with more and more amenities and more luxurious characteristics.

CONCLUSION

What can be gleaned from these data on land-use trends and housing preferences? First, issues of land development are primarily local concerns. Nation wide, very little land is used for development. In fact, three-quarters of the U.S. population lives on about 4 percent of the land. While recent estimates of development trends from the Natural Resource Inventory suggest urbanization has increased dramatically—doubling its rate from 1992 to 1997 compared to earlier periods—land development has not significantly eroded the availability of open space on a national or state level. Moreover, the nation's farm economy continues to be very productive, and little evidence suggests that urbanization significantly threatens agriculture production on a national, state, or local level. These trends are complimented by the fact that Americans are building homes that are bigger, taller, and loaded with more amenities. Finally, despite widespread land availability and rising demand for more spacious and luxurious homes, new homes are consuming less land per unit.

Pressure to develop land is likely to increase, although the pressures will be felt most acutely in existing metropolitan areas. U.S. metropolitan areas grew from 177.3 million people in 1980 to 211.8 million in 1996, a 19.5 percent increase. The proportion of the U.S. population living in metropolitan areas increased from 78.3 percent to 79.8 percent over this period. The nonmetropolitan population increased as well, growing from 49.3 million to 53.5 million (an 8.5 percent increase), but not by enough to offset the increasing concentration of people in metropolitan areas.

Despite the increasingly urbanized character of the American population, the nation's land area in metropolitan areas remained stable at 19.9 percent between 1980 and 1996. In part, this stability reflects the existence of large tracts of vacant land within these areas. Thus, despite the fact that one-fifth of the nation's surface area is within metropolitan areas, substantial amounts of land remain undeveloped or in agricultural use.

These population shifts imply that urbanization occurs primarily near existing urban areas, a well-documented process (e.g., Vesterby and Heimlich 1991). In fact, 70 percent of the nation's metropolitan population stills lives in urban areas with populations exceeding one million. Just 25 percent live in metropolitan areas with fewer than 500,000 people. The result is pressure to develop new land for housing, both to accommodate the growth in the native population as well as meet needs of new residents, most often on the urban fringe.

The implications for growth management are important. While concern over urban sprawl and development continues to grab headlines and be a catalyst for public policy, growth-management policies still need to grapple with the tensions and conflicts inherent in a political and social system structured to accommodate the rising aspirations of its citizens. A potentially efficient way to address these concerns is through market mechanisms rather than using rhetorical approaches to promote public policies that ultimately limit choice in an artificially constrained environment.

Chapter 3

The Geography of Transportation and Land Use

PETER GORDON AND HARRY W. RICHARDSON

Discussions of transportation and land use are no longer restricted to specialists but are now in full public view in the debate over "urban sprawl." In our view, the critics of suburban development are mostly wrong. Their most fundamental error is to underestimate the importance of land market adjustments to alleviate highway congestion. Traffic congestion, where it occurs, is the consequence of the absence of pricing, a policy failure. The real news is that by any comparison, international or intertemporal, traffic conditions in the United States are quite favorable. The most plausible explanation for this is the suburbanization of origins and destinations. Turning the logic of sprawl's critics on its head, it appears that land markets flexible enough to allow such adjustments are the market's way to remedy the consequences of a policy failure.

While several reports (e.g. Cox and Alm, 1999; Easterlin 2000; Lebergott 1993; Moore and Simon 1999) document stunning advances in health, longevity, and material well-being, and while it is no longer disreputable to credit the market economy, most current discussions of cities and land use see only market failures. A representative example is a recent magazine article by Bruce Katz and Jennifer Bradley (1999), ominously named "Divided We Sprawl." It blames most U.S. social ills on how cities are growing (especially suburbanization) and supports draconian interventions by politicians and planners to set the world right. Indeed, a flurry of growth management measures either passed by or being presented to voters across the land are unabashedly replacing markets with planning interventions. It is difficult to understand how acknowledged market successes and renascent statism can coexist side-by-side.

Urban sprawl is now widely used to explain increasing income inequality, job insecurity, central city decline, receding housing affordability, long commutes, environmental problems (especially dire global warming and ozone depletion concerns), species extinction, farmland losses, a sense of isolation, elevated blood pressure, muscle tension, intolerance, psychological disorientation, obesity, even murder and mayhem, and for good measure, "racial and income segregation, oppression of women, and ecological rape" (Thomas 1994). Some have blamed the Littleton, Colorado, shootings on the "anomie and ennui that's being produced in these environments" (James Kunstler, in Peirce 1999). One critic noted that "the American people are coming to the conclusion that sprawl is to blame for a good deal of the discontent that attaches to end-of-century middle-class life. And this change of mind will shake up politics in many places in the first decade of the 21st century" (Ehrenhalt 1999a). It is worth noting that Anthony Downs, by no means a defender of sprawl, ran hundreds of regressions of a sprawl index against two measures of urban decline (central city population change, 1980-90) and a nine-variable decline index (poverty, crime, per capita income, age composition of the housing stock, etc.). To his surprise and perhaps disappointment, he found no meaningful and significant statistical relationship (Downs 1999, p. 961).

According to the critics, sprawl is the problem and Smart Growth is the solution. Smart Growth advocates see "a growing sense that the suburban paradigm, which has dominated since the 1940s and 1950s, cannot sustain another generation of growth" (Katz, 1994, p. ix). Peter Calthorpe is fairly specific when he suggests a "New Urbanism" where

there should be defined edges (i.e., urban growth boundaries), the circulation system should function for the pedestrian (i.e., supported by regional transit systems), public space should be formative rather than residual (i.e., preservation of major open-space networks), civic and private domains should form a complementary hierarchy (i.e., related cultural centers, commercial districts and residential neighborhoods) and population and use should be diverse (i.e., created by adequate affordable housing and a jobs/housing balance). (in Katz 1994, p. xiii)

There is little analysis or discussion of the costs, the implied trade-offs, the consistency or even the consumer's desire for such forms. There is certainly no anxiety over the loss of property rights nor over their politicization. Even the New Urbanist fall-back position that, "building walkable neighborhoods may not get people out of their cars and building front porches may not create an integrated convivial communities, . . . but people should be given a choice" (Calthorpe 1993, p. 10) never acknowledges the fact that markets regularly generate most feasible choices while discarding the infeasible ones, based on how opportunity costs compare to consumers' willingness to pay.

There is a widespread presumption that planning should strive for mixed-use and more compact land development (including "infill," but only on any vacant lands and parking lots) with plenty of transit, walkways, and bikeways (Schmidt 1998). This evokes Peter Hall's discussion of the 1952 General Plan for Stockholm, which reads like a plan for a high-density transit metropolis:

It proposed establishing new suburban districts, each for 10,000 to 15,000 inhabitants, strung like beads along the lines of a new subway system. Within them, apartment blocks were to be built within 500 yards of subway stops; single-family houses, constituting no more than 10-15 percent of housing units in each district, were to be built within 1000 yards of the stops but no further ... the city's policy was that each station on the subway should generate enough traffic to make it self-supporting (1966, pp. 862, 863).

Plans often fail to materialize. Hall notes that "surveys in the late 1970s reaffirmed the fact that 90 percent of people preferred single-family homes" (p. 876). Not surprisingly, a more recent Swedish development is described as " a vast linear edge City of business parks and hotels and out-of-town shopping centers, stretching along the E4 highway, for twelve miles and more towards the Arlanda Airport. It is almost indistinguishable from its counterparts in California and Texas" (p. 878).

Critics of U.S. suburban development cite Europe and Canada as favorite models but have avoided taking a hard look at Europe and other developed countries (see Bruegmann, chapter 9). If they had, they would have found increasing suburbanization and growing auto use under (and in spite of) a policy milieu carefully designed to prevent precisely these outcomes. Planners in the United States point to a wide array of U. S. policies (favorable federal tax treatment of home ownership, comparatively low gasoline taxes, extensive highway systems, large-lot residential zoning, local tax incentives to mobile firms, etc.) that could account for observed dispersed settlement patterns.

Some U.S. policies have had a suburbanizing impact, beyond a doubt, but the question is: How much? That question is seldom asked or answered. An exception is Richard Voith (1999), who estimates that the federal tax treatment of housing is responsible for a 15 percent decrease in residential densities. The critics have paid far less attention to the many policies that favor central cities, such as downtown renewal, subsidized stadiums placed in central cities, and heavily subsidized downtown-focused rail transit systems. It may be that U.S. policies that bear on land development do not point in a single direction of spatial development. A recent General Accounting Office (GAO) report reaches similar conclusions (U.S. General Accounting Office, 1999).

Elsewhere, we have noted (Gordon and Richardson 1999) that widespread auto ownership with suburban land-use patterns are evolving in Western Europe and Canada where policies are very different, most of them strongly favoring compact development (Gerondeau 1997; Giuliano 1998; Morrill 1991). A recent compilation from the U.S. Department of Transportation (1999) shows that among the G-7 countries, Japan—not the U.S.—is the outlier when it comes to the share of total domestic passenger kilometers traveled by personal vehicles. Most of the evidence suggests that land use and transportation trends in foreign cities, although difficult to measure and compare, are very similar to those in U.S. cities, with the differences largely explained by a moderate lag (see also Bruegmann, Chapter 9). These events and facts have gone almost unnoticed in the U.S. sprawl debate.

In sharp contrast, Pietro Nivola sees the decentralization of U.S. cities as "path dependent: technological innovations helped chart an early course that has determined, and been amplified by, subsequent events" (1999, p. 11). The trouble with this view of technology is that it leaves no room for people's preferences as a driver of technological change. The view that technological change is an exogenous juggernaut has been challenged by Paul Romer (1996) and others. Nivola also calls attention to America's interstate highway program, begun in 1956. This is too large an investment to have had no impact. Yet there was significant suburbanization before 1956 and there is much of it in countries without infrastructure programs of this type. The relative sparseness of highway networks in other countries helps to explain their high levels of traffic congestion, especially in cities or along major interurban corridors. In this way, the lack of highways can be seen as a decentralizing force. By asserting that peculiar U.S. policies are the explanation for sprawl, the critics accomplish two things: (1) they divert attention from universally preferred lifestyle choices, and (2) they point to a simple fix, which is to move U.S. policies closer to those found elsewhere.

The futility of the transit/high-density model in the modern world can be seen in the miserable traffic and commuting conditions in places like Seoul, Athens, Rome, Tokyo, Jakarta, and Paris. Newly affluent households are increasingly opting for the automobile in spite of widely available transit, the absence of freeways, and U.S.-style highway networks. The long-run income elasticities of demand are greater than one (the demand for automobile travel increases faster than income), while the price elasticities of demand are much lower. Thus, income matters more than gasoline prices. But because people have fewer suburb-to-suburb commuting opportunities, the result is congestion levels and traffic conditions that would appall Americans.

Many of the Smart Growth gurus are architects and urban designers not easily reconciled to a world of order without the benefit of human design. They fail to appreciate the idea that the uncountable number of trial-and-error processes that occur in a free society best manage complex trade-offs, leading to discovery and progress. Instead, they are likely to see the need for grand strategies to implement their visions. Consumer choice is not high on their list. Yet the grand strategies are extreme, even dangerous. The idea that cities and neighborhoods can be adequately represented via the pretty mock-ups and models found in university architecture studios is disturbing. James Scott refers to all this as "high modernism," noting that "the carriers of high modernism tended to see rational order in remarkably visual aesthetic terms. For them, an efficient rationally organized village, city or farm was a city that looked regimented and orderly in a geometrical sense." And, *a propos* the apparent oddity that Smart

Growth rhetoric follows so close after the collapse of central economic planning, "the carriers of high modernism, once their plans miscarried or were thwarted, tended to retreat to . . . miniaturization: the creation of a more easily controlled micro-order in model cities, model villages, and model farms" (Scott, 1998, p. 4).

The technocratic view of cities as places that will benefit from intelligent design is shared by many outside architecture studios. Two prominent operations researchers, George Dantzig and Thomas Saaty, published *Compact City: A Plan for a Livable Urban Environment* as long ago as 1973. The authors employed what they called "total-system models" to refigure many aspects of city life. The last line in their book is the fully capitalized sentence: "THE ULTIMATE GOAL IS A RICHER QUALITY OF LIFE" (p. 224). While this is a refreshing alternative to Le Corbusier's unabashed authoritarianism, it is inadequate because nowhere do the authors pay any attention to the choices that people have been making in the real world, inconsistent with compact cities. This is the well-known fatal flaw of the technocratic approach.

Wholly planned new cities such as Brasilia and Chandigarh that are more monumental than inviting have been built by architectural visionaries. They have been spectacular and costly failures, rejected by most of the people for whom they were designed. No matter. Today's interventionists, in pursuit of a new design dream, promise that the specifics of Smart Growth plans will be conjured up and wisely implemented by the powers that be. They will specify minimum and maximum allowable densities for various locations plus a raft of other specifications, asserting repeatedly that any departures from these standards would be, by definition, wasteful.

SUBURBANIZATION

Historical Trends

The suburbanization of population and employment is not a new phenomenon. Most societies have been urbanizing while their cities have been expanding outward for many years. In the process, most urban population densities have been falling. There are many reasons why economic activity becomes more efficient when other activities are located nearby—this is why cities evolved. Yet the definition of "nearby" continues to change. The association of urban expansion with improved ease of movement is clear. As the "friction of distance" subsides, people and firms access more sites and more opportunities without incurring substantially greater costs. They also can forego the huge capital costs of high-rise development as well as many of the costs of crowding and congestion. Geographers (e.g., Mueller, 1986) have linked city expansion with the dominant transportation technology of the time, calling attention to the "Walking-Horsecar Era" (1800–1890), the "Electric Streetcar Era" (1890–1920), the "Recreational Automobile Era" (1920–1945), and the "Freeway Era" (1945–the present). The current era of Moore's Law, expanding bandwidth, electronic commerce, and extraordinarily cheap (and rapidly declining) communications costs, continues (and probably accelerates) a longstanding trend. The forces that induce firms to cluster, agglomeration economies, now exert an influence over a more extensive geographical space.

This is why official metropolitan boundaries are regularly adjusted outward to keep up with suburbanization. Yet, in the United States, change outpaces the mapmakers and substantial employment growth in recent years has occurred far beyond the officially recognized boundaries of metropolitan areas (Beyers 1998; Gordon, Richardson, Yu 1998). Many of the more dynamic sites are far more peripheral than Garreau's "Edge Cities." It is not surprising that the U.S. Census reported that in 1995–96 a quarter million more people left U.S. metropolitan areas than moved into them (www.bls.census.gov/cps/pub/1997/mobility.htm).

One approach that has been used to minimize the boundary problem is the U.S. Census Bureau's effort to define urbanized areas (UAs) for each census year. This avoids the use of counties as the building blocks (as with the MSAs and CMSAs) by delineating functional boundaries ("where the lights start when you fly in at night", according to one observer). Unfortunately, most of the important data, notably employment, are not compiled using these areas. Population data for the Census years going back to the 1950s (Table 3.1) show that, in general, in larger UAs population densities have been declining throughout the 1950–1990 period. As might be expected, the exceptions have been the fast-growing sunbelt cities. Los Angeles and Miami, which absorb large numbers of immigrant populations, were the two highest-density places in 1990, surpassing even New York, where in spite of an immigrant influx, population densities continue their long-term decline. Many people choose to relocate to lower-density settlements as soon as it becomes feasible (the noncore counties of large MSAs, counties in small MSAs, and non-metropolitan counties adjacent to MSAs being the major beneficiaries; see Table 3.2).

Most firms, especially manufacturers, were once primarily attracted to raw material sites, transshipment points, major highway intersections, or harbors. Once established, many experienced economies of scale in production, both internal and external (both localization and urbanization economies). Workers had to settle in the vicinity of these clusters of factories and facilities to keep commuting costs in check. Much of this has now been reversed. A variety of technological advances in transport and communications makes it possible for increasing numbers of firms to become "footloose." These footloose firms tend to follow the labor force into the suburbs and exurban areas. Most households, all things considered, prefer to live and work in suburban environments where single-family homes (the average size of which increases every year) dominate the housing stock. They can do this without paying for the privilege with long commutes. This is because many jobs are now in the suburbs and commutes are on faster suburb-to-suburb routes. Measures to enforce compact development are more likely to make matters worse. Yet the conventional wisdom takes a different line (from a recent newspaper editorial): "here's hoping that planners, communities and government officials make a serious effort to fight a key cause of traffic congestion: sprawl. It's sprawl that creates housing that's far removed from jobs, schools, shopping and the like. What's better? Sensibly planned communities where jobs and housing are close, where essential trips can be measured in terms of a few blocks instead of miles and where people are able to

Table 3.1
Urbanized Area Population Densities, 1950 - 1990

	1998 Pop	1990 UA Pop Dens	1950 - 90 UA % Pop Dens Chge	1980 - 90 UA % Pop Dens Chge
New York-Northern NJ-Long Island CMSA	20124	5408.5	-44.9	-2.6
Los Angeles-Riverside-Orange CMSA	15781	5800.8	26.4	11.8
Chicago-Gary-Kenosha CMSA	8809	4286.6	-38.2	-5.3
Washington-Baltimore CMSA	7285	3560.1	-50.8	3.9
San Francisco-Oakland-San Jose CMSA	6816	4152.3	-41	3.6
Philadelphia-Wilmington-Atlantic City CMSA	5988	3626.7	-61.3	-10.5
Boston-Worcester-Lawrence-Lowell-Brockton CMSA	5633	3114.1	-51.9	-0.4
Detroit-Ann Arbor-Flint CMSA	5458	3303	-49.2	-9.4
Dallas-Ft. Worth CMSA	4802	2216.3	-31.2	15.7
Houston-Galveston-Brazoria CMSA	4408	2464.8	-5	7.2
Atlanta MSA	3746	1898.4	-60.3	6.4
Miami-Ft. Lauderdale CMSA	3656	5429	38.3	14.7
Seattle-Tacoma-Bremerton CMSA	3424	2966.6	-41.3	3.3
Phoenix-Mesa MSA	2931	2707.2	-31.1	23.2
Cleveland-Akron CMSA	2912	2638	-42.8	-5.3
Minneapolis-St. Paul MSA	2831	1956.5	-54.2	7.2
San Diego MSA	2781	3402.7	4.5	22
St. Louis MSA	2563	2673.1	-56.5	-13.6
Denver-Boulder-Greeley CMSA	2365	3307	-30.4	7.4
Pittsburgh MSA	2346	2157.6	-64.3	-15
Tampa-St. Petersburg-Clearwater	2257	2630	16	2.4
Portland-Salem CMSA	2149	3021	-32.9	2.7
Cincinnati-Hamilton CMSA	1948	2367	-57.5	-11.5
Kansas City MSA	1737	1673	-64.3	-10.2
Sacramento-Yolo CMSA	1686	3284	-34.9	14.7
Milwaukee-Racine CMSA	1646	2395	-70.5	-1.6
Norfolk-Va Beach-Newport News	1542	1992	-67.9	8.2
San Antonio MSA	1538	2578	-48.4	-3.4
Indianapolis MSA	1519			
Orlando MSA	1504			

Source: http://www.publicpurpose.com/new-ix.htm

Table 3.2
Average Annual Population Growth Rate
USDA Area Groups

	1969-97	1969-78	1978-89	1989-95	1995-97
Metro Counties					
Large—counties in metro areas with 1 million or more pop					
Core Counties	0.65%	0.34%	0.89%	0.67%	0.63%
Non-core counties	1.30%	1.26%	1.33%	1.30%	1.32%
Small—counties in metro areas with LT 1 million pop	1.21%	1.43%	1.08%	1.23%	0.93%
Non-metro Counties					
Adjacent to Large Metro Areas					
Contain all or part of a city with 10,000 or more pop	1.05%	1.23%	0.82%	1.22%	1.01%
Contain no part of a city that large	.20%	.46%	.85%	.32%	1.56%
Adjacent to Small Metro Areas					
Contain all or part of a city of 10,000 or more pop	0.79%	1.25%	0.47%	0.74%	0.60%
Contain no part of a city that large	.90%	.28%	.51%	.98%	1.06%
Not adjacent to Metro Areas					
Contain all or part of a city of 10,000 or more pop	0.82%	1.32%	0.48%	0.82%	0.46%
Contain all or part of a town of 2,500 or 9,999 pop	0.61%	1.21%	0.10%	0.67%	0.55%
Totally rural, contain no part of a town as large as 2,500 pop	0.27%	0.71%	-0.22%	0.42%	0.51%
US Total	1.02%	1.10%	0.96%	1.05%	0.94%

Source: Calculated from Regional Economic Information System 1969-1997, Bureau of Economic Analysis, U.S. Department of Commerce, May 1999.

leave their cars at home in some instances" (*Los Angeles Times* January 2, 2000, p. M4). This approach errs on three counts: (1) most suburbanites do not have long commutes (see discussion that follows); (2) people make complex and personal trade-offs when choosing a place to live; and 3) it is naive to think that better spatial arrangements would result from a politicized, "sensible" approach.

Manufacturing industries began leaving large cities many years ago when trucks and highways made deliveries far away from rail yards economic. Of all the spatial groupings, the core counties in the million-plus metropolitan areas experienced the most rapid manufacturing decline from 1969 to 1997, while the most rural counties exhibited the most rapid metropolitan employment growth (Table 3.3). But the trends for total private employment growth are not too dissimilar, with the core counties in large MSAs growing more slowly, except that the non-core counties in these MSAs were the best performers between 1969 and 1997 (although 1989-95 was a notable exception; Table 3.4).

Table 3.3
Average Annual Manufacturing Employment Growth Rate
USDA Area Groups

	1969-97	1969-78	1978-89	1989-95	1995-97
Metro Counties					
Large—counties in metro areas with 1 million or more pop					
Core Counties	-1.22%	-0.82%	-1.36%	-2.30%	1.05%
Non-core counties	-0.03%	0.24%	0.07%	-1.09%	1.46%
Small—counties in metro areas with LT 1 million pop	0.00%	0.61%	-0.39%	-0.22%	0.12%
Non-metro Counties					
Adjacent to Large Metro Areas					
Contain all or part of a city with 10,000 or more pop	0.55%	1.21%	-0.18%	0.96%	0.38%
Contain no part of a city that large	.95%	.07%	.34%	.66%	0.17%
Adjacent to Small Metro Areas					
Contain all or part of a city of 10,000 or more pop	0.43%	1.20%	-0.01%	0.20%	0.06%
Contain no part of a city that large	.02%	.86%	.69%	.97%	-0.81%
Not adjacent to Metro Areas					
Contain all or part of a city of 10,000 or more pop	0.85%	1.67%	-0.03%	1.26%	0.70%
Contain all or part of a town of 2,500 or 9,999 pop	1.12%	2.48%	0.30%	1.26%	-0.96%
Totally rural, contain no part of a town as large as 2,500 pop	1.44%	2.55%	1.53%	0.61%	-1.55%
US Total	-0.15%	0.33%	-0.39%	-0.66%	0.56%

Source: Calculated from Regional Economic Information System 1969-1997, Bureau of Economic Analysis, U.S. Department of Commerce, May 1999.

Table 3.4
U.S. Private Employment Growth Rates
USDA Area Groups

	1969-97	1969-78	1978-89	1989-95	1995-97
Metro Counties					
Large—counties in metro areas with 1 million or more pop					
Core Counties	1.55%	1.35%	2.02%	0.58%	2.75%
Non-core counties	2.81%	2.91%	3.31%	1.62%	3.17%
Small—counties in metro areas with LT 1 million pop	2.48%	2.84%	2.34%	2.14%	2.68%
Non-metro Counties					
Adjacent to Large Metro Areas					
Contain all or part of a city with 10,000 or more pop	2.18%	2.49%	1.73%	2.48%	2.4%
Contain no part of a city that large	.43%	.73%	.87%	.86%	2.87%
Adjacent to Small Metro Areas					
Contain all or part of a city of 10,000 or more pop	1.91%	2.42%	1.48%	1.82%	2.22%
Contain no part of a city that large	.11%	.60%	.61%	.3%	2.02%
Not adjacent to Metro Areas					
Contain all or part of a city of 10,000 or more pop	2.32%	3.16%	1.52%	2.55%	2.19%
Contain all or part of a town of 2,500 or 9,999 pop	2.08%	3.07%	1.14%	2.35%	1.91%
Totally rural, contain no part of a town as large as 2,500 pop	2.00%	2.69%	1.11%	2.57%	2.04%
US Total	2.23%	2.39%	2.35%	1.61%	2.74%

Source: Calculated from Regional Economic Information System, U.S. Department of Commerce, Economics and Statistics Administration Bureau of Economic Analysis, Regional Economic Measurement Division.

Downtowns, Centers, and Subcenters

Most traditional central city functions, including the "incubation" of new industries, can now function efficiently in the large metro areas' suburbs and subcenters. This is why, within declining central cities, the biggest losers have been the traditional downtowns. Spatial delineations vary among the few data sources but it is clear, despite city boosterism, that there is no discernible link between metropolitan area success and downtown vitality. In 1996, the twenty-five largest central business districts (CBDs) employed only 5 percent of the surrounding metropolitan areas' jobs (Table 3.5). Without New York City's 1.4 million downtown jobs (40 percent of the Top 25), the number would be lower. Between 1994 and 1996, a period of substantial economic prosperity, nine of the major downtowns (including Los Angeles, Washington, Boston, and Houston) lost employment. Retail and services job growth in the CBDs between the 1987 and 1992 economic censuses was negative and zero, respectively (Gordon and Richardson 1997). Similar results are found from another data source: the Wharton Urban Decentralization Project reports zero employment growth for the top ten CBDs between 1976 and 1980 and slightly more than 1 percent average annual job growth for the same areas between 1980 and 1986. Thus, downtown stagnation is no new phenomenon.

This decline is happening despite expensive downtown renewal programs, many of which we augmented by equally costly convention centers, sports stadiums, and other baubles placed in declining areas at huge taxpayer expense with the stated purpose of "revitalizing downtown." Downtown-focused rail transit, discussed below, is merely one of many costly policy mistakes. Downtown boosterism and porkbarrel politics have been assisted by a widespread failure to understand that the era of strong downtowns dominating the major cities is, with very few exceptions (city quarters with historic districts and some small tourist downtowns), long gone and will never return. Many Americans seek out such places when they do a tour of Europe, treating them as large-scale museums to be visited and enjoyed, and may pay lip service to having one closer to home but their actual lifestyle choices tell the opposite story.

Current events in Los Angeles suggest that the highest and best use of the downtown's regional centrality is for high-tech switching equipment, not for residents or office workers. A recent *Los Angeles Times* front-page article ran under the headline "Telecom Invasion Rattles Downtown L.A. Boosters" and continued, "with more high-tech firms filling space with machines, visions of a revitalized central city are clouded . . . The telecommunications companies are clustered downtown because nearly all of the major local, national and international fiber-optic trunk lines carrying voice and data run underneath downtown streets. The firms want to be close to one another so that they can easily and cheaply hand off calls and other information between their networks" (November 2, 1999, p. A1). The story noted that very few people work in these new facilities. Meanwhile, approximately sixty miles to the south, California's Irvine Ranch Properties includes in its promotional brochures an aerial view of the Southern California coastline, stretching all the way from Santa Barbara to San Diego, wherein the ranch is highlighted and the accompanying text notes that "the Irvine Ranch is strategically located in the heart of Southern California's Technology Coast." The idea of centrality has changed (Kotkin 1999). It is very different from the days before ubiquitous access and communications links.

Table 3.5
CBD Employment, 1994, 1996

	1998 pop	1994	1996	1996	1996
		Principal CBD Empl	Principal CBD Empl	94 - 96 CBD Job Growth	CBD Empl Prop of Metro
New York-Northern NJ-Long Island CMSA	20124	1354.3	1388.8	0.025474	0.156168
Los Angeles-Riverside-Orange CMSA	15781	241.5	239.9	-0.006625	0.039762
Chicago-Gary-Kenosha CMSA	8809	173.5	182.6	0.052450	0.042270
Washington-Baltimore CMSA	7285	119.6	114.2	-0.045151	0.031930
San Francisco-Oakland-San Jose CMSA	6816	245.5	261.5	0.065173	0.082589
Philadelphia-Wilmington-Atlantic City CMSA	5988	82.5	82.8	0.003636	0.030241
Boston-Worcester-Lawrence-Lowell-Brockton	5633	24.5	24.9	0.016327	0.010691
Detroit-Ann Arbor-Flint CMSA	5458	42	37.6	-0.104762	0.015080
Dallas-Ft. Worth CMSA	4802	96	97.4	0.014583	0.041645
Houston-Galveston-Brazoria CMSA	4408	83.3	79.8	-0.042017	0.040590
Atlanta MSA	3746	50.1	64.3	0.283433	0.033743
Miami-Ft. Lauderdale CMSA	3656	12.6	10.9	-0.134921	0.007042
Seattle-Tacoma-Bremerton CMSA	3424	114.4	115.5	0.009615	0.071156
Phoenix-Mesa MSA	2931	48.2	51.6	0.070539	0.039404
Cleveland-Akron CMSA	2912	112.6	119.9	0.064831	0.083461
Minneapolis-St. Paul MSA	2831	99.2	105.3	0.061492	0.066684
San Diego MSA	2781	65.8	64.4	-0.021277	0.064464
St. Louis MSA	2563	84.1	85.7	0.019025	0.067560
Denver-Boulder-Greeley CMSA	2365	59.1	61.8	0.045685	0.050207
Pittsburgh MSA	2346				
Tampa-St. Petersburg-Clearwater MSA	2257				
Portland-Salem CMSA	2149	46.5	43.9	-0.055914	0.043591
Cincinnati-Hamilton CMSA	1948	78.7	77.9	-0.010165	0.083387
Kansas City MSA	1737	69.7	73.1	0.048780	0.083201
Sacramento-Yolo CMSA	1686				
Milwaukee-Racine CMSA	1646	101.7	101.4	-0.002950	0.113474
Norfolk-Va Beach-Newport News CMSA	1542				
San Antonio MSA	1538				
Indianapolis MSA	1519	39.9	41.5	0.040100	0.051102
Orlando MSA	1504				

Source: Zip Code Business Patterns 1996, U.S. Department of Commerce, Economics and Statistics Administration, U.S. Census Bureau, issued August 1999.

Conventional public transit, especially rail, best serves traditional dense employment clusters found in the now declining central business districts. Yet high levels of investment in transit systems continue with little attention to the fact that these places are fading fast. The universal justification is that these investments will reverse the decline of downtowns. There is no evidence to justify this conclusion.

The demise of downtowns does not necessarily mean that strong subcenters (metropolitan polycentricity) represent the new prototypical urban form. A serious problem is that the employment data are reported in terms of small spatial units, such as census tracts, only every ten years. We used these data to study metropolitan dispersion in the Los Angeles metropolitan area. Using 1970, 1980, and 1990 employment data to identify and define activity centers in each year, we found increasingly generalized job dispersion. We identified the number and the proportion of the region's jobs in each of the three years that show up in each year's centers (12 to 18, depending on the year). We found the proportion of jobs in each year's centers fell consistently and dramatically, from 19 percent in 1970 to 12 percent in 1990. In the period 1980–1990, even the number of jobs in centers fell.

Generalized dispersion does not imply an even spread of jobs. The pattern is rather a few "spikes" and many low-rise "hills" on a three-dimensional job density map. Again, agglomeration economies remain, but they are spread over larger geographical spaces. Using sales price data on office space for Los Angeles county locations, Rena Sivitanidou reached similar conclusions (1996). Whereas these economies had once been limited to the small radius of pedestrian access, and later over a much wider radius of auto access, their reach will now probably expand considerably with the use of electronic "highways."

Los Angeles downtown (approximated by a slightly larger L.A. core) has been the recipient of approximately $2.5 billion in urban renewal funds (in constant 1992 dollars) over the last twenty-five years. This does not include more than $500 million for the new convention center, $375 million for the new Staples Center stadium, and billions more on a downtown-focused rail transit plan. What is there to show in terms of the core's development? Visitors to L.A.'s downtown already know that (with the exception of a vibrant Latino street, Broadway) it is mostly barren. Nightlife is almost nonexistent, certainly in comparison with the Sunset Strip on the borders of Beverly Hills and West Hollywood some nine miles way. Office and hotel vacancy rates in downtown have been among the highest in the United States. Employment in the mid-Wilshire corridor to the west of downtown is declining. Between 1980 and 1990, absolute job growth in downtown was only 8,800 (2.5 percent), while regional jobs grew by 35 percent; the differential has not narrowed in the 1990s (with the takeover of the *Los Angeles Times* by the Chicago *Tribune* in March 2000, and the imminent approval of the takeover of ARCO by BP, there will be only two Fortune 500 corporate headquarters remaining in downtown Los Angeles).

Spatial Mismatch

Perhaps the most important market failure claim involving cities is the allegation that the suburbanization of jobs has left large numbers of minorities and the poor isolated from many jobs and, therefore, more likely to be unemployed. The "spacial mismatch" hypothesis has important implications for transportation access and the geographic dispersion of some ethnic and racial minorities, particularly those with lower incomes. If the mismatch exists, inner-city unemployment has a spatial explanation as well as a seemingly simple spatial policy antidote: balance jobs with housing in various zones of the region by implementing the managed growth agenda. "Balancing" can be done in a variety of ways: influence the location of low-skill jobs, manage the location of affordable housing, promote more mixed land uses, and improve access. Some proponents want to draw jobs back to the central cities while others want to pull them to "job-poor" parts of the suburbs to create shorter commuting opportunities. In any event, spatial mismatch reasoning is seen as a way to expand local government's already substantial role in income redistribution. This is a role that big-city governments have already embraced even though economists have argued that the cities are ill-equipped to perform them. Local governments have minimal policy instruments to make a difference, and they are open economies subject to selective migration (the poor move in while the highly taxed move out; Oates 1999).

Even if we overlook the impossible scale of a regional land-use matching task ("smart" growth advocates are not shy about fatal conceits), the premise is false. Involuntary unemployment and poor job prospects are human capital (including social networks) problems, rather than the result of inaccessibility. Moreover, the decentralization of jobs is not skewed in ways that remove only the best jobs from traditional centers. Rather, decentralization is across-the-board, affecting all major economic sectors (Gordon, Richardson, and Yu 1998). The problem of poverty is complex but the good news about U.S. labor markets is that there are relatively few working poor; once in the labor force, a person is unlikely to remain in poverty.

There is only one sure way to create jobs: improved education and training. Education, however, is related most closely to land-use issues due to the fact that parents compete for better schools by bidding up suburban home values in the better school districts (Crone 1998). The most promising way to achieve better schooling is via competition and parental choice, facilitated by school vouchers (Hoxby 1994). Better central city schools would slow suburbanization. Yet the voucher movement has had only moderate success because of vigorous opposition from the politically connected education establishment and constitutional obstacles. On-the-job training in the form of apprenticeships and on-the-job preparation has been almost wiped out by minimum wage legislation, and its local if misnamed version, "livable wage" ordinances. The substitution of government training programs for the lost apprenticeships has not worked.

The empirical case for a spatial mismatch explanation of inner city unemployment is unconvincing. To make the connection, Katherine O'Regan and John Quigley (1998) rely on general measures of "social isolation and social access," moving the discussion beyond the conventional focus on geographical urban space and commuting costs. Their findings for four New Jersey MSAs, however, add perspective to the spatial mismatch discussion; the employment rate differential between white and minority youth is explained more by human capital differences than by differences in geographic access. A similar ranking of the effects of space versus human capital is reported by Immergluck (1998).

Critics also ignore the fact that minorities are suburbanizing faster than the population as a whole. In the 1980s, while the white suburban resident population grew by 9.2 percent, the black suburban population grew by 34.4 percent and the Hispanic suburban population grew by 69.3 percent. These trends accelerated between 1990 and 1996 when the white suburban population grew by 10.8 percent, while blacks and Hispanics grew by 35 and 70.6 percent, respectively. The 2000 Census data will no doubt reinforce these trends. In addition, on a related theme, the growth rates in mortgage originations, business ownership, and college degrees are much higher for all minority groups than for whites.

Used cars are the favored transportation mode of the poor, reinforcing trends that further decentralize cities and lower population densities. Even among the poorest (those with incomes below $15,000), 80 percent of travel is by auto, and less than 10 percent is by public transit. The fact that many of the very elderly continue to operate private autos (even after they have lost some of the necessary skills) shows the strength of preferences for personal transportation.

In real world tests of the spatial mismatch hypothesis, some cities have added conventional transit lines to connect inner city areas with job centers. None of these have had a measurable impact on unemployment. Non-auto accessibility is most favorable in the nation's transit capital, New York, with transit use per capita seven times that of the United States as a whole (in fact, 37 percent of all 1997 U.S. transit boardings were in the New York metropolitan area). Yet among the ten largest U.S. central cities, unemployment in New York City was highest in every month of that year except one (it was surpassed by Detroit in July).

Mismatch-based arguments for transit investments are undermined by the fact that the addition of new rail transit has actually reduced accessibility because bus service has often been reduced or cut to pay for the high costs of rail. In Los Angeles, a coalition of minority and poor sued the transit agency to stop rail transit construction on these grounds. They argued successfully that the lion's share of transit costs pay for commuter rail lines that predominantly serve non-poor suburbanites. This suggests inefficient targeting: many highly subsidized rail systems, such as that of Washington D.C., serve large numbers of the middle and upper-middle class. User subsidies and expanded jitney-type services serve the poor and the elderly, but are strongly opposed by the transit lobby.

To explain inner-city unemployment in terms of the spatial mismatch story is flawed. Analysts overlook that prior to 1970, hundreds of thousands of poor blacks migrated long distances from southern farms to northern cities in search of better lives. Despite limited employment opportunities and blatant discrimination in destination cities, their lives improved. That dramatic historical trend makes "the hypothesized deterrent effect of a ten-mile bus trip to the suburbs in search of a job appear a little thin" (Mills and Lubuele 1997, pp. 733–34). Most long distance migrations are by the very poor. Currently, many immigrant domestic workers put up with the longest commutes in order to work.

A major problem that flows from smart growth plans and the manipulation of the supply of buildable sites is rising housing costs, contributing to the widely lamented housing affordability problem. Twenty years ago, Bernard Frieden warned that "(e)nvironmental and growth controls have laid heavy cost burdens on California homebuyers" (Frieden 1979). Residential densities throughout most of California are now rising, primarily the result of high land values; this is the major explanation of why the Los Angeles urbanized area, the nation's so-called sprawl capital, is in fact the most densely populated metropolis in the United States.

Sprawl's critics might applaud California's "progress." Yet, Portland's Urban Growth Boundary, in place since 1979, demonstrates the downside. Portland housing prices appreciated by 56 percent in the years 1990–1995, making the area one of the least affordable in the United States (Staley, Edgens, and Mildner 1999). Landowners inside the boundary were spectacularly rewarded while renters and first-time home buyers, generally among the less well off, were hurt. Similarly, as with the U. K. green-belt experience, leapfrogging into areas beyond the no-build zone resulted in very long commutes for those who continued to work inside the boundary and incurred significantly higher infrastructure costs.

The balancing strategy is complex and underscores the difficulty of social engineering. Businesses are "beginning in some cases to recognize the opportunity to expand in central cities and to employ central city residents to meet their labor needs" but "improving residential mobility is another way to increase the access of urban residents to better housing, jobs and educational opportunities. For inner city residents who desire this mobility, a combination of barriers exist, which must be overcome; these include a lack of affordable housing in the suburbs and social barriers related to race and ethnicity" (Final Report of the 95th American Assembly 1999, p. 14). Housing regulations crimp supply and create opportunities for politicized antidotes, in this case more subsidized housing programs. The low end of the housing market is no longer served by an unassisted private sector and the long-established filtering process. Rather, it is the almost exclusive province of tax credits, bonds, and public-private partnerships. Paradoxically, affordable housing units are brought to market only at a very high cost (Cummings and DiPasquale 1999). Once again, if subsidies are appropriate, they should be targeted at the demand not the supply side.

People are more likely to get the shelter they want at prices they can afford in freely functioning housing markets. Moreover, suburban lifestyles are chosen by the majority because they offer job, shopping, and social arrangements that work out better. Net migration out of the higher density nineteenth-century central cities continues unabated even in metro areas that show little or no growth. Critics who assert that "sprawl systematically deprives inner-city residents of opportunities and adequate services" (Freilich and Peschoff 1997) have the cause and effect backwards. In any migration, there are push and pull forces.

People are making moves that are in their best interests; they are choosing to leave less attractive environments.

Inner cities in the United States include greater concentrations of poor people than the central cities of other developed countries. This has resulted in the problem of poverty being identified in many people's minds with the problems of the inner cities. Critics of sprawl often talk about decaying inner cities and central cities losing jobs, people, and capital. All these commentators are describing places, not people. They focus on the inanimate rather than on the actors. They embrace a "place-prosperity" argument, losing sight of what should count most, the welfare of people ("people prosperity"). Phyllis Myers (1999) has shown, in his concept of "demographic dynamism," that immigrants move up (e.g., to home ownership) and move out. The idea of "saving" places is the politically preferred way to fight poverty. The place-prosperity approach invites politicization and waste and ignores the more important human capital discussions (Jacoby and Siegel 1999). This is similar to protectionist concerns that focus on job losses rather than on the highest and best use of human capital that could generate more and better paid jobs in the long run. In the fast-paced modern economy, the key to prosperity lies in flexible markets where participants are able to exploit new opportunities quickly. Augmenting the role of regulators, especially growth managers, is more costly than ever. The recent example of a stipulated $1,000 per employee annual exaction to be levied by a Portland suburban county on Intel if they hire beyond a negotiated employment ceiling evokes comparisons to European-style anti-job policies. Of course, in attractive locations in periods of prosperity, such constraints are considered less bothersome and hence are widely tolerated.

TRANSPORTATION ISSUES

The Auto-Highway System

Unpriced highway access falls within the textbook market failure category. Yet, in spite of this, average highway speeds keep rising as more commuting occurs on less congested suburb-to-suburb roads. In a recent letter to the editor (*Wall Street Journal* June 7, 1999, p. A23), the president of the American Society of Landscape Architects wrote that "sprawl is the kind of unchecked and unplanned growth that creates appalling lifestyles marked by two-hour commutes between decaying cities and traffic-choked suburbs." The writer does not reveal how many two-hour commutes there are. In fact, average (one-way) commuting time in 1990 (Pisarski 1996) was 22.4 minutes (all modes, even lower if transit was excluded). Suburb-to-suburb commutes (within the same metro areas) were even shorter, averaging 20.8 minutes. Suburb-to-suburb commuting accounted for 44 percent of all metropolitan commuting in 1990 and is the fastest growing commuting flow. In 1990, just 12.5 percent commuted more than 45 minutes and less than 6 percent commuted longer than 60 minutes (the longer trips included disproportionately greater numbers of transit users). By way of contrast, almost one-half of Greater Tokyo commuters, with more dependence on transit, travel more than 60 minutes one-way (Sato and Spinks, 1996).

Trip time changes from 1980 have been minor, with an average increase of 40 seconds for the United States as a whole, in spite of significant population growth and much faster growth in vehicle miles traveled (data are from Pisarski 1996). However, the Census data make no allowances for the documented increase in multi-stop, multi-purpose trips ("trip-chaining"; Gordon, Richardson, and Liao 1998) stimulated by more two-worker households. This suggests that the 40-second intercensal increase is an overstatement.

The Nationwide Personal Transportation Survey (NPTS) data highlight good news over a longer time span: average commuting durations fell from 22 minutes in 1969 to 20.7 minutes in 1995. Yet in the sixty-five largest U.S. urbanized areas, vehicle miles traveled grew much faster than lane-miles resulting in a substantial increase in average traffic densities; nationwide, in the last ten years, urban vehicle miles traveled grew at almost 2.5 times the rate of urban lane-miles (Hartgen and Curley 1999). The combination of more people in more autos traveling more miles at faster speeds without concomitant highway capacity growth is an amazing example of beneficial market adjustments. It also exposes the erroneous interpretations routinely attached to "congestion indices"; that is, comparisons of available metropolitan lane-miles to recorded area vehicle miles traveled (Schrank and Lomax 1999).

"*Impending* gridlock" is forever. Those subscribing to gridlock stories typically assume that all new metropolitan growth will be in established centers. In the 1980s, for example, the Greater Los Angeles area added more than 3 million people, growing from slightly more than 12 million to almost 15.5 million. In spite of this growth, average commuting times and speeds ranked fifth in the top ten U.S. metro areas. Traffic doomsday scenarios are, of course, helpful to the promoters of expensive subway projects. In Los Angeles, the metropolitan planning agencies predicted crawling highway speeds without building rail transit.

Despite the predictions of standard urban economic theory, most households do not choose where to live by focusing only on the journey to work. Instead, they consider trade-offs among a wide variety of possible destinations and other locational considerations. Most notably, families with children rank access to good schools and other family services at the top. Some urban economists have, unfortunately, concluded that these households indulge in "excess commuting." This conclusion is undermined by Alan Pisarski's calculation for 1990 that if 70 percent of all workers live in multi-worker households then it is unclear that there are relocations that could substantially reduce aggregate commuting distances (Pisarski, 1996). The rapid rise in home-based businesses also complicates this picture.

In the absence of efficient highway pricing some congestion is inevitable. It is the default roadway capacity rationing device. The real news is how little highway congestion there is. Dynamic market adjustments, the suburbanization of jobs for example, is the explanation—"rational relocation" by both firms and households is the solution, not the problem. Given these market responses, it is puzzling why Anthony Downs subscribes to the opinion that the "single most aggravating problem associated with sprawl is rising traffic congestion—

particularly in suburban communities" (Downs, 1999a, p. 968). His subsequent discussion suggests a confusion between peak-hour congestion on *some* routes and systemic worsening congestion throughout a metropolitan region; the former is inevitable, the latter is not.

Although historical commuting data are rare, the few available examples show long-term stability. A 1967 Los Angeles Regional Transportation Study found that average commuting times were 24 minutes each way (Gordon and Richardson 1993), whereas the 1995 NPTS entry for Los Angeles (Table 3.6) is also 24 minutes. Comparisons of entire travel time distributions are even harder to find, but the best information available suggests that the shape of the entire distribution appears not to have changed at all in a half century. Beneficial land-use adjustments are the only convincing explanation.

The data from self-reported travel time surveys are not only more reliable and more plausible than modeled travel time results (such as those from the Texas Transportation Institute and the Federal Highway Administration) but also tell a diametrically opposite story. Area-wide averages of vehicle-miles per lane-mile mask the important spatial redistributions that explain the good news. The commuting paradox (stable regional travel times coexisting with substantial, but not ubiquitous, increases in route congestion) explains how and why flexible land markets allow people (as rational relocators) to adjust to road and highway bottlenecks. All the doomsday forecasts of traffic gridlock are wrong because they build on a static model that assumes away such adjustments. In fact, there would be less spatial decentralization if road and highway pricing were efficient.

Efforts to reduce external costs and charge travelers the full marginal costs of each trip are economists' favorite urban transportation policy prescription (see Poole, Chapter 4). Supporting this view is the fact that most peak-hour traffic in U.S. cities is for non-work purposes. Many of these trips could efficiently be diverted to off-peak periods. Without pricing, there are likely to be severe inefficiencies. Mobility is a good, but newly generated traffic provides a perpetual justification to oppose new proposed developments, unless it pays its way. Mark De Lucchi (1996) has estimated that full-cost pricing would add between 17 and 26 percent to the annual costs of auto use. Even without political obstacles, there are transaction costs involved in getting the prices right. Economists are as skeptical about achieving a congestion-free world as a pollution-free world.

An additional question is whether public officials can be expected to behave like profit-maximizing private owners and make the necessary pricing and road improvements to reduce congestion. This suggests road privatization as the best way to achieve efficient use. But extensive highway privatization in the United States is unlikely. The states would have to take the lead, but they are holding on to a huge and politically popular highway trust fund that they are unlikely to let go (Roth 1995).

There are several significant congestion pricing projects now underway, one of which (Southern California's SR-91) was privately financed and built (see Poole, Chapter 4). Numerous lessons are being learned, including the difficulties and pitfalls that emerge when private owner-operators manage very small pieces of a state-run network. Many commuters, on the other hand, are learning first-

Table 3.6
Average Trip Times, 1995
(selected NPTS trip purposes, one-way, POVs)

	1998 pop	1995	1995	1995	1995
		(NPTS 1) To/From Work	(NPTS3) Shopping	(NPTS4) Fam Pers	(NPTS 10) Soc Rec
		All POV Mins	All POV Mins	All POV Mins	All POV Mins
New York-Northern NJ-Long Island CMSA	20124	25.4	12.2	14.1	19.0
Los Angeles-Riverside-Orange CMSA	15781	24.1	12.4	13.6	16.1
Chicago-Gary-Kenosha CMSA	8809	23.7	12.0	16.9	16.0
Washington-Baltimore CMSA	7285	25.1	14.8	17.0	18.0
San Francisco-Oakland-San Jose CMSA	6816	21.4	11.3	14.1	16.4
Philadelphia-Wilmington-Atlantic City CMSA	5988	20.6	11.8	13.3	19.1
Boston-Worcester-Lawrence-Lowell-Brockton CMSA	5633	22.2	12.0	13.1	17.2
Detroit-Ann Arbor-Flint CMSA	5458	20.6	11.9	11.7	14.3
Dallas-Ft. Worth CMSA	4802	21.2	13.3	13.1	18.7
Houston-Galveston-Brazoria CMSA	4408	21.2	12.0	14.2	17.6
Atlanta MSA	3746	23.1	11.5	14.9	15.3
Miami-Ft. Lauderdale CMSA	3656	21.7	11.4	14.1	16.4
Seattle-Tacoma-Bremerton CMSA	3424	27.1	12.5	14.9	19.0
Phoenix-Mesa MSA	2931	18.5	13.5	13.4	16.0
Cleveland-Akron CMSA	2912	18.9	13.5	19.4	15.6
Minneapolis-St. Paul MSA	2831	19.5	12.3	14.5	17.4
San Diego MSA	2781	11.8	5.8	8.1	11.4
St. Louis MSA	2563	21.2	14.8	12.8	15.2
Denver-Boulder-Greeley CMSA	2365	21.4	10.7	11.1	17.7
Pittsburgh MSA	2346	22.7	11.8	12.4	15.8
Tampa-St. Petersburg-Clearwater MSA	2257	18.9	11.3	16.2	20.2
Portland-Salem CMSA	2149	18.5	13.3	11.6	19.7
Cincinnati-Hamilton CMSA	1948	20.2	12.4	14.4	19.1
Kansas City MSA	1737	19.7	11.4	11.5	15.7
Sacramento-Yolo CMSA	1686	17.0	11.0	13.5	14.8
Milwaukee-Racine CMSA	1646	17.5	19.0	13.0	16.3
Norfolk-Va Beach-Newport News CMSA	1542	20.6	15.6	13.4	18.4
San Antonio MSA	1538	19.0	12.1	12.8	21.2
Indianapolis MSA	1519	17.0	11.1	15.0	14.0
Orlando MSA	1504	20.3	14.4	14.5	24.8
All CMSAs		23.6	12.4	14.4	17.8

Source: Nationwide Personal Transportation Survey, October 1997, Federal Highway
Administration, United States Department of Transportation.

hand that they have an opportunity to exchange money for time whenever they want.

Nevertheless, there is the widespread impression that road pricing is inequitable (for an opposite view, see Richardson and Bae 1998). The lengths to which transportation planners and others will go to avoid the pricing option is illustrated by the willingness to build or try almost any other alternative to avoid gridlock. New urbanists now propose traffic calming; that is, impediments to the flow of traffic, such as roadway narrowing, "neckdowns and chokers," closures, traffic circles, forced turns, and speed humps. These are capacity reductions designed to change the behavior of motorists (Dittmar and Poticha 1999, p. 5) by making driving less attractive so that people will walk, bike, or use transit instead.

Of course, any pricing scheme is likely to create both winners as well and losers. The real problem is that most people enjoy the personal mobility provided by the auto-highway system and suburban lifestyles, while simultaneously bemoaning pockets of congestion and resisting their logical antidote—peak-load pricing. Free access continues to be widely regarded as an entitlement even though congestion might be avoided by restraining consumption by charging the full opportunity costs.

Many solutions are offered as an escape from this dilemma, including strict, and usually counterproductive, land-use controls and hugely expensive transit investments, especially high-capacity rail transit systems. A recent San Francisco Bay Area Council opinion survey showed that 40 percent of respondents ranked transportation as "the most important problem facing the Bay Area today" (education was second at 14 percent); the same poll found that "expand public transit" was the first choice (favored by 82 percent) for "effective ways to improve quality of life" (Wall Street Journal, Dec. 9, 1998). But is the diagnosis and prescription in line with individual behavior?

Urban Transit

Many politicians, planners, environmentalists, and Smart Growth advocates continue to stress the importance of expanding public transit, especially the much more expensive rail transit, despite conventional transit's long history as a declining industry; after more than $360 billion of public subsidies since the mid-1960s, transit use per capita is at a historic low (www.publicpurpose.com). Falling ridership in the face of rising subsidies has become the industry norm. There are only slightly more transit users in the whole of the United States than in the city of Shanghai. Only 1.8 percent of all person-trips (2.1 percent of all person-miles) are via transit. This is substantially less than walking (5.4 percent of person-trips) but slightly more than school bus use (1.7 percent of person-trips; U.S. Department of Transportation 1997, Figure 15). Transit work-trips are 3.5 percent of person-trips (U.S. Department of Transportation 1997, Figure 21). Yet public transit received more than 15 percent of all public expenditures on transportation between 1977 and 1995.

Per capita transit use in almost all of the nation's largest metro areas fell by double-digit rates in the period 1980–1997 (Table 3.7; the data measure board-

Table 3.7
Per Capita Transit Use, 1980 - 1997
(unlinked trips)

	1998 Pop	1980 - 97	1990 - 97
		Prop Chge Unlinked Transit Trips/Cap	Prop Chge Unlinked Transit Trips/Cap
New York-Northern NJ-Long Island CMSA	20124	-15.4	-0.1
Los Angeles-Riverside-Orange CMSA	15781	-15.6	-2.6
Chicago-Gary-Kenosha CMSA	8809	-36.3	-25.1
Washington-Baltimore CMSA	7285	-19.8	-14.6
San Francisco-Oakland-San Jose CMSA	6816	-21.9	-5.4
Philadelphia-Wilmington-Atlantic City CMSA	5988	-22.8	-14.8
Boston-Worcester-Lawrence-Lowell-Brockton CMSA	5633	-11.0	-4.2
Detroit-Ann Arbor-Flint CMSA	5458	-51.0	-31.1
Dallas-Ft. Worth CMSA	4802	-10.6	0.2
Houston-Galveston-Brazoria CMSA	4408	34.2	-16.8
Atlanta MSA	3746	-15.3	-5.8
Miami-Ft. Lauderdale CMSA	3656	-8.0	3.2
Seattle-Tacoma-Bremerton CMSA	3424	-21.9	7.8
Phoenix-Mesa MSA	2931	28.9	-12.0
Cleveland-Akron CMSA	2912	-41.2	-10.9
Minneapolis-St. Paul MSA	2831	-54.8	-18.9
San Diego MSA	2781	27.5	12.6
St. Louis MSA	2563	-40.2	19.0
Denver-Boulder-Greeley CMSA	2365	5.8	9.1
Pittsburgh MSA	2346	-31.8	-15.6
Tampa-St. Petersburg-Clearwater MSA	2257	-38.8	-24.8
Portland-Salem CMSA	2149	-1.2	12.6
Cincinnati-Hamilton CMSA	1948	-41.2	-20.9
Kansas City MSA	1737	-53.3	-27.2
Sacramento-Yolo CMSA	1686	14.6	28.4
Milwaukee-Racine CMSA	1646	-21.1	4.7
Norfolk-Va Beach-Newport News CMSA	1542	-47.4	7.5
San Antonio MSA	1538	-27.0	-20.5
Indianapolis MSA	1519	-53.7	-28.7
Orlando MSA	1504	33.8	78.0

Source: http://www.publicpurpose.com/new-ix.htm

ings or unlinked trips, avoiding the misleading mixing of trips involving trans
fers with those that do not). Houston and Phoenix started from a low ridership
base and grew in the 1980s but suffered reversals between 1900 and 1997. Only
four (Denver, Orlando, San Diego and Sacramento) of the thirty largest metro
areas show a sustained seventeen-year growth in per capita use; these four also

started the period with very low levels of ridership and still have minuscule transit use.

Increasingly dispersed origins and destinations, rising auto affordability, and the widespread appeal of auto use have been widely cited as the explanations for transit's decline. One important dimension of the convenience and flexibility of auto travel is the increasing propensity to make incidental stops to and from work (trip chaining). The 1995 NPTS data show that 20 percent of all trips to work between 6 and 9 a.m. involve at least one intermediate stop. In the afternoons, between 4 and 7 p.m., 30 percent of commuters do not go directly home but make a stop (e.g., shop, school, etc.). Contemporary lifestyles cannot easily be accommodated by conventional transit or by carpools. This is also why extensive systems of HOV lanes and even more expensive exclusive freeway-to-freeway carpool lane ramps have had negligible impacts and why they will never redeem their high costs. Further increases in the female labor force participation rate will likely expand the demand for trip-chaining and more auto use.

Nevertheless, vast sums have been spent on the wrong projects (mostly rail transit) administered by unresponsive yet politicized (and unionized) agencies. Dan Pickrell (1990) examined eight new rail systems and found that (1) four new heavy-rail systems experienced ridership shortfalls averaging 35 percent; (2) four new light-rail systems had patronage shortfalls that averaged 65 percent; (3) full costs per boarding were $8.66 (average) for the subways and $7.99 (average) for the trolleys; and (4) three of the eight cities experienced lower systemwide patronage after rail systems opened. Each new transit trip cost almost $20. The annual cost of one new transit commuter was more than $10,000 (it would almost have been cheaper to pay low-wage workers to stay home). Pickrell's findings are notable because the transit industry rarely elaborates full costs, focusing on operating costs while most capital cost data remain obscure and hard to get.

Updating the Pickrell findings, the 1985-1995 systemwide performance in these eight cities reveals net transit ridership losses in four of the eight. Taken as a group, their ridership grew by only 3 percent over the ten-year period. Roughly speaking, it cost society $15 billion in capital costs plus operating expenses to effect this increase. Assuming that capital costs per year are annualized at 10 percent and using Pickrell's average operating cost for rail service, the 25 million net new transit trips cost $1.85 billion per year or almost $75 per new boarding! These fares are not even competitive with limousines. Approximately 75 percent of transit costs are subsidized by taxpayers, some of it from the highway trust fund. In contrast, FHWA's most recent cost-allocation study puts auto subsidies at 10 to 30 percent, although Randall Podenza (1995) argued that auto use more than pays for itself. Transit advocates say that they want "balance." A better option is to phase out any auto subsidies (perhaps via an "optimum" fuel tax, as suggested by Mills 1999) and, at the same time, end the new rail programs.

In the face of the bad news, rail boosters have retreated to an emphasis on light rail. These systems tend to be even less cost-effective (Rubin, Moore, and Lee 1999). The ten U.S. cities that added light rail in the years 1980-1995 experienced a collective system-wide ridership loss of 2 percent. Even the few systems that showed modest gains are not close to being cost-effective (Richmond 1999, Table 2-15). Fifteen light-rail systems that opened their books to the U.S. Federal Transit Authority (FTA) show considerable taxpayer subsidies. Farebox recovery of only *operating costs* ranged from 10 percent in Los Angeles to 66 percent in San Diego. When capital costs are added, the subsidies become much larger. In return, these systems serve .27 percent of their metropolitan areas' travel (Richmond 1999, Table 5). Rail transit cannot pay its way because no one values its service to cover its huge costs. This is, of course, why the promotion of transit is expressed in terms of other goals: saving energy, cleaning the air, decongesting the roads, and promoting new (and "better") land-use patterns. Paradoxically, none of these additional benefits are possible while transit's ridership gains are negligible.

Even though the failure of rail transit has been widely documented, expensive proposals for new rail projects are still being sold as a way to "get people out of their cars." The transit industry's trade magazine recently noted: "At first glance, the largesse of the Transportation Equity Act for the 21st Century (TEA-21) seems to have turned the U.S. rail projects pipeline into a gusher. Indeed, the law enacted in 1999, the nation's largest public transport bill in history, authorized funding for more than 200 specifically identified projects over the six-year life of the law" (Henke, 1999, p 32). At the height of the Cold War, it was said that there was at least one military base in every congressional district; analogously, there soon may be a light-rail transit system in each U.S. metropolitan area.

Responding to the poor record of recently installed rail transit facilities, advocates now promote "transit-oriented development" (TOD) or Transit Villages, a key element of Smart Growth, as a way to create development densities around train stations to assure adequate patronage. Homes, stores, and social services would be clustered around transit stations. Residential densities would be in the range of 12 to 20 dwelling units per acre. In support, some studies have found slightly higher transit use by people living near stations (Cervero 1993). From this, it is inferred that somehow forcing more such densities will generate greater transit use. Yet the obvious logical fallacy is ignored. Even if there are some people willing to trade off density for transit access (perhaps because they like transit or have used it in the past), it does not follow that others compelled to live at higher densities would choose the same trade-off (Brindle, 1995).

The widespread and powerful preference for personal mobility cannot be easily dismissed. A survey showed that 88 percent of French car owners look on their car as "an important part of their personal freedom" (Gerondeau 1997, p. 229). In the United States there were 1.78 vehicles per household but only 0.68 children per household in 1995. Even scholars have recognized the empowerment that accompanies the release from fixed routes and schedules. Carpooling in the United States is negligible for precisely this reason, and declined by 19 percent in the 1980s. Average commuting vehicle occupancy in metro areas in 1990 was only 1.09. These statistics do not purge the data of spontaneous intrahousehold carpooling, thereby overstating induced ridesharing. James Dunn adds that "the auto provides a sort of individualist equality that is particularly well suited to American values" (1999, p. 2). The international allure of American popular culture suggests that American freedoms appeal to people everywhere. Hence, a universal fondness of autos is no surprise.

All this fuels the fire. For many, the private auto is too democratic while public transit is properly collective and politically correct. The leaders of the former east-bloc nations understood quite well that "a mobile population is a population essentially out of control of centralized government" (Yates, quoted in Smith 1990). The complementarity of auto use with privacy and individual single-family housing incites the critics.

Compact development and growth management advocates hate to admit that while there are just negligible differences in auto trips per capita in TOD-type areas (Cervero 1993), their higher densities result in more traffic congestion. Evidence across the largest U.S. urbanized areas points to positive, if moderate, correlations between population density and commuting trip times. The 1995 NPTS data for the thirty largest metropolitan areas can be disaggregated by trip purpose and travel mode (see Table 3.6). At this level, sample sizes are large enough (greater than 100) to distinguish among four major trip types (working, shopping, family and personal purposes, social and recreational purposes) and trips by autos and by all privately operated vehicles (autos, vans, trucks, SUVs, etc.). The simple correlation between auto commute times and 1990 densities is 0.55; between all privately operated vehicle commute times and 1990 densities, it is 0.32. Correlations between the other three trip types and urbanized area population density are near zero.

Dan Pickrell and Paul Schimek (1999) demonstrate that, after controlling for income and other household characteristics, the elasticity of household vehicle miles traveled with respect to residential density is approximately -0.1. In other words, a doubling of densities would decrease vehicle miles traveled per household by 10 percent. However, with twice as many households, there would be many more trips. Other cross-sectional studies corroborate the intuitively obvious thought that high development densities are associated with high congestion (Hartgen and Curley 1999). Kenneth Orski (1999) reports that: "The Ballston rail transit station in Northern Virginia, often cited as a national model of a compact transit-oriented village that is supposed to encourage walking and reduce car use, is a case in point. With density five times higher than its neighboring spread-out Fairfax City/Oakton area, Ballston creates more than four times as many daily vehicle trips than its low-density neighbor." It appears that even when everything is within walking distance and everyone rides bicycles, people will continue to use their autos.

Household trip frequencies are often the wild card. It is by no means clear that they remain unaffected when access is improved. In most cases, we consume more when the price drops. This contributes to one more of many Smart Growth ironies. The EPA, through its Clean Air Act mandates, and hundreds of other federal, state, and local planning agencies do whatever they can to promote compact land-use arrangements in the belief that these will contribute to less auto use and cleaner air. Bun in fact, auto use may increase and certainly the air gets dirtier. The theory behind this multi-billion dollar effort is unsound (see also Green, Chapter 5).

There are no plausible policies that "get people out of their cars" in significant numbers. The steepest transit ridership losses in recent years were in transit's strongest markets where conditions are most favorable, including New York, Chicago, Boston, Philadelphia, Washington, D.C., and Baltimore (Taylor and McCullough 1998). It is for this reason that the last refuge of true believers, those who disregard all news of discomforting trends, is faith in some imminent U-turn. What if it happened?

Going back to the 1990 Census data and excluding those who work at home (and are least likely to switch modes), commuting mode shares across the United States were 91.4 percent private auto, 5.5 percent public transit, and 3.1 percent for other modes. Assume that an ambitious transit program were to succeed and increase transit's share by 25 percent (unprecedented, even after $360 billion in subsidies). Assume also that all new transit riders come from automobiles (historically, at most a one-third shift). Even under these conditions, auto use would still account for more than 90 percent of all commuting. Would the expenditures needed for such an expansion in mass transit be justified in terms of external economies or other benefits?

A variant of the TOD argument holds that sprawl can be avoided and land use can be shaped by the introduction of transit service, especially rail. Low and declining preferences for transit and powerful suburbanization trends are the Achilles Heels of this argument. A recent study by John Landis and Robert Cervero (1999) that examines twenty years of development trends around stations of the oldest of the post-World War II subways, San Francisco's Bay Area Transit (BART), finds that "population has grown faster away from BART than near it" (Landis and Cervero 1999, p. 4). The authors report the same for employment growth in the Bay Area. A system that in 1999 had not yet reached its 1975 ridership forecasts, even with the aid of a 30 percent population growth, cannot be expected to have any significant secondary impacts. This is the real problem, rather than the regulatory barriers to land-use changes cited in an accompanying article (Levine, 1999).

Unconventional transit (including private transit) and transportation management approaches, including deregulation and proper pricing, have received only moderate attention in U.S. cities. Being low-cost items (sometimes unsubsidized), they lack the built-in pork-barrel constituencies attached to rail projects and are unable to compete politically. Transit systems configured in ways to take advantage of commuters' preferences, such as express buses running on separate rights-of-way (busways or transitways), could achieve high operating speeds but are not political favorites. Because they typically do not require feeders, they can reduce the need for transfers and generate more demand than rail, at a cost per passenger trip that is between 10 and 20 percent of that of light rail (Kain 1999). Light rail is often not grade separated and, therefore, slower than buses on grade-separated busways. The political preference for rail is explained by the fact that it is primarily a jobs program, reinforced by an opportunity for politicians to harness massive public funds with the support of environmentalists. Rail transit evaluations have consistently overestimated expected ridership (and other benefits) and underestimated capital and operating costs (Kain 1992, Pickrell 1990, Wachs 1985).

The preference for driving is so powerful that transit will always be a marginal alternative in the United States. But it should be easy to improve on recent performance. The trouble is that the politics of pork ensure the neglect of common sense, low-cost transportation programs. Policy recommendations might proceed on four complementary lines: (1) getting the prices right, including congestion pricing and the privatization of some highways (see Poole, Chapter 4); (2) deregulation to allow more private transit provision while bringing the various informal suppliers out of the shadows and offering shuttle services beyond the typical fixed-routes or airport origins and destinations; (3) user-side subsidies, such as taxi vouchers, transit passes for students, and so forth, to replace or scale down the much abused supplier-side subsidies; and (4) busways to accommodate transit and HOV vehicles.

The specifics of all of these would vary from place to place. For example, user-side subsidies have received some recent attention in the form of "eco-pass" experiments, whereby employers buy inexpensive bulk access rights to public transit in much the way that they secure group health insurance. Transit agencies then sell unused capacity at bulk rates to employers, who award or sell passes to employees at low rates. Local governments could partner with such employers, using available transit funds to make the passes even more attractive. Donald Shoup (1999) reports that the Santa Clara Valley (California) Transportation Authority charges from $10 to $80 per employee per year, depending on the employer's location and the number of passes purchased. The price is much lower than for conventional transit passes because the frequency of use by each employee is lower than that of the conventional transit pass user. Transit vouchers of this type could be redeemable when using conventional or private transit (if significant deregulation occurred).

Private transportation would be a realistic option if deregulation were fully implemented (see Klein, Moore, and Reja 1997). After passing the normal safety and insurance requirements, any and all providers should be permitted to operate. The clandestine jitney-type services operating in the immigrant and low-income communities of New York, Miami, Los Angeles, Detroit, and other cities strongly suggest that the established transit and taxi monopolies serve the poor badly. Legalization would impose significant costs on "underground" operators and user-side subsidies might be needed persuade them to become legal; they might even induce new suppliers. Another important benefit is that competition would force public transit to become more efficient if it wishes to survive.

The "HOT"-lane (high-occupancy-toll) proposal also embraces all four parts of common sense urban transportation and may be the most promising way to reintroduce market mechanisms to the highway system (Poole, Chapter 4; Fielding and Klein, 1993). Existing high-occupancy lanes would be made accessible to solo drivers if they paid tolls that varied by time-of-day demand conditions; new electronic toll collection, scanning, and feedback technologies make this approach quite feasible. HOT lanes in large metropolitan areas would be open to the usual ride-sharers of underutilized HOV lanes, as well as solo drivers paying peak-hour tolls, buses, and private and other kinds of transit (Poole and Orski 1999). There would be more transit users if deregulation were jointly implemented with eco-passes, both on HOT/HOV lanes and exclusive busways.

Finally, tolls could be a new source of highway funding. The sum of these policy approaches, if implemented simultaneously, is greater than their individual parts.

In an effort to sidestep the record of poor performance of public transit in the United States, Paul Weyrich and William Lind (1999) suggest that transit's critics have been asking the wrong questions. Rather, they ask: What share of "transit competitive trips" does transit really serve? "Transit competitive" has three parts: "First, transit must be available. Second, the available transit must be high quality. And third, the trip purpose must be one for which transit can compete." For Weyrich and Lind, high-quality transit means rail transit; availability means easy pedestrian access, presumably at both ends of the trip; and work trips are the logical trip purpose—although the authors also see a new recreation market, such as riding trolley lines for fun at the Atlanta Olympics.

Is transit less widely available because it is little used? Or, is it little used because it is less widely available? Inevitably, both are true to some extent. Which matters most? Weyrich and Lind emphasize the latter in spite of the fact that most people prefer to live in a world of consumer sovereignty where resource allocation and use responds to demand rather than the reverse.

Demand still matters even where provision is highly politicized, as in public transit, although the link between quantities supplied and demanded is tenuous. In the United States, transit use per capita is now at a historic low despite massive public subsidies. The recent spate of rail transit building has added significant capacity but not in forms or in places where people seem to want it. In spite of all the new capacity, there is no reversal in the long-term decline of transit use.

Conventional transit worked best in a world with high concentrations of origins and destinations (where employment and population densities are high) and with large numbers of people too poor to own and operate an automobile. Both conditions have been declining in the United States and in many other developed and developing nations, explaining the decline of conventional transit both here and abroad. The three preconditions that Weyrich and Lind insist on are receding precisely because transit competes so poorly. Population and employment densities are falling in most places, and most people and employers are choosing *not* to locate near transit stations because collective transportation is inconvenient and expensive in terms of what really counts, economizing on time. In low-density settings where origins and destinations are dispersed, transit that best serves high-volume corridors competes poorly. Thus, high-capacity rail systems are inevitably underutilized and very expensive.

CONCLUSIONS

Are modern cities a market failure? Or will the statistic interventions widely prescribed for cities do more harm than good? Do we need more than the urban equivalent of minimal "Night Watchman" governance (Nozick 1977)? Do urban land and housing markets fail, requiring the intelligent arbitration of the state?

The entitlement process has become an intricate and very costly obstacle course in the way of development. In the case of Los Angeles' massive Playa Vista development, the site remained empty during a decade of permitting and lawsuits. Spontaneous privately agreed controls, such as covenants or developer-planned communities, have emerged to reduce the risk of externalities. Levittown, New York, with its community swimming pools, schools, and recreation areas, and its many successors and imitators are now staples of modern American history, documented and celebrated in literature (Hise 1993). Developers have always been planners. They are now becoming more involved, packaging governance procedures with residential and mixed-use developments (Beaudreaux and Holcombe forthcoming; Foldvary 1995; Nelson 1999). In Hayekian fashion, homebuilders see a demand for transparent property rules and procedures and are prompted to design and offer them in ways that appeal to prospective buyers. This is often criticized as "private government" outside the accepted federal, state, and municipal system. However, this is merely a response to the fact that Exit (suburbanization and exurbanization) has trumped Voice; alternative arrangements have developed because conventional governments offer unacceptable property rights arrangements.

"Perfect" markets exist only in textbooks.

The market works precisely because it is not perfect. The great strength of the private property market economy is not the optimality properties of a state of affairs where all the gains from exchange have been exhausted, but the fact that the market is in constant state of flux where existing errors provide the incentives for future corrections and this leads individuals to be less erroneous than before. It is this constant activity that is the source of the adaptability to changing circumstances and the spur for innovation. (Boetke 2000, p. 39-40)

The profits of developers depend on giving people what they want. The competitive nature of the U.S. construction industry is apparent. There are many producers competing for the consumers' dollars: there were 168,400 general building contractors in the U.S. in 1992 (1998 Statistical Abstract of the U.S. Table 1190). Moreover, Dun & Bradstreet data reveal that construction industry business starts are more frequent than in most other industries, an indicator of above-average ease of entry. Wide real estate price swings imply competition and numerous surveys show consistency between people's overwhelming stated preferences for low-density living and the revealed preferences of home purchase (Morrill 1991). The new houses entering the market are, on average, bigger and better than ever (see Staley, Chapter 2). The preferences for size and space are most likely to be met in outlying locations where land and access costs combined are lower. Between 1970 and 1997, the typical new home increased substantially in size and the list of amenities became longer (Cox and Alm 1999, Table 1.1). Moreover, home ownership in the United States (including minority home ownership) has reached an all-time high. Clearing the market of more than 1 million new units per year could only be accomplished by a competitive industry keenly attentive to the wishes of consumers.

If consumer tastes change, the product line will change. There are several, often expensive, developments already on the ground that include New Urbanist features. Research published by the Urban Land Institute suggests a "new urbanism premium" of 4 to 25 percent of the value ($5,000 - $30,000) of new single-family residential units (Eppli and Tu 1999). If valid, this is a clear signal to developers to incorporate New Urbanist features in their projects. The good news is that market tests of alternative development types are available and are much preferred to the 240 Smart Growth initiatives on state and local ballots in 1998, 72 percent of which passed (Myers 1999). The bad news for the Congress for New Urbanism platform is that these developments are unlikely to have the desired traffic impacts.

The answer to questions about market failure has two parts. First, there is considerable competition with predictable positive results. Second, inefficiencies can be best mitigated via market-based incentive schemes. But these clash with political priorities, such as the emphasis on Smart Growth.

Urban economists argue that minimum-lot-size residential zoning is exclusionary. Where property taxes are used to fund local public goods, notably public schools, a poor family may get a "free ride" by sending its children to the local school while avoiding much of the tax burden by consuming small amounts of residential space. Communities cannot enforce income requirements on new arrivals, but they can enforce minimum-lot-size zoning. Despite some corroboration for this idea, the suburbs are much more heterogeneous than often assumed. The 1995 American Housing Survey, for example, shows that of 30.7 million "attached and multiple" housing units, one-half were in the suburbs. Also, the distribution of income in the suburbs is much more similar to the central city income distribution than the literature suggests (Table 3.8), an important point missed by the constant references to increasing income segregation between inner cities and the suburbs. Two tidy spatial units, the central cities and the suburbs, are too few for convincing analysis.

Critics of sprawl focus on policies that they believe are peculiar to the United States They note, for example, that minimum-lot-size zoning stands in the way of "more efficient" uses of land. Yet replacing this type of zoning with other planning instruments such as urban growth boundaries may have the same exclusionary impact on low-income households. When these become binding constraints, housing prices rise, giving windfall gains to existing homeowners but shutting out new entrants of modest means (Staley, Edgens, and Mildner 1999).

Faith in the potential for upward mobility is a core societal value in the United States. In prosperous times, people (of all races) move up and out, both socially and spatially. They leave behind old jobs, lifestyles, and neighborhoods. They make their own trade-offs. Fred Siegel (1999) reminds us that the lifestyles of the first mass upper middle class are an expression of explicit preferences. Yet sprawl's critics argue that people are consistently making the "wrong" choices and/or that they have only very poor choices available. Neither argument is plausible.

Table 3.8
Household Income Distribution in U.S. Urbanized Areas
Central Cities and Suburbs, 1989

	Central Place	Urban Fringe
< $5,000	0.0808	0.0335
$5,000 - $9,000	0.1081	0.0594
$10,000 - $14,999	0.0954	0.0643
$15,000 - $24,999	0.1833	0.1458
$25,000 - $34,999	0.1562	0.1519
$35,000 - $49,999	0.1645	0.1985
$50,000 - $74,999	0.1300	0.1995
$75,000 - $99,999	0.0431	0.0784
> $100,000	0.0385	0.0687

Source: 1990 Census of Population: Social and Economic Characteristics, Table 3:
Summary of Occupation, Income, and Poverty Characteristics Washington, DC: 1990.

Suburbanization in response to residential preferences and technological change is efficient. The Smart Growth movement has many romantic roots: the benevolent state, activist environmentalism, the vision of urban designers. The ideals override the facts. As an example, in his September 1998 talk at the Brookings Institution, Vice-President Gore praised Portland and its light-rail system, saying that "it has attracted 40 percent of all commuters." In fact, all transit in Portland services slightly more than 5 percent of the workforce, and light rail carries 15 percent of the transit total. Although off by a factor of more than fifty, Gore's statement has been routinely repeated without challenge.

The favored political model of Smart Growth and slow-growth advocates is regional government. According to Anthony Downs, the "socioeconomic isolation" of the poor results from a "regionwide hierarchy of neighborhoods caused by deliberately exclusionary policies of the suburbs. . . . Thus the responsibility for creating impoverished inner-city neighborhoods is to some extent regional" (1994, p. 28). Of course, even in a world without racism and without exclusionary zoning, income constraints would keep many of us out of wealthy neighborhoods. As noted, however, the suburbs are more heterogeneous than assumed, with an overall income distribution only moderately different from that of the central cities.

Many planners believe that a variety of many economic, social, and environmental problems cut across municipal boundaries leading to the prescription of regional government. A related argument holds that central cities provide critical regional functions that benefit outlying areas and provide services for suburban commuters, justifying the idea that suburban areas have "exploited" the central city, and ought to do more to support it. This argument was much stronger when suburbs were bedroom communities and jobs were more centralized; it has much less appeal in a world of edge cities and ex-urban development. In fact, little evidence exists that more regional or expansive government promotes economic development or income growth (Blair, Staley, and Zhang, 1996). However, the problem with regional government is that it seriously limits the people's choice of governance. The goal of forcing higher residential densities in the suburbs would be facilitated by cartelizing local government and land use. Competition would suffer, because more households and firms relocate within than between metropolitan areas. Operating efficiencies and tax constraints would be under less pressure. Structural reforms in government typically occur when governments compete. More homogeneity in the supply of public goods and services means more mismatches with local demand (Oates 1999). Regional power-sharing agreements among local governments (e.g., via special districts) for addressing such problems as air quality and transportation exist and can easily be expanded. But these should be the exceptions, not a substitute for local sovereignty.

Siegel reminds us that there are no success stories among metro governments that have been formed in recent years. "What's striking about Metro-Dade [Florida] is that it has delivered neither efficiency nor equity nor effective planning while squelching local self-determination" (Siegel 1999, pp. 88-89). His other examples are no better. New York City's consolidation has been good for Manhattan but ruined Brooklyn. The removal of local jurisdictional competition is not benign. The spatial wealth redistribution mandate of regionalism is a poor substitute for wealth expansion.

Chapter 4

Congestion and Traffic Management

ROBERT W. POOLE, JR.

America's urban areas are being overwhelmed by traffic. According to the most recent annual study by the Texas Transportation Institute (TTI), the cost of congestion to motorists (the sum of extra travel time and wasted fuel) in the nation's 68 largest urban areas was $72 billion in 1997, the latest year for which the data have been analyzed (Schrank and Lomax 1999).[1] That was a 9 percent increase from the $66 billion cost calculated for 1996 by TTI. Annual congestion cost per driver ranged from $50 in Brownsville, Texas, to $1,370 in Los Angeles.The peak-period time penalties imposed on drivers more than doubled in the 68 urban areas between 1982 and 1997.

Urban traffic congestion is a problem for a number of reasons. Mobility is an important component of people's quality of life; an area plagued by poor mobility will, over time, become less and less attractive as a place to live and work. Congestion worsens air quality, because vehicles in stop-and-go conditions produce several times the emissions per mile as vehicles traveling at steady speeds. Congestion, for some, is a source of stress and even "road rage." And the sheer waste of time involved reduces people's productive work hours or their important personal and family time.

Clearly, reducing or eliminating urban traffic congestion is desirable. Yet the nation's opinion-makers appear increasingly resigned to the conclusion that the situation is nearly hopeless. Anthony Downs of the Brookings Institution terms traffic congestion "a problem that cannot be solved . . . there is no such thing as a solution to the traffic congestion problem" (Downs 1999b). Many environmental groups, no-growth or slow-growth advocates, and urban planners have been quite effective in gaining public acceptance of the idea that "we can't build our way out of congestion" by adding lanes to freeways or building new ones. On the other hand, their preferred option—spending billions of taxpayer dollars to create rail transit systems in America's mostly low-density urban areas—is increasingly seen to be a bad investment, as noted in Chapter 3.

In contrast to urban planners and opinion leaders, many transportation economists believe that a solution to the congestion problem is achievable—at least in theory. They note that many other services—telephones, airline flights, even restaurants and movie theaters—are also characterized by large differences between busy and non-busy times, with a tendency for the most popular times to become congested. But these other service industries deal with the problem by charging higher prices at the most popular times and lower prices during the less popular times. That does several worthwhile things. First, it suggests to those who are most price-sensitive that they can save money by shifting their usage to off-peak times, which some do. Second, it suggests to the service provider that it might be worthwhile to add capacity during the peak-demand periods. Third, and most important, the increased revenues generated by higher prices at peak hours makes it more feasible to accommodate that capacity (in other words, it makes sense to add as much capacity as can be supported by the higher peak-hour revenues).

In other words, transportation economists view urban traffic congestion as an imbalance of demand and supply, caused by the lack of market pricing of roadway use. Their solution is to introduce pricing—assuming that it is technically and politically feasible to do so. But road pricing would reduce the total amount of investment needed in the highway system. Instead of attempting to build the amount of capacity needed for (unpriced) peak demand, highway providers could build a more modest amount, which would be more fully utilized at non-peak hours than most of today's freeways.

ROAD PRICING: THE HISTORY OF AN IDEA

Applying market pricing to roadway use was first proposed in some detail by economist Alan Walters in the mid-1950s (Walters 1954). In 1959, economist William Vickrey (later to win the Nobel Prize) testified before a congressional committee on the feasibility of implementing road pricing using electronics (Vickrey 1959). These ideas were taken up in the mid-1960s by officials in Britain's Ministry of Transport, following a 1962 visit to London by Vickrey. The resulting landmark report by a panel headed by Reyben Smeed, director of the Road Research Laboratory, set out principles and techniques for road pricing which are still cited in the transportation literature (Smeed 1964). But two significant problems—technical issues involving how to implement variable pricing and political opposition to direct payment for existing (free) roads—prevented any serious attempts to implement the idea in either the United States or Britain during those years.

In the 1970s, the Urban Mass Transportation Administration (UMTA, the predecessor of today's Federal Transit Administration) funded a series of studies by Urban Institute researchers to flesh out the case for road pricing and to deal with implementation issues. The UMTA offered grants to cities willing to serve as test sites for some forms of road pricing, but received no takers. Likewise, when a special California task force on transportation appointed by then-Governor Jerry Brown proposed the introduction of road pricing in 1976, the idea was perceived as an anti-auto measure and was dropped as politically infeasible.

The only country that implemented road pricing before the 1990s was Singapore. In 1975 its somewhat authoritarian government imposed access control, via pricing, on its central business district. Cars were not permitted to enter the Central Business District (CBD) during morning rush hours unless they displayed a purchased windshield sticker. Rather quickly, the number of cars on the CBD streets during rush hours decreased by about 40 percent, thereby demonstrating to skeptics that a crude form of pricing can work. During the late 1980s and early 1990s, Norway's three largest cities (Bergen, Oslo, and Trondheim) implemented "toll rings" around their CBDs, charging a toll to enter via any major route during daylight hours. The key to the political acceptability of this change appears to be the government's pledge to use the revenues to expand and improve highway (and to some extent, mass transit) capacity. Also during the 1990s, several existing toll facility operators in France and South Korea implemented peak/off-peak differentials, which succeeded in alleviating peak-period congestion by shifting some traffic out of peak periods. Toward the end of the 1990s, Singapore replaced its crude sticker-based access control system with a comprehensive electronic road-pricing system, involving prices that vary by roadway and time of day.

In the United States, the federal International Surface Transportation Efficiency Act (ISTEA) legislation enacted in 1991 included a Congestion Pricing Pilot Program. It offered funds to local metropolitan planning organizations (MPOs) to develop specific proposals for implementing road pricing with the aim of reducing congestion. In addition, it provided modest funding and legal authority to implement up to five pricing projects in urban areas, three of which could be on Interstate facilities (which are otherwise off-limits to the addition of tolls, under federal law). Under that pilot program, two agencies with existing toll bridges (in Florida and New York) introduced peak/off-peak differentials. Two other agencies (in San Diego and Houston) converted under-utilized high-occupancy vehicle (HOV) lanes to what are now called HOT (high-occupancy/toll) lanes, by allowing vehicles not meeting the car-pooling requirement to purchase excess capacity in those lanes. In addition, a private firm in California developed and implemented a form of HOT lane in the median of the Riverside Freeway, called the 91 Express Lanes.

The two California projects make use of nonstop electronic toll collection (ETC). Drivers who wish to use the HOT lanes open an account with the road company and pay the charge via an electronic tag on their windshield, which is read by a radio beam as they pass beneath an overhead gantry at highway speed. This system dispenses with toll booths and permits prices to be changed far more flexibly than would have been possible with traditional coin-based toll booth systems.

This very limited implementation of road pricing nevertheless demonstrated two important points. First, the limitations of technology that were cited previous to the 1980s as obstacles to road pricing have been substantially overcome via today's electronics technology. Indeed, both Australia and Canada now have new toll roads in operation that dispense with toll booths not merely for individual access-controlled lanes but for the entire facility. Cars not equipped with windshield-mounted transponders are identified via sophisticated video license-plate recognition systems, permitting them to be billed or cited, as the case may be. Second, the perception of the political impossibility of introducing road pricing into an urban area served previously only by free roads has been at least weakened by the popularity of the HOT lane projects in California and by Toronto's very popular all-electronic Highway 407.

Since the passage of ISTEA in 1992, Anthony Downs (1992) has produced a book-length assessment of 23 possible anti-congestion policy measures and concluded that only two could produce significant reductions in peak-hour congestion: peak-hour pricing on major traffic arteries and/or charging sizeable amounts for all parking during morning hours. The Transportation Research Board (of the National Academy of Sciences) has also continued to provide a forum for the exploration of road pricing during the 1990s. Its committee of experts produced a major, book-length report on the subject in 1994, concluding that such pricing was the most appropriate solution to this growing national problem (Wachs, 1994).

Congress responded to the small but growing interest in pricing by creating TEA-21, a successor to the ISTEA pilot program. The TEA-21 legislation enacted in 1998 includes a Value Pricing Program under which fifteen additional implementation projects are authorized, any or all of which can be on urban Interstate facilities.

RESISTANCE TO URBAN ROAD PRICING

While the case for road pricing is sound, and the limited evidence we have from places like Singapore and California indicates that charging more for road use during peak hours does reduce congestion during those hours, there remains the enormous problem of political feasibility.

There is strong, organized opposition to road pricing. First, the traditional highway user groups (e.g., the various auto clubs and trucking associations) consider the addition of tolls to a system already being funded by user taxes to be double taxation. They have something of a case. Careful analysis of the sources and uses of highway funding in America reveals that highway users are already paying more in user taxes than is being spent on the costs of building, operating, and maintaining the U.S. roadway system.

For example, a case study using California figures for 1993 showed that motorists paid a total of $14.1 billion in transportation-specific taxes and fees (see Table 4.1). With an additional $1.7 billion in local property tax support for local roads, the total road-related revenues were $15.8 billion. In comparison to this total, just $4.3 billion was spent on state highways (including the interstates) and $3.1 billion on city/county roads, for a total of $7.4 billion. What happened to the rest of the money? Nearly $4.5 billion was spent on mass transit, $.3 billion was transferred to transportation uses in other states (California is a "donor state" in the federal surface transportation system), and the remaining $4.2 billion was spent on non-transportation purposes (Pozdena, 1995).

As this example illustrates, highway user groups may feel quite justified in opposing any effort to add tolls to existing highways, because they already pay so many existing excise taxes and other fees. They are generally also opposed—though not as strenuously—to the addition of new toll roads to the highway system, arguing that it is unfair for the users of those roads to pay both the tolls and fuel taxes earmarked for transportation.

Despite these concerns, however, a number of fast-growing urban areas have relied on tolled expressways for a considerable portion of their limited-access networks in the past two decades—including Miami and Orlando, Dallas and Houston, Denver, and Orange County, California. User groups in those localities have generally conceded that without the use of tolls, high quality expressway systems could not have been built soon enough to cope with traffic growth, given the competition for limited highway funds in those states.

But in several other states, efforts to add tolled expressways to existing freeway systems have been stopped due to political opposition. During the 1990s, the legislatures of Arizona, Minnesota, and Washington each passed transportation public-private partnership measures, under which private firms were invited to submit proposals to design, finance, build, and operate tolled additions to the existing freeway systems. Competitions were held, projects were selected, and franchise agreements were awarded in the Phoenix, Minneapolis/St. Paul, and Seattle areas. But out of nearly a dozen proposed projects, only one has survived grass-roots political opposition (a second span for the congested Tacoma Narrows Bridge near Seattle). All the others fell victim to angry campaigns equating tolls with new taxes and/or arguing that adding toll roads in certain portions of the metro area discriminated against those living in those areas, given that similar expressways in other parts of the metro area would continue to be "free."

The only pricing approach that appears to be having success in congested U.S. urban areas is that of High Occupancy Toll lanes, or HOT lanes. The two California HOT lanes projects—four lanes of new capacity in the median of the 91 Freeway in Orange County and the conversion of two lanes of underutilized HOV lanes in the median of I-15 in San Diego County—have been both technical and operational successes, with thousands of users happy to have the option

Table 4.1
Major Sources and Uses of Transportation Revenue in California

Sources		Units	Revenue $Mil-lions	State Hwys, Bridges	Cnty Roads	City Streets	CA Transit, Transp. Planning	Non-CA Hwys	Non-CA Tran-sit, Transp Planning	Other
1.	**Federal Taxes**									
	Gasoline Excise Tax	Gallons	$2,346							
	Diesel Excise Tax	Gallons	407							
	Truck & Trailer Use Tax	Value	155							
	Use Tax (est.)	Weight	81							
	Tire Tax (est.)	Sales	34							
	Total		$3,023	$1,918	$87	$88	$463	($82)	($244)	$794
2.	**State Taxes**									
	Vehicle Fuel License Tax (gas)	Gallons	2,295							
	Use Fuel Tax (diesel, et al.)	Gallons	301							
	Subtotal		$2,596	$1,304	$460	$470	$362			
	Retail Sales & Use		$863				863			
	Bridge Tolls		171	146			25			
	Total		$3,630							
3.	**Registration & License Fees**									
	Registration Fees		$1,488	$935						$553
	Vehicle License Fees		$2,901		$9	$57				$2,835
	Total		$4,389							
4.	**Local Taxes and Fees**									
	Sales and Use									
	• County Trans.	Gen. Sales	690		72		583			23
	• Spec. Dist. Taxes	Gen. Sales					1,761			46
	Road & Street	Varies	157		23	134				
	Transit Fares	Varies	421				421			
	General Fund	Varies	655		32	623				
	Other Local Sources	Varies	$1,009		213	796				
	Total		$4,737							
	Grand Total		$15,780	$4,303	$896	$2,168	$4,478	($82)	($244)	$4,251

Source: Pozdena 1995

of choosing, on a day-to-day basis, whether to stay with the regular congested lanes or to save time by paying the current price to use the HOT lanes.

Indeed, based on the limited evidence available thus far, adding a HOT lane to a congested freeway appears to be a win-win proposition, benefiting both those who opt for the limited-access lane and those who remain in the general-purpose lanes. A study of the 91 express lanes found that the new lanes reduced the length of rush hour in the adjacent free lanes and doubled average rush hour speeds in the free lanes (from 15 to 32 mph), as well as saving significant time for those choosing to pay for premium service (Sullivan 1998). Some may argue that the addition of any new capacity—whether tolled or un-tolled—would produce these same effects. But the superiority of adding a HOT lane rather than a free lane is that the former (assuming pricing flexibility) can remain uncongested indefinitely, while a free lane will likely become congested in future years, due to traffic growth.[2]

In response to the success of those projects, HOT lane proposals have been springing up across the country. At the end of 1999, nearly a dozen projects were on the drawing boards in California alone, with others being seriously considered in Baltimore, Dallas, Denver, Houston, Phoenix, and elsewhere (see Table 4.2). Thus, an incrementalist approach to urban congestion relief via pricing would concentrate on adding HOT lanes to as many congested freeways as possible, in some cases by converting existing, mostly underutilized, HOV lanes and in other cases by adding tolled express lanes (Poole and Orski 1999).

While this appears to be a politically feasible approach, it does not address congestion on the remaining freeway lanes, nor the congestion on arterials. Because of the opposition by highway users to "paying twice," the only way that widespread pricing is likely to be feasible is if it could be put in place as a replacement for much or all of the current excise tax system. But due to the complexities of the federal, state, and local highway financing system, that is a daunting task.

RETHINKING HIGHWAY FINANCE

If Houston officials had total control over all highway revenues used for the Houston roadway system and total control over the management and operation of that system, then, in principle, it would be feasible for those officials to decide to switch from a largely fuel tax-based highway finance system to one based on variable pricing. In other words, if the metro area's roadway network were analogous to its electricity or water network—i.e., under a single owner, which charges users directly for their use of the network—such a change would be relatively straightforward.

Unfortunately, as Table 4.1 suggested, the financing and ownership of America's roadways is hugely convoluted. Within a typical metro area such as Houston, there are federal highways (such as I-10), state highways, and city and

Table 4.2
Current HOT Lane Projects

State	Location	Facility	Status
AZ	Phoenix	all freeways	study
CA	Alameda County	1-680, 1-880	study
	Contra Costa	SR 4W	study
	Los Angeles	various	study/post-study
	Marin County	US 101	study
	Orange County	SR 91 Exp. Ln.	operational
	Orange County	SR 57	study
	Riverside County	SR 91 ext.	study
	San Diego County	I-15	operational
	Santa Cruz County	SR 1	approved
	Sonoma County	US 101	post-study
CO	Denver	I-25	study
FL	Miami	I-95, SR 836	study
MD	Baltimore suburbs	various	study
MN	Minneapolis	all freeways	study
OR	Portland	various	post-study
PA	Philadelphia	US 1	study
TX	Austin	I-35	study
	Dallas	I-635	MIS
	Houston	I-10	operational
	Houston	I-10	MIS
VA	Hampton Roads	I-64	approved/hold
WI	Milwaukee	I-94	study

Source: Poole and Orski, 1999.

county roadways. The federal government provides much of the funding for federal highways (but does not own them; the state does) and a portion of the funding for many state highways (which the state also owns). The state government, in turn, usually provides part of the money for the urban area's major roadways, some of which are state highways and others of which are owned and maintained by the cities or the county government. These local governments may use a wide variety of funding sources—in addition to state funds and local property taxes, they may use local-option gas taxes (Florida), local-option sales taxes (California), and any number of other general fund or specialized sources.

Federal funding, in particular, complicates the picture, because with federal funding comes significant federal controls. Until the 1990s, when Congress authorized first the Congestion Pricing Pilot Program and later the Value Pricing Program, charging a toll on any federal-aid highway was illegal. Even the Value Pricing Program provides only 15 exceptions to this general rule for pricing projects on urban interstates. Hence, a state that wished to switch from fuel taxes to direct pricing would be unable to do so on many of its most important and heavily traveled roadways. Federal funding also comes with numerous cost-increasing strings attached, including the Davis-Bacon Act prevailing wage provisions, Buy America provisions, minimum drinking age provisions, and so forth. The redistributive aspect of the federal surface transportation program creates donor states and recipient states, with most of today's fastest growing states (like California, Florida, Texas, and Virginia)—the very places that need the greatest highway investment—sending funds to slow growth or low-population states such as Alaska, Montana, and Rhode Island (Poole 1996).

Despite the complexity of today's highway funding system, it is worth seriously considering the case for major change. One major reason is the coming obsolescence of the gasoline tax. Using figures for California, Figure 4.1 shows how the gasoline tax has been failing to keep pace with highway travel since the mid-1960s. There are two principal reasons for this trend. First, like most state fuel taxes (and the federal gas tax), California's is not adjusted for inflation; yet the cost of building, rebuilding, and maintaining the highway system obviously does reflect inflation. Second, ever since the automakers started emphasizing improved fuel economy in the 1970s, the amount of gas-tax revenue generated per mile driven has been decreasing.[3] Note also that Figure 4.1 already takes into account several significant increases in federal and state gas taxes enacted since the mid-1960s.

This dismal trend, which is representative of most states, will very likely get worse in coming decades. The federal government and the auto companies are committed to a program called the Partnership for a New Generation of Vehicles, whose goal is a mid-size family car that gets 80 miles per gallon—about four times more than the average car in the fleet today. That would cut the real value of gas-tax revenues to 25 percent of what they are now, per mile driven. Also, for environmental reasons, it is quite possible that twenty years from now the internal combustion engine will be on its way out, replaced by fuel cells or other alternative forms of motive power. Because fuel taxes constitute the lion's share of federal and state highway user taxes, these trends suggest that it is time to look seriously at a replacement system.

HIGHWAY FINANCE REFORM

In 1999, with support from the Federal Highway Administration, a multi-state task force launched a study to examine the potential for a mileage-based fee or tax, which could supplement or replace the gasoline tax.[4] The effort is being led by Dr. David Forkenbrock of the University of Iowa and Dr. Max Donath of the University of Minnesota.

Several policy groups in California have looked into the possibility of implementing a direct charge for each mile traveled on any roadway in the state. Assuming the technology to do this existed (and was affordable and reliable), a VMT (vehicle-miles-travelled) fee would serve as a replacement funding source that was independent of the type of propulsion used. It could be applied to all driving, on all roads within the state, as a kind of baseline charge for the use of uncongested roads. Higher rates could be charged at those times and those loca-

Figure 4.1
Inflation-Adjusted Gas Tax Collected per Vehicle Mile of Travel in California (% of 1950 value)

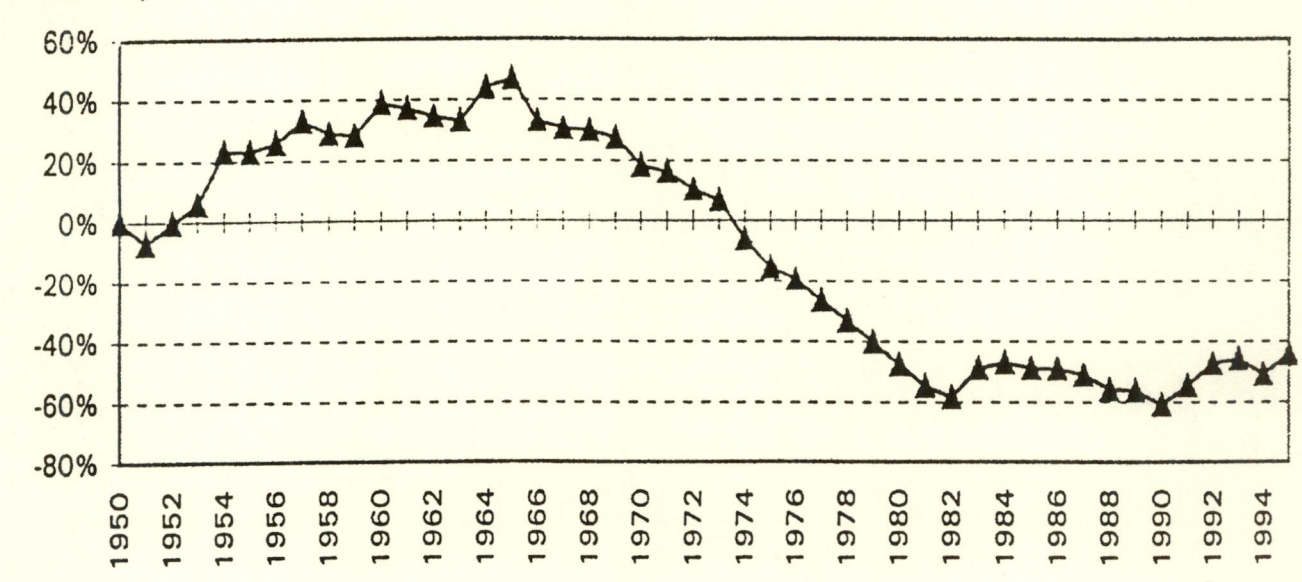

Source: Brown 1999.

tions where there was congestion. Higher rates per VMT also would be charged for various types of larger and heavier vehicles, such as trucks and buses, which impose greater wear and tear on the roadways.

In a detailed analysis of California's roadway system, economist Randall Pozdena (1995) estimated that (using 1993 data) the average road user charge paid by cars (primarily via fuel taxes) is 2.1 cents per VMT. This charge does not vary between rural roads and urban freeways; nor does it vary between uncongested streets and heavily congested freeways and arterials. Pozdena also calculated what it actually costs to drive (in economically meaningful terms, reflecting both the costs to build and maintain various types of roadway and the cost imposed on others by congestion). He found that on rural and uncongested roads, the actual cost for cars is around 1 cent per VMT. But on heavily congested urban freeways, it's in the vicinity of 18 cents per VMT. He concluded that the present fuel tax-based system overcharges rural drivers twofold while undercharging urban rush-hour drivers ninefold. Thus, from the standpoint of economic efficiency (as well as the impending obsolescence of fuel taxes), there is good reason to work toward fundamental reform of the way we pay for roadways.

There is also public misunderstanding of highway costs. Traditionally, tolls are sold to the public as temporary—a means of paying for the initial construction of a new road or bridge. Once the initial bonds have been paid off, there is widespread popular expectation that the tolls will be removed (as they occasionally have been). Yet this common perception ignores the fact that roads begin wearing out as soon as they start being used. Particularly with the pavement designs and thicknesses typical of U.S. (as opposed to European) practice, a highway will last only 20 to 40 years before needing to be completely rebuilt. Thus, in a market-based highway financing system, tolls would be understood as a permanent, ongoing funding source—not as a temporary expedient.

EQUITY ISSUES

One basic question that arises in considering a new highway funding system is who should pay for what. The current convoluted system has everyone paying for everything—i.e., Los Angeles drivers are paying federal fuel taxes to help pay for highways in Montana and mass transit in Cleveland and state fuel taxes to pay for San Francisco's BART and rural roads in the Gold Country. Increasingly, transportation economists are concluding that major infrastructure such as highways should be funded on a *user-pays* basis. While the fuel tax is a crude form of user tax (and would be somewhat better if it were collected and spent in the same geographical area), direct pricing along the lines suggested by Pozdena would be far superior. The team of University of California researchers who recently evaluated California's highway finance system recommended that, "Major new expansions in the highway system should be financed by even more direct user fees, such as electronically collected tolls that are dedicated to financing the facility on which they are collected" (Brown 1999).

Economist Marlon Boarnet has done extensive research seeking to quantify the benefits of highway investment. His conclusion is that most of the economic benefits of new investment in highway projects occur locally (Boarnet 1999). Consequently, Boarnet recommends that highway funding be decentralized, and that greater use be made of variable tolls supporting specific facilities.

Should even local streets and roads be financed directly and entirely by motorists? Traditionally, this portion of the roadway system has been funded primarily from property taxes and other local general-fund revenues. The case for doing so is that local roads provide access to the rest of the roadway network, which increases the value of properties that have such access. Even people without cars benefit from the services made available to them by local roads— emergency vehicles can get to them when needed; delivery trucks, repair services, newspaper carriers, and meter readers can reach them; and taxis, jitneys, and buses use these streets to provide mobility for non-drivers. So it is not strictly true that general fund support for such roads constitutes a "subsidy to the automobile" as claimed by some.

On the other hand, since over 90 percent of Americans own personal vehicles, local streets and roads funded by auto-related payments would be reasonably congruent with our notions of user-pays and efficiency. If a state's major roadways (intercity highways, urban expressways) were to be funded by some form of a direct user payment or toll, a user-based source of funding for local streets and roads could be a revamped version of today's annual registration and licensing fees. As Table 4.1 shows for California, the $4.4 billion produced by these fees is well in excess of the $3.1 billion actually spent on local streets and roads.

CAN NEW TECHNOLOGY MAKE PRICING FEASIBLE?

Electronic Toll Collection Systems

Current and near-future technologies appear to provide the basis for direct pricing that could be applied to all types of road use. Already in widespread use on existing toll-road systems is first-generation electronic toll collection (ETC) technology. To use the system, each vehicle must be equipped with a windshield-mounted tag the size of a deck of playing cards. The tag is programmed with a user's account number. That number is "read" by a radio signal as the vehicle passes an antenna, which is typically mounted on an overhead gantry at the toll collection point. The toll system's computer then applies the charge that is in effect at that time and location, and either adds it to the user's monthly bill or debits the balance in the user's account (the system can be set up on either a credit or a debit basis).

Early applications simply provide a way to speed up passage of vehicles through conventional toll lanes. On new toll roads, however, tag-equipped users can pay their tolls at highway speeds; only those not equipped have to leave the main traffic lanes in order to wait in line at toll booths off to the side. The most advanced automated toll road system is on Toronto's Highway 407, a 43-mile toll road with dozens of on-ramps and off-ramps in a dense urban area. This facility, which opened in 1997, was designed from the outset without any toll booths. Regular users pay via windshield-mounted tags, which are read at the on-ramp and again at the off-ramp, so that the user can be charged for the exact number of miles driven. Users without tags have their license plate videotaped at the on-ramp and again at the off-ramp. The video images are deciphered (in most cases electronically) and used to identify the vehicle via motor vehicle department records, from which a bill is generated. This fully automated system went on-line in late 1997, and has worked well. Total daily traffic on Highway 407 by late 1999 was in the 300,000 range—a high number representing overwhelming acceptance of automated tolling.

One of the concerns raised by first-generation ETC systems is privacy. In several locations, including Dallas, Orange County (Calif.), and Toronto, the toll-road operators offer cash-based anonymous accounts (analogous to Swiss bank accounts), under which a unique account number is established for the person's dashboard tag, but no record is made of the identity of the account-holder. Such a system can only operate on a debit basis, with an account balance maintained in cash, but it protects user privacy. Interestingly, the demand for these accounts has been only a fraction of 1 percent in each case where they have been offered.

Second-generation ETC systems are being developed primarily in Europe (and are now in use in Singapore), offering privacy protection to all tag-holders. These systems use a more expensive vehicle-mounted transponder device, into which the user inserts a stored-value smart card (similar to the stored-value fare cards used on the San Francisco BART and Washington Metro subway systems). As the vehicle passes each toll-collection point, the value of the toll in effect at that time and place is deducted from the balance on the smart card, without the need for any tag or vehicle ID number.

Vehicle-Miles-Travelled Technologies

ETC is well-suited to limited access highways and bridges with high traffic volumes where the cost of installing gantries, antennas, and video enforcement equipment can be spread over a large number of users. It would be much less cost-effective on low traffic inter-city routes and on urban streets and roads, where the number of tolling points would be enormous. Hence, we need to review what technology may exist to reliably measure vehicle miles travelled, so that a per-mile fee could be applied to those miles.

In a report for the Los Angeles area REACH (Reduce Emissions and Congestion on Highways) Task Force, Wilbur Smith Associates (WSA) reviewed a number of alternative approaches (Wilbur Smith Associates 1996). A summary of their findings follows.

Manual Odometer Readings This approach would require no new technology. It would require that all vehicles in the jurisdiction (state, county, etc.) be brought periodically (perhaps quarterly) to an official odometer reading kiosk. For the five-county Los Angeles region, WSA estimated that such a system would require 40 million readings per year, using 1,000 kiosks around the region.

While technologically simple, this approach has several serious drawbacks. Current odometers are easily rolled back; hence, evasion of the fee would not be difficult. In addition, there would be problems charging the fees to out-of-region vehicles that do some of their driving within the region, as well as problems in giving rebates for miles traveled outside the region by in-region vehicles. In addition, significant customer (i.e., voter) resistance might exist to having to go in for quarterly odometer readings.

Computed VMT at Refueling This new-technology approach would equip all vehicles with a hypothetical device that identifies the vehicle type and its average miles per gallon. This device would be read at the gas pump each time the driver fueled up, and the miles travelled charge would be calculated (based on mpg times quantity of fuel pumped) and added to the fuel charge, instead of today's fuel tax. This approach has the advantage of being far less fraud-prone than odometer readings; it also does not require a unique vehicle account number, so it could be designed to protect privacy. It could also be designed to charge a conventional fuel tax to out-of-jurisdiction vehicles not equipped with the tag. Costs would include equipping every registered vehicle and gas pump within the jurisdiction and enforcing those requirements. But it would be no more intrusive to users than paying today's fuel tax each time the vehicle is refueled.

VMT Measured by Electronic Odometer This approach would also charge the VMT fee at each refueling, but would do so via an electronic odometer that keeps track of the actual miles driven since the last reading (refueling stop). Again, for non-equipped vehicles from outside the jurisdiction, a per-gallon fuel tax would apply. Costs would include equipping every vehicle and every fuel pump within the jurisdiction. Privacy would be protected, since there would be no need for a unique ID number.

Electronic Odometer plus Border Stations This approach adds to the concept of roadside communication stations at the jurisdiction's border crossings, so that mileage driven within and outside the region can be differentiated. This would be more complex, and hence more costly, than the previous approach. Once again, however, it does not require a unique ID number, as long as the out-of-region mileage information can be stored on the onboard electronic odometer in a reasonably tamper-proof manner.

Electronic Odometer with Onboard GPS Computer The Global Positioning System (GPS) is a worldwide complex of satellites operated by the U.S. Air Force, broadcasting position-locating signals 24 hours a day over most of the globe (and available at no charge). Civilian use of GPS has grown enormously in the latter years of the 1990s, and inexpensive GPS receivers are now available for hikers, boaters, drivers, and pilots (with further price decreases likely as technology improves and volume production continues to increase). WSA proposed that an onboard GPS receiver be linked with the electronic odometer in a car so as to avoid the need for border crossing stations.

None of these schemes requires any technological breakthroughs, but aside from GPS receivers, the other components do not yet exist—not the on-board transponder pre-programmed with the car's average MPG, not the gas pump that can communicate with such a device, not the electronic odometer with communications capability. To be suitable as a replacement for the present fuel-tax system, they would have to be mandated for all vehicles and all service stations within a jurisdiction. However, if the on-vehicle device became standard equipment on all new vehicles within a jurisdiction, a dual system could exist for many years under which new vehicles would pay the VMT fee while all other vehicles would continue to pay the fuel tax (with the two adjusted so that the average per-mile cost was lower under the new system, to encourage people to shift to new—or retrofitted—vehicles).

A GPS-Based Virtual Tolling System

If the geographic location information provided by GPS is combined with ubiquitous two-way communications capabilities (such as are likely to be available this decade from low earth-orbit satellite systems), another approach to road pricing is possible. Under this concept, each vehicle would be equipped with an "electronic license plate," consisting of a GPS receiver and a two-way communications unit, with associated on-board computer capability. Various road owners—such as private franchisees for specific tolled expressways or a county government's local street network—would define the pricing policies to be applied, creating "virtual" tolling points in geographical terms. In other words, lines of code would replace toll booths and gantries.

This technology would permit both pricing per mile travelled and variable rates per mile at specific times and locations. The GPS system would know the vehicle's location at all times, and the always-on two-way communications system would be in continual contact with the billing system. Charges to use specific roadways would be widely publicized, so that a driver would know in advance what it would cost to choose different routes at various times of day. While it is easy to visualize the use of virtual tolling on limited-access roadways (such as major inter-city highways and urban freeways), this approach will also make pricing possible on local streets and roads. Planned enhancements to the GPS system (such as the Federal Aviation Administration's Local Area Access System) will increase the location-accuracy of civilian GPS signals to tens of feet. This level of accuracy will permit charging for local trips based on reasonably accurate calculations of distance traveled. As the recently retired executive director of the American Association of State Highway and Transportation Officials, Francis Francois, recently noted,

Looking into the future, 10 to 20 years from now, with the satellite systems that we have and electronic toll collection systems that are now possible, it is conceivable that every new vehicle will come equipped with a meter to measure where and when you drive. Each month you'd receive a detailed printed bill similar to your electric or telephone bill. I think that will happen. (Francois 1999)

Prospects for Pricing Technology

How likely are the technologies just summarized to be available and usable for the pricing applications discussed here? First-generation ETC technology is being rapidly adopted by existing toll operators across the United States; *Toll Roads Newsletter* estimates that at the end of 1999, between 5 and 6 million in-vehicle tags were in use. A standardized national specification for next-generation ETC systems is being developed by the National Institute of Standards and Technology. Thus far, however, smart-card-based systems appear to be confined primarily to Europe and Singapore, and their addition to U.S. ETC systems remains to be seen.

Highly tamper-resistant electronic odometers are starting to appear on luxury cars, and may become standard on new cars within the decade. The auto industry is also moving toward a "standard bus" configuration in which all electronic elements will go through a common microcomputer interface. This will facilitate the emergence of the kind of electronic license plate envisioned for virtual tolling systems. GPS receivers continue to evolve toward smaller size and weight and lower prices; some are being incorporated into cellular phones and luxury vehicles. And a number of low earth orbit (LEO) satellite communications systems (Globalstar, Orbcom, Teledesic, etc.) are under development and should be in service early this decade. Thus, except for the kinds of gas-pump devices suggested by WSA in their discussion of VMT fee collection, all the technological components needed for sophisticated road pricing systems—including local streets and roads—are either in existence or under development.

A NEW PARADIGM FOR URBAN ROADWAYS

Technology is changing roads from a classic public good (which everyone uses but cannot easily be charged for) to a more ordinary commercial service—something like a public utility. This suggests a new approach—a new paradigm—in which the road system (or at least the limited-access portion of the roadway system) becomes a public utility, akin to the electric, gas, phone, and water utilities familiar to everyone. They could be run either as government utilities (i.e., operated as businesses, with pricing, but owned wholly by a governmental unit) or franchised to private firms on a long-term basis (as with most gas, telephone, and electric utilities in the United States).

Why franchise expressways to private companies? The main reason is to change the relationship between road users and road providers, turning the former into customers who express their demand in the roadway marketplace. Whereas state highway agencies have offered a standardized product—a typical one size fits all approach, under which we must all sit in the same congestion regardless of the value of our time or the urgency of this particular trip—private franchise-holders will be likely to try out various levels of service targeted at different customer groups. While few individuals might be willing to pay an extra premium for guaranteed arrival times, time-sensitive delivery services (e.g., FedEx) might well jump at the chance. The wearing-out of many urban expressways in the first two decades of the twenty-first century offers a golden opportunity to rebuild them with several different types and sizes of lanes, aimed at different categories of customer (Samuel 1999). As of this writing, both Dallas and Houston are planning such major reconstruction of their undersized and heavily congested LBJ and Katy freeways.

Today's freeways could easily be managed by expressway operating companies, under competitively bid long-term franchise agreements (Roth 1996). Precursors of such arrangements exist in new public-private tolled expressway and bridge projects in operation or under development in California, Missouri, Puerto Rico, South Carolina, Texas, Virginia, and Washington State. They are likely to begin with first- or second-generation ETC technology (a la Toronto's Highway 407), but could adapt to virtual tolling if and as it evolved. Since the un-tolled freeways in today's metro areas were designed without space for toll plazas, they will be converted only when fully automated, boothless toll collection technology is judged acceptable (as it seems to have been in Toronto and Melbourne).

Peter Samuel has also suggested that major arterials could be franchised out to companies "with the right to electronically toll traffic in return for converting them into 'super-arterials' in which vehicle sensors would work with optimizing algorithms to manage traffic signals to maximize the use of green time. At selected places the concessionaire might install and electronically toll an overpass [or underpass] to allow free flow on the super-arterial" (Samuel 2000) While such tolling could be done using current ETC technology, an arterial has far more open access than an expressway. This suggests that practical implementation of this idea might need to wait for the implementation of electronic license plates and virtual-tolling technology.

If direct pricing is limited initially to limited-access expressways (and later, to selected arterials, as well), there will be incentives for some drivers to avoid the charges by rerouting their trips through local neighborhoods. In some urban areas, this kind of shortcutting—to avoid nearly gridlocked freeways—is already a significant problem. Few neighborhood residents would accept pricing for major roadways if it leads to the conversion of their formerly safe and quiet neighborhood streets into quasi-arterials crowded with traffic.

The answer to this problem is the selective use of a variety of techniques known as traffic calming. Among these techniques are adding speed humps to certain streets to prevent excessive speed, preventing through traffic on certain streets via barriers (which, needless to say, must be used very selectively to avoid serious inconvenience to residents), reducing lane widths, and changing the design of intersections to make them less attractive for turns and heavy traffic.

GETTING FROM HERE TO THERE

Pricing is the missing ingredient in addressing urban traffic congestion. If we are serious about using pricing to manage urban traffic, we must aim to replace the present largely fuel tax-based highway funding system with one based directly on the time and location of road use. We should also encourage the shift toward a new institutional model of road provision, in which roadways—at least expressways and major arterials—become customer-responsive utilities far more like telecom networks than today's take-it-or-leave-it roadway system. What policy changes would move us significantly in that direction?

Defederalize the Highway System   Today's three-level funding system fragments responsibility and control and makes the replacement of fuel taxes by pricing nearly impossible. With the interstate system completed, there is little real justification for continuing the federal fuel tax and trust fund program, with its costly array of federal controls. The state is a far simpler jurisdiction in which to reform highway funding along the lines suggested in this chapter.

Convert HOV Lanes to HOT Lanes   Just as a picture is worth a thousand words, so is a first-hand experience of congestion-relief via pricing worth hundreds of journal articles and policy papers. California's first two HOT lanes have demonstrated that people in congested commuter corridors have different time-urgencies and willingness to pay, even from one day to the next. America's several thousand miles of unpopular and not very effective HOV lanes offer a unique opportunity to demonstrate the benefits of pricing in our congested metro areas. First-hand experience using HOT lanes will help to lay the basis for broader moves to replace fuel taxes with pricing.

Use Annual Registration Fees for Local Streets and Roads   The battle for road pricing can more readily win the support of some environmental groups and others who are not generally pro-highway if 100 percent of the cost of the highway system (including local streets and roads) are borne by highway users. It would therefore be wise for state legislators to reserve funds generated by annual vehicle registration and licensing solely for road-related functions. A portion could be used for such state purposes as operating the highway patrol, but enough should be returned to the counties of origin to permit them to eliminate their reliance on property taxes and all other local general revenues for streets and roads.

End "Double-Taxation"   The shift to a user-responsive, priced roadway system cannot be accomplished unless user groups perceive it to be in their interest. The historical opposition of auto clubs and trucking organizations to tolls must be overcome. The best way to do this is to eliminate their most powerful argument—that paying tolls and fuel taxes constitutes double taxation. As ETC becomes widespread, and it becomes easy to count all miles driven on tolled facilities, users of toll roads and bridges should be offered rebates of the amount of fuel tax they paid for those miles (based on the average miles-per-gallon of their registered vehicle). This change will make the phase-in of tolled roads significantly more feasible.

Enact Public-Private Partnership Laws   One key to transforming major roadways into customer-responsive utilities is to bring in the private sector as developer/operators of such facilities, under carefully drafted franchise agreements that serve both public and private interests. At the end of 1999, fifteen states had such measures on their books, but only some of those measures (e.g., Texas, Virginia) were flexible and broad enough to be good models. State-of-the-art enabling legislation is needed in every state, or at least every state with major metro areas suffering from congestion.

Develop National Standards for Electronic Tolling   The phase-in of pricing along the lines discussed here would be far easier if we had national standards such that auto makers could begin building in the ETC transponders and (ultimately) electronic license plates (combining GPS with two-way communications) that will facilitate such pricing on all types of roadways.

CONCLUSION

The message of this chapter is twofold. First, pricing can address the problem of urban traffic congestion. And we now have empirical evidence that road pricing works. We have electronic technology that permits flexible pricing, at least on limited-access facilities, and technology likely to be available within the next decade or so will extend that capability to local streets and roads. Second, the political obstacles to road pricing can be overcome. The two main tools for doing so are to remove federal obstacles (by decentralizing highway finance to the state level) and to use pricing to replace—not supplement—existing fuel taxes.

NOTES

1.   As measured by TTI, congestion includes delays on both freeways and major arterials.

2.   Since Profesor Sullivan's evaluation of the 91 Express Lanes was published, that project's financial performance has deteriorated (in 1999) due to the completion of the Foothill/Eastern toll road in Orange County which has diverted 15 to 20 percent of the traffic formerly using the express lanes, at least on a short-term basis. Partly due to that impact, in December 1999 the company that holds the franchise attempted to sell the express lanes to a newly created non-profit corporation, which would have refinanced the project with tax-exempt revenue bonds. The proposed sale was cancelled after a variety of political objections were raised. Despite these short-term difficulties, the express lanes remain a landmark project in terms of demonstrating the viability of value pricing and all-electronic tolling.

3.   Tolls are typically charged based more or less on miles driven, but the gasoline tax "user fee" is based only on gallons of gas consumed; if you can go much further on a gallon, you pay much less to use the road.

4.   Participating states are California, Iowa, Kansas, Michigan, Minnesota, Washington, Wisconsin, and Texas.

Chapter 5

Air Quality, Density, and Environmental Degradation

Human development impacts the environment in diverse ways. There are, of course, the emissions that human society produces in the course of daily living: chemical emissions to the air, the land, and the water. Beyond the emission of chemicals, the physical elements of human development have significant impact on the environment.

For example, with development comes the construction of roadway systems that may alter the flow of surface waters. The creation of sub-surface sewage systems, often combined with storm drains, can distort the natural flow patterns of water, both downward percolation and lateral flow through the soil. The installation of underground tanks not only interferes with sub-surface water flow, but they almost invariably leak, presenting a contamination hazard. In addition, paved areas (such as parking lots and driveways) and other impermeable surfaces (such as rooftops, foundations, and decks) cover areas that are normally foliated and porous, and disrupt these important recharge areas for surface and groundwaters. Development also can interfere with such environmental dynamics as air-flow patterns; local temperature and precipitation levels, wildlife habitat and movement, and so on.

Some environmental advocacy groups have asserted that certain forms of development are more environmentally destructive than others. Most notably, groups such as Greenpeace, the Natural Resources Defense Council, and Friends of the Earth are campaigning against decentralized and lower-density development (which they call "sprawl") and are agitating for regulatory restraints against such development.[1] Policy approaches like these have consequences, and can infringe upon people's rights to economic and lifestyle freedom. As will be discussed later, it is not at all clear that decentralized development is more harmful to the environment than dense development. Further, public policy, when implemented under conditions of high uncertainty, tends to fail as well as create new problems, as noted policy analyst Aaron Wildavsky has shown in innumerable ways in his landmark book, *Searching for Safety* (1988).

Wildavsky demonstrates that it is not what we do know that constrains the effectiveness and beneficence of advance-planning types of public policy—it is our uncertainties that most strongly influence the probability that a given approach is likely to be efficacious. This is so primarily because the conditions needed to assure a reasonable chance of success for policy actions that are intended to head off the development of predicted or modeled problems are quite stringent. Systems evolve more quickly than regulations do, and when one picks an approach before one has sufficient information to eliminate possible errors, there are far more ways to get things wrong than to get them right.

As Wildavsky points out, situations with significant uncertainty should favor approaches he defines as "resilient." These are problem-solving approaches that nurture society's ability to respond to problems if and when they occur by maintaining a dynamic, market-based, knowledge-building social structure, rather than trying to intercept a suggested problem before it appears. As Samuel Staley (1999) and others have pointed out, development patterns driven by market forces are strongly resilient and dynamic.

Wildavsky and others give several reasons why resilient approaches should be considered the default in situations where there is significant uncertainty. First, as any number of researchers have demonstrated, an unmistakable linkage exists between a society's resilient social and economic structures and its prosperity, safety, and environmental cleanliness. Because of the tendencies of resilient systems to build knowledge through research and to build safety through efficient use of resources, we have overwhelming evidence that resilient approaches that maintain a market-based, knowledge-building, and dynamic structure are highly effective, enhancing our ability to respond over time to risks and to reduce environmental degradation (see Bailey 2000). Second, resilient approaches make maximal use of the highest quality local knowledge at the appropriate point of exploration. Resilient approaches do not try to boil down a multidimensional problem into one of two dimensions—to spread out, or not to spread out. Finally, resilient approaches are the only type that can be as dynamic as the dynamic systems under discussion. Resilient approaches, contrary to frequent characterizations by environmental advocates, are not "do nothing" solutions, simply because "do nothing" is never a choice in a dynamic system. As often as not, taking a resilient approach will include actions that reverse various mistakenly adopted or no-longer-fruitful interceptive measures that are blocking the resilient process. This may include removal of zoning requirements that exacerbate environmental degradation, or replacement of less market-based measures, such as a hydraulic approach to storm-water management, with more market-based measures, such as watershed utilities (see discussion later).

The purpose of this chapter is to assess whether the claims linking decentralized development to environmental degradation are rigorous and are sufficiently well defined to suggest that the proposed remedy of Smart Growth (e.g., increasing compactness and residential/commercial densities) would be effective at addressing the various problems laid at the feet of decentralization.

DENSITY AND AIR QUALITY

Air quality data is the highest resolution environmental data available. The U.S. Environmental Protection Agency (EPA) collects such information via thousands of air quality monitors across the country. But is the developmental density of an area a primary causal factor in air pollution levels? The evidence is mixed.

Air quality degradation is a function of the type of emissions, the quantity of emissions, the post-release processing of emissions, and the concentrating elements of the local geography. The air pollutants that get the most attention are those that impact human health, including carbon monoxide, lead, nitrogen dioxide, ozone, PM_{10} (soot), and sulfur dioxide.

At the macro level, the EPA has published ambient air emission levels as they relate to development type, categorizing areas as "rural," "urban," or "suburban." Figures 5.1 through 5.6 show the measured ambient levels of primary pollutants as they relate to these classifications.[2] As the figures show, four out of the six criteria pollutant concentrations were higher in suburban areas than in rural areas from 1988 to 1997, and higher still in urban areas. The exceptions to the rule are ozone, which, has had higher levels in suburbs than in urban centers, and sulfur dioxide, which showed a suburban concentration exceeding urban levels in 1997. These figures appear to suggest that increasing density increases ambient air pollution levels, while the higher population densities in urban areas exposes more people to these higher pollutant levels.

This relationship was also observed by Randal O'Toole (1997), who, working with the EPA's classifications for pollution attainment (or non-attainment) and U.S. Census bureau data, showed that both central cities and metropolitan statistical areas with higher development levels have higher levels of air pollution. As Figures 5.7 and 5.8 show, there is a strong positive correlation between pollution attainment status and both metropolitan area population density and central city population density.

Such broad-brush conglomerations may not reflect reality. Using data from the EPA and from the Federal Highway Administration, one can correlate the ambient air pollutant levels with developmental density for specific pollutants in

Figure 5.1
Ambient Lead Concentration by Year and Development Classification

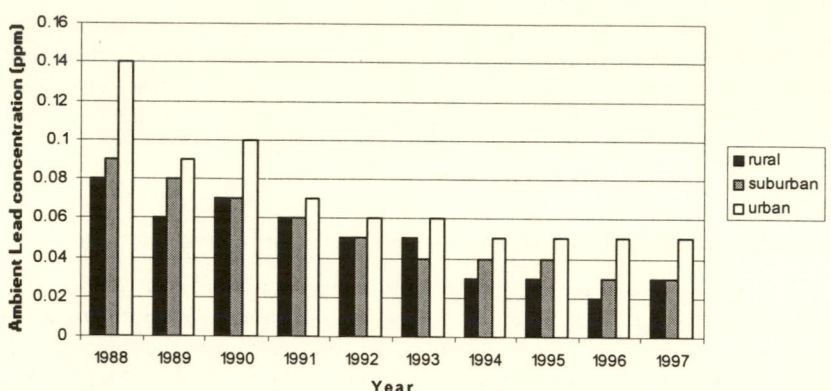

Figure 5.2
Ambient Nitrogen Dioxide Concentration by Year and Development Classification

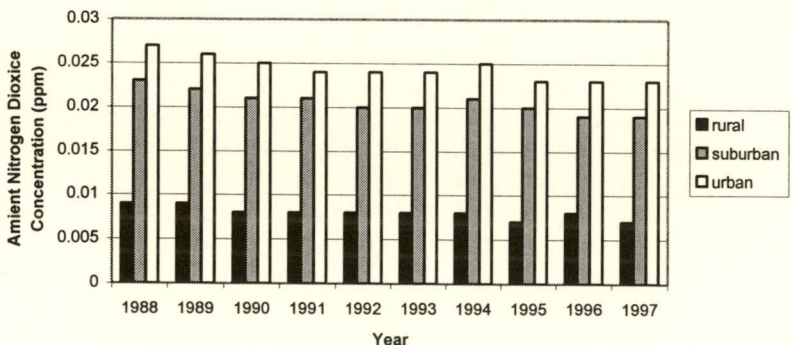

Figure 5.3
Ambient Carbon Monoxide Concentration by Year and Development Classification

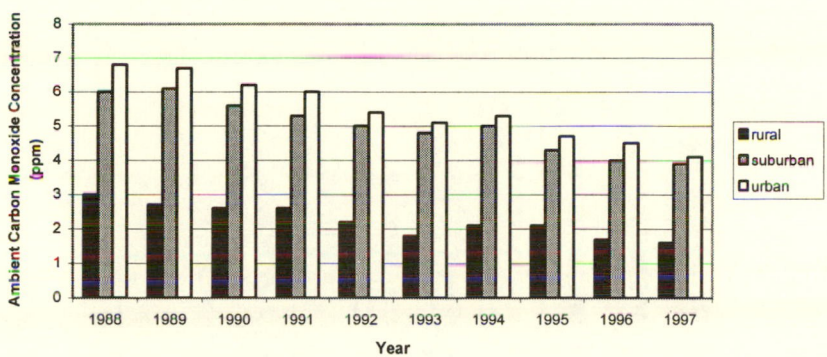

Figure 5.4
Ambient Sulfur Dioxide Concentration by Year and Development Classification

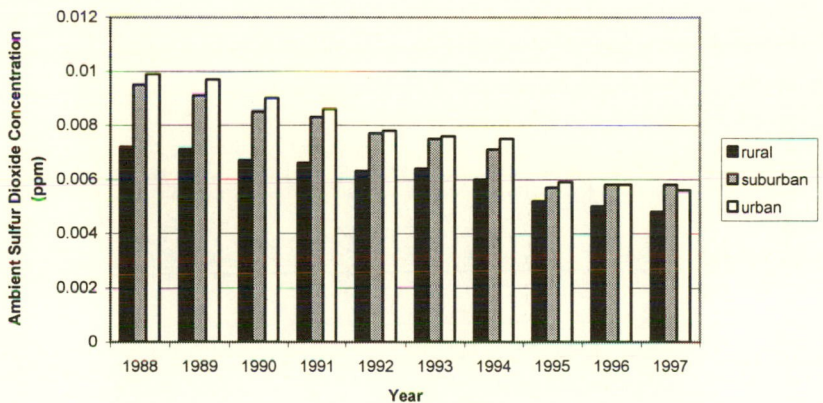

Figure 5.5
PM-10 Concentration by Year and Development Classification

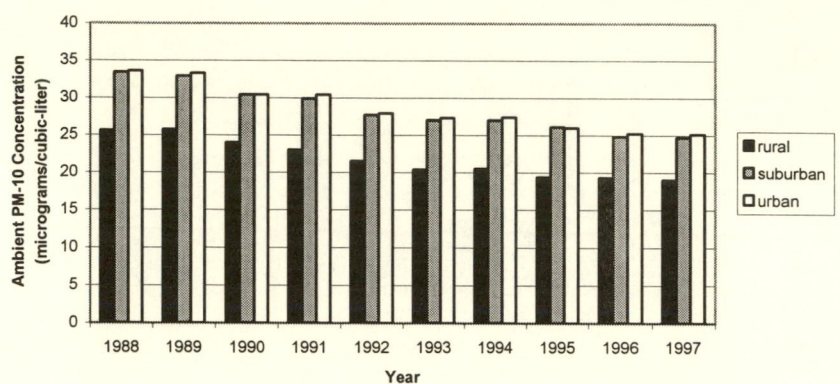

Figure 5.6
Ambient Ozone Concentration by Year and Development Classification

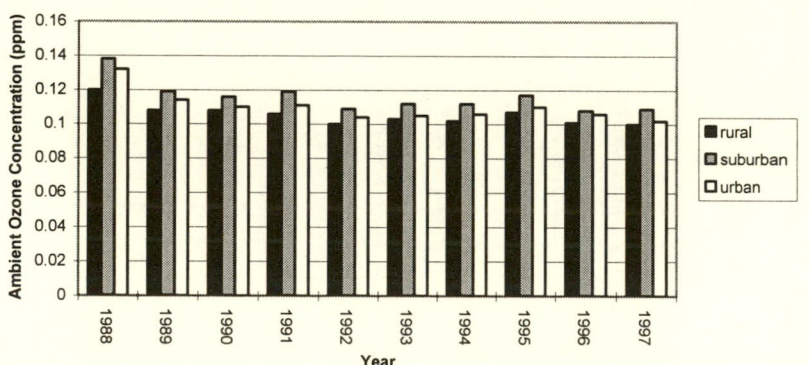

Figure 5.7
Metropolitan Area Average Density and Nonattainment Status

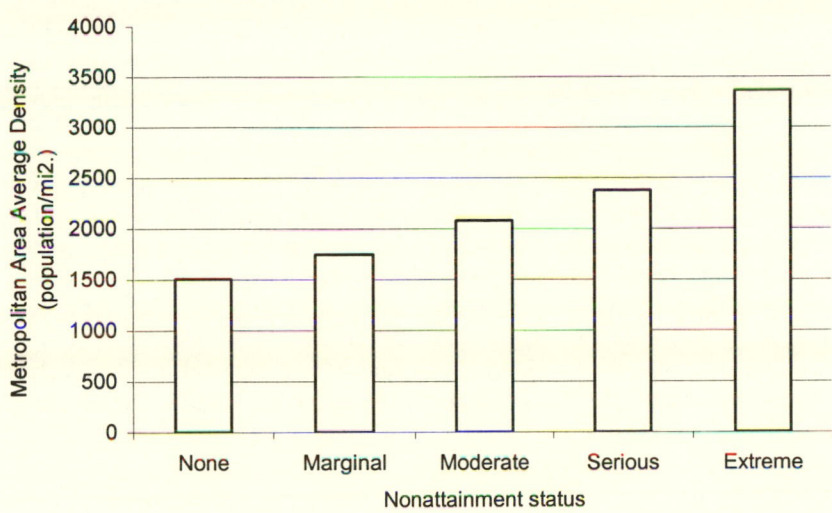

Figure 5.8
Central City Population Density and Nonattainment Status

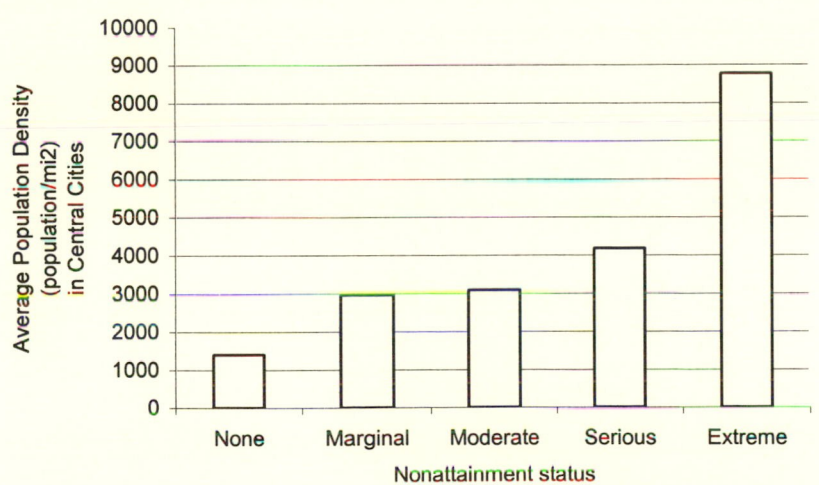

many of the nation's metropolitan statistical areas. An examination of several hundred of the nation's MSAs reveals little or no correlation between air pollution and density levels. Figures 5.9 through 5.12 show how the maximum concentrations of ozone and particulate matter correlate with density for between 175 and 200 MSAs where high-quality air pollution data is available.[3] This lack of correlation should not be surprising. Air pollution creation is a complex phenomenon, with far more factors involved than the simplistic "more driving-more smog" paradigm often put forward by opponents of decentralized development. Anti-sprawl advocates, taking simple measures of air pollution and density, fail to capture the wealth of data necessary for either forming a robust hypothesis of correlation or to put forward a solution with a strong suggestion of efficacy. Factors that aren't measured by such ad-hoc correlations include local meteorology, local air quality planning and regulation, and local fluctuations in economic and industrial activity. The uncertainty in the air pollution/decentralization relationship demonstrated by the mixed data just discussed, combined with the uncertainties introduced by ignoring relevant meteorological and other factors, suggest that claims that Smart Growth will reduce air pollution levels are questionable.

Figure 5.9
PM10 Concentration (2nd maximum) Vs. Density

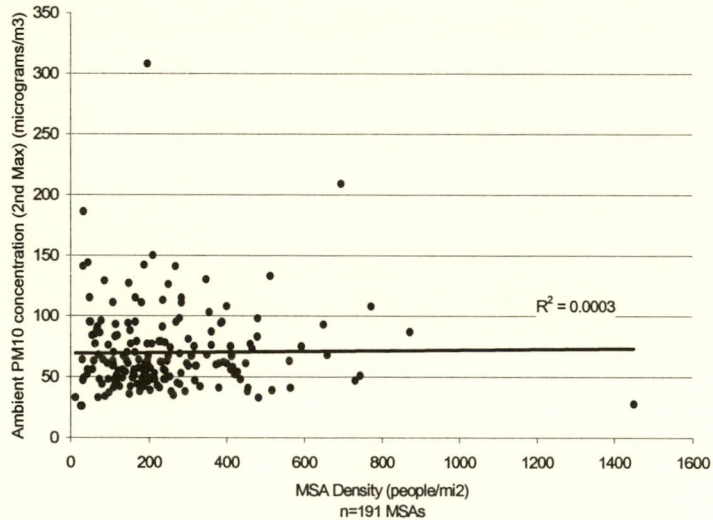

Figure 5.10
PM10 Concentration (ninety-ninth percentile) Vs. Density

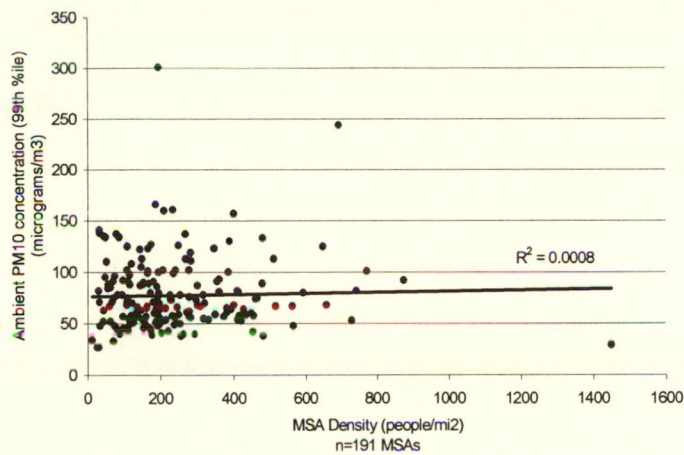

Figure 5.11
Ozone Concentration (8-hr) Vs. Density

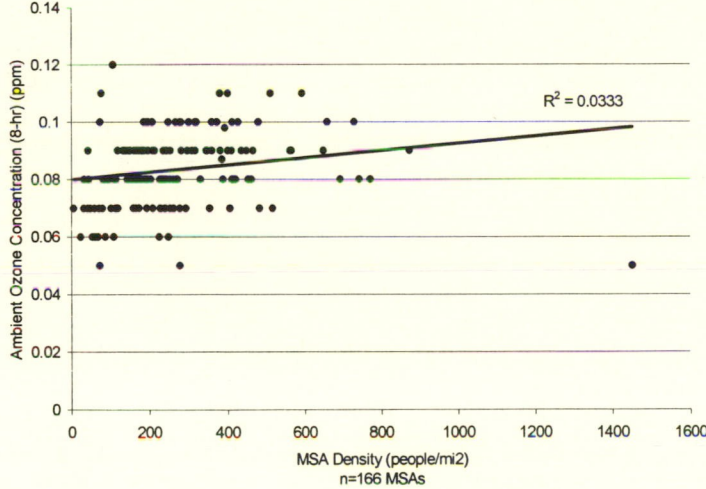

Figure 5.12
Ozone Concentration (1-hr) Vs. Density

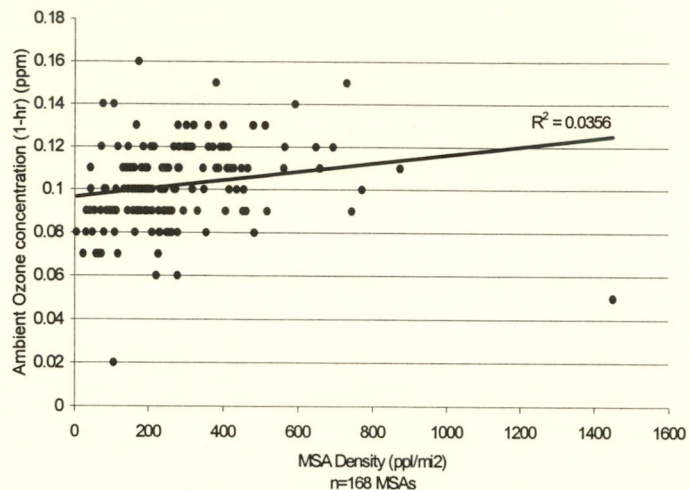

MSA Density (ppl/mi2)
n=168 MSAs

DENSITY AND WATER QUALITY

As discussed at the beginning of this chapter, water quality can be impacted by several aspects of development including the run-off of pollutants into waterways and the physical characteristics of wastewater or stormwater control systems. But the extent to which this occurs is not known. As the U.S. General Accounting Office (GAO) reported recently, the National Water Quality Inventory, a set of data intended to detail water quality levels across the country, "does not accurately portray water quality conditions nationwide" (U.S. General Accounting Office 2000). The GAO report goes on to state that "only 19 percent of the nation's rivers and streams were assessed for the 1996 Inventory [the latest report], as were 6 percent of ocean and other shoreline waters." While recognizing that the monitoring of all waterways would be prohibitively expensive, the GAO report observes that the current inventory gathering methodology fails to perform in a way that would lead to a statistically useful sample from which general trends could be determined.

Evidence gathered from specific incidences of water quality degradation suggests that the key factor that determines the impact of development on surface and ground water is not population density, but primarily the level of impervious surfacing and the control of run-off. Impervious surfacing materials disturb the natural sub-surface flows of water and provide a surface where wastes such as pesticides, motor oil, or automobile lubricants can accumulate and become concentrated. A growing body of scientific evidence supports the dominance of the linkage between impervious cover and stream health (City of Olympia 1995). Where impervious cover exceeds 5 percent, stream health begins to decline in some regions (May et al. 1997). With more than 10 percent impervious cover, stream health is biologically impaired. At 25 percent cover streams become biologically non-supportive.

Decentralized development, which can be accompanied by marked increases in the use of impervious surfaces, now covers 5 percent of the land area in the United States. East of the Mississippi, the median amount of development—the mid-point when the states are ranked by their degree of development—is almost 10 percent. Examining different types of development, at the low end of the scale, residential development on estate lots covers 12 to 20 percent of the land with impervious surfaces. At the high end of the scale, shopping center development results in over 90 percent surface imperviousness (Arnold and Gibbons 1996).

Runoff is another problem that can accompany development, decentralized or centralized. New construction, if done without proper concern for environmental degradation, can be particularly harmful, as was shown in a landmark study on the effects of urbanization on stream channels conducted by the U.S. Geological Survey (USGS) in the early 1950s. The USGS study showed that a surge of sediment enters streams when land is opened for construction. Less well recognized is the long-term effect of increased runoff from paved roads, rooftops, and parking lots. The increase in impermeable area results in an increased volume of runoff that is rapidly conveyed by storm drains into streams. The development-induced surge of runoff from each storm then erodes stream channels draining the area, gradually enlarging them and depositing sediment downstream (Leopold 1994, p. 164).

In the past, cities dealt with problems of bank erosion and channel enlargement by burying headwater streams in underground culverts and constraining larger tributaries in concrete or stone-lined channels. Some urban areas continue to bury and channelize streams despite widespread recognition that the practice worsens flooding and exports polluted water to communities downstream. While surface and groundwater impacts of development can be extensive, the assertion that dense development is less likely to cause harm than decentralized development is not supportable by data.

Surface and groundwater impacts are not unique to new development. In fact, the situation can be worse in older, highly urbanized areas where sewage and storm drains are often combined, causing stormwater mixed with sewage to overflow as aging systems become overburdened. During dry weather, sewage flows to treatment plants, but during rainstorms the combined systems become overburdened and overflow into surface streams through relief pipes called combined sewer overflows (CSOs). Another common problem in many urban areas is the illicit connection of sewer lines from homes and businesses to enclosed storm drains. CSOs and illicit connections add to the problem of stormwater runoff. Further, the cost of repairing the aging CSOs in the areas favored for densification is likely to exceed the costs of constructing newer, higher technology systems in new suburban development.

Finally, a deeper examination of the issue suggests that it is not development per se that produces water quality degradation. Rather, it is the incentives that guide the nature of development and the control of runoff. As Barrett Walker (2001) demonstrates, alternative institutional arrangements can sever the linkage between new construction or decentralized development and water quality degradation.

Walker gives the example of Bellevue, Washington, where instead of using the traditional engineering approach that concretizes and channelizes stormwater flows, a stormwater utility attacked the problem where it lived: at the level of impermeable surfacing. After citizens worked with local government to study the problem and identified stormwater runoff from impervious surfaces and loss of ecosystem function as the main problems, a user fee-based stormwater utility was established in 1974. The system charged property owners a stormwater utility fee based on the amount of impervious surface they had on their property. Now, an advanced Geographic Information System (GIS) is used for ecosystem management that overlays elements of the built environment with elements of the natural environment. Despite one of the highest rate structures in the nation, property values and approval ratings for the utility remain high, and Bellevue's waterways are protected.

Data on water quality nationwide is scarce. At regional levels, data exists showing that development can degrade water quality, but countervailing data also exists suggesting that impermeable surfacing, and not development per se, is the inherent cause of water quality degradation. The smart growth proposal presumes that the linkage between water quality degradation and decentralized development is clear, and that stopping decentralization will protect water quality. This claim is questionable, particularly in light of the problems with the combined stormwater/sewage systems of many dense urban environments in the United States, the favored site of additional development in the Smart Growth agenda. As with air quality, the uncertainties in the relationship between density and water quality degradation make claims that the Smart Growth solution will work to protect water quality questionable. At the same time, by decreasing the resilience of market-driven development, the Smart Growth movement is likely to produce a social form that is less capable of dealing with future environmental problems when and if they appear.

DENSITY AND SOIL CONTAMINATION

Besides releasing pollutants into the air and water, human activity also releases contaminants into the soil, both intentionally and inadvertently. Waste disposal is one way that contaminants find their way into the soil, but chemical disposal into leaky sewer systems and leakage on roadways or from underground tanks offer other contamination pathways. Soil contamination also can happen in areas used for farming, where pesticides and fertilizer contaminants can, over time, build up in the soil.

There are two national data sets that could offer insight into the relationship between development patterns and soil contamination. The EPA's Toxics Release Inventory (TRI) gathers data regarding the release of a long list of chemicals currently being disposed of by burial. TRI data has known limitations that make it unreliable for assessments of risk, and its accuracy as reported by EPA has also been questioned (Volokh et al. 1998). However, TRI data might serve as a general indicator of soil contamination.

For a retrospective look at the question, the nation's list of Superfund sites (the National Priorities List) offers a view of the distribution of past sites of soil contamination. Table 5.1 shows the states with the highest number of hazardous waste sites on the National Priorities List as of 1993, while the percentage of urban population in each state was calculated in the 1990 census. As Figure 5.13 shows, there is a positive correlation between the number of Superfund sites that a state had, and the level of its urbanized population. This would suggest that centralized living arrangements in the past were associated with greater levels of industrial activity, and hence, greater levels of soil contamination. This finding, which is fairly intuitive, is weakly supported by TRI data as well. Figure 5.14 shows the relationship of TRI releases and the percentage of urban population, by state. The percentage of urban population is from 1993, while the TRI releases are from 1994, to facilitate comparison.

Table 5.1
States with the Highest Number of Hazardous Waste Sites on the National Priorities List in 1993, and the Urban Population Percentage in Each State

State	No. of sites on the National Priorities List	Percent urban population
New Jersey	109	89.4
Pennsylvania	99	68.9
California	95	92.6
New York	85	84.3
Michigan	76	70.5
Florida	55	84.8
Washington	55	76.4
Minnesota	41	69.9
Wisconsin	40	65.7
Illinois	37	84.6
Ohio	36	74.1
Indiana	33	64.9
Massachusetts	31	84.3
Texas	30	80.3
Virginia	24	69.4
South Carolina	24	54.6

Note: Data on number of NPL sites is from Samuel R. Staley, "Environmental Policy and Urban Revitalization: The Role of Lender Liability, *Capital University Law Review*, 1996, p. 61. Percent urban population is for 1992, from Samuel Staley, "The Sprawling of America: In Defense of the Dynamic City," Policy Study No. 251 (Los Angeles: Reason Public Policy Institute, January 1999).

Figure 5.13
Number of Sites on NPL Vs. Percent Urban Population in Highly Urbanized States

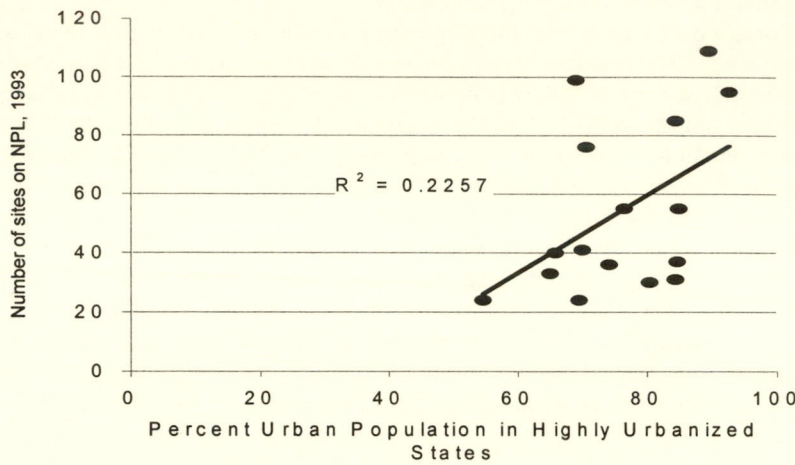

Figure 5.14
TRI Releases Vs. Percent Urban Population (all States)

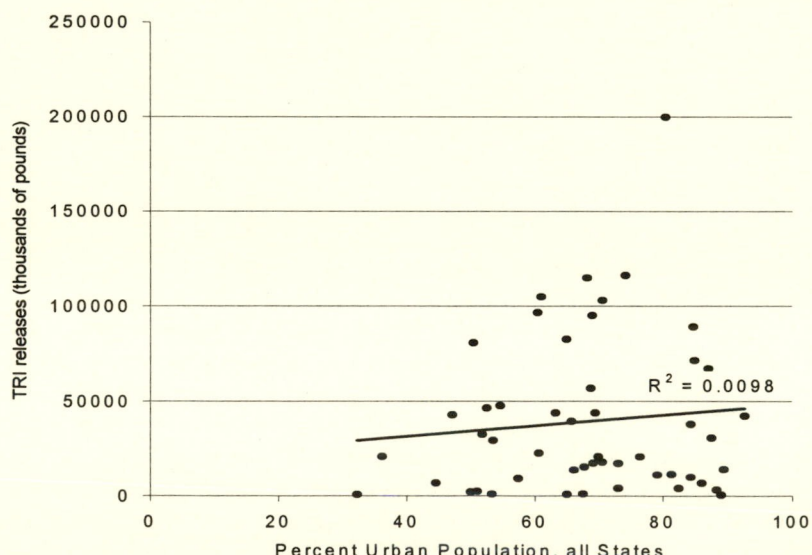

Thus, the most recent data for which both ground-discharge metrics and urbanization metrics were available suggest that increasing density, not decreasing density, is associated with a higher likelihood of living near a hazardous waste site, or being in the proximity of larger waste discharges. But as with air and water quality, one has to be mindful of how little information is captured in a simple correlation of these types, even when such correlations may be the only hard data available. As mentioned earlier, TRI data has many known flaws that make it less than useful as an indicator of risk, or even of environmental contamination. The simple number of Superfund sites tells us nothing about when the sites were first contaminated, what the density was at those times, or whether current laws regarding waste burial would prevent more such soil contamination regardless of developmental density levels. TRI releases are not meaningful indicators of risk, and our knowledge of population density immediately adjacent to the sites of TRI releases is minimal.

CONCLUSION

While human development certainly has the potential for damaging environmental systems through both physical elements and emitted contaminants, what little data is available does not permit strong conclusions to be drawn regarding how such potential damage relates to developmental density. Several data sets suggest that higher levels of air pollution may correlate with higher population densities, but a more detailed data set throws this correlation into doubt. This is not surprising, because simple correlations of emission levels and population density cannot capture such important elements as local geography, wind flow patterns, industrial development, and other factors affecting pollution levels. Available data on water quality, whether ground water, surface water, or coastal water is insufficient to derive general trends of any sort, much less those associated with population density. Data does exist suggesting that the critical factor in protecting ground and surface waters is the extent of impervious surfacing, rather than the density of development or population. Finally, examinations of soil contamination from two data sets, the Toxics Release Inventory and the National Priorities List of Superfund Sites, suggests that more urbanized populations risk exposure to either hazardous waste sites or to toxic discharge areas. But correlating Superfund site frequency with density runs into a historical perspective problem: we do not have data detailing what the density is like immediately surrounding Superfund sites, nor what it was historically when the site was created. The same lack of data applies to the sites of TRI releases today.

Advocates of higher population densities and dense forms of urban development assert that lower density lifestyles contribute to environmental degradation such as air pollution, water pollution, and soil contamination. Secondary to these effects, other health advocacy groups claim that human health is suffering from exposure to air, water, and soil pollutants (American Lung Association 1996; Colborn et al. 1996; National Resources Defense Council 1996). On the basis of such claims, advocates of high urban densities lobby for regulations limiting suburban expansion and low-density development. In addition to the known side-effects of such interventionist policy on the economic and civil rights of the population, such interventionist policies are likely to be environmentally counterproductive. They will surely result in increased pollution levels in areas where people live, thus producing a negative impact on human health, and there is no evidence that higher density development is good for the environment in general.

NOTES

1. See the Sierra Club's anti-sprawl faq (http://www.sierraclub.org/sprawl/factsheet asp#Polluters). The Natural Resources Defense Council website (www.ndrc.org) carries numerous anti-sprawl documents and Friends of the Earth lay the blame for environmental degradation at the feet of road building (http://www.foe.org/eco/transportation/index.html).

2. Data are from *National Air Quality and Emissions Trends Report*, 1997, U.S. Environmental Protection Agency (http://www.epa.gov/oar/aqtrnd97/).

3. The different charts look at a different selection of MSAs, based on the availability of pollutant concentration data in those areas. The number (n) of MSAs plotted on each chart are noted along the x-axis. Data for the MSA population densities are from the U.S. Census (www.census.gov/Press-Release/metro06.prn).

Chapter 6

National Land-Use Planning Through Environmental Policy

JEFFERSON G. EDGENS

As Chapter 1 pointed out, growth management policy issues have risen to the forefront on public policy debate at the national, state, and local levels. For the first time in U.S. history, land-use issues have become part of a national policy debate. The Clinton administration solidified the position of these issues as federal policy when it introduced the Livability Agenda in January 1999. The Livability Agenda is relatively modest by contemporary federal policy standards, but nevertheless reinforces a long-term trend toward national land-use regulation and development control. More importantly, the Livability Agenda may signal a new era of aggressive federal regulation in the area of land-use planning.

Is the federal government moving toward local land-use management? National land use planning management was contemplated in 1976 as part of a general environmental regulatory effort, but failed. Since then, environmentalists and others have continued to voice concern about the environmental impacts of land-use patterns and have attempted to use environmental policy to regulate land-use activities that potentially harm the environment and ecosystems. As this chapter will show, the federal government is becoming increasingly active on local land-use issues, particularly through policymaking and implementation at the Environmental Protection Agency (EPA).

The most overt example of this trend is currently playing out in Atlanta (Antonelli 2000). In 1999, the Georgia legislature established a regional transportation agency in the Atlanta metropolitan area as a direct result of federal environmental policy. Because the Atlanta area was considered a high pollution area (a serious nonattainment area), the federal government withheld transportation funds until the region establishes, and the EPA approves, a regional development plan (RDP) to address air quality problems. While federal funds for transportation infrastructure have been released for projects already in the pipeline, the EPA and other federal agencies are wielding significant power over state and local governments because they are in a position to approve or disapprove individual components of the plan. Indeed, the Clean Air Act of 1990 gives the federal government sweeping powers over local governments, and can even stop investment by refusing to grant permits to new or expanding manufacturing facilities, utilities, and other businesses considered potentially harmful to the environment. The Atlanta experience, discussed in detail later in the chapter, demonstrates how an aggressive stand by the federal government can influence a wide range of issues outside traditional environmental policy issues.

While some environmental policies, such as air quality control, have received substantial attention in the media, water quality issues have received scant attention. This is unfortunate because water pollution control policies, particularly watershed management, may have far more pervasive influences on local land-use policy and federal efforts to influence development patterns. This chapter assesses trends toward greater federal control over land-use policy within the context of water quality policy and watershed management in particular.

NONPOINT SOURCE WATER POLLUTION

One area in which environmental policy is becoming a type of federal land-use policy is the regulation of nonpoint source (NPS) water pollution. Nonpoint source pollution is diffuse runoff from farms, streets, and houses that flows across the ground and into surface waters such as lakes, ponds, and rivers. Policies influencing water policy could affect virtually all major urban areas in the United States. The Mississippi River watershed, for example, includes 31 states and major metropolitan areas such as St. Louis, Memphis, and New Orleans. Similarly, the Hudson River watershed includes cities such as Albany and New York City. The EPA, as the lead federal agency, is developing a unified process to protect and monitor water quality through a series of initiatives and agency rulemaking that directly impact land use and development patterns. These efforts go beyond the statutory requirements of the Clean Water Act, because the Act is silent as to nonpoint source control. At the heart of these initiatives is greater federal control of state and local land-use planning. In fact, one can argue that the EPA is essentially implementing a federal growth management program through watersheds and water quality regulation and enforcement.

The mechanism for this is ecosystem management, a goal federal agencies have pursued since the early 1980s. The concept has been criticized for its lack of definition and controlling legal authority (Fitzsimmons 1994), but several statutes hint at federally driven ecosystem management. The two most important are the Clean Water Act (CWA) and the Multiple Use Sustained Yield Act, but they stop short of authorizing it. Nevertheless, the EPA and other federal agencies are implementing ecosystem management despite limited statutory authority and the legal ambiguity of administrative rulemaking (which bypasses Congress).

Rather than implement ecosystem management *per se*, the EPA's central organizing principle is watershed management. A number of practical reasons explain this. Watersheds are more easily defined and identified (Ruhl 1999). Water quality is a means of assessing watershed/ecosystem health. Thus, with the goal of improving water quality, federal policy attempts to control land-use activities by identifying and managing ecosystems in order to protect watershed health (Ruhl 2000).

A wide array of issues fall into watershed management, including sprawl, agricultural policy, silviculture, and building construction (DiLorenzo 1999). Through a coordinated approach spearheaded by the EPA's Clean Water Action Plan (CWAP) requirements, federal resources are leveraged to improve water quality in a manner that centralizes control at the federal level and compromises independent land-use decisions by state and local governments.

One CWAP requirement mandates an open space set aside for watershed management. This is accomplished through the President's Land Legacy Initiative in which the federal government directly, or through grants, buys open space, farmland, and other areas sensitive to watershed health and wildlife habitat. The federal government can accomplish a simultaneous goal of controlling urban development by placing some land permanently off limits to development (because land purchased by the government will never be developed), irrespective of market trends or consumer preferences (Doppelt, Scurlock, Fissell, and Karr 1993; Ruhl 2000). Another example of federal watershed management is the Clinton administration's directive instructing the U.S. Forest Service to set aside over 40 million acres in the national forests, protecting them from further road building. In furtherance of this goal, U.S. Forest Service Chief Michael Dombeck has issued a plan to manage national forests on a watershed basis.

Similarly, the Conservation and Reinvestment Act (CARA) creates an off-budget fund for open space preservation. In order to tap into the federal funds, which would allocate $2.8 billion to states under the legislation passed by the Congress in 2000, each state will have to submit a plan outlining how funds would be used, their priorities, and objectives (VanHelmond and Antonelli 2000, pp. 6-8). The act would require states to consult with local and federal agencies, and gives the Secretary of the U.S. Department of the Interior substantial discretion in determining whether projects and priorities were appropriate.

Water quality assessments and federally approved pollution caps in water bodies throughout the nation also can be used to control land use by regulating how much sediment or nutrient enters the watershed. This becomes a form of back-door land-use control. One scenario under a watershed regime would be to require EPA approval of water "pollution caps" prior to building or expanding new facilities (Edgens 1999b). Thus, federal agencies, through rulemaking, indirectly control land-use planning, usurping local control (Edgens 1999a).

ECOSYSTEM PROTECTION VIA WATERSHED MANAGEMENT

Environmental protection involves a multi-media approach—land, air, and water. Perturbations to any of these separate but connected systems can create problems for ecosystem health. As a result, many scientists have pushed for an ecosystem approach because, in principle, it can accommodate a multi-media approach. Defining the ecosystem, though, has been fraught with problems (Fitzsimmons 1994). An ecosystem can be defined as a parcel of land as narrow as a backyard, small woodlot, lake, or lakeshore. Ecosystem management is also difficult because natural systems do not recognize political boundaries of national, state, or local governments (Ruhl 1999). Complicating matters further is the issue of how to balance economic needs within this larger organizing framework. Management philosophies tend to embrace cooperative intergovernmental efforts to manage across jurisdictions.

To address the deficiencies of ecosystem management, policymakers and environmentalists increasingly rely on watershed management, because watersheds can be identified and monitored. Watersheds, as defined by Andrew Dzurik (1990), include land over which water drains to a particular point in a stream. The Mississippi River watershed, for example, consists of 31 states all made up of tiny watersheds with an outlet to the Mississippi River. The basin itself is a watershed with the river as an outlet to the Gulf of Mexico. Watersheds are also ecosystems because land, air, and water are interconnected in these small geographic units. In turn this makes for easier delineation of watersheds as demonstrated by the U.S Geological Surveys Hydrologic Unit Code (HUC) numbering system. All watersheds are numbered and reflected on maps.

Watersheds are an effective means of managing ecosystems because ecosystem health can be determined based on water quality and quantity within a watershed. In other words, poor water quality is an indicator of an unhealthy ecosystem. Algal blooms, for example, can tell environmental managers that more phosphorus is entering the watershed than it can safely assimilate. This can lead managers to search for other sources of phosphorus in a watershed, such as livestock operations, nearby residential areas, or water treatment plants.

EPA AUTHORITY UNDER THE CLEAN WATER ACT

The Clinton/Gore administration began to change federal environmental policy through the regulatory process rather than through legislation. The EPA, in particular, appears to be particularly aggressive in using new administrative rules to enforce new environmental standards, from air quality to brownfield liability. In part, this may be explained by the deference courts have given to regulatory agencies. Courts have traditionally presumed that agencies have the relevant expertise needed to manage complex problems (Adler 2000). Thus, an activist administration could use agency rulemaking as an effective way to design and implement new policies. One can see the rationale for such a strategy predicated on controlling urban sprawl. By leveraging federal, state, and local resources, nonpoint source activities like agriculture, silviculture, and construction can be targeted for management and permitting.

Federal legislation to control nonpoint source pollution, however, is not only absent, but the scientific data identifying impaired waters is spotty. State environmental monitoring normally focuses on known hot spots or known polluted waters, so it is difficult to get an accurate picture of water quality problems caused by nonpoint sources of pollution.

The EPA's proposal to broaden their Total Maximum Daily Load (TMDL) program for nonpoint source pollution provides an example of the way in which environmental regulations have expanded to cover land-use issues. In August 1999 the EPA proposed new rules that bring agriculture and silviculture into the TMDL program. The TMDL is a calculation to determine the maximum amount of pollution that a water body can assimilate without violating water quality standards, resulting in a pollution cap. The TMDL program is used for point sources to decide how much of a given chemical can be discharged by a treatment facility. Thus, the program evaluates the potential harm of proposed activities (e.g., development, road building) based on a maximum load the environment could tolerate, according to EPA-set guidelines. Activities that exceed the estimated TMDL would be prohibited until an impaired water body met the established water quality standards. Under the TMDL program, specific activities like prescribed burning, site preparation, and road construction require landowners to obtain permits from the EPA before proceeding. Clearly, this is potentially a very intrusive regulatory approach because the EPA would be able to approve and disapprove specific activities based on standards it promulgates, often without adequate scientific evidence to support the standards. The agency's application of the TMDL program to *nonpoint source pollution*, however, is not statutorily authorized for four reasons.

1.　*CWA provisions used to implement the TMDL program (Sec. 303(d)) apply solely to point sources.* The Clean Water Act was signed into law in 1972 for the purpose of making the nation's waters fishable, swimmable, and drinkable. Section 303(d) covers identification of areas with insufficient controls; maximum daily loads; and certain effluent limitation revisions required under section 301b(1A) (setting best practicable control technology for point sources) and 301b(1B) (effluent limitations for secondary treatment at public water treatment facilities). This implies that 303(d), the provision of the CWA that authorizes the use of TMDL, is not applicable to nonpoint sources.

2.　*Legislative history strongly reinforces the idea the nonpoint sources of pollution are to be treated differently than point sources.* The EPA is broadly interpreting the CWA and its various amendments to give it the legal authority to regulate nonpoint sources. By 1987 Congress recognized that the act was inadequate to address NPS pollution, and created a separate Section 319 to apply to nonpoint sources rather than linking NPS control to the existing point source permit system (U.S. GAO 1999). Section 319 is the incentive-based nonpoint source section of the CWA, a grant program for states to adopt NPS management programs and to make further reductions in NPS pollution. Absent from Section 319, is any reference to establishing TMDLs for nonpoint sources. Congressional debate reflects this reasoning:

Senator Stafford: A new Section 319 establishes a program to begin the process of addressing this hitherto unregulated source of water degradation. The addition of a nonpoint source control program to the Act is thus a reasonable and necessary extension of the Act's existing requirements. It does not signal the discovery of a new problem. We have known about the problem for years and have taken pains to collect the information and carry out the planning needed to deal with it effectively. Nor does it imply that the point source control program at the heart of the Act has been a failure.

Senator Durenberger: Mr. President, this new Section 319 represents a *first step* in controlling pollution from nonpoint sources. *We have been persuaded to take a path somewhat different from that taken for point sources.* States are given flexibility to identify priorities.

Senator Simpson: For the *first time* we have included a provision in the Clean Water Act related to nonpoint source pollution that comes from farm lands, timber operations, and other sources of *runoff which are not considered "point sources."* (Barrett 1999; emphasis added)

The EPA is nonetheless continuing to aggressively pursue agriculture and development controls through the TMDL process and a variety of other regional water quality initiatives regardless of congressional intent.

   3. *The EPA's aggressive use of its regulatory authority runs counter to the intent of Congress, which is to give states more flexibility in designing and implementing environmental policy.* Each step, when examined closely, shifts regulatory authority and oversight from the state and local level to the federal government. Some raise legal questions as to whether the TMDL program is applicable to nonpoint sources of pollution. TMDLs naturally lend themselves to engineering solutions because a wastewater treatment system is contained in a single system and constantly monitored. In contrast, a farmer's field contains natural amounts of phosphorus and wet-weather events can exacerbate phosphorous loadings to the water even with the best of conservation efforts. Thus, the methods, technologies, and standards of measurement are not easily transferable. What is an appropriate amount of phosphorus to leave a farm and enter surface water compared to a water treatment facility? How should natural or background sources of phosphorus be balanced?

   4. *Executive orders, guidance documents, and expansive rules are used to legitimize nonpoint source controls.* Through a variety of administrative tools, the EPA is expanding its control of NPS pollution and consequently, land-use activities. The administration and EPA have creatively used executive orders, guidance documents, and memoranda of agreement connected via its Clean Wa-

ter Action Plan, giving EPA illusory authority to regulate nonpoint source pollution.

EXPANDING THE EPA'S NONSTATUTORY REGULATORY CONTROL

Despite the lack of statutory authority for the EPA's aggressive application of regulatory policy, the EPA has applied regulations to a wide range of activities through a number of administrative mechanisms. The most important tools have been the Clean Water Action Plan, executive orders, guidance documents, and memoranda of agreements.

Clean Water Action Plan

When the Congress failed to re-authorize the Clean Water Act, the Clinton administration created a regulatory strategy to plug what they considered critical gaps in the act—one of which was the control of nonpoint sources of pollution via a permit system. The administration produced the Clean Water Action Plan (CWAP) with 111 key action items to improve the nation's waters. The plan's genesis was in the EPA, not Congress. This is significant because the EPA's authority to regulate NPS through the CWA is dubious at best. In addition, the promulgation of a national CWAP represents a major policy shift because in the past significant policy decisions typically have been left to elected representatives in Congress. In essence, the administration made an end-run around Congress to patch the perceived failings of the CWA passed by Congress.

Two years ago the administration released its CWAP with proposals for improving water quality in lakes, rivers, and streams. The CWAP has not been authorized by Congress nor has it undergone administrative approval in accordance with the Administrative Procedures Act. Yet Congress approved the CWAP budget for 1998 and 1999 with the latest appropriation greater than the previous request. The executive branch is implementing the goals of the CWAP through presidential executive orders and EPA guidance documents and regulations.

Executive Orders

Wilson Olson and Alan Woll (1999) point out that presidents have come to apply executive orders (EOs) to bypass Congress. President Clinton was quick to use EOs to make policy decisions when he believed Congress would not support administration policies. A number of these EOs show an interest in significantly expanding the roles and scope of federal involvement in what has been traditionally state and local affairs. Executive Order 13083 on Federalism was quietly signed (and later rescinded after significant opposition from Congress and the public) in May 1998. Several portions of the executive order triggered direct federal involvement in affairs of state and local governments. Subsection 3(d), titled "Federalism and Policymaking Criteria," outlined the conditions under which federal policy would take precedence over local interests:

Matters of national or multi-state scope that justify federal action may arise in a variety of circumstances, including: 1.) when the matter to be addressed by federal action occurs interstate, 2.) when the source of the matter to be addressed occurs in a state different from the state (or states) where a significant amount of the harm occurs, 3.) when there is a need for national uniform standards, [sections four and five have less application] 6.) when states would be reluctant to impose necessary regulations because of fears that regulated business activity will relocate to other states, 7.) when regulatory authority at state or local level would undermine regulatory goals due to high costs or demands for specialized expertise beyond the resources of state authorities, 8.) when the matter relates to federally owned or managed property or natural resources, 9.) when the matter to be regulated significantly or uniquely affects Indian tribal governments.

While reasonable at first glance, these criteria would essentially enable federal control and regulation of every significant watershed in the United States, bypassing state and local environmental authorities. These criteria imply that any pollutant in a state stream, whether originating in that state or a neighboring state, is subject to federal regulation. The EPA is currently pursuing unified watershed assessments or uniform national standards for water quality. Because states may not closely regulate large farms (e.g., corporate hog and poultry farms), new standards would allow the federal EPA to intervene in a state where the pollution originates using the justification that the state may not have sufficiently strong rules to avoid impairing water bodies downstream. Technical costs, insufficient scientific knowledge, pollution from federal lands and impaired tribal waters would also trigger federal involvement under Subsection 3(d). Clearly the federalism criteria would expand almost any source of pollution to federal control. Concerns about the environmental impacts of land development could trigger federal intervention if the EPA determines state laws are too weak. The hue and cry of state and local governments led to the rescission of EO 13084 four months after it was signed.

Guidance Documents

When the EPA is in doubt about its authority, it drafts guidance documents (GD). Agency guidance is meant to be advisory in nature and thus does not need to undergo review expected under the Administrative Procedures Act. "Nonlegislative rules have no legal binding effect, but practical binding effect when used to establish criteria to control individual rights and obligations of private persons" (Anthony 1998). Guidance documents can become important policymaking tools. New air emissions standards, for example, were nearly established through a GD and would have dramatically increased EPA involvement in environmental, land use, and economic policy at the state and local level. In fact, much of the support behind regional transportation and land use planning in Georgia is directly tied to federal environmental policy. In order to maintain federal funding for road and highway projects, the Atlanta metropolitan area had to establish a regional planning agency, conforming to federal guidelines, to bring the region into compliance with air quality standards set by the EPA. In a U.S. Court of Appeals case in the D.C. Circuit regarding air emissions, EPA guidance was struck down as unenforceable. It remains to be seen what effect, if any, this ruling will have for other areas of environmental policy. At this point, however, guidance documents like the CWAP have not been challenged and so remain viable.

Memoranda of Agreements

The EPA is working with other federal agencies via signed Memoranda of Agreements (MOA) and Memoranda of Understanding (MOU) to coordinate federal activities with respect to watershed management. In far reaching MOAs, the EPA and the U.S. Fish and Wildlife Service have tackled the coordination of TMDL and water quality as it relates to aquatic habitat. Specifically, both agencies address endangered species protection with implementation of TMDLs. If runoff creates algal blooms and subsequent fish kill of a threatened or endangered species, then the landowner can be fined for a "take" (e.g., species death or destruction of habitat) under section seven of the Endangered Species Act.

In another example, the U.S. Army Corps of Engineers, under considerable pressure by environmental groups and the EPA, revised their wetlands permitting rule. The EPA signed a MOA that connects CWAP goals with the new Corps wetland rules. The Corps regulates navigable waters and wetlands under the Clean Water Act. By restricting the size of development along river corridors, the Corps protects wetlands and the EPA indirectly controls land use along these waterways. If wetland quality is impaired, waterfowl (subject to authority of the U.S. Fish and Wildlife Service) might be harmed, thus drawing attention to the source of water impairment and nearby landowners and any land activities. What holds all of these administrative devices together is the Clean Water Action Plan.

With assistance from state and federal courts, the EPA is rewriting the language of the Clean Water Act. Two cases, one from New York and another from Washington state, redefined nonpoint source pollution, giving the EPA much broader authority and discretion over environmental compliance and enforcement. In *CARE v. Southview Farms*, a New York farmer's manure spreader was declared a point source and subject to EPA rules (Martin 1997). In a related case, *CARE v. Henry Bosma Dairy,* a manure pile on a Washington dairy farm was defined as a point source because an inspector could "point" to the manure pile as a the source of runoff.

An Oregon case arrived at a totally separate decision and one much closer to the language of the Clean Water Act. In *Oregon Natural Desert Association (ONDA) v. Dombeck*, an environmental group wanted to define cattle a point source for section 401 certification under the CWA. The judge opined that cattle grazing is a nonpoint activity and, further, that the act does not mention "nonpoint source discharge" or "discharge by a nonpoint source," so the grazing cattle did not require federal permits.

Undeterred by the *ONDA* decision and repeatedly having its hands slapped by other court decisions, EPA aggressively continues to expand their regulatory authority over nonpoint source activities with the aid of the New York and Washington courts. Evidence of this was EPA Assistant Administrator for Water Chuck Fox's testimony before the House Subcommittee on Oversight, Nutrition, and Forestry chaired by Representative Bob Goodlatte (R-VA). Before a packed committee and after significant bipartisan questioning, Goodlatte pointedly asked Fox why the EPA had not asked Congress for authorizing legislation for the TMDL process. Fox responded that "Congress has ample authority to intervene under the Congressional Review Act and raise objections." Goodlatte responded, "that's not how democracy is supposed to work. Its not up to the regulatory body to take action and then sit back and see if it gets past Congress" (Edgens 2000). In fact congressional acquiescence emboldens EPA authority. The EPA testimony raises the question of TMDL and permit application to nonpoint sources, and whether the agency has the legislated authority to control nonpoint sources in the same manner as point sources.

Much of what the EPA is contemplating is in its nascent stages. How would it implement land-use control? Again visiting the CWAP, the EPA is the lead agency of a dozen federal agencies with some sort of responsibility in managing federal lands, wildlife habitat, or construction and economic activities. The EPA is overseer to the CWAP. Federal agencies are in an oversight role in which local land and water plans are subject to approval or disapproval by federal agencies, in effect granting the EPA or another federal agency veto authority over local land-use decisions. The agency's rationale is that polluted waters are caused by private land-use activities and that these activities need to be controlled for states to meet water quality standards and pollution caps. This is beyond the authority of federal agency mission as expressed in the statute (Clean Water Act).

Watershed management through the TMDL process and other water initiatives that appear at first irrelevant to land-use planning will place the EPA in the driver's seat for state and local land-use decisions. For example, over the last seven years the EPA has created a host of initiatives that reinforce regional watershed management and federal oversight, such as the Chesapeake Bay Initiative, Great Lakes Initiative, Great Basin Initiative, and Gulf of Mexico Program to Control hypoxia. The Chesapeake Bay Initiative attempts to protect water quality and aquatic habitat in three states. Maryland, Virginia, and Delaware had to agree to watershed plans consistent with federal objectives. On close inspection, one finds that the Chesapeake Bay agreement has some far reaching goals, including a watershed-wide 30 percent reduction in the growth rate of harmful sprawl, the protection of 20 percent of open space, and the removal of the Bay from the impaired waters list by 2010 (Gilmore 2000). Virginia delayed signing the agreement until the EPA threatened to withhold funding for its watershed plan.

THE EPA AND FEDERAL GROWTH MANAGEMENT

The Case of Atlanta

Federal growth management is demonstrably more clear in Atlanta, Georgia. Atlanta's air pollution woes attracted the attention of the EPA when it consistently violated air quality standards set by the agency. Most of Atlanta's smog and air quality problems are a result of nitrogen oxides (NOx). Most NOx are manmade, and growth management advocates charged that automobiles were the source of much of Atlanta's smog conditions. Sixty percent of metropolitan Atlanta's NOx emission, however, are from point sources (e.g., factories, power generation facilities, etc.), not nonpoint or mobile sources such as automobiles (Green 1999). Even if all potential implementation strategies were used to control NOx emissions, controls on mobile sources would reduce emissions by only 5 percent compared to 46 percent for point sources (Green 1999, p. 4). The EPA and the U.S. Department of Transportation, a signor of the CWAP, threatened to withhold Georgia's highway funds until Atlanta was in compliance with its air pollution plan. Governor Roy Barnes in 1999 created a super agency in 1999, the Georgia Regional Transportation Authority (GRTA), charged with coordinating transportation planning in a thirteen-county region of metro Atlanta, focusing almost exclusively on controlling mobile sources (e.g., automobiles). The key to spurring Georgia in this direction was the threat of withholding federal funds because the region was out of compliance with federal environmental regulations and guidance documents (Antonelli 2000).

The Atlanta case is illustrative of how the EPA and federal agencies can influence the details of regional land-use planning. In order to mitigate air pollution, the EPA's (and U.S. Department of Transportation's) preferred policy strategy is to emphasize mass transit over direct congestion reliefs such as expanding highway capacity or instituting variable pricing on highways (see Chapter 4). This implies a greater reliance on buses and extensions of the Metropolitan Atlanta Rapid Transit Authority (MARTA) heavy rail system. In order to encourage greater mass transit (particularly rail use), residential and commercial densities have to increase significantly. In order to conform to the transportation plan, the GRTA also has authority to mandate higher density and mixed-use zoning at the local level consistent with ensuring the success of the transportation plan. *Thus, the federal government, by setting the rules of the game, has effectively intervened or heavily influenced local land-use planning to achieve a federal objective.* More importantly, the traditional solutions to air quality problems—mass transit, less automobile dependence, higher densities—have a low likelihood of success (Green 1999; Chapters 2,3,4,5). The final outcome is federally driven land-use planning and heavily subsidized mass transit without improvements in air quality, along with a subsequent loss in local control of land-use activities.

The next two examples, the American Heritage Rivers Initiative and the Gulf of Mexico hypoxia program, demonstrate how EPA decisions can influence local government planning through grants, technical assistance, and land-use regulation.

AMERICAN HERITAGE RIVERS INITIATIVE AND
THE GULF OF MEXICO INITIATIVE

In 1997, President Clinton signed Executive Order 13061 proclaiming the creation of the American Heritage Rivers Initiative (AHRI). As stated in the EO, the primary purpose of the initiative is to leverage federal resources to assist state and local communities to improve redevelopment along rivers, establish trails and green space, and improve economic development. To guide this over-arching process, a river guide is hired by local communities to interact and coordinate with a host of federal agencies.

The AHRI works when local communities nominate a river for consideration in the program (communities can opt out of the process as well). A list of parameters are considered to evaluate whether the rivers qualify under the initiative, such as cultural heritage, natural resources, economic development, and community. In its first year, President Clinton named ten rivers to the AHRI program with the understanding that the administration would name ten rivers every year.

Overall management of AHRI programs is based in the Council of Environmental Quality (CEQ) within the White House Executive Office. The CEQ director serves as a co-chair of the committee with the other co-chair rotating annually among the various federal agencies. On the surface the AHRI seems like a good program, but it may be used in the future to overrule local decisions.

AHRI initiatives appear to be stand-alone programs until one connects the dots and discovers that each program fits together and serves as a backdoor method for federal land-use planning. All federal agencies are working together to coordinate diverse programs to achieve one simple goal—environmental protection through control of land-use activities organized around the watershed framework.

Take, for example, the Upper and Lower Mississippi rivers included in the AHRI. The Mississippi watershed covers nearly three dozen states and empties into the Gulf of Mexico. The Gulf is home to a variety of activities: fisheries, breeding grounds for young fish, human recreation, and offshore oil drilling. But the Gulf, at the mouth of the Mississippi River, contains a hypoxic zone (an area of low oxygen waters) (Halpern 2000). Low oxygen can create fish kills and impact habitat. Scientists believe the hypoxic zone is caused by a huge seasonal influx of nutrients (phosphorus and nitrogen) originating from farms within the Mississippi river basin. To protect the fisheries, the EPA wants to ensure that clean water flows into the Gulf. But to improve water quality, land-use activities must be controlled, according to the agency, allowing the EPA to subvert local control of planning and economic development.

The EPA created the Gulf of Mexico Initiative as a multi-state partnership to manage the hypoxic zone. A proposal from this group recommends that farmers in the river basin reduce nutrients by 20 percent. Congress even passed legislation (P.L. 105-383) to control hypoxic condition in the Gulf of Mexico on March 30, 2000.

On close inspection, it is clear that water quality can be the driving force for both initiatives. AHRI activities for the Mississippi River would have to consider hypoxic concerns when applying for grants or technical assistance for communities. Under the AHRI, the riverkeeper can guide grant money to local communities along the river. In fact, if one accesses the World Wide Web and goes to the AHRI website to look at the Upper and Lower Mississippi rivers, a link to the Index of Watershed Indicators (IWI) is listed. The IWI reports water quality via watersheds identified by the hydrologic unit code. This is consistent with the EPA's goal of unified watershed assessments to be conducted across watersheds, communities, and states. The GAO, however, reports that the IWI is misleading and that comparing water quality conditions across watersheds is inconsistent since methodology and local conditions vary (U.S. GAO 2000).

By recognizing the connection of these initiatives (AHRI and Gulf of Mexico), it becomes evident that federal resources can be leveraged through grants, communication strategies, and technical assistance for local communities in a way that places federal priorities at the top of the list. Although AHRI supporters claim that AHRI is a locally led effort, the goals of the program are set and plans made to coincide and coordinate with other federal laws and objectives. For instance, if sprawl is a concern to water quality, program administrators can direct resources with EPA and other federal agency guidance consistent with wastewater treatment outcomes.

Because communities must develop plans to improve wastewater treatment plants and file for grants to cover the cost of upgrades, plans are submitted to the governing agency for funding review. In such a scenario, the EPA could deny funding for additional wastewater treatment if it decided that too much residential development would overload existing wastewater treatment plants. Funding to upgrade could then be denied until the local government restrained sprawling development, even though the upgrade would have addressed the problems of development by expanding capacity. Moreover, other local governments could expect grant funds to be withheld until supposed "sprawl-related problems" are corrected. Once the stipulations are taken care of, a new grant proposal for wastewater upgrades could be approved. Thus the federal government could control local land use decisions and subsequent economic development through the granting process. Ironically, environmental protection could easily become secondary to the broader goals of controlling land use (as appears to be the case in Atlanta).

In the context of the AHRI, most grant requests could be approved or denied at the regional level. Regional approval would accomplish a key step many critics say is missing from the Clean Water Act—regional planning. Because the EPA regions are already established, Congress would not have to authorize a new federal land-use planning agency. This is consistent with the watershed approach because all EPA regions cover more than one state and include multiple major and minor river systems.

Under these circumstances, water quality becomes the standard from which all progress along the watershed is measured. If hypoxic areas get worse, then the EPA can target any one of the various programs it coordinates with other agencies and increase or decrease funding to be consistent with the agency's plans. In combination with new administrative rules being drafted by the EPA, certain land-use activities could be prohibited or heavily regulated if they cause violations to water quality standards and disturb wildlife habitat.

Again, the example of Atlanta's GRTA is a case in point. The regional transportation authority, in order to conform to EPA guidelines and standards, is implementing a mass transit plan despite little evidence suggesting it will substantially improve air quality. In fact, federal highway funds were withheld even though improving the traffic flow and circulation in the metropolitan area is crucial to reducing mobile sources of pollutants, effectively forcing the GRTA to use its authority to supercede local land-use plans to require high densities and mixed uses along the transportation corridor to enhance mass transit's potential for success.

EPA AUTHORITY OVER NONPOINT SOURCES

In 1999 a California farm family challenged the EPA's authority to control nonpoint sources of pollution under the Clean Water Act. Guido and Betty Pronsolino sued the EPA for overstepping its authority under the Clean Water Act to regulate nonpoint sources of pollution under the TMDL program. In 1960, the Pronsolinos purchased 800 acres of heavily logged timberland along the Garcia River in Mendocino County, California. The family began immediately to replant trees on the property. The Pronsolino's obtained a permit in 1998 from the California Department of Forestry to harvest 1.5 million board feet over 15 years.

Back in 1992, the EPA had overruled California state regulators and placed the Garcia River on its list of polluted waters. In March 1998, as part of this listing, the EPA restricted the amount of sediment runoff to the Garcia River coming from timber harvesting and certain regional activities, making it the first TMDL in the state for nonpoint sources.

The EPA's decision required the Pronsolinos to inventory and control sediment loading on their ranch, and restricted them from harvesting certain areas of the farm and from harvesting certain areas during six and a half months of the year. The Pronsolinos were prevented from using roads and skid trails in certain areas. These restrictions would result in significant economic losses for the family, according to the lawsuit. The EPA's requirements go beyond the California law on which the owners relied in making their timber harvesting plans. In essence, what the Pronsolinos took nearly forty years to create and plan has changed on a bureaucratic whim and throws landowner and agency cooperation to the wind. The Pronsolino suit asked the court to overrule the EPA's decision to regulate the Garcia River for nonpoint sources and also contended that the EPA lacks clear authority to control nonpoint sources of pollution through the TMDL process. Judge William Alsup's decision stopped short of halting the EPA's TMDL rules for agriculture, but reaffirmed that the EPA *does not* have authority to regulate agriculture and silviculture activities under the Clean Water

Act (*Pronsolino v. Marcus* 2000). Furthermore, Judge Alsup ruled that EPA guidelines are an advisory for states, not a mandate.

GUIDELINES FOR POLICY

Federal regulatory aggressiveness has accelerated on land-use issues as Smart Growth has become more popular and entrenched in federal decisionmaking. The EPA may be the most invasive of the federal agencies. In fact, its court record under the Clinton administration provides ample testimony to this aggressiveness. Although the courts have tended to give agencies discretion in determining how rules are made and enforced, 53 percent of challenges to the EPA's rulings have been overturned by the courts (Adler 2000). The EPA is undeterred and is "picking up the pace" in controlling nonpoint sources of pollution. Using watershed management as an organizing principle, the EPA has become a federal growth management agency.

The EPA's authority as it relates to agriculture, nonpoint sources of pollution, and land use needs to be clarified. The following are seven recommendations for improving EPA policy in this area, some of which may require changes to the Clean Water Act.

1. *Watershed management should be limited to regional and local levels.* This is desirable because (1) it fits better with local decisionmaking and established political boundaries; (2) the principal component of watershed management is land-use control, which is a uniquely local concern; (3) local watershed management allows citizens to keep government closer to the people for better accountability; and (4) regional planning agencies will result in resources being diverted to another level of government with less accountability and conflicting land use management. Regional coordination and planning implies that each county or local government must surrender sovereignty, lose additional tax dollars, and place local economies under yet more regional central planning.
2. *Congress should clarify the intent of the Clean Water Act to control nonpoint source pollution.* As this chapter has discussed, the EPA has been extending is regulatory authority via administrative procedures, without the expressed intent of Congress. Congress needs to clearly outline the boundaries of the EPA and other federal agencies in land use, watershed, and air quality management. In 2000, three members of Congress from the Arkansas delegation put forth three separate bipartisan measures to exempt agriculture and silviculture from the expansive EPA rules regarding TMDLs. Landowners and the forestry industry held several public meetings in late 1999 and early 2000. One meeting in El Dorado, Arkansas, was attended by several hundred people criticizing the EPA's lack of authority to regulate nonpoint sources. It was this meeting and nationwide complaints that spurred the Arkansas delegation to make the proposals.
3. *Congress should establish a congressional regulatory office to oversee the regulatory actions of federal agencies.* Passage of the Congressional Review Act illustrates members' concerns about broadly worded regulations with an impact on small businesses. The Unfunded Mandates Reform Act was passed to inform states about impending executive agency rules that could force states to shoulder exorbitant costs

with little regard given to a states' resources. States have been reluctant to impose TMDL for their waterbodies due to a lack of personnel and budgets.

Through guidance, executive orders and memoranda of agreements the EPA and other federal agencies are capitalizing on congressional inattention to rulemaking for the purpose of creating new laws. It is important, then, that a Congressional Office of Regulatory Analysis similar to the Congressional Budget Office be created and adequately funded to give Congress the resources to monitor and act on executive rulemaking (Antonelli 1998).

At a minimum, Congress should identify sweeping agency initiatives similar to the Clean Water Action Plan and determine the proper congressional oversight and committee of jurisdiction. This means that a single committee should have approval over CWAP budgets with input provided from other congressional committees. Because EPA oversight is spread over thirteen disparate congressional committees, it only makes sense that one group have oversight of these all encompassing initiatives.

4. *Congress should amend the Clean Water Act to specifically encourage trading between point and nonpoint sources as a means of meeting requirements of a TMDL.* Emissions trading is already being used successfully to control air pollution among point sources. The concept is relatively simple: the EPA establishes a regional pollution threshold for identifiable pollutants. Then, each potential source of pollution (e.g., farms, cities, industrial parks, etc.) is given an allowable level of pollution. The sources can then trade with each other, so those sources (e.g., farms) that have higher pollution requirements can trade with less polluting sources. All participants have incentives to reduce the level of pollution so they can sell their allotment on the open market. A similar system can be created for nonpoint source pollution. Some EPA regional offices interpret the trading rules to be implemented after both sources attain a TMDL. Critical to trading is quantifiable and surplus credits to trade. Nothing is surplus if both sources must meet the TMDL, because all pollution caps are already established. Trading offers great promise for NPS to meet water quality standards in an environmentally friendly way that is also cost-effective for the farmer. Such a policy would allow farmers to make cost-effective pollution reductions that can contribute to reductions in water pollution.

5. *Congress should amend the Clean Water Act and allow for water quality reports to be submitted every five years instead of every two years.* Two years is not enough time for many overworked and underfunded state environmental agencies to meet the biennial April deadline. (The EPA claims states are tardy in submitting their section 305(b) reports in a timely manner and repeatedly allows states to submit reports six months past the required date with no threat of punitive action.) Another reason 305(b) reports should be extended is that two years is not enough time to properly monitor water quality conditions in many watersheds. Nonpoint source pollution varies over time, stream flow, and weather conditions. Sometimes the effect seasonality has on pollution loads varies and it may take five years for certain trends to emerge. With 5 year increments states can make better use of their resources and submit reports with more useful data.

6. *Rather than compelling states to conduct TMDL analysis with limited funds, the EPA should provide increased direct funding for water quality monitoring.* Since the inception of the Clean Water Act in 1972, point sources have benefited from federal grants to expand, improve, and build new wastewater treatment systems in order to meet the goals of the act. Monitoring is now in place and point sources are aware of the penalties associated with permit violations. Out of fairness, if for no other reason, Congress should make funds available for NPS to implement best management

practices and for state water quality monitoring efforts. Environmentalists argue farmers should have been doing the right thing all along and do not deserve funding. But wastewater facilities received funds to ease their transition to a regulatory permit system. If the EPA's goal is to regulate NPS in the same manner, then making sufficient funds available is important.

7. *Congress must stress to the EPA its intent to make NPS reductions voluntary and state-based.* States have a good track record of enforceable and voluntary devices for controlling NPS. States should be the proper authority to make decisions that may impact local resources and economies.

CONCLUSION

Through ecosystem management and aggressive rulemaking and integrated planning, federal agencies have gained a foothold in local land-use planning. This is troubling not only because the federal agencies do not have the legal authority, but the scientific evidence often does not support the proposals recommended by the agencies.

Ecosystem management, though a novel concept, is not authorized through legislation. Congress must take a stronger roll in overseeing federal agency activities. The EPA's scientific analysis in many respects is questionable; it tries to use monitored data in combination with evaluated data, thus contaminating the entire data set, and it attempts to link all impaired waters within a watershed to agricultural contributions. The EPA's science process needs serious improvement and further verifiable data must be collected before satisfactory policy can be designed to solve the problems. Vigilance and proper congressional oversight is necessary at a minimum.

The details of the EPA's activities to regulate land use raise important questions, but there is a larger issue related to land-use planning. The EPA was created to protect the environment, and land-use planning has remained within the realm of state and local government control, on paper at least. There has been some discussion in the political arena about creating federal policies to try to implement some of the goals of the Smart Growth movement. This chapter shows that even as the debate about the role of the federal government in land-use planning is going on, the federal government already has a significant presence in land-use planning which has been undertaken through the EPA's environmental policy. One troubling aspect about the EPA's actions is that they appear to go well beyond what has been authorized by Congress.

Chapter 7

Regionalism and the Growth Management Movement

GERARD C. S. MILDNER

If the Smart Growth movement were a religious movement or a voluntary self-help movement, there would be little about it to complain. Devotees of Smart Growth could benignly persuade citizens to reduce their automobile usage or their housing consumption in order to lead a better life. Housing consumers could persuade developers to build homes with single-car garages (or none at all), with front porches, and with small backyards. Architects could sell plans for walkable communities and transit-oriented homes and compete in the land market with developers of more traditional designs. Such a movement would be remarkable and innovative, but of little cause for concern.

However, the Smart Growth movement has little to do with changing people's consumption tastes or introducing a new housing development technique. Instead, the advocates of Smart Growth have formed a political movement that intends not just to persuade people to lead better lives, but to force communities to make leading these new lifestyles mandatory. They argue that communities would be better off if more compact development was required and more dense building designs were utilized.

The evidence for such claims is stark indeed. As this and other chapters in this volume argue, there is little evidence that land-use changes have positive impacts on the efficiency of public services or the costs of transportation. This chapter will discuss the history of growth management and regionalism in the United States and focus on the trade-off involved in producing more compact urban development and competition in the real estate market. In particular, the risk from regional growth management comes in two areas—a loss of diversity in local government services and an increase in the cost of housing provision.

THE DEVELOPMENT OF COMPREHENSIVE LAND-USE PLANNING

One of the first models for growth management in the United States came from post-World War II innovations in Great Britain, where the Town and Country Planning Act of 1947 created county planning bodies to manage and plan development in rural England. The 1947 legislation called for "stop lines" around urban settlements and for a compensation fund of 300 million pounds to compensate rural landowners for the taking of their development rights by the state (Nelson 1983, p. 18). As a result, greenbelts and relatively high density towns and villages surround British cities. Not all the effects of the Town and Country Act are benign. Despite the endowment of a dense network of rail services dating from the eighteenth century, Britons have experienced increased travel commute times and energy consumption in recent decades. In addition, several studies have demonstrated that housing prices in Britain are significantly higher as a result of development constraints (Evans 1988, 1998).

The British example gave a framework by which Americans could compare their relatively loose zoning practices and untrammeled development procedures. The orderly appearance of the traditional British village contrasts sharply with the commercialism and vitality of the traditional American suburb. However, the desire and ability of growth control advocates to change land development patterns would converge only in the 1970s, primarily as an outgrowth of the environmental movement. Accompanied by visions of population explosion and environmental decay, activists across the country developed new legislation for the control of suburban expansion.

In the late 1960s and 1970s, environmentalists pushed for the development of a National Land Use Policy Act. Although this movement ended in failure, a number of states developed comprehensive land-use planning systems during the 1970s and 1980s as an outgrowth of this movement. We will briefly discuss six states that can be described as having comprehensive statewide planning systems: Hawaii, Vermont, Florida, California, Oregon, and New Jersey.

Two of earliest states to adopt comprehensive land-use planning are also two of the smallest states geographically: Hawaii and Vermont. Hawaii is an unusual case given the high concentration of land ownership in the Bishop Trust and a highly centralized government structure, a product of its small size, plantation agriculture heritage, and geographic isolation. Hawaii approved a comprehensive land-use law as early as 1961, which was later modified by the State Plan in 1978. Hawaii's land-use laws are focused primarily on the intensive development of urban areas and preservation of key agricultural and conservation areas (Cullingworth 1993). By comparison, Vermont is also a small state, but with a tradition of more decentralized local government. Vermont passed a growth management act in 1970, focusing on preserving the rural character of the state against strong development pressures. In a review of the Vermont system, Barry Cullingworth (1993) described it as a reactive system that empowered regional commissions within a framework of various statewide goals and policies.

Following several decades of fast growth, Florida and California, two of the largest and fastest growing states, initiated new land-use planning systems in the early 1970s. In Florida, the initial effort was primarily to preserve distinct areas of natural beauty in the Environmental Land and Water Management Act of 1972, which led to the protection of the Big Cypress Area, the Florida Keys, the Green Swamp, and the Apalachicola Bay Area. While the geographic scope of this initial effort was limited, Florida's 1985 Omnibus Growth Management Act was significantly more comprehensive (see Chapter 8). According to Cullingworth (1993), the 1985 legislation gave Florida a highly centralized form of growth management with local government plans needing to pass review by higher forms of government or face the loss of state funds. Another key feature of the Florida law is the requirement that local infrastructure must be ready before development can take place. However, as Gerald Koenig (1990) and others have noted, this requirement has not meant that infrastructure is developed where needed, but that development has been pushed to areas that happen to have existing infrastructure.

California's growth management system grew incrementally from a 1972 voter initiative to protect coastal areas. This initiative led to the California Coastal Zone Conservation Commission in 1973, the Coastal Act of 1976, and the California Coastal Conservancy in 1976, all of which focused on the preservation of scenic beauty and other qualities of the unique forest lands, wetlands, and agricultural lands on California's coast. Due to intense political opposition, the Commission was abolished and the planning system was converted into a statewide mandate that local governments establish local coastal plans. The Conservancy has aimed at preserving public access to beaches and coastline through property acquisition and focused on the restoration and preservation of wetland areas (Cullingworth 1993).

In the last thirty years, Oregon has developed the most comprehensive statewide land-use planning system in the United States. Following a series of voter initiatives for environmental protection, the state legislature passed the Land Conservation and Development Act of 1973. The act specifies a statewide system of goals administered by the Land Conservation and Development Commission that local governments must adhere to. Each urban area has a specified urban growth boundary, beyond which public services are not to be extended and urban development is restricted (Abbott, Howe, and Adler 1994;

Knaap and Nelson 1992). Because Oregon's example is the most comprehensive, we will discuss it later in greater detail.

Like Florida, New Jersey developed its statewide planning system by initially approving planning processes for special geographic areas—in this case, the Pinelands, the Hackensack Meadows, and the New Jersey coast. An unusual development in this process was the imposition by the state supreme court of a Statewide Development Plan in the *Mount Laurel* decision in the 1980s, which mandated affordable housing production in suburbs. Under the court's prodding, the state legislature adopted the 1985 State Planning Act and the 1989 Preliminary State Plan, whose goals emphasized redevelopment of cities, the containment of suburban sprawl, and the promotion of mass transit. However, the effectiveness of the state plan has been greatly limited by citizens' preference for local control and resistance to state authority. Five years after the first plan was adopted and twelve years after the state's planning act was signed into law, just 11.1 percent of the state's cities, towns, and villages were participating in the plan (Staley 1999, pp. 40-41). These cities covered just 16.5 percent of the state's population. Despite the ability to tap into state infrastructure funds, just thirty-six cities and towns (out of a total of 323) have applied for "center" designation (Staley 1999). State officials have recognized that resistance and created a process of "cross acceptance" that as much adjusts the state plan to local plans as forces local plans to accommodate the statewide plan (Cullingworth 1993).

The modest progress of these six states suggests that comprehensive statewide land-use planning has limited political appeal in the United States. In most states, land-use regulation and zoning remain a local concern over which state officials and legislators have little jurisdiction. Those states with the most comprehensive form of statewide planning tend to be relatively small in population, suggesting that national land-use planning will likely remain an unopened Pandora's box. As a result of the weakness of the national and statewide planning movements, most of the attention of growth management advocates has focused on implementing regional government at the metropolitan area level. At the metropolitan level political attitudes are likely to be more homogenous than at a statewide level, and federal policies for the last forty years have promoted regional planning for transportation and other purposes (Beimborn 1995).

REGIONAL PLANNING AND FISCAL EQUITY

Planners and advocates of growth management place a high value on the coordination and unity of decisionmaking in metropolitan areas. Because the goals of the Smart Growth movement are at odds with individual decisionmaking and local government decisionmaking, the sheer number of local governments becomes a source of concern. According to one author, the greatest constraint on land development and protection is "the overlapping jurisdiction of different governments, authorities, and regulatory agencies, making piecemeal and often redundant claims over policy making and development permissions at the fringe" (Daniels 1999, p. 137). From this perspective, the American government tradition of a large number of local units of governmental power acting independently becomes a source of weakness rather than strength.

The movement for metropolitan planning also finds allies among those wanting to ease the fiscal burden of central cities. In his book *Cities without Suburbs*, David Rusk, former mayor of Albuquerque, New Mexico, makes a comprehensive case for regional government on the grounds of assisting the poor. Rusk's argument for regional government focuses on the fiscal disparities between central cities and suburbs in the United States. He argues that as higher income whites flee central cities, their local economies and schools fall into an inexorable decline. To remedy these imbalances, Rusk identifies "elastic" central cities, which through luck and perseverance have been allowed to expand their borders so the city has little income and racial difference than the adjoining suburban communities. He argues that elastic cities have been much more successful economically and socially than their inelastic counterparts. Whether elasticity can explain the socioeconomic health of a city, however, is disputed empirically (Blair, Staley, and Zhang 1996; Nelson and Foster 1999). Rusk advocates policies that will create more economically integrated regional government, including the formation of regional government or allowing central cities greater latitude to annex their surrounding territory or merge with the local county government.

Tax Revenue Sharing and Metropolitan Governance in Minneapolis-St. Paul

One of the best known examples of regional government and revenue sharing is the Minneapolis-St. Paul metropolitan area. Regional planning takes on two forms: coordination of core infrastructure by establishing an urban service area managed by the metropolitan council, and regional tax revenue sharing. In 1971, the Minneapolis legislature enacted a regional compact that permits revenue sharing among counties in the Minneapolis-St. Paul metropolitan area. Under this plan, 40 percent of the increase in the commercial and industrial property valuation is put into a common fund for all the municipalities in the region (Rusk 1995). This program addresses the fiscal imbalances between rich and poor communities in the region, and, in theory, makes each community less likely to promote, subsidize, or entice commercial and industrial development from neighboring communities. In a separate policy, the state legislature established the Metropolitan Council in 1967 as a governor-appointed board of local citizens, responsible for solid waste, sewer, transportation, and land-use planning in the region. The total budget for the Met Council has reached one-half billion dollars per year (Daniels 1999).

In recent years, the state legislature has been embroiled in discussions of whether to expand the powers of the Met Council to promote greater regional equity. State Representative Myron Orfield proposed reforming the water and sewer policies of the Met Council so that charges paid by inner-city residents would no longer support the infrastructure expansion required by new suburban development (Rusk 1999). Although unsuccessful, Orfield's work has highlighted how the regional government in Minneapolis has been used to socialize the cost of new suburban growth at the expense of the poor. Rather than promoting Rusk's vision of income equity, the Met Council has exacerbated the disparities between central cities and suburbs.

Another effort of Orfield's coalition has been to promote a "fair share" housing plan for the region. Under the plan, municipalities in the region having less than their "fair share" of low cost housing would be required to remove local exclusionary zoning, to support affordable housing providers in their community, and to support the maintenance of local affordable housing. A related effort by Orfield has been to convert the Met Council from an appointed body to an elected body (Orfield 1998). The Republican governor at that time, Arne Carlson, vetoed both proposals, but these ideas remain actively supported by a coalition of inner metropolitan representatives (Rusk 1999).

In regard to the Smart Growth movement, the Twin Cities are only just beginning to experiment with regional planning policies. Smart Growth advocates have characterized Minneapolis-St. Paul as the third least densely settled metropolitan area in the United States, following Atlanta and Kansas City. In 1997, Minnesota established a voluntary system of local planning that calls for state review of local plans and the establishment of statewide goals (Daniels 1999). The Smart Growth bandwagon has been supported by Minnesota's Independent Governor Jesse Ventura, who has initiated a Smart Growth Initiative calling for agricultural land preservation, economic development, and reductions in pollution and waste (Metropolitan Council 2000). At this point, however, much of the governor's initiative appears very formative.

The experience with regional government in Minnesota shows that even when regional governments are limited in their activities, it is still difficult to get them to work productively. The Met Council is a limited form of regional government that handles relatively few government functions. Still, policies taken by the governor through the Met Council remain highly controversial, and efforts to introduce a form of redistributive policy through the Met Council are strongly resisted by suburban legislators and suburban town officials

Inefficiency of Regionalism

Regional coordination of governmental activity has been a desire of environmental activists and government reformers for many decades. From an economic perspective, the support for regional government or regional planning hinges on two key issues. First, is regional planning a public good that can only be provided by regional or central government? Second, does local government experience economies of scale such that large metropolitan governments can provide such services at lower per unit costs?

The evidence on both these issues is very limited. The best evidence of economies of scale in public services at a metropolitan level exists for water and sewerage services (Hines 1969). However, most government services reach their efficient level at population sizes much less than the metropolitan level. In a review of the literature, Arthur O'Sullivan (2000) finds that public services such as police, fire, and schools have economies of scale at no more than 100,000 in city population. Ronald Fisher (1996) notes that the efficient size of cities varies considerably among the services in question. Services like water and sewer can be provided efficiently by special districts or by a central city, which sells its services to smaller suburban governments. Committing a wide range of services to a central regional agency would likely drive up the costs of providing those services. Rising administrative and bureaucratic costs could result in higher overall spending.

In addition to the risk of higher operation costs and management difficulties, regional governments also reduce consumer choice about the type of communities and neighborhoods available and the level of services in those communities. The economic literature on community choice and decentralization dates to University of Washington economist Charles Tiebout (1956). Tiebout argued that citizens choose a community within a metropolitan area based in part on the local public goods and services offered and the taxes required to pay for those local public services. Under certain conditions, the competition among communities for residents will ensure that local public goods are provided efficiently and provided in different levels depending on the diverse tastes of local residents. In fact, substantial empirical research shows that competition among local governments reduces costs and improves the quality of services (Boyne 1992; Staley and Blair 1995).

Following Tiebout, subsequent work by Bruce Hamilton (1975) pointed out that local governments reliant on property taxes have a strong incentive to use zoning to regulate the size of homes and insure that local property tax contributions from each household pay for the local services that each household receives. Existing residents in communities with high house values will be wary of permitting new homes to be built of significantly lower value. By mandating larger homes through zoning, the existing residents can be assured of a minimum level of property tax payments by each household to support local services, thereby preventing the "free rider" problem.

Tiebout's theory illustrates the risk of forming regional government. First, competition among local governments insures that each metropolitan area has a diverse set of communities in terms of the local government services. Creating a regional government with a uniform service level will narrow the range of choice for residents whose preferences for local government services will differ from that of the majority. Some households will have to pay for services they don't want; others may not be able to get the full service levels they prefer. Second, many Smart Growth advocates want to use regional government to homogenize local zoning ordinances and encourage significantly smaller homes than would otherwise be permitted. Because the new housing units are of less value, existing homeowners will be required to pay for a much larger share of local spending. As a result, this policy will increase established residents' resistance to new housing construction because new residents will pay a disproportionately smaller share of local government services. The outcome will be either rising antagonism toward new residents in the community or declining support for local government services.

Finally, it is not entirely clear that the movement toward growth management has as benign an intention as helping the poor. In his recent book *New Vi-*

sions for Metropolitan America, which otherwise endorses the Smart Growth movement, Anthony Downs identifies an ulterior motive for many slow growth advocates—to prevent low-income households from moving to high-income suburban areas (Downs 1994, p. 33). This "fiscal zoning motive" for local government action may have serious consequences for housing affordability for the poor when implemented comprehensively at the regional level.

Regional Government and Housing Affordability

Under a unified growth management regime, regional government can constrain housing development and increase housing costs for poor households. While this effect is almost certainly unintentional, it is also unavoidable given conventional Smart Growth tools and tactics (see also the discussion in Chapter 11). One of the most clearly articulated goals of the Smart Growth movement is to increase the density of residential development. To achieve that result, restrictions on the conversion of rural land to urban usage are imposed. Once those restrictions are binding, a dual land market is created whereby rural land prices are depressed and urban land prices increase due to the scarcity of vacant land. Because land is necessary for housing production and capital cannot easily substitute for land, the increase in land costs inside the urban area increases the prices for new and existing homes (Knaap and Nelson 1992; O'Sullivan 2000).

For existing homeowners, this problem is relatively easy to ignore: although the opportunity cost of housing has increased, so has the value of the home they currently occupy. As a result, home ownership is a form of insurance against housing price appreciation enjoyed by approximately two-thirds of U.S. households. The wealth increase experienced by those households becomes a source of retirement income and borrowing power, which they likely attribute to their own astute investment. Of course, this illusory wealth effect disappears if the households want to move somewhere else within the region. For the one-third of households who rent, home price appreciation creates a significant cost burden that is hard to avoid. In the language of economics, housing is income inelastic, meaning that low-income households pay a significantly higher proportion of their expenditures for housing than do higher income households. Housing is a necessity, and the poor suffer greatest from its appreciation. Smart Growth's impact on housing affordability has played out most dramatically in the home of growth management: Portland, Oregon.

LAND-USE PLANNING IN PORTLAND, OREGON

In the 1970s, the Oregon State Legislature established a system of statewide land-use planning. The centerpiece of that legislation, the Land Conservation and Development Act of 1973, imposed a mandate on local jurisdictions to form city and county plans that would conform with statewide planning goals and mandates. Higher levels of government must review local plans for consistency and conformity. As compared to planning in California, Vermont, and elsewhere, land-use planning in Oregon is a top-down system in terms of goals, mandates, and responsibilities (Daniels 1999).

The act was passed during a period of rapid population growth and economic development within the state. Growth management proponents, headed by Governor Tom McCall, warned that Oregon would become like "another California," with the all the accompanying imagery of pollution and environmental damage (Cullingworth 1993). The primary concern of the legislation was the preservation of the rural character of the Willamette Valley, which contains 80 percent of the state's population as well as the state's most productive farmland.

In the special case of the Portland metropolitan area, the metropolitan planning organization (MPO) was assigned the task of overseeing planning at the city and county levels. In most metropolitan areas, the MPO is an advisory planning body whose membership is appointed by local officials. In Portland, the MPO was converted into a new layer of government, the Metropolitan Service District, later renamed Metro. Following the passage of a new charter in 1992, Metro became an elected government with a renewed mandate for comprehensive regional land-use planning. Metro oversees local plans within its territory, determines whether the urban growth boundary should be adjusted, and reports its findings and actions to the Oregon Department of Land Conservation and Development. In the last decade, however, rapid changes in population, housing prices, and land prices, particularly in the Portland area, have put the land-use system under considerable economic and political stress. Population growth has tripled since the early 1980s, land prices have doubled since 1990, and housing prices have risen by more than 60 percent.

Housing Price Appreciation in Portland

Since 1992, the community in the Portland metropolitan region has been engaged in a decision-making process regarding how to adapt the urban growth boundary to population growth and meet the legislative mandate that the growth boundary contain a "20-year land supply." This debate, known as the "Region 2040 Planning Process," has taken place within the context of a rapid population growth (see Table 7.1), with the 1990–95 growth rate more than 3 times the 1980-85 growth rate. Since 1990, housing prices in the Portland region have risen 10 percent annually, changing the metropolitan area from one of the lowest-cost places for housing on the West Coast to one of the most expensive. The National Association of Homebuilders recently identified the Portland metropolitan area as the sixth least affordable region in the country (Staley and Mildner 1999). The rise in housing prices has created a burden for young and low-income households, particularly those that are seeking new homes or renting.

Portland's house prices have appreciated faster than almost all other metropolitan areas in the United States. Table 7.2 lists the average existing housing appreciation rate and population growth rate for fifty metropolitan areas in the United States between 1990-1995, using data from the National Association of Realtors. Portland has been among the fastest growing metropolitan areas in the country during this period, along with other cities in the west and southeast.

Table 7.1
Portland Metro Population, 1970-95

Year	Population (in thousands)	5-Year Growth Rate
1970	1,009	
1975	1,098	1.70%
1980	1,240	2.46%
1985	1,284	0.70%
1990	1,412	1.92%
1995	1,597	2.49%

Source: Statistical Abstract of the United States, various years.

Unlike the other cities, Portland's rate of housing price appreciation was much higher.

Housing price appreciation in Portland has also been accompanied by rapid appreciation in inner-city neighborhoods, creating substantial burdens for low-income renters and minorities. As shown in Table 7.3, the Portland-area housing market in the early 1980s was quite depressed, due to the national recession and low timber prices. During the late 1980s, the economy picked up and housing prices began to rise primarily in the higher-income communities, such as Lake Oswego, West and Northwest Portland, Tigard, and Wilsonville. Inner-city Portland saw very little investment and housing price appreciation during this period. From 1990 to 1995, however, housing prices appreciated rapidly in inner-city neighborhoods. The three fastest appreciating communities have been the low-income areas of North, Southeast, and Northeast Portland. This pattern has been confirmed in a separate study looking at Census data for rents and housing prices. Halstead and Mildner (1998) found that housing prices had increased by 102 percent and rents by 35 percent from 1990 to 1998, with the greatest appreciation rates occurring in low-income Census tracts closest to downtown Portland.

For advocates of the growth management system, this turn of events is a symbol of success, believing that investments in transit projects and downtown revitalization have caused an increase in the amenities of close-in neighborhoods, thereby leading to new investment and a new vitality. But it is the tightness of the urban growth boundary that has forced investment inwards and led to inner-city revitalization. A less sanguine view of these developments would describe this reinvestment and revitalization process as gentrification. As land supplies became tighter on the fringe of the metropolitan area, housing demand is pushed inwards, and the increased land prices have led to higher density development in suburbs and city neighborhoods alike. And as these suburban neighborhoods achieve higher density and become less distinguishable from inner-city neighborhoods in physical form, higher-income households compete with lower-income households for inner-city locations.

Table 7.2
Population Growth and Housing Price Appreciation for 51 U.S. Metropolitan Areas, 1990-95

Rank		Population Growth		Housing Price Appreciation
1	Las Vegas	33.51%	Salt Lake City	63.83%
2	Phoenix	14.55%	**PORTLAND, OR**	**61.51%**
3	Riverside	13.92%	Denver	47.34%
4	Orlando	13.52%	Louisville	42.11%
5	**PORTLAND, OR**	**12.89%**	Milwaukee	35.90%
6	Denver	12.83%	Oklahoma City	32.33%
7	West Palm B.	12.51%	Nashville	31.17%
8	Ft. Lauderdale	12.44%	Cleveland	29.90%
9	Salt Lake City	11.88%	Birmingham	28.09%
10	Houston	11.70%	Detroit	28.03%
11	Nashville	11.05%	San Antonio	27.04%
12	Charlotte	10.95%	Chicago	26.63%
13	San Antonio	10.25%	Indianapolis	26.47%
14	Ft. Worth	9.63%	Cincinnati	25.81%
15	Sacramento	8.73%	Kansas City	23.75%
16	Seattle	8.09%	Las Vegas	22.04%
17	Jacksonville	7.94%	Columbus	21.45%
18	Minneapolis	7.25%	Minneapolis	20.41%
19	Richmond	7.09%	Miami	19.93%
20	Indianapolis	7.02%	Richmond	17.83%
21	Columbus	6.88%	Pittsburgh	17.12%
22	Washington	6.79%	Charlotte	15.79%
23	Anaheim	6.35%	Phoenix	15.24%
24	Memphis	6.15%	New Orleans	15.04%
25	Oklahoma City	5.86%	Jacksonville	14.78%
26	San Diego	5.85%	Ft. Lauderdale	14.36%
27	Tampa	5.44%	St. Louis	14.34%
28	Dallas	5.25%	West Palm B.	12.31%
29	Kansas City	5.09%	Houston	12.02%
30	Birmingham	4.98%	Seattle	11.97%
31	Honolulu	4.93%	Memphis	10.76%
32	Miami	4.87%	Tampa	9.66%
33	Cincinnati	4.31%	Philadelphia	9.20%
34	Chicago	4.23%	Ft. Worth	9.13%
35	Louisville	4.01%	Orlando	7.73%
36	Baltimore	3.69%	Dallas	7.71%
37	Los Angeles	3.11%	Rochester	6.52%
38	San Francisco	2.61%	Buffalo	5.31%
39	Rochester	2.50%	Baltimore	5.10%
40	New Orleans	2.36%	Washington	3.99%
41	St. Louis	2.24%	Boston	2.81%
42	Milwaukee	1.81%	Honolulu	-0.85%
43	Albany	1.42%	Albany	-0.94%
44	Detroit	1.25%	San Francisco	-1.89%
45	Boston	1.05%	New York	-2.97%
46	Cleveland	1.04%	San Diego	-6.33%
47	Philadelphia	0.59%	Riverside	-8.48%
48	New York	0.27%	Sacramento	-12.58%
49	Pittsburgh	-0.01%	Anaheim	-13.86%
50	Buffalo	-0.41%	Los Angeles	-15.18%
51	Hartford	-0.79%	Hartford	-15.19%

Source: Statistical Abstract of the United States, various years.

Table 7.3
Average Housing Prices by Portland Sub-Market, 1982-95

	Prices (in thousands)				Appreciation Rate		
	1982	1985	1990	1995	1982-85	1985-90	1990-95
N. Portland	42.9	35.4	41.3	83.8	-17.48%	16.67%	102.91%
NE Portland	56.8	51.6	64.2	114.5	-9.15%	24.42%	78.35%
SE Portland	53.2	48.5	59.2	109.7	-8.83%	22.06%	85.30%
Gresham/Troutdale	70.3	66.1	88.9	132.9	-5.97%	34.49%	49.49%
Milwaukie/Gladstone	68.9	65.6	94.0	144.8	-4.79%	43.29%	54.04%
Oregon City/Mollala	58.5	64.7	89.2	144.5	10.60%	37.87%	62.00%
Lake Oswego/West Linn	119.1	118.8	183.6	244.4	-0.25%	54.55%	33.12%
West Portland	97.1	94.9	143.4	210.2	-2.27%	51.11%	46.58%
NW Portland	99.1	99.6	144.2	195.9	0.50%	44.78%	35.85%
Beaverton/Aloha	75.3	73.0	105.5	141.7	-3.05%	44.52%	34.31%
Tigard/Wilsonville	86.2	77.7	125.6	174.9	-9.86%	61.65%	39.25%
Hillsboro/Forest Grove	69.5	64.9	87.0	134.5	-6.62%	34.05%	54.60%
Unweighted Averages	**74.7**	**71.7**	**102.2**	**152.7**	**-4.76%**	**39.12%**	**56.32%**

Source: Higgins 1999.

Shortage of Available Land

The boom in housing prices and rents in the region has many causes, local and national, economic and political, including the decline in interest rates and the strong national economic growth. However, the exceptional increase in the Portland market is also partly explained by the restrictiveness of the region's Urban Growth Boundary (UGB) (Knapp 1985). Originally established in 1979, the region's UGB was set far beyond existing development to provide twenty years' worth of land supply for future development (as required by law). Since the regional economy soon fell into an extended recession that saw both nominal housing price declines and population stagnation, the original UGB was never a significant constraint on the housing supply (Knaap and Nelson 1992).

In the current boom, the UGB has become a binding constraint. According to a recent Metro study, the amount of vacant land available for new development has been reduced from 75,000 acres to 55,000 acres between 1985 and 1995. As this inventory has dwindled, the quality of the vacant land available for development has become less attractive, whether in terms of slope, soil, view amenities, or transportation access. For example, of the remaining 55,000 acres, 16,000 were deemed to be too steep, too wet, or environmentally constrained to be usable; and 13,000 acres were identified as necessary for schools, streets, and parks. Approximately 12,000 "vacant" acres are currently active farms receiving farm tax deferral and owners would need to pay significant penalties in order for that property to be developed (Metro, 1996). Therefore, the reduction in vacant land from 75,000 to 55,000 acres is more significant than first appears because of environmental and regulatory constraints on their actual development.

This increased competition for land has translated into higher land prices, although the extent is difficult to determine. Good data on land prices is hard to come by. For comparative purposes, Metro officials have used data from the Urban Land Institute's Market Profiles. However, much of this information is drawn from very small or narrow samples. For example, the Los Angeles data comes from developments in a single place, the Antelope Valley, and the Las Vegas data is a per lot price estimate derived from builders' cost information.

As an alternative, I collected land price data from the Washington County (OR) Tax Assessor. Washington County is the most populous suburban county in the 4-county Portland region and the county with the greatest new home production. The Washington County Tax Assessor reviews sales prices and determines an average ratio of sales price to assessed value for each class of property. These assessment ratios are used to adjust assessments, which then can be used to compute the average percentage price increase in lot prices in Washington County. As the data in Table 7.4 indicate, land prices were fairly stable in the 1980s, with single digit annual rates of increase. However, since 1990, land prices have grown at a rapid pace, doubling in the last five years. Adjusting the tax assessor data for inflation, lot prices in Washington County have increased by 79 percent between 1990 and 1995.

Table 7.4
Residential Lot Prices, Washington County, 1986-95

Year	Annual Increase	Lot Price Index 1990=100	Inflation-Adjusted Price Index 1990=100
1986	2%	89	106
1987	3	92	105
1988	4	95	105
1989	-1	94	99
1990	6	100	100
1991	17	117	112
1992	8	126	117
1993	20	152	137
1994	20	182	160
1995	15	209	179

Source: Washington County Tax Assessor, *Ratio Study Report*, various years.

Density and Zoning

A large part of the growth boundary debate reflects the goal of increasing residential population densities as a means to reduce urban land use. Since achieving higher density is a formal goal of the planning system, planners need to know the degree that zoning changes or land price changes can induce housing developers (and ultimately buyers) to build at higher densities. In the early years of the land-use planning system, the increase in density was encouraged by establishing the urban growth boundary itself and liberalized zoning rules. Under the Metropolitan Housing Rule, local governments were required to increase permitted density levels in their zoning code and then permit more land to be allocated for apartments and mobile homes (Knaap and Nelson 1992; Toulan 1994). However, the results of this liberalization have been mixed. Actual housing densities for new development have been much lower—as much as two-thirds lower—than the level permitted by zoning codes (1,000 Friends of Oregon 1991; Howe 1993). Part of the reason for the reduced total density was increased allocation of space for open space, streets, and various easements, as well as the lack of demand for very small residential lots (Mildner, Dueker, and Rufolo 1996).

In response, Portland increased its recommended minimum densities for new development from an average of five homes per acre to eight homes per acre from 1994 to 1997. In turn, the amount of vacant land converted to residential use has declined as the share of new residential construction for multi-family housing increased from 25 to 49 percent of building permits between 1992 and 1997 (Metro 1998). However, despite these dramatic increases in density, the housing density produced remains below that projected under current plans, so that the current land supply will have a deficit of over 8,000 housing units (Metro 1998). This shortage of land for housing has led Metro to require local governments to impose minimum density levels for new development. The combination of maximum and minimum zoning constraints on new development may yet create a scissors-like action to choke off new housing development.

The Political Economy of Zero Growth

In Portland, Metro and local governments in the region have planned for adjustments in the UGB to account for the region's future growth in the so-called Region 2040 Planning Process. However, this process has avoided viewing the UGB decision in terms of its impact on housing markets and housing prices. Instead, the focus has been on the narrow legal requirement of establishing a twenty-year land supply and preserving farmland and forestland. Public surveys taken early in the process showed strong support for zero expansion. Due to these political pressures, Metro planners have sought new and innovative ways to accommodate housing development within the available land supply, thereby minimizing the need for expansion. These methods include assuming a rising proportion of homes be built as redevelopment properties and as infill housing and requiring local governments to increase zoning on vacant land by an average of 60 percent (Mildner, Dueker, and Rufolo, 1996). Local city planners, who view planning at Metro as the ultimate career objective, have readily acceded to these ideas and have "volunteered" their cities for increased housing capacity. This shift in regulation has led to a number of conflicts. An attempt to rezone single-family neighborhoods in Southwest Portland and suburban Milwaukee for row houses and apartments brought a fierce negative reaction by local residents. Thus, the attempt by regional planners to force densification plans on local homeowners may not be politically feasible.

Early on in the 2040 Process, the environmental group 1,000 Friends of Oregon, along with other advocates of zero expansion, formed a pressure group, the Coalition for a Livable Future, to merge the efforts of environmental advocates and low-income housing advocates. To attract the housing advocates, the coalition added to their recommended policies the idea of enhancing local trust funds for low-income housing with real estate transfer taxes and land sales taxes and imposing an inclusionary zoning mandate on new housing development in the UGB expansion areas (Orfield, 1998). Both of these planks had appeal to the environmental community in that they further diminished the possibility that the metropolitan area would be expanded at all. Developers on the urban fringe would be required to build at a inner-city density, pay for local service expansion, and either build low-income housing or pay funds into a low-income housing trust fund.

The economic effect of these policies would be to raise the threshold price at which any new housing gets built. First, high-density housing is more expensive to build. Impact fees and low-income housing subsidies will reduce the value of development to landowners and indirectly lead to higher rents and prices for housing consumers. And by raising the supply price of new housing, these policies would unambiguously raise the market price of housing, creating significant burdens for low-income households.

Why did the housing advocates accept this package of policies? First, many housing "advocates" are actually landlords and developers, and the housing trust fund promises the creation of an income stream to support their development plans. As federal funds for low-income housing have been reduced in recent years, local nonprofit housing developers will either need to find a state or local source of funds or face the contraction of their operations.

Second, the political ideology of low-income housing advocacy is distinctly anti-capitalist, and hence unfavorable to the idea of a coalition with private housing developers. For years, housing advocates have painted a picture of helpless low-income households vulnerable to escalating rents on the private market. A policy of higher rents and prices perpetuates the housing crisis and increases the solvency of non-profit housing operations.

Third, the connection between development constraints and rising housing prices is an indirect effect and easy to ignore. Easing development constraints would largely cause new housing for the middle- and upper-income households to be built. Those households would move out of less desirable housing that would, after several iterations, filter down to lower-income households (O'Flaherty 1996; O'Sullivan, 2000; Pozdena, 1998). This phenomenon, known as the "filter hypothesis," is either dismissed or ignored by housing advocates, who usually focus on the unaffordability of new housing to low-income households. However, just as an affordable automobile is usually a used car, an affordable home is typically a house built years ago that has depreciated. New development for upper-income households hastens the day that the older housing is vacated and made available for lower-income households.

Fourth, the interests of low-income households and nonprofit housing providers are not overlapping. Federal studies have consistently pointed out that housing vouchers and portable certificates are a better way of serving the poor, while nonprofit providers are better served by receiving project-based assistance (O'Sullivan, 2000; Pozdena, 1998). While housing subsidies are required for all the providers of new affordable housing developments, over 80 percent of low-income renters find housing in the private market (Salins 1987). Thus, the advocates represent the select 20 percent of low-income renters in assisted housing, not the 80 percent suffering from rising rents.

Finally, many low-income housing advocates are also political environmentalists, and the easiest way to resolve a policy that involves a trade-off between those two causes is to deny that any trade-off exists at all. In hindsight, the Coalition for a Liveable Future was a vehicle to prevent advocates of low-income housing from forming a coalition with developers and favoring an expansion of the boundary.

The Political Stability of the UGB

The outcome of the Region 2040 Process was a vote in October 1997 by the Metro Council to expand the urban growth boundary by 4,500 acres. This vote was seen as a compromise between pro-environmental, zero-expansion advocates and pro-development advocates who had been favoring an expansion of at least 10,000 acres, and a sign of how the planning system can adapt to growth, rather than stop growth. However, two-and-a-half years later and eight years after the planning process began, this decision is still being adjudicated by the courts and no new land has been converted to urban use. The slowness of this process suggests that land-use politics will remain a contentious issue for many years to come in Oregon. A recent Metro report suggests that raw land just inside the UGB sells for six times the value of land just outside the UGB, where urban housing and commercial development is permitted (Metro 1997). With such large gains to be achieved with the expansion of the UGB, large political contributions can be raised to challenge the existing planning system.

This analysis suggests that growth management in Oregon's Willamette Valley is likely to be politically unstable, unlike, for example, the experience of Britain with greenbelt planning. In the fifty-year history of its greenbelt policy, the UK government compensated landowners for the loss of the development rights. Thus, a farmer in Essex would see little benefit from being designated part of the London area without also receiving the development rights, which are zealously guarded by local planning commissions (Evans 1999). In Oregon, however, land-use planning was sold as a way to enhance the profitability of farming by guaranteeing permanence and protecting farmers from urban encroachment. However, to keep this regulation less costly and to ensure support from the agricultural community, farmers retained the right to develop their properties should their land be included in the UGB at a later point. In the future, the agricultural community is likely to divide between the landed farmers who want to see their land reach its highest value and the farming implements and supplier lobby who want to preserve their customer base.

Bursting the Bubble

How and when will the rapid escalation in regional housing prices come to a halt? This analysis suggests several alternative scenarios, some economic and some political. The political scenarios would begin with a more vocal articulation of the interests of low-income households in the Portland region who are suffering disproportionately from the rise in housing prices. This scenario would require new leadership to mobilize the low-income community. Another variant of this scenario involves some enlightenment of the nonprofit housing advocates. The current environmental-housing advocate coalition has produced no movement of the UGB, in exchange for a promise of housing assistance later, either in the form of a real estate transfer tax or development linkage fees. Because the opposition to either of these two housing proposals is strong, the position of the low-income housing advocates may change once they realize that the bargain was one-sided. The other political scenarios involve changes in the state political climate or changes in public attitudes. These kinds of changes are inherently more difficult to predict, but some of the fault lines are clear. Landowners, property rights groups, and communities outside the Willamette Valley have been agitated by the Oregon planning system for some time (Knaap 1994). Those groups may find additional support from first-time homebuyers, renters, and developers in the Portland region, as the regulations become ever tighter.

The economic scenarios revolve around when metropolitan growth will come to a halt. Already, some analysts have noted the rapid growth in suburban and exurban communities not constrained by the Portland UGB (Mildner, Dueker, and Rufolo 1996). That is, as housing prices rise inside the Portland UGB, an increasing number of home buyers have turned to Clark County, Washington and the Salem metropolitan area, or exurban communities like McMinnville, Newberg, and Mollala. In this scenario, ironically, growth management is an inducement to creating greater regional sprawl. This kind of diffusion of excess housing demand in the wider regional market in reaction to tight zoning restrictions has long been noted in analysis of growth management in individual towns (Evans 1998; Fischel 1997). That is, if Pasadena has exclusionary zoning, housing prices don't rise disproportionately in Pasadena since consumers can choose a close substitute in Los Angeles, Glendale, or another nearby community. Growth management in Boulder, Colorado, has led potential residents to commute from Denver or nearby towns (Staley, Edgens and Mildner 1999). The difference in Oregon is, that unlike Pasadena and Boulder, the Portland UGB dominates the wider housing market. Given the limited capacity of the outlying communities to handle the extra growth, sharply rising house prices in Portland mean sharply rising house prices in Vancouver, Salem, McMinnville, and elsewhere.

The other economic scenario involves an end to the regional economic boom. Oregon's land-use planning system is still a novel system that has yet to experience a full business cycle. For over a decade, Portland planners have echoed the mantra that growth management, dense settlement, and rural preservation will enhance the quality of life in the region and perpetuate the economic investment and employment growth. However, recent decisions by Nike and high tech firms in the region to consider expansion in places like Austin, Salt Lake City, and Phoenix where housing and development costs were important factors suggest the investment in the region may be slowing down.

CONCLUSION

The proponents for Smart Growth rely heavily on the experience of communities like Minneapolis, Minnesota, and Portland, Oregon, in advocating their vision of equity, efficiency, and sustainability. These advocates recognize that without strong regional powers, such as the Met Council in Minneapolis or Metro in Portland, the regulatory efforts to promote dense development, fixed rail mass transit, and other features of Smart Growth will be impossible. This chapter has examined the history of comprehensive land-use planning and regionalism and evaluated impacts on community choice and housing costs. These two cases illustrate that developing a regional consensus about housing and tax-base sharing is an extraordinarily difficult task. Redistributional policies are most efficiently handled at larger levels of government, due to the possibility of migration.

Since Tiebout (1956), economists and other social scientists have come to see migration as an important process maintaining the efficiency of local government and the diversity of local government services. Thus, if effective implementation of Smart Growth policies requires a strong regional government, considerable costs in the efficiency and representativeness of local government will occur. Indeed, a degree of personal liberty is at stake. That threat is most clearly seen in the drive to maintain higher densities in the Portland metropolitan area by Portland's Metro government. Under the guise of limiting urban sprawl, protecting agriculture, and reducing public infrastructure costs, a process of land appreciation and housing appreciation is well underway. Portland has been converted from a traditionally low-cost housing city to one of the least affordable communities in the country. The response to this crisis by local and state officials has been to follow the process of growth boundary expansion, which in eight years has little to show for itself. Proposals have emerged to create new mechanisms for affordable housing, which are only likely to create further reductions in housing supply and increases in housing prices. Given these difficulties, the political consensus behind the Region 2040 Plan cannot be guaranteed.

For the rest of the United States, applying the Portland model or the Minneapolis model to other communities seems even more far-fetched. Both Oregon and Minnesota are relatively small, homogenous states with histories of regional politics and healthy local economies. Indeed, Portland and Minneapolis have very little racial, ethnic, and economic diversity when compared to other metropolitan areas in the United States. The next challenge for the Smart Growth movement will be applying regional government in a community with greater political and social divisions.

Chapter 8

Growth Management in Action: The Case of Florida

RANDALL G. HOLCOMBE

Florida's current growth management laws are based on Florida's Growth Management Act of 1985. Florida had passed growth management legislation before, but there was a consensus among those in the state—both citizens and elected officials—that prior laws were ineffective, and that the state was suffering from undesirable development as a result of rapid population growth. Florida's population had grown by 44 percent in the 1980s, and by another 16 percent from 1980 to 1985, creating a construction boom, but infrastructure development did not keep up with the private development of residential subdivisions and commercial establishments. Michael Gannon, a prominent Florida historian, noted, "Business and housing development . . . had been almost without plan or design, with the result that in many places Florida's once pristine landscapes were marred by uncontrolled urban sprawl with its ugly strip malls, garish signs, crackerbox architecture, overstretched utilities, and congested streets" (1993, p. 144). Gannon's observations reflected the opinions of Florida's citizens, and in response, the Florida legislature passed the Growth Management Act of 1985 with broad support from Florida's citizens.

Florida's Growth Management Act has lofty goals, but the goals are vague. The Act was supposed to provide, for example, affordable housing and environmental protection. It was supposed to control urban sprawl, and was supposed to ensure that the infrastructure to support development would be produced concurrent with the development, thus easing traffic congestion, which was the primary infrastructure concern. Almost everybody would agree with these objectives, but by themselves the goals are so vague that it is unclear how they can be achieved, and the Act gives no guidance. What constitutes affordable housing? What is urban sprawl? Lacking specific definitions, the Act provides little direction for action. Even in the case of transportation infrastructure, where definitions of traffic congestion were made specific, the Act does not explain what actions are to take place to relieve it. Although the Act is vague about the actions necessary to achieve the goals of growth management, it is specific about the bureaucratic structure under which growth management is to take place. All local governments are required to draw up comprehensive plans for development, following the guidelines of the Act. The local plans are then be submitted to Florida's Department of Community Affairs, which reviews them to see that they are in compliance with the Act. In essence, Florida's Growth Management Act has developed a procedure for growth management, and specified its goals in this area, but it doesn't specify how the procedure would accomplish the goals.

Florida is ahead of most of the nation in its growth management activities, having been spurred into action by the rapid population growth of the 1970s and 1980s, but similar sentiments are widely shared throughout the United States. Thus, Florida provides an interesting case study that allows one to look at the effects of the Growth Management Act, to consider how well it has been able to achieve its goals, and to reflect on some of the problems Florida has had it. This line of inquiry may help not only to identify improvements that could be made in Florida, but to offer insights on how growth management can be carried out effectively in the rest of the nation.[1]

FLORIDA'S 1985 GROWTH MANAGEMENT ACT

While there were many lofty motivations for passing the 1985 Growth Management Act, the two main reasons for its widespread political support probably were, first, the increased traffic congestion that came along with rapid population growth, and second, the increased commercial development in low-density residential areas that replaced the local character of cities and towns with strip malls and convenience stores, paving over what many Floridians thought were Florida's finest assets. Goals like affordable housing and environmental protection were popular and widely supported, but they do not directly affect one's quality of life as much as increased traffic congestion and the revamping of the suburban landscape. Floridians were motivated to support the concept of growth management because their neighborhoods were being blighted by strip malls and because their commuting times lengthened as traffic congestion worsened due to population growth. Few Floridians spend much time in the Everglades; they were motivated more by the environment they saw on their daily commutes than anything else. The Growth Management Act was crafted with this motivation in mind.

Another factor shaping the design of the Act—and indeed, legislation in general—is that it is much easier to reach agreement on things that people want to improve than it is to reach agreement on how to implement improvement. Thus, as already noted, the Growth Management Act put forth lofty goals, but did not propose how those goals could be accomplished. That, presumably, would be the work of the bureaucracy that was charged with administering growth management.

Following the passage of the Act, the actual management of growth takes place through local comprehensive plans that are required of all local governments in the state. As originally envisioned, the planning was done primarily at the local level, with local governments having the responsibility of drawing up their own growth management plans. At the state level, the Department of Community Affairs (DCA) was charged with the responsibility of evaluating the local comprehensive plans to see that they were in compliance with the state law. Compliance is partly a technical matter; plans must have certain specified components in order to meet the Act's goals. The DCA has gone beyond that, however, and has taken it upon itself to evaluate whether the local plan actually will further the goals of the Act. As a result, many local comprehensive plans have been rejected by the DCA for being out of compliance because the DCA determined that the local plan, as written, would be ineffective. Local governments that are not in compliance with the Act can lose state funds, so there is a financial incentive to produce a comprehensive plan that meets with DCA approval.

To comply with state law, the local comprehensive plan must have many elements, but the most significant element is the land-use map that specifies how all land within the local government's jurisdiction may be used. When the Act was originally passed, the consensus of opinion was that its most restrictive feature was that land could not be approved for development without a plan for the infrastructure to service the development to be in place concurrent with the completion of the development. In fact, as will be discussed, this concurrency requirement did not turn out to be as restrictive as was initially envisioned, while other provisions turned out to be more restrictive.

Another reason for DCA oversight of the comprehensive planning process is to see that local plans are consistent with each other.[2] This coordinating aspect has had relatively little impact on the growth management process. The biggest effect that the DCA has had on the local planning process has been to impose their own views of what constitutes desirable development patterns on the local governments that have submitted plans. Needless to say, this has led to controversy, and will be discussed further below.

Although the Growth Management Act was passed in 1985, local governments were given half a decade or more to begin the planning process and submit their local comprehensive plans to the state for approval. A staggered schedule was set up for plans to be submitted, and as the state began to evaluate them in 1990 and 1991, local governments were stunned to find that many of their plans were rejected by the DCA for being out of compliance. The most common reason for noncompliance was that the plans allowed for too much urban sprawl. With the DCA's guidance, the plans were redrawn, and while there was considerable tension between local governments and DCA in the early 1990s, that tension has eased as the governments involved in the process have adjusted to each others' expectations.

Plans should be rigid enough to provide a structure for future development, but flexible enough to adjust with changing circumstances. Rigidity is provided by state law and DCA oversight, while flexibility is provided by the ability to amend the plans, and by some slight but significant changes that the legislature has made to the growth management process. Toward that end, local comprehensive plans can be amended as often as twice a year, but the amended plans then must go through the same DCA approval process. With regard to land-use planning, the two most significant aspects of the comprehensive planning process are the concurrency requirement for infrastructure and the DCA's policies on urban sprawl. As it has turned out, the infrastructure concurrency requirements have not been as binding as were originally feared, whereas the urban sprawl policies have had a much bigger impact than was anticipated when the law was passed.

CONCURRENCY

The concurrency rule requires "that public facilities and services needed to support development shall be available concurrent with the impacts of such development."[3] As part of a forward-looking comprehensive plan, what the concurrency requirement implies is that the public services and infrastructure that will serve a development must be planned so that when the development is completed, the support services also will be ready. For example, roads to service a development do not need to be in place before the development can begin, but they must be completed by the time the development generates traffic. The concurrency requirement applies to infrastructure and services generally, including wastewater treatment, police and fire protection, schools, and parks. In practice, however, the binding effect of concurrency is on roads. If the roads to service a development cannot be completed concurrent with the completion of the development, then the concurrency requirement means that the development cannot proceed.

The concurrency of roads to service new developments was a key element in the Growth Management Act. As noted earlier, the growth in traffic congestion was one of the significant motivating factors behind the Act, and the concurrency requirement addressed that issue by making additional development illegal unless the infrastructure was in place. Notably absent from the Act, however, was any mention about how this new infrastructure was to be financed. Current residents liked the requirement because seemingly it would prevent new development from further clogging the already congested roads. Developers favored the requirement too, because they wanted roads available to service their developments and believed that with the support of the law, local governments would be pressured into raising the money to build them. The construction industry is a major employer in Florida and an important component in many of the state's local economies. Thus, when faced with the choice of halting development or devoting resources toward the construction of roads, those in the construction industry believed that concurrency would force the roads to be built.

The mechanism by which roads are deemed adequate for new development is relevant for understanding how the process works. All roads within a local government's jurisdiction are given target "levels of service" in the local comprehensive plan, based on the amount of congestion that the plan allows for the road. New development can take place only if it will not lower the levels of service of roads below their target levels or place additional traffic burdens on roads already below their target levels of service. This requirement, combined with the goal of infilling already developed areas (discussed further later on), was designed to ensure that new development not only did not further degrade traffic flow, but in many cases could even improve it. The concurrency requirement mandated that roads would have to be built or widened to accommodate any additional traffic, and in areas where the traffic already was below target levels of service, roads would have to be improved not only enough to accommodate new traffic but also to improve the flow of existing traffic to acceptable levels before development would be allowed. The concurrency requirement would create a demand from developers as well as drivers for traffic improvements.

Everyone agreed on the traffic goals set out in the Act, but the specifics of how the additional infrastructure would be financed were not spelled out. This was not an oversight, but an intentional strategy. It would have been difficult to agree on a taxing mechanism, or on a system whereby some individual or group would have the authority to mandate revenues to finance the infrastructure. The idea was that if the Act became law, it would place local governments in the position of having to make the hard choices to comply with the law, and money would be appropriated to build the roads. Taub (1988) argued that unless local governments rose to the financial challenge of concurrency, the 1985 act would produce a moratorium on development, and 1,000 Friends of Florida (1988), which strongly supports growth management and environmental preservation, saw concurrency as the key element in Florida's Growth Management Act. Holcombe (1990a) argued that the burden of concurrency would fall on those Floridians who could least afford it, and Wilson (1989), in the widely read *Florida Trend* magazine, argued that strict adherence to concurrency would create such problems that taxpayers, developers, and Floridians in general would oppose the concept once they found out its true implications. In the half decade between the passage of the Act and the submission of the first local comprehensive plans for DCA approval, the consensus of opinion was that concurrency would be the most significant component of Florida's growth management process.

As events actually unfolded in the 1990s, however, concurrency was not as significant to the growth management process as most analysts thought, for two reasons. First, another issue—urban sprawl—came to dominate the growth management process, and second, there were several avenues of relief from the constraints of concurrency. The first avenue of relief was that people who already had development permits were grandfathered in. This created an incentive to get permits prior to the submission of the local plans, and a huge amount of land was vested and placed beyond the reach of the growth management planning process. The second avenue of relief was the possibility of development in less developed areas where traffic was not congested. Downtown development might be prohibitively expensive because of the obligation to relieve existing traffic congestion, but development away from the urban core would place traffic on less-traveled rural roads, perhaps necessitating no road improvements at all to meet the concurrency requirement. Of course, this type of development was contrary to the philosophy behind growth management, but often it was a less costly response to the law, and often the vesting of development rights put this kind of leapfrog development beyond the reach of the planners.

An unintended consequence of the concurrency requirement, then, was to create incentives for the very kind of development that the planners were trying to prevent. As a result, the incentives have been modified in two ways. First, the concurrency requirement has been made more flexible, especially in already urbanized areas like Dade County. The DCA would accept local comprehensive plans that allowed for additional development that would add traffic to roads below their target levels of service if it would help achieve other goals, such as urban infill. In addition, the legislature amended the Act to allow for local comprehensive plans to designate concurrency areas within their land-use plan. Within these areas, if developers wanted to develop but roads were already at or below their levels of service, the requirement could be satisfied by contributing money to improve the transportation infrastructure, even if the level of service would be below the plan's target level. Thus, in already developed areas where traffic was already congested, development could still take place. This was meant to help produce more compact development and to contain urban sprawl.

The bottom line is that the concurrency requirement, initially considered to be the most significant aspect of Florida's Growth Management Act, turned out to be less binding and less significant than originally anticipated for a number of reasons. Developers and local governments have learned how to work together to avoid the most pessimistic predictions surrounding the requirement. This also has meant that the concurrency requirement has been less effective at relieving traffic congestion than was originally anticipated. In many ways the requirement, once thought to be the cornerstone of growth management, has been ineffective. It has imposed costs on developers and on the local governments that administer it, and perhaps because it has made growth more costly, it may have slowed development down. It also may have shifted development away from areas that the Act's designers would have liked to have seen developed toward areas that they would have preferred to remain undeveloped.

The concurrency requirement was the result of political compromise to try to accomplish a widely-held goal without specifying the means. Any legislation, including growth management legislation, must be the product of compromise in order to get political support to get it passed. Even though the intended results were widely supported, the actual effects of this requirement fell short, and in some cases were the opposite of what was intended. This suggests the limits of growth management legislation in general, because of limitations in the political framework within which it must be designed and implemented.

URBAN SPRAWL

In contrast to the concurrency requirement, the urban sprawl provisions in Florida's Growth Management Act were barely noticed it was passed. Once again, the Act was not very specific, but merely stated that one of the goals was to "prevent the proliferation of urban sprawl." Nowhere in the Act was urban sprawl defined. Thus, while the focus of concern was on how local governments would meet the concurrency requirement, the urban sprawl provision of the Act was overlooked. The issue became important, however, when the first plans were submitted to the DCA and many of them were rejected because they did not do enough to prevent urban sprawl. The DCA, in turn, provided specific guidance to those local governments that did not, in the DCA's view, do enough to curb sprawl, and in response, some local governments amended their plans based on the DCA suggestions so that the DCA would find them in compliance, while others objected to the DCA's rejection of their plans. From a legal standpoint, the question was what was meant by urban sprawl and whether the DCA really had the authority to reject local comprehensive plans on such a vague basis. While these aspects were the focus of the urban sprawl controversy, from a broader perspective, there is the issue of whether the DCA, though its sprawl policy, was turning the local comprehensive planning process into one in which the local plans really became the DCA's plans for each locality.

The critics of the DCA argued that the department was creating arbitrary criteria for identifying urban sprawl, which amounted to the DCA's using urban sprawl as a reason for rejecting any plan that it did not like. Because there was no definition of urban sprawl in the Act, the local governments found themselves in the uncomfortable position of not being able to tell ahead of time whether the DCA would find their plan in compliance or not. Drawing up local comprehensive plans is costly for the local governments, both in dollar terms and politically. The political costs arise because agreement about future development must be agreed on by various parties who have conflicting interests, and if a plan is rejected, those political battles must be fought again. Some local governments wanted to fight what they viewed as the DCA's heavy-handed imposition of its views on local government—Why should a group of state bureaucrats in Tallahassee be able to tell local residents all over the state how their communities should develop? Other local governments just wanted to know what the DCA's criteria for accepted plans were, so that they could design their plans to be accepted the first time.

In response to this controversy, the DCA issued a technical memo in 1989 that laid out its criteria for identifying urban sprawl. That memo listed three indicators of urban sprawl: leapfrog development; strip or ribbon development; and low-density, single-dimensional development. The memo described each type of development and explained why the DCA viewed those development patterns as undesirable. In addition to the indicators listed in the memo, the department had another indicator that was not written down, but became well-known among those who were responsible for drawing up local comprehensive plans. The DCA would look at population projections for growth within the local government's boundaries, and would not approve local plans that allowed for more development than was necessary to accommodate 120 percent of the projected population.

The DCA's clarified policy on urban sprawl met with two different reactions. Some people were grateful for the clarification because it would make the planning process easier, while others argued that the DCA's policy went well beyond the intent of the Growth Management Act, and that the DCA was over-stepping its bounds to, in effect, create new law. In part the issue was whether the DCA had the authority to create their sprawl policy and to reject local comprehensive plans based on criteria they developed rather than those that had been created by the legislature, but surely there would have been little objection if the DCA's critics had liked the department's policy. The policy could be criticized on two grounds. One was that the policy, as stated, would produce undesirable results, and the other was that Florida's Growth Management Act originally intended that local comprehensive plans were to be the product of local governments, not state government. The DCA's detailed analysis of local development patterns via their sprawl policy essentially transformed the local planning process into a state planning process. In effect, the local governments still did the work, but because of the DCA's proclivity to reject plans it did not like, plans were drawn up to the DCA's specifications, not the specifications of the local governments or even of the original Act.

The planning issue aims at the heart of land-use planning in general. Before getting into the larger issue of planning, however, it is worth analyzing in more detail the DCA's sprawl criteria to see how planning, in fact, takes place.

The 120 Percent Rule

While the 120 percent rule is not part of Florida's written guidelines on urban sprawl, it remained an important part of the DCA's policy throughout the 1990s, and has some similarity to the policy of designating urban service areas (USAs) beyond which growth is sharply limited. Florida allows but does not require USA boundaries, but the land-use map coupled with the 120 percent rule and the other sprawl policies create similar results. A key element in every local comprehensive plan is the land-use map, which indicates the allowable uses of all land within the government's jurisdiction. The reasoning behind the 120 percent rule is that even with other sprawl policies in place, if too much currently undeveloped land is allowed to be developed, it can still create developed areas that are scattered among undeveloped areas, raising infrastructure costs and weakening restrictions on development. At the end of the 1990s the DCA was questioning whether this type of restriction was good policy, but it has remained a part of their policy nonetheless.

From an economic perspective, several objections can be raised to this type of growth restriction. The first is that it substitutes the judgment of government planners for market forces in determining how development should proceed. Government planning has not worked well in other areas of the economy, and it is not clear why government planners should have more success in this area. A second objection is that by restricting the amount of land available for development, the supply of available land is reduced, and a reduction in the supply will raise the price of that land. Thus, development will be more expensive solely because of an artificial scarcity created by the planning process.

Some of the highest housing prices in the United States are found in San Francisco, and for good reason. The city is almost entirely developed and it is surrounded on three sides by water. With the supply of land limited by nature in this way, the demand for housing has pushed the market price of housing up. Except on parts of the east coast, Florida does not have these same natural barriers to development, yet a similar type of artificial barrier is created when growth management policies restrict the amount of developable land. Another of the goals of Florida's Growth Management Act is to provide affordable housing, but the entire growth management process, as it actually works, is geared toward making housing more expensive.

By imposing the 120 percent rule along with preventing leapfrog development and strip or ribbon development, the rule essentially mandates that development take place within the urban core, and from there, outward into the land nearest the urban core until that is developed and the urbanized area is expanded again. This places more traffic in the areas that already have the most congestion, and more pollution in areas that are already the most polluted. While other chapters in this book deal with these issues more directly, the point is that Florida's unwritten 120 percent rule creates results similar to the designating of a USA to contain development.

Leapfrog Development

Leapfrog development occurs when new development is located away from an existing urban area, bypassing vacant parcels suitable for development that are located closer to the urban area. For developers and home buyers, leapfrog development makes sense because land further from the urban core is likely to be less expensive, allowing homeowners to have larger lots and bigger houses for the same amount of money, or alternatively, to pay less than for equivalent housing closer in. Critics of leapfrog development argue that it increases infrastructure costs when infrastructure has to be extended beyond currently undeveloped areas, that it increases commuting distances, and that it harms the environment by fragmenting ecosystems. This raises a number of issues worth considering, both for the purpose of analyzing leapfrog development specifically and for the purpose of analyzing growth management more generally.

Consider the argument that leapfrog development fragments ecosystems. If one is interested in long-run environmental preservation, this argument makes sense only if the area that is leapfrogged will remain undeveloped. If, years or even decades down the road, the leapfrogged area will be developed, then the ecosystem argument is irrelevant, because the developed area will encompass both the current development and the leapfrogged area eventually anyway. The question is really the timing of development, and which areas should be developed first, rather than which areas should remain undeveloped. The question of leapfrog development is not whether it is a good idea to leave undeveloped areas between developed areas, but rather as an area develops, whether it is a good idea to develop some areas further out before developing some areas closer in.

Framing the question this way reveals the strong argument in favor of leapfrog development. People who undertake higher-density business and commercial development prefer to have those developments centrally located, and leapfrog development helps produce tracts of centrally located undeveloped land. Once leapfrogged, that land has an improved location because it is centrally located, encouraging higher density development, and should also go up in price, again encouraging it to be developed more intensively. Thus, leapfrog development is a mechanism to encourage high density development. Conversely, discouraging leapfrog development results in lower density development in the long run, and increases the type of sprawl that the policy was intended to reduce.

In addition, by creating areas away from the central city that are ripe for higher density business and commercial development, leapfrog development encourages the growth of many nodes of activity in a metropolitan area. Because most people will tend to live closer to one of these activity nodes than to the central city, it can also help to reduce overall commuting distances and times. If everybody shops and works in the central city and lives in suburbs in the periphery, commutes will be increasingly longer as an area develops, and traffic will tend to be heavy into the downtown area in the morning, and heavy out in the afternoon and evening. By encouraging additional nodes of business and commercial activity, leapfrog development can reduce commute times by allowing people to live close to where they work and shop.[4]

This discussion does not imply that leapfrog development is always a good thing, but rather that it can be a desirable development pattern. In Florida, because it is—according to Florida law—one indicator of urban sprawl, and because Florida's local comprehensive plans are supposed to discourage the proliferation of urban sprawl, leapfrog development in Florida is a violation of the law. In practice, there is some flexibility in DCA policy to allow some instances of leapfrog development, but what this means is that, once again, urban sprawl becomes an arbitrary concept that allows land-use planners to approve or disapprove of development plans based on their own preferences rather than any objective criteria.

Critics of leapfrog development correctly argue that often it is subsidized by government policies that provide infrastructure to leapfrogged developments at less than the true cost. A market-oriented growth policy would be neutral toward leapfrog development, so would not subsidize it but also would not discourage it. The subsidy to leapfrog development may sometimes be overstated, because critics argue that infrastructure was extended beyond undeveloped land to reach the leapfrogged development, but that infrastructure can also be used to service the leapfrogged area when it is developed. Nevertheless, if the problem is that leapfrog development has been inappropriately subsidized, the solution is to change government policy so that it is neutral toward leapfrog development rather than to be critical of it.

This section makes two major points. First, leapfrog development can be a desirable development pattern, and in the long run can lead to higher-density development and improved land-use patterns. Second, leapfrog development violates Florida law, so if the law is enforced literally, Florida will have less desirable land-use patterns as a result. If the law is not applied literally, what at first appears to be an objective policy toward leapfrog development instead ends up being arbitrary, and gives land-use planners the latitude to impose their own preferences as they see fit.

Strip or Ribbon Development

Strip, or ribbon, development occurs when high amounts of commercial, retail, and office development occur in a linear pattern along both sides of major arterial roadways. Critics oppose it because it creates traffic congestion as thoroughfares become clogged with traffic trying to access the businesses, and because it extends development beyond the central city while leaving tracts of undeveloped land between the ribbons of development. Many of the comments on leapfrog development apply here as well. Strip development is often efficient because it puts businesses on high-traffic roads, providing easier access for potential customers. Because the roads will have higher-than-average volumes of traffic, the surrounding business locations will be more intensively used. Furthermore, land between the developed ribbons becomes prime locations for residential development. People like to live in areas that are conveniently located to shopping and employment, but away from busy thoroughfares. Strip or ribbon development creates just such locations for residential development. Because shopping and jobs are closer to residential locations, traffic congestion can be lessened by this type of development.[5]

The problems that critics cite with strip or ribbon development tend to be more the result of poor planning for land use in the vicinity of the major thoroughfares rather than problems with the development itself. Too often, road planners build roads for current traffic conditions and do not plan for future growth, leading to traffic congestion and the unsightly development around major thoroughfares that creates the negative reaction toward urban sprawl. When major thoroughfares are initially built, they should be constructed with sufficient right-of-way to widen the road as development spreads outward, and to provide visual buffers and access roads around commercial development. That way, when commercial development occurs, it can be separated from the thoroughfare with landscaping, and curb cuts into the thoroughfare can be minimized.

This would allow the benefits of strip or ribbon development, while minimizing the costs.

This introduces one of the most important points this chapter has to make about government growth management policies. As it stands, growth management polices deal almost entirely with how private landowners can use their resources, but tend to overlook the government's responsibility to manage its resources effectively. The problems with strip development are not primarily the results of private landowners making inappropriate use of their property, but of inadequate government management of roads. One of the main conclusions of this chapter, which I will develop further, is that growth management should be focused on the management of government resources, not on government management of private resources.

Low-Density, Single-Dimensional Development

The final indicator of urban sprawl in Florida's taxonomy is low-density, single-dimensional development. Large residential subdivisions are good examples of this type of development. Houses have relatively large lots and residents must drive everywhere they go because the subdivisions contain nothing other than residences. The big advantage of this type of development is that many people like to live in single-family homes with their own yards. The fact that widespread automobile ownership has allowed this type of development only in the past half-century is an indicator of the nation's increased standard of living and quality of life. At the same time, people like to live in close proximity to shopping and work. Thus, the ideal situation would be to create development that allows the advantages of detached single-family housing, while placing business and commercial development in closer proximity to residences.

One factor behind the isolation of residential subdivisions is zoning laws. Often business and commercial establishments are prohibited from locating near residences, and as Bernard Siegan (1970) notes, minimum lot sizes and setback requirements incorporated into zoning laws often decrease housing density via government mandate. Thus, reducing government restrictions on land use can often help alleviate the undesirable side effects of low-density residential development. Another way to reduce those side effects is to encourage leapfrog development and strip development. As already noted, these types of development tend to put business and commercial establishments in closer proximity to residences. Ironically, the development patterns that are opposed by those who fight urban sprawl can help offset its worst features. Policies promoted by the opponents of sprawl end up creating the problems that turn public opinion toward growth regulation, so as is often the case, the negative side effects of government regulation create the demand for more regulation.

LESSONS FROM FLORIDA'S URBAN SPRAWL POLICY

Florida's urban sprawl policy through the 1990s provides a number of general insights about the growth management process. The first is that policies, as implemented, can often evolve significantly from their original intent. As Florida's Growth Management Act was originally intended, local governments were supposed to draw up their own local comprehensive plans which would then be checked for compliance with the law by the DCA. The provision that those local plans were supposed to prevent the proliferation of urban sprawl was thought to be of minor importance in 1985 when the Act was passed. Once implemented, however, urban sprawl policy became the major vehicle through which the DCA enforced the Act, and through which the DCA was able to impose its own ideas on local planners. Through Florida's urban sprawl policy, what was supposed to be a local planning process became a state planning process, with local governments being put in the position of implementing state policy.[6]

A second insight from Florida's growth management process is that the bureaucracies that oversee the growth management process can expand their oversight powers to become central planners of the growth process. The intention of Florida's Growth Management Act was not to create a state-level central planning bureaucracy for land-use management, but the effect was that through their oversight powers, the DCA was able to dictate to local governments the specifications of their plans. Certainly, the DCA did not do this with malicious intent; rather, the public servants employed by the DCA believed that the requirements they placed on local governments to get their plans approved would produce improvements that would be in the public interest. This is quite irrelevant for the present point, which is that the power of oversight given to the DCA expanded into the role of central planner for growth management.

A third insight that emerges is that the vagueness of the whole concept of efficient land-use planning means that either inflexible rules must be created and adhered to, which in many cases will work against the goal of efficient land use, or that land-use policies will be arbitrarily determined by the land-use bureaucracy. Florida's urban sprawl guidelines illustrate this because it is clear that in some instances, development patterns such as leapfrog development and strip or ribbon development can be efficient patterns. If the guidelines are rigidly enforced, then development patterns will be less efficient as a result; if they are not rigidly enforced, then what development is allowable and what is not is up to the judgment of the bureaucracy with the final authority to approve or disapprove the development. In Florida, the DCA has shown some flexibility in applying their guidelines to local comprehensive plans, which means that what is allowed and what is not remains at the discretion of those in charge of the planning process.

While these insights are derived from Florida's experience with state-wide growth management, they surely provide lessons for growth management more generally. The incentives inherent in bureaucratic organizations tend to push them to expand their power, to seek larger budgets and more control, and to overlook the costs they impose on others because, unlike in the private market, the bottom line in a bureaucracy is insulated from those costs because the bureaucracy is funded by tax dollars, not revenues from customers. Because bureaucrats are not motivated by profits and losses as are business people, they have wider latitude for discretion in their jobs, and have the motivation to use it. It is less professionally rewarding to see one's job as following the orders of others than to see how one can work within the constraints one has to exercise discretion and implement one's own agenda. Again, the argument is not that bureaucrats act against what they perceive as the public interest, but rather that they have the incentive to implement their own ideas and have little incentive to take account of the costs they impose on others.[7]

Thus, there is good reason to believe that if states pursue large-scale growth management in a manner similar to Florida, they will get similar results. Because of the incentives inherent in bureaucracy, government authority over growth management will tend to differ significantly from its original intent, the process will tend to become increasingly centralized so that growth management becomes central planning for land use, and those in charge of the process will tend to implement policies at their discretion rather than according to a well-defined set of rules.

GROWTH MANAGEMENT AS CENTRAL PLANNING

Throughout most of the twentieth century there was a serious debate about the merits of central planning versus the market system as a method for allocating economic resources and running the economy. Reputable scholars argued that the economy could grow faster and could allocate resources more efficiently under central planning than if left to the uncertainties of the market.[8] By the end of the twentieth century, that debate had been resolved in favor of the market system.[9] Despite the almost universal recognition that the market system works better than central planning for the production of goods and services, in other areas, including land-use planning, people continue to make the argument that central planning is needed to overcome the shortcomings of the market. Is growth management, as practiced in Florida, really like the central economic planning that used to take place in the former Soviet Union? Yes. The process is exactly the same.

In the former Soviet Union, the central plan was implemented by the drawing up of a five-year plan for the economy by the Central Committee in Moscow. Within the constraints of this plan, each individual factory manager would draw up his own plan for his facility, including what inputs the facility would need to produce its output and what output would be produced. The Central Committee would then evaluate the plans to ensure that they were consistent with each other and with the five-year plan, and if they were not, would send them back to be redone. Thus, individual factories drew up their own plans following the guidelines of the Central Committee, and the factory plans were subject to the approval of the Central Committee. Florida's growth management process works exactly the same way. Local governments draw up their own plans following the guidelines of the DCA, and are subject to the approval of the DCA. Plans that are inconsistent with each other (for example, a city plan that is inconsistent with the county plan where the city is located) or that do not follow DCA guidelines are sent back for revision, with DCA advice on how to modify the plans to secure approval. Thus, the land-use planning process in Florida is institutionally exactly the same as central economic planning in the former Soviet Union.

When confronted with this argument, DCA personnel are inclined to deny that land-use planning in Florida is central planning. Local governments draw up their own plans, the rebuttal goes, and the DCA simply checks them to see that they are in compliance with the law. One reason for this denial may be that DCA employees are not economists and are probably not familiar with the way that central planning actually worked in the former Soviet Union. But factories drew up their own plans there, just like local governments draw up their own plans in Florida. Another reason for the denial is that the DCA's argument is that they are merely checking for compliance with the law, not dictating the nature of the overall plan. The discussion on Florida's urban sprawl policies showed this is not true, however. The central planners in the DCA drew up the policies themselves and proceeded to enforce them by rejecting plans based on their noncompliance with those policies, thus forcing the local governments to reconfigure their plans as the DCA dictated in order to get them approved.

Quite clearly, Florida-style land-use planning is central planning and is institutionally identical to central economic planning in socialist economies. Even if one disagrees with this characterization, however, it is still worth considering the similarities between government land-use planning and central economic planning to try to get some idea about why central economic planning, once held in high regard by respected economists, failed, and whether government land-use planning might face some of the same problems. Doing so has the potential to improve the planning process, regardless of whether one sees the similarity to central economic planning.

The problems with central economic planning can be analyzed in detail,[10] but when compared with the market allocation of resources, the key difference is that with central planning, the planners dictate to those in the economy what they may and may not do in order to comply with the plan, whereas in the market economy, people do whatever they choose and their behavior is steered by incentives. The same principles can be applied to land-use planning. As it currently stands, planning takes place by telling landowners what they can and cannot do with their land. Land-use planning faces an additional obstacle that central economic planning did not. Whereas land-use planners can come up with a plan for how some land ideally should be used, and while government can prevent landowners from pursuing other uses, land owners cannot be forced to undertake particular investments in the same way that economic planners could (try to) force factories to use resources in a certain way. Pursuing urban infill, for example, planners might designate a certain site for commercial development. That may prevent other uses, but as matters presently stand, land-use planners cannot force the landowners to invest in the structures that will transform currently unused land into a commercial site.

Seeing the parallel between land-use planning and central economic planning, a better strategy for land-use planning would be to undertake it in such a way that landowners have the incentive to develop their land in an optimal manner. Thus, some of the problems that bought down Soviet-style central planning could be avoided, and land-use planning could proceed along more productive lines.

PLANNING FOR PRIVATE AND PUBLIC RESOURCES

One striking feature of land-use planning in Florida is that the local comprehensive plans contain land-use maps and detailed requirements regarding how private landowners can use their resources, but there are no requirements for governments to plan out the development of their resources. The closest that Florida's growth management process comes to requiring government planning for its own resources is the requirement mandating that infrastructure be available concurrently with development. However, merely meeting this concurrency requirement is insufficient for private landowners to draw up optimal plans for the use of their property. A plan that looks ahead five years would indicate where roads would be constructed (or widened) within that time frame, but land-use decisions are much more permanent than this. Determining whether a site is better suited for residential or commercial development, or for apartments or single-family homes, requires looking out decades ahead to see where infrastructure development, and in particular, highway development, will take place. Thus, the planning horizon for public resources, and especially roads, should be much longer, and if this is done, optimal land-use patterns can be realized by having longer-range planning for government resources and eliminating government planning for private land uses. In short, government should do more planning for its own actions and less planning for the actions of others.

Land-use patterns have always been determined by transportation patterns. For most of history, this meant settling in areas near navigable rivers or seaports. In the mid- to late-1800s the railroad changed that, and population growth concentrated around rail lines. Then again, following World War II, widespread automobile ownership changed the nature of transportation and allowed lower density development and the spread of suburban living. In the same way that the structure of navigable waterways determined development patterns for most of human history, the structure of roads now determines development patterns. Thus, following the line of reasoning above, if one wants to create a more market-oriented method of land-use planning, then rather than dictating how people can use their property, land-use planning can be directed by planning the transportation infrastructure, especially the highway system, and then allowing market forces to produce land-use patterns that efficiently access the transportation system.

Reflecting on the impact that transportation systems have on land-use patterns, it is understandable why public interest in land-use planning accelerated at the end of the twentieth century. Waterborne commerce evolved slowly over the centuries, and while rail transportation evolved more rapidly, the change was not as rapid as with auto transportation in the last half of the twentieth century, it was more centralized because there were relatively few railroads, and those railroads made their plans in conjunction with government. People had to go where the railroads went, but with the automobile, people gained the freedom to travel wherever they wanted, when they wanted, by themselves. This freedom really only came to the masses after World War II, and this transportation revolution led to a revolution in land-use patterns. People no longer have to live within walking distance of their destinations, or take account of mass transit, when planning where to live or work. Thus, the movement out of the cities and into the suburbs began, and people could enjoy lifestyles they preferred.

The trend toward more decentralized development hit Florida harder than most states because Florida was growing faster. Florida's population grew 43.5 percent from 1970 to 1980, while the total U.S. population only grew by 11.4 percent, and Florida's population grew another 32.8 percent in from 1980 to 1990, compared to a 9.9 percent increase in the U.S. population. With a population growth well over three times the national average in the 1970s and 1980s, construction was booming to keep up with the growth and communities throughout the state were transformed by that growth. As noted earlier, one of the major complaints that Floridians had about the impact of growth was the increase in traffic congestion. Congestion increased because of rapid population growth, but also because of a decline in highway expenditures. In 1960 highway expenditures in Florida made up 30.2 percent of the state's budget, and 2.2 percent of the state's personal income. By 1985, when Florida's Growth Management Act was passed, highway expenditures had fallen to 7.6 percent of the state's budget, and 1.1 percent of personal income.[11] Surely, if Florida had maintained its expenditure levels on roads, congestion would have been less severe.[12] The data on state highway expenditures in Florida support the idea that the construction of roads was not keeping up with real estate development as Florida expanded.

From the standpoint of land-use planning, this lack of highway development creates more harm than just increasing traffic congestion. If optimal development patterns are determined by the transportation infrastructure, but that infrastructure is not designed until after the development has occurred, development patterns will be suboptimal. The manifestations of suboptimal development patterns in relation to roads are apparent throughout Florida. New thoroughfares, including limited access highways, have been cut through already-developed areas, disrupting formerly quiet residential subdivisions. Narrow roads in commercial areas have been widened, leaving commercial establishments very near the road, with limited space for parking, no opportunity for landscaping and visual buffers, and no room for access roads to minimize traffic slowdowns on thoroughfares. Development comes right up to the roadways at major intersections, limiting the ability of planners to create interchanges that could increase traffic flow. These problems exist outside of Florida, of course, but are notewor-thy because the kind of growth management that Florida has implemented is not well-suited to dealing with these problems. The key to effective land-use plan-ning is to recognize the central role that transportation infrastructure plays, and have more government planning of its own infrastructure and less government mandates about how people can use their own property. By appropriately plan-ning the infrastructure, private land-use decisions will occur in a manner that will produce efficient land-use patterns.

PLANNING FOR TRANSPORTATION AND LAND-USE PATTERNS

Growth management legislation in Florida and elsewhere stands on the foundation of strong popular support for its underlying goal of producing more livable communities. The problems associated with urban sprawl came to Flor-ida more suddenly than in other parts of the country because of Florida's more rapid population growth coupled with its reduction in highway expenditures. These more sudden pressures also brought growth management legislation to Florida to deal with those problems, and Florida's experience as one of the pio-neers in this area can be used to develop more effective strategies for growth management, both in Florida and in the rest of the nation. Despite widespread support for the stated goals of growth management, experience has shown that growth management legislation as it is currently designed is insufficient to ac-complish its goals.

In recent decades, the thrust of growth management has been to try to create more desirable land-use patterns. Many other goals have been associated with growth management, such as the creation of affordable housing and the protec-tion of the environment, but as the rules actually have been developed, the em-phasis has been on the design of land-use patterns, hopefully consistent with these other objectives. To that end, it is essential to consider how growth man-agement can be redesigned to foster better land-use patterns, consistent with other goals of growth management. That can be done by having government planning focus on future infrastructure development, and most especially the development of transportation corridors, rather than dictating how private land-owners can use their property. In most cases, roads are the crucial transportation link, so roads are what government needs to plan. If government plans its infra-structure, then market forces will make more efficient land-use decisions than if the planners try to plan those land use decisions directly.

This alternative to the current method of land-use planning would call for governments to develop a land-use map not of how private property could be used, but rather for the location of future infrastructure, and especially roads. Ideally, these plans would be made decades ahead, so that current landowners can have a good idea about the relationship of future transportation corridors to their property. With this information, landowners can make their own plans for future development in a manner much more sensible than the current system of mapping out permissible uses for privately owned property.

The first step in the process would be to map out the area's major transportation corridors. In a growing area, this may mean determining where major thoroughfares will go in areas that are now primarily rural in character. The second step is to secure the right-of-way, which should be done early for several reasons. First, securing the right-of-way in undeveloped areas will be cheaper than trying to buy up land in already-developed areas; indeed, landowners will often be willing to donate some of their holdings in order to secure a major transportation corridor that will increase the value of the rest of their land holdings. Second, securing the right-of-way long before it is needed demonstrates a commitment to actually build a road there. Hypothetical plans can easily be changed, and are more subject to political manipulation. If the right-of-way is already in the government's hands, then the government's plan to build a road there is more credible. Third, securing the right-of-way well ahead of time minimizes the disruptions caused by the creation of transportation corridors. Rather than putting major thoroughfares through those low-density, single-dimensional developments, the locations of thoroughfares will be known before the developments are undertaken.

When the right-of-way is secured, it must be adequate to its future purpose, and thus be wide enough to accommodate limited access divided highways, perhaps a rail line, interchanges at points where major thoroughfares will meet, and access roads so that local traffic will not be congesting major traffic thoroughfares. A sufficiently wide right-of-way also will minimize the negative impact of the transportation corridor on the surrounding property, and enhance the positive impact for those who desire ready access to roads. Too often, only enough right-of-way is secured to build a road for present levels of traffic, making it costly to widen the road at a later date, and often making it infeasible to add access roads and interchanges at busy intersections.

There are several problems with securing the right-of-way ahead of time. One is that the government must find the resources to buy it. The second problem—perhaps more significant—is that any plan to build roads will meet with political opposition. It is hard enough to get political support for roads when they would provide obvious and immediate benefits, it is even harder to get support for roads that are not yet needed. Some opponents will argue that rather than roads light rail or bike paths should be built. Others applaud congestion as a method of forcing drivers onto mass transit, although experience with congestion shows that this does not happen. This is why a comprehensive planning process directed by the state government, mandating transportation planning by local governments, makes sense. For political reasons, local governments will be reluctant to do this planning otherwise. The state government, which regulates the activities of local governments, should mandate that this planning takes place.

Once the right-of-way is secured, the next step is to build the roads. However, while the right-of-way to accommodate future traffic must be secured, roads only need to be built to accommodate the current level of traffic. For example, in the right-of-way secured for a limited access divided highway, a two-lane road can be built on one side of the right-of-way, leaving room on the other side to build another two lanes when traffic warrants. Following this plan, four-laning can occur without disrupting the current flow of traffic. Another possibility is to plan for a limited access highway with access roads on either side, parallel to the major thoroughfare. With little traffic, the access roads can be built first and used as the main thoroughfare, leaving green space between the access roads. The access roads then intersect with other roads at ground-level intersections. When traffic warrants, the main thoroughfare can be built between the access roads, along with bridges and interchanges to create a limited access road. Again, following this plan, new construction will cause minimal disruption on the existing roads.

If major transportation arteries are planned in this way, and if the right-of-way is secured and two-lane roads are built until more capacity is needed, land-use patterns will evolve efficiently without any government planning for private land use. There is a natural segregation of land uses that minimizes incompatibilities and that results in efficient use patterns, if only developers know where major thoroughfares will be located, as Siegan (1972) pointed out long ago. For example, shopping centers and other commercial activities that draw large numbers of people are best located at major intersections. This benefits the businesses because they want to locate in areas that are accessible and that have a large traffic flow. It also improves the flow of traffic because destinations for large numbers of people are located near roads that can handle the traffic. While locations at major intersections and near busy thoroughfares are good for commercial activities, they are undesirable residential locations, so if people know ahead of time where major thoroughfares and intersections will be, commercial users will be attracted there, and residential users repelled. There is no need to tell private landowners how they can use their property.

Contrast this with a system that creates a land-use map for private landowners but does not secure the right-of-way for major thoroughfares. Over time, commercial developers may find their properties decline in value if traffic is routed away from them. Poor transportation planning thus causes urban blight. Meanwhile, when new arterial roads are needed because of inadequate past planning, some residential areas will find themselves in the path of major thoroughfares, often requiring costly acquisition to build the roads, and placing major traffic arteries near formerly quiet residential areas. Again, if the traffic arteries are planned ahead of time, government does not need to intervene in private land-use decisions to create efficient land-use patterns. If traffic arteries are not planned ahead of time, then neither government planners nor private landowners can know the optimal uses for specific parcels of land.

Residential users like to be located conveniently close to major transportation arteries, but not close enough that those arteries become nuisances. Thus, by planning major thoroughfares that creates strips or ribbons of commercial development, the areas between those strips of commercial development are ideal residential locations. They are conveniently located to commercial establishments and commercial arteries, yet not right on them, where the traffic would disturb residents. Areas even a block or two from major thoroughfares are not good commercial locations because they do not have the traffic flow that benefits businesses. Gas stations and convenience stores would rather locate on thoroughfares than on less-traveled streets; similarly, people would rather live on those less traveled streets than on the major thoroughfares. Creating efficient land-use patterns requires knowing ahead of time where the transportation corridors will be, however.

One of the disadvantages of strip development as it is currently undertaken is that it creates unsightly rows of buildings and parking lots along major thoroughfares. Another is that traffic entering and exiting those businesses slows down through traffic. These problems are not the result of development patterns themselves, and can be addressed if sufficient right-of-way is obtained before development takes place. With sufficient right-of-way, visual buffers can be created through landscaping, and access roads can be provided to aid in the flow of through traffic. To do this, it is not enough to simply designate where roads will be built. The right-of-way must be acquired early on in order to keep development from encroaching on the transportation corridor. Otherwise, the result is that as roads are widened, they use up space adjacent to the roadway that could have been used for access roads and visual buffers, creating an imperfect solution. Also, it is more costly to acquire already-developed property to widen a road, rather than acquiring it well ahead of development.

Environmental protection is another important motivator for growth management, but one must separate out the issues of what areas should be preserved in their natural state from issues regarding the sequence of development. Leapfrog development is criticized because it develops land further from the urban core before land closer in, but as suggested earlier, this can be an efficient method of development. If that land further out is environmentally important, and should be preserved, then the solution to that is to have the state purchase the land to remove it from development entirely. The issue of regulatory takings is beyond the scope of this chapter; the point here is simply that if environmental amenities should be preserved, then the state may have a role in doing so, but that issue is completely separate from the issue of whether leapfrog development should be allowed. In other areas too, infrastructure planning can aid in protecting the environment. In Florida, for example, one of the more significant environmental problems is stormwater runoff, which is best managed through retention ponds that allow the runoff to seep back into the water table rather than removing it through storm drains. This requires sufficient land area to build the retention ponds which, however, requires advance planning not only for the location of roads, but for sufficient right-of-way for environmental amenities. In general, lower density development does not have to be worse for the environment than high-density development if it allows for more natural areas. Higher density typically brings with it more paved areas, more concentrated sources of pollution, and less ability of the environment to absorb pollutants.

Too often, issues of environmental preservation are confounded with issues of the optimal sequencing of land development, and effective growth management must treat them separately. Environmental preservation means setting land aside for the long term, whereas issues of leapfrogging and strip development are more about which areas should be developed first. Leapfrog development and strip development often lead to higher density development over the long run, and to more efficient land-use patterns, and thus can be environmentally beneficial.

Another area of concern in growth management is affordable housing, and the traditional method of setting some areas aside as off limits to development works against affordable housing. Housing prices are determined by supply and demand. In areas where there is little available developable land, like San Francisco, housing prices are higher than in areas like Tallahassee, Florida, where there is a significant amount of developable land. Restricting development in some areas reduces the amount of land available for development, and so raises housing prices. By allowing landowners to determine when they develop their land, there will be competition among various locations, thus lowering housing prices and creating more affordable housing. There is a difference between affordable housing and cheaply built housing. Government can mandate that some housing be built cheaply, and that housing units are small, but the price at which those units will sell will still be determined by supply and demand (unless the government also controls housing prices and rents, which creates other problems). The source of housing for most lower-income people is used housing, and the best way to allow lower-income people access to high-quality affordable housing is to increase the housing stock. Every upper-income person who moves to a new house makes a housing unit available to someone else, so allowing good housing to trickle down to lower-income people is a good way to provide affordable housing, not just cheaply built housing.

This chapter suggests a major overhaul in the way that growth management is practiced. Rather than assigning government the power to dictate how private landowners can use their property, a more efficient alternative is to require governments themselves to plan out their transportation infrastructure well into the future. Land-use patterns have always tended to reflect the transportation infrastructure. When that meant waterways, it was easy to foresee transportation patterns well into the future. Now that the transportation infrastructure is highways, it is important for government to do its planning well ahead so that private landowners can plan for effective use of their property. Many local governments used to plan along the lines suggested here in the 1950s and 1960s, but with the energy crisis in the 1970s, planners started to look for ways to reduce automobile travel rather than accommodate it, resulting in increased congestion. The suggestions put forward here might be looked at as a call to return to at least some of the planning principles that governments used to implement. If government planning for its own infrastructure were effectively undertaken, private land-use patterns would naturally evolve efficiently, without government mandates.

As it stands now, a land-use map dictating allowable private uses for land without an effective long-term plan for government infrastructure cannot produce efficient land-use patterns. Property owners cannot know how intensively they should develop their property without knowing where future transportation corridors will lie, and without knowing where major intersections will be located. This lowers land values, and means that developers cannot risk higher-density developments that would be optimal if they knew where transportation thoroughfares would be located. Ironically, the way planning is done now creates lower densities and more traffic congestion, even though its goals are just the opposite. Planning for government infrastructure rather than for private land-use can vastly improve the process of growth management.

IMPEDIMENTS TO INFRASTRUCTURE PLANNING

Why is planning not done like this now? There are several possible answers, all of which may contribute to the nature of growth management. One factor is that it is difficult to achieve political consensus on how development should take place. As noted earlier, the benefits of long-range planning come in the future, but many political costs of such planning are immediate. People who do not want roads built, or do not want new thoroughfares near them, can object, and in a mobile society, most of the beneficiaries of long-range planning may not even live in the area yet. Thus, political decisions are made looking at the short-run costs and benefits rather than thinking for the long term. Another factor is that some planners sincerely believe that they know what is best for everyone else, and if they could just dictate land-use patterns to everyone, the world would be a better place. Central planning has not fared well in other areas of the economy, which should make observers skeptical about the merits of central planning for land use. Nevertheless, the advocates of centralized land-use planning rest on the same types of arguments—and have constructed the same types of planning systems—as the central economic planners of the former Soviet bloc.

Politically, it is more popular to mandate how private landowners can use their property than to make the hard decisions on future infrastructure and to come up with the funding to implement them. Part of the problem is that because of past neglect, many areas are now having to try to implement expensive solutions in response to inadequate past planning for infrastructure. When one must buy and bulldoze existing homes and businesses to build thoroughfares through developed areas to relieve current congestion, it is hard to devote the funds and political energy to securing the right-of-way now to prevent the same thing from happening in other areas decades in the future. That is why there is good reason not to argue against growth management in general, but to argue for changing the way growth is managed, so the emphasis is shifted from government planning for private land use to government planning for infrastructure development.

CONCLUSION

Florida has been one of the pioneers in growth management, and Florida's experiences can lend valuable insight into how the growth management process can be improved, both in Florida and elsewhere. Florida initiated statewide growth management for the same reasons that are typically given for government oversight of growth. Floridians wanted to relieve traffic congestion, they wanted to preserve their existing neighborhoods and way of life in the face of substantial growth, and they favored other goals such as environmental preservation and the creation of affordable housing. While the process is still relatively new in Florida, it is apparent to both the supporters and detractors of growth management that it has been less successful at achieving its goals than its proponents had hoped, and as this analysis has suggested, in many cases the actual effects of growth management laws were opposite of their stated intentions. After analyzing growth management in Florida, one can see not only that it could work better, but how it could work better. If Florida's governments focused their attention on planning for their own activities, and especially for their future infrastructure development, rather than on dictating what private individuals can do with their property, the whole process of growth management would work more effectively, and land-use decisions would be more efficient.

NOTES

1.   Along these lines, see Holcombe (1990b).
2.   Colburn and deHaven Smith (1999, p. 131) note that this coordination among plans has been a key feature of growth management planning in Florida since the early 1970s.
3.   Excerpted from Florida Statute 163.3177(9).
4.   See Gordon and Richardson (1989) for a further discussion of this type of development. Also see Holcombe (1995) for a discussion of leapfrog development and these other types of development that indicate urban sprawl.
5.   Siegan (1970, 1972) remarks on the efficiency of this type of development, and also on how market forces tend to provide it.
6.   The institutional reasons of why a little planning tends to grow into a lot of planning are discussed well by Ikeda (1997).
7.   See Niskanen (1971, 1975) for an analysis that makes these points, and that has served as the foundation for much of the current theory of bureaucratic organizations.
8.   For example, Samuelson (1973, p. 883), a Nobel laureate in economics, argued that even though the U.S. economy at that time had roughly twice the per capita income as the Soviet Union, the Soviet Union's superior economic system would result in the U.S.S.R. catching up with the United States perhaps as soon as 1990, and almost surely by 2010. See also Holcombe (1995, ch. 2) for a discussion of markets versus planning.
9.   Fukuyama (1992) provides an insightful discussion of this topic.
10.   Ikeda (1997) does an excellent job.
11.   These figures calculated by the author from data in the *Statistical Abstract of the United States,* 1961 and 1987 editions.
12.   The national trends, while in the same direction, were not as severe. Nationally, all state highway expenditures were 1.8 percent of income in 1960 and 1.4 percent in 1985. Thus, even though Florida's population was growing faster than the national average during that 25-year period, its highway expenditures fell from above the national average to below the national average.

Chapter 9

Urban Density and Sprawl: An Historic Perspective

ROBERT BRUEGMANN

According to current opinion, urban sprawl represents a crisis. Anti-sprawl reformers would like to institute new policies that will stop or severely restrict sprawl and instead promote Smart Growth. Because other authors in this book ask whether sprawl is, in fact, bad, or Smart Growth good, I will instead focus on a key factor in sprawl: This chapter will examine some historical trends in urban density.

For many people advocating a fight against sprawl, it is important to believe that the sprawling of our cities is a recent and accelerating phenomenon, peculiar to the United States, and caused by specific conditions or policies that can be readily changed. Otherwise it would be difficult to convince the public at large that stopping sprawl or encouraging Smart Growth is a plausible policy option and not an exercise in tilting at windmills. I will look at the subject of urban densities in an historical and comparative perspective, arguing that the kind of lowering of densities associated with sprawl is neither recent, nor peculiarly American. Nor is it accelerating. In most cities in the United States, in fact, decentralization is either moderating or has disappeared altogether. Contrary to opinion on the subject, a growing number of American cities are becoming denser. If this is true, the fight against urban sprawl has been founded on a very poor understanding of the current condition of American cities. It can be seen more as a prescription for the woes of the city of the immediate postwar decades than as a useful formula for dealing with the cities we actually have today.

I will also argue that the usual reasons given for sprawl are insufficient to explain the phenomenon. The processes both of decentralization and centralization are much more complex than the anti-sprawl literature suggests. This makes it highly unlikely that the policy changes suggested by anti-sprawl reformers would have the effects that they are expected to have. In fact, there is good historical evidence to suggest that, like many large-scale planning solutions, they are just as likely to backfire or cause unintended consequences as they are to solve the original problem.

SPRAWL AND DENSITY

There has always been a great deal of confusion over the term *sprawl*. The use of sprawl as a noun with something like its current meaning seems to have occurred first in Britain between the wars. It was then used primarily to indicate discontinuities or lack of order in the settlement pattern. Scattered villas in the countryside and "ribbon" development, (building along roadways leading out from towns) were among the things most distasteful to the opponents of middle-class occupation of the countryside (Bruegmann, forthcoming b). Scattered or discontinuous development, although it has survived in many definitions of sprawl, however, has always been problematic. It has been shown by many authors that discontinuous settlement in one era is often just a stage in the creation of a compact, continuous settlement pattern at a later date (Lessinger 1962; Holcombe, chapter 8). Likewise, there are several difficulties in trying to define sprawl as chaotic or disorderly development. In any kind of objective sense, it is clear that there is a great deal of order in the processes by which development has happened in virtually any city. This is obvious from the way cities across the world have changed in ways that have been fairly constant and predictable (Muth 1969).

Although, at first glance, *unplanned* has a more objective meaning, it becomes apparent on closer examination that it, too, is fraught with ambiguity. At the most basic level, it is obvious that no development can be unplanned. It is simply a matter of who is doing the planning. Thus the apparently random placement of houses along a roadway leading out of London in the early twentieth century required a great deal of planning by owners, builders, and many others. What planning has really meant in this context is city planning or regional planning by professional planners working for governmental agencies. But even here there is the obvious objection that there is quite a bit more land-use planning by professionally trained planners today than ever before in history. If lack of planning causes sprawl, it should stand to reason that we would have had maximum sprawl in the late nineteenth century and minimal sprawl today, which is certainly not what anti-sprawl reformers believe. It is certainly odd to hear them hold up earlier urban forms, whether turn-of-the-century cities or smaller towns in the interwar years, as models of good planning since these were usually the product of very little professional planning. In any case, whether development is planned or not appears to be a very subjective indicator of sprawl.

Many of the recent definitions of sprawl are related to the way sprawling metropolitan areas supposedly function. For many authors sprawl is defined as settlement that fosters automobile dependency or results in low accessibility to jobs, shopping, and recreation or public open space (Ewing 1997). This, too, provides little specific guidance for what is and what is not sprawl. Automobile ownership and use appear to be at least as much a result of income level and other factors than of land-use patterns. The question of whether open space is public or private and its degree of accessibility are also obviously very subjective matters. One could argue, for example, that for most people the most accessible open space they can have is their own yard.

The one factor that consistently has been part of almost everyone's definition of sprawl and is amenable to objective study is low density. Most writers on sprawl believe that cities today have densities that are too low. They need to be more compact. They believe that this would reverse a decentralization trend that has been largely in evidence since World War II in which urban dwellers have been moving continuously outward, "consuming" land at a disproportionate and ever-increasing pace. Let's examine this proposition.

DENSITY: A COMPACT HISTORY

Trying to chart a history of urban densities is surprisingly difficult, in part because of the complexity of urban systems, in part because of the inadequacy of available data, and in part because of the partisan nature of much writing about the subject. One thing can be stated with some certainty, however. Both decentralization and centralization have operated in cities simultaneously, producing complicated patterns of density increases and declines throughout urban areas over the years (Muller 1977). The pattern that is usually described by most historians involves a vast concentration of people and jobs at the center of cities in the Western world at the beginning of the industrial revolution through the nineteenth century, and then an equally vast deconcentration of both out of these central cities in the twentieth century, particularly after World War II. There is also the assumption that these changes were caused by changes in the economy and particularly changes in transportation patterns.

Although there is some truth to this historic plot line, it reduces the extremely complex process of urban growth to an overly simplified formulation that obscures as much as it reveals about historic or current urban trends. The 1880s, a moment of enormous job growth in the central business districts of American cities and of increasing population density in areas well served by new means of transportation, for example, also was a period that saw some of the most dramatic outward residential and industrial expansion at the periphery. Both trends were made possible by the same means of transportation. Or, conversely, in recent decades when many areas near the center of metropolitan areas are still losing population, there has been a major increase in density in other places, for example, in the west side of Los Angeles which has been rebuilding at much higher residential and commercial densities. Although New York and Chicago were still, at least until recently, decentralizing, there have been major new surges of residential construction near the core, for example, in the Chicago Loop and the South Bronx. Both the decentralization and the increasing density have been made possible by the use of the private automobile, which is currently the primary means of urban transportation for the vast majority of citizens in every American city, even those living quite close to the center of cities. These conflicting trends, in which every movement in the city sets in motion a vast net of consequences and counter-movements throughout the system, have been visible since the earliest days of city building. All urban areas, like all complex systems, natural or manmade, tend to act like an organism. They confound attempts at simple description or reduction to unitary cause-and-effect analyses.

A corollary of this is that every change affects people in very different ways. For example, when land prices in any specific area drop significantly, this loss on someone's part almost always creates opportunities sooner or later for others. In any such case, it is misleading to try to characterize a change as inherently good or bad. The commonly held notion that neighborhoods are in decline when existing residents are replaced by families with lower incomes, for example, tells only half the story. For the people moving in, the neighborhood often represents affordable housing and upward mobility. Over long periods of time most areas of any city go through cycles of this kind. Sometimes it results in higher densities or higher incomes, sometimes in lower densities or lower incomes. The economic "failures" of many cities in one era are exactly the reason that they are considered so attractive in a successive era, as the story of Charleston, South Carolina, or Prague, Czechoslovakia, demonstrate. Making value judgments about whether an extremely complicated process like a rise or fall in urban densities is good or bad seems almost certain to miss the complicated system of trade-offs that happen throughout the urban system with any change and the way all urban changes help some people and harm others.

Surprisingly little is known about urban densities through history. Although there was a large literature in the nineteenth and early twentieth centuries trying to demonstrate the evils of excessively high urban densities, and there has been a large literature starting in the mid-twentieth century arguing that there are problems with excessively low urban densities, there has been remarkably little on the actual history of decentralization and density over the years. However, what little is known is very instructive. It appears that very high densities characterized large cities from a very early date but that when people have been able to afford lower densities they have generally done so. This probably goes a long way toward explaining the difference between the low densities of American and European urban areas today, many of them under 5,000 people per square mile, with the tightly bounded large cities throughout history that registered well over 100,000 people per square mile.

Archaeologists have estimated that in Mesopotamian times, cities had residential densities over 125,000 per square mile. Figures like these appear to be fairly consistent over centuries for very different kinds of cities. It might represent the upper threshold of tolerable densities before the time of the industrial revolution (Clark 1951, 496). In Rome, the population of about one million people in the early Republic was piled up in the small area enclosed by city walls, creating residential densities estimated to be on the order of 160,000 people per square mile. This figure included areas occupied by an urban elite at fairly low densities, at one extreme, and vast areas of the city where the population was warehoused in high-density apartment blocks called *insulae* that, in many cases, appear to have been urban slums from the moment of their erection. There was a great deal of complaint about these densities and the lack of planning in the city generally. To escape the congestion, pollution, and noise of the city, a large number of Romans who could afford to do it built themselves villas in the *suburbium*, the countryside around Rome, where they could retreat on weekends and vacation periods (Friedlaender 1910; Morley 1996). Also outside the city walls were what we would think of today as industrial areas, places where noxious or space-intensive activities took place. Ancient Rome can certainly be said to have been a sprawling metropolis, and it called forth virtually all the complaints we hear today about congested, polluted, disorderly cities.

From what is known of them, cities in the medieval and early modern period exhibited densities similar to those in antiquity. Paris in the fourteenth century, was estimated to have 125,000 people per square mile, and London at the end of the seventeenth century something like 140,000 per square mile (Clark 1951, 496). Once again, those who could afford to escape the city for periods of time did so, to villas or country houses. But, at least by the end of the seventeenth century in London, and probably much earlier, there was also the phenomenon of wealthy residents building permanent year-round residences at the urban periphery at much lower densities than those found in the city itself. This involved what was then long-distance commuting back into the city by carriages (Hall 1966). Thus was born a large suburban region in what is now called the central West End of London laid out along private parks with gated streets (Olsen 1982).

After the advent of the industrial revolution even denser cities appeared as new developments in infrastructure, particularly transportation, allowed very large production facilities to bring in a constant supply of materials and take away the finished products for distribution. These production facilities also required a huge daily labor force, much of which needed to live within walking distance because it could not afford public transportation. This caused a massive residential densification near industrial areas. Central city densities reportedly reached 180,000 people per square mile in the four central arrondissements of Paris in the mid-nineteenth century, and perhaps peaked at figures as high as 350,000 on the Lower East Side of New York City in the first years of the twentieth century (Hall 1966). This may have been the highest density ever recorded, although there is some evidence that residential densities in the central areas of cities like Hong Kong, Manila, or Cairo in recent decades might approach or even surpass these figures. It is important to keep in mind that the densities in all these places rose in an era when a mass transportation network was already in operation, allowing sharply lower densities in other parts of the city. Obviously, density patterns in various parts of an urban area do not necessarily move in the same direction and are affected in quite different ways by infrastructure and technology.

In the twentieth century, in virtually every city in the economically developed world, a marked decentralization of both jobs and residence has been underway. Unfortunately, despite decades of scholarship, trying to describe this phenomenon in any detail is difficult. Although there is a great deal of information, it is often incomplete and inadequately organized. Because, in the United States and many other countries, administrative units are most often used as the basic categories for aggregating data, most density figures have been given for specific cities or their suburbs. The problem is that political boundaries do not correspond in any systematic way with urban patterns. The newer the city the more problematic the situation. The popular notion of Los Angeles as a low-density city, for example, is in great part a statistical artifact, the result of merely dividing a given population into the total land area of a political jurisdiction. In fact, from a very early date it seems that it would have been more appropriate to describe Los Angeles as a dispersed cluster of relatively high-density settlements than a low-density city. Likewise today, contrary to common perceptions, the urbanized part of the Los Angeles area that is the inhabited part of the region, is quite high in density. Although the central area does not have the densities of Manhattan or central Chicago, the outlying areas are actually quite a bit denser than those in older cities with a result that Los Angeles is the single densest urbanized area in the country (Wendell Cox, www.publicpurpose.com)

The notion that the decentralization of jobs and residences sped up greatly after World War II in American cities is another artifact of the way historians have used Census data. Actually, decentralization of jobs was very important in most American cities throughout the entire first half of the twentieth century. Historians have tended to ignore this and concentrate instead on the move of jobs after World War II because it was more noticeable in the Census figures when jobs crossed municipal boundaries. In most cities before this time, many of the jobs simply moved further out within the central cities, which were constantly expanding. It was the eventual consequence of the end of easy annexation more than any dramatic speed-up in decentralization that caused the apparent sudden decentralization of jobs in the postwar years (Bruegmann 1993).

Another major problem in describing the history of decentralization is that residential density in the twentieth century has been fairly independent of employment density. In fact, it is precisely the fact that the location of jobs forms quite a different pattern from the location of residences that causes many of the perceived problems in our cities today. The current literature on urban sprawl tends to suggest that the "jobs-housing imbalance" has been a relatively recent phenomenon, something that was aggravated by the appearance of automobiles which allowed people to live far from their place of work. This does not seem to be an accurate view of the subject. As we have seen, long before the automobile and even before public transportation, the center of a city like London was decanting its residential population outwards at the same time as it was intensifying its employment base. In the early years of the twentieth century the jobs/housing imbalance in American cities was probably at its most extreme as a vast expansion of office jobs in cities' central business districts coincided with a very rapid outward dispersal of the residential population. With the advent of the automobile and motor truck and a rapid decentralization of employment, this imbalance has, if anything, declined.

In many ways, therefore, many of the really important questions about density, past or present, cannot be answered using the available research. This is particularly true with what logically ought to be central questions about the current patterns of decentralization and sprawl. In any given city or in cities more generally is the current decentralization pattern recent or long-standing? Is it continuing at the same pace as in the past, accelerating, or declining? What has caused it in the past and is causing it now? These questions have received surprisingly little sustained attention, and the conclusions reached are often reductive and skewed by ideological bias.

A useful measure of decentralization would need to tie together the rate and specific location of population change. For this reason the best measure of decentralization in cities, at least until recently when multi-nucleated urban areas may have made it more problematic, has been the plotting of densities by Census tract and the creation of charts showing how average densities fall with distance from a given city center. Starting with the efforts of Colin Clark in the early 1950s, there has been a good deal of work with density gradients. This work, although often used to establish theoretical models rather than to describe actual conditions, has been useful in demonstrating that although there have been some fluctuations, the flattening of the residential density curve, or the decline of density in the center and an increasing density at the periphery, has been one of the most constant features of virtually every city in the developed world in the twentieth century (Clark 1951; Edmonston 1975; Light 1983).

AMERICAN CITIES AND EUROPEAN CITIES

One of the most important features of the study of the density gradient is that it allows useful comparisons between very different kinds of cities. For example, the flattening of the residential density gradient in Chicago in the first half of the twentieth century was quite similar to that for London in the same period, suggesting that the same processes were at work even though London, because of the much larger and denser pre-existing fabric, had overall densities that were higher than Chicago's. This finding, that despite very different policies, social systems, and economic systems, cities have tended to have similar reductions in density gradients when they became mature and affluent, has enormous implications. One of the things that it strongly suggests is the fundamental similarity of American and European cities despite the commonly held belief that they are different in fundamental ways. According to the usual wisdom on this subject, Europeans have had a different attitude toward the land, density, energy use, and the automobile, which led to cities that are denser and more pedestrian-friendly. Europeans also, according to this point of view, have a higher tolerance for high-density living, public transit use, and multi-family dwellings than Americans (Jackson 1985).

The empirical evidence showing similar residential density gradient reductions suggests otherwise. It suggests that although at any given point in time overall densities might be higher in European cities than in American cities, or automobile ownership lower, or transit use greater, the trends are quite similar. Of course European cities are denser overall than American ones. Large parts of them were built at very high densities before the advent of public transportation and the private automobile. If, however, density gradients in European cities are flattening, automobile ownership rising, and the percentage of public transportation ridership falling very much as in American cities, it suggests that attitudes about density and about the use of private versus collective transportation might not be fundamentally different. People in central Paris may, indeed, live in apartment buildings and use public transportation more than Americans but not necessarily because they want to or will continue to do so given a choice.

In fact, the research done on Parisian housing preferences consistently shows that residents of the Parisian area who live in single-family houses are more satisfied with their dwellings than those who live in apartments and that the majority would prefer single-family detached dwellings (Bernard 1992, 27–32, Evenson; 1979, p. 251). Likewise with public transportation. Historically it was enormously expensive for European city dwellers to own automobiles. But with increasing affluence, this is changing rapidly. By 1990 something like three-quarters of all families in the Paris agglomeration owned private automobiles, and these accounted for some 66 percent of all trips in the region. Even in the Netherlands, despite the fact that this country is the densest in Europe and has one of the most extensive public transportation systems, the percentage of inhabitants who use public transportation to commute to work is less than 10 percent. The reasons are easy to understand. On average transit trips take much longer than automobile trips. In the Parisian region, for example, the average trip by car takes 20 minutes whereas the average trip by public transportation lasts 46 minutes (Gerondeau 1997, pp. 223, 227, 254; Giuliano; 1998, U.S. Department of Transportation, Bureau of Transportation Statistics, 1999). As a result of citizen preferences for private housing and private transportation, many of the most stringent European planning laws of the postwar years have fallen victim to the desire on the part of a large and growing middle class for space, privacy, and mobility. All evidence seems to suggest that, despite continuing governmental policy restrictions, the Paris region and other European metropolitan areas will continue to decentralize and as they do, automobile ownership and single-family homeownership will continue to rise and per capita transit use and apartment living continue to fall.

Another flawed assumption has been the notion that European and American cities have had a fundamentally different history in the way various classes have segregated themselves out in metropolitan areas. A standard old chestnut is that in American cities the poor live in the central city and the rich live in the suburbs and in European cities the reverse occurs. While it is true that in a number of European cities the highest-status residential area is part of the central city, it is rarely the case that these residential areas are in the oldest areas at the very heart of the city. The most desirable areas are usually those parts of metropolitan areas built in the late nineteenth and early twentieth century at the edge of the metropolitan area. That is to say they are located at a place where development was occurring at the end of the long-term segregating-out process that happened in the wake of the industrial revolution. The same could be said for American cities.

Paris can again serve as a good example. The Parisian elite for many years inhabited quarters near the center of the city. In the seventeenth century, a great many of the wealthiest Parisians were found east of the Ile de la Cité in the area known as the Marais. By the eighteenth century, as the central arrondissements grew dramatically in population and in commercial activity, the elite started a westward movement, partly pushed by noise and congestion and partly pulled by the lure of less dense, greener quarters. After reaching what was then the western limits of the city, they spilled out into what were then the western suburbs, notably the Faubourg St. Honoré, literally the St. Honoré suburb. The westward march continued in the late nineteenth and early twentieth century into the 16th arrondissement, and finally into the near western suburbs such as Neuilly. At the same time, however, affluent Parisians desiring lower density and more land often moved much further out into the small villages and new suburbs far from central Paris. It is true that the majority of the Parisian elite did not move out to anything like the distances that their counterparts in the United States did. Part of this can be explained by the enormous and continuous subsidy of the central city, particularly the capital cities in each country, by the national governments. European countries have had a long tradition of much greater intervention by central governmental authorities, whether the monarch or the national government, into local land markets, and this central administration has virtually always privileged the center (Nivola 1999).The high amenity level of affluent residential neighborhoods near the center with their heavy concentration of parks, museums, and cultural facilities was effectively subsidized by the entire population of the country. This fact also explains why the centers of Liverpool, Lille, or Liege, and other provincial cities have fared far much less well than the capital cities in the same countries.

Other parts of the Parisian region have changed in ways much like American cities. The residential density in the municipality of Paris peaked about 1920 at 27,576 people per square kilometer (71,400 people per square mile) and has declined since. In the meantime the suburbs continued to grow very quickly. In the interwar years the inner suburbs saw the development of a vast number of single-family homes. This kind of development was strenuously discouraged after World War II and in its place occurred a great governmental effort to produce large apartment complexes or "grands ensembles" (Bastié 1964). The inner ring of suburbs, where a large percentage of this social housing was built, reached its peak of density in the 1970s and is now declining in density as well. These areas contain the poorest and most troubled neighborhoods in the Parisian region and have been marked by widespread violence in the 1990s (Economist, 1996). During the last several decades, the vast majority of growth in the Parisian region has been in the outer ring of suburbs. Here, in place of the *grands ensembles* the single-family house and the automobile have become the norm (Fouchier 1997, p. 73). By 1990 the city of Paris accounted for only about 20 percent of the population in the Parisian region. In all these ways, despite a very different political system in which the national government and regional planning bodies exert a much greater control than is the case in any American city, the overall pattern of recent development is not really much different from that found in American cities (Louchard and Ronsac c. 1991).

Another factor, one rarely discussed in comparisons between European and American cities, is the importance of the second house. Since the days of ancient Rome one of the most important models for wealthy Europeans was a town house or an apartment in the city and a country house in the surrounding territory. In this fashion the lack of space in the city became more tolerable because of the large amount of space at the country house. It is conspicuous on a map of the Parisian region in the late eighteenth century, for example, that enormous tracts of land in the areas west of the city were devoted to the country houses of the French urban elite. The pattern of house, garden, and park, with nearby village, seen in its grandest form at Versailles, was repeated hundreds of times around the French capital by lesser members of the nobility, covering vast areas of the most attractive countryside. This was really suburban living at very low densities and ought to be thought of as integral to the Parisian metropolis. As more intense development has moved outward, this area of second homes, increasingly bourgeois rather than aristocratic and with individual houses more modest but much more numerous, has simply migrated farther out.

The second-house phenomenon sped up dramatically with the increase in affluence across a wide part of the population following World War II and grew even faster with the urban unrest in the late 1960s. In the 1970s Hugh D. Clout demonstrated the importance of the trend and the way the second home had become integral in the urban systems of Europe. He showed that by the end of the 1960s nearly one in five urban households in affluent Sweden used country houses. He used the very appropriate term "seasonal suburbanization" to describe the second-house phenomenon and suggested that there were at least two rings of these houses starting with a week-end dormitory zone nearest the suburbs and a summer dormitory zone at a greater distance (Clout 1974). At the time Clout was writing the weekend suburbs extended over 160 kilometers from Paris and municipal jurisdictions in which summer houses constituted more than 75 percent of the entire housing stock extended all the way to the Normandy coast (1974, p. 111). This was before the full effects of the unrest of 1968 had registered on the metropolitan area or the full development of the extensive Parisian area superhighway system.

The number and extent of secondary residences has grown enormously since then. By 1990 there were nearly 400,000 secondary residences within the Parisian basin outside the Ile de France. This accounted for close to 10 percent of the entire housing stock in the area (Louchart and Ronsac 1991). These are very substantial figures and suggest that as French urbanites have grown wealthier they, like their American counterparts, have used vastly more space. This process of very low-density development beyond the suburban fringe has been designated "periurbanisation" or "rurbanisation" in France (Bauer and Roux 1976; Dézert, Methong and Steinberg 1991). However, because most English-speaking scholars are familiar with the center of Paris and not its periphery, and because of a strong tendency to think of landscape in aesthetic terms, they have failed to pick up on Clout's lead and have continued to describe the city and suburbs as urban and the surrounding countryside as rural. The result, in both European and American cities, has been to obscure some of the most important features of the urban use of space and to contribute fuel to the erroneous conclusions made about "non-metropolitan" population growth (Lang 1986; Nelson 1992). A great deal of this non-metropolitan growth is really a low-density expansion of urban areas.

A good corrective can be found in the work of Javier Francisco Monclús, who has studied the decentralization of Barcelona. This city, like many southern European cities, maintained a very compact form and actually saw increased densities through the early interwar period. The rapid economic growth from the 1950s to the 1970s triggered a process of very rapid decentralization starting in the 1980s. Population in the municipality of Barcelona peaked about 1981 and then started to decline as growth outward occurred. In the process, the percentage of single-family houses in the metropolitan area jumped from 22 percent to 39.5 percent as middle- and upper-middle-class citizens moved to the suburbs. There also was an enormous increase in the ownership of second houses, either isolated villas or units in gentrified villages, often well beyond the continuously built-up part of the city. Areas many miles from the city are increasingly part of the weekly, if not daily, urban system (Monclús 1998a, 1998b). In their overall patterns of decentralization, southern European cities seem to be following the trajectory of cities in the north of Europe, just as cities in Northern Europe are following the lead of those in North America; but in both cases with a time lag that appears to be related to the rate of growth in personal income.

Returning for a moment to American cities, a look at the history of any major city will show that the usual formulation about the poor at the center and the rich at the edge is also very inadequate. It is clear, first of all, that up until some point in the process of industrialization, usually in the late nineteenth century for many large cities in the Northeast and Midwest, most wealthy inhabitants lived close to the center. Probably the majority of Chicago's wealthiest citizens lived on the near south side of Chicago until the last decades of the century. It is true that many of the very affluent left the central city to settle in the suburbs starting in the late nineteenth century. This happened at a point when the city had reached a level of economic maturity and industrialization seen considerably earlier in European cities. It is not true, any more than in Europe, that the wealthiest citizens have retreated constantly further afield. In the case of Chicago, the elite suburbs that were established in the period from the 1880s to the 1920s, places like Kenilworth, Lake Forest, or Hinsdale, are the most exclusive suburbs to this day. Many, if not most, of the very exclusive neighborhoods are still located closer to the center than the edge of the built-up area. Very few are located at the extreme periphery, which has become increasingly the domain of middle and lower-middle income groups. In this respect, as in many others, American and European cities seem to be converging.

This convergence is also noticeable at the center of the city. The number of families of high socio-economic character near the center of American cities has expanded very dramatically in recent years. In Chicago, for example, it is clear that the initial gentrification activity of the postwar decades, concentrated in an area of a few dozen blocks in the Gold Coast and Old Town neighborhoods, has spread throughout much of the north side of the city and has jumped over the Chicago River into a long corridor that extends along Milwaukee Avenue for miles out from the Loop. The same process is happening in the near west and near south sides of the city and even into areas like the Gap and North Kenwood in the mid-south side that, until a few years ago, seemed to be involved in an inevitable downward trend in socio-economic indicators. The same process of gentrification also can be seen in several near suburbs, such as Evanston or Oak Park, often leading to the phenomenon of suburban gentrification creeping back into adjacent city neighborhoods.

The full extent of the gentrification process is still largely unknown because the usual social science tools are far too crude to measure it. Population figures and income levels, often used to try to track gentrification, can lead to completely false conclusions because gentrification is more about social class than it is about income levels. In fact, both population and income levels usually decline in the early stages of gentrification because urban pioneers often form small and relatively young households without large yearly income streams, at least initially. The result has been that, even though vast areas of the city are obviously and visibly gentrifying, the uptick in indicators can be canceled out by a slow loss of affluence elsewhere in the central city leading analysts to reach the false conclusion that because they could not measure it, gentrification wasn't important (Bourne 1993). This gentrification represents another convergence between American and many European cities.

In short, when we compare the history of an American city like Chicago with that of a European city like Paris, it becomes apparent that the differences are not nearly as great as received opinion would suggest. Despite the obvious weight of pre-existing building stock in the central area of European cities and a certain time lag in developments at the periphery, the trend of populations moving outward and the creation of new lower-density settlements at the urban periphery has been remarkably similar. Since the 1970s, particularly, the convergence of many European and American cities, where both have witnessed a rapid gentrification at the center and a continuing settlement at the periphery of middle- and working-class residents, is striking.

DECENTRALIZATION AND DENSITY TODAY

Clearly both residential and employment decentralization have been major forces in cities in developed countries for much of the twentieth century. In many ways the most important question about densities, decentralization, and sprawl today is to determine how these processes compare with those in the past. To read almost any account of the sprawl "crisis" one would assume that decentralization is accelerating, that the decline in overall densities is speeding up as people who can afford to do it are constantly moving further out, and using more and more land per person in the process. Speakers at any conference on Smart Growth are likely to bemoan the 5 and 10 acre "ranchettes" and other large-lot developments. Rather startlingly, there is very little evidence for increasing per capita land use in most American cities, and, in fact, quite a bit of evidence that the reverse is happening: the decentralization process has slowed, densities are not being reduced at nearly the same rate as in the past, and an increasing number of American cities may be entering a period of increasing density.

In Chicago, the statement most commonly used by anti-sprawl reformers is that between 1970 and 1990 the population grew by 4 percent but the amount of land used for urban purposes grew by 46 percent. To begin, it might be useful to consider several assumptions built into the Chicago anti-sprawl campaign slogan. The first is the assumption that normal growth ought to mean that the amount of land used should not exceed population growth. But why should this be assumed? Why not assume that as population grows and society becomes more wealthy it is perfectly justifiable to use more land for urban purposes? Even if it is assumed that land use should track in some way demographic trends, why the assumption that population growth, rather than, for example, growth in the number of households or growth in the number of jobs, would be the appropriate factor to use?

A more basic question is what the Chicago figures really mean. Would the apparent disproportionate use of land be considered a crisis if the change from farmland and open space to urban purposes in the period 1970-1990 actually represented a decline from previous levels? What if Chicago had stopped decentralization altogether and was in the process of getting denser rather than less dense? Wouldn't this suggest that sprawl, or at least land use disproportionate to population growth, might be stopping on its own without any planning effort? There seems to be considerable evidence that all these things are, in fact, happening. If so, the most basic factual underpinnings of the current anti-sprawl argument would appear to be questionable or even fundamentally wrong.

The chief difficulty in trying to document these trends is the discontinuity of evidence. Virtually all anti-sprawl arguments tend to rely on extrapolations into the future of statistics like the ones used in Chicago; that is, statistics from a single recent decade or at most two and usually a decade already some time in the past. The question is, how can these figures be put into a larger historic perspective? The most easily accessible measure of this trend is contained in the figures the Census Bureau has collected for America's urbanized areas since 1950. The idea of the urbanized area was to give a functional definition of the city rather than one that followed governmental boundaries, making it by far the best measure for studying density. Evidence from these figures clearly shows a decline in the rate of residential decentralization. For example, Chicago, which experienced a decline in density of 15.3 percent in the 1960s, showed a decline of 13.9 percent in the following decade, and of only 5.3 percent in the 1980s. In a more sophisticated analysis prepared by the Urban Transportation Center at the University of Illinois at Chicago, an index of decentralization based on the average distance of any pair of inhabitants in the region using the townships as population centroids registers a period of maximum decentralization up to the end of the 1960s and then a declining rate of decentralization for each decade after that up until 1990, the last year a full set of figures were available (Sen 1998, Appendix 10). Figures from the Northeast Illinois Planning Commission indicate that by the mid-1990s the use of land was tracking fairly closely the growth in population in the Chicago region. From almost any perspective, it appears to be clear that after the 1960s the rate of residential decentralization has slowed down considerably, and the urbanized region may be in the process of becoming more dense.

Similar patterns can be seen in most large cities in the Midwest and Northeast. In many of the cities in the South and West, on the other hand, particularly in the fastest growing ones, recent decades have witnessed not just a slowing of the decline in residential density but a reversal of it. For example, from 1950 to 1990 Los Angeles increased in density over 26.4 percent. Because Los Angeles was already one of the densest of the sunbelt cities at the end of World War II and because it grew in density in virtually every decade since then while urbanized areas in the Midwest and Northeast were losing density, it found itself by the 1990s as America's single densest urbanized area (Wendell Cox, www.Publicpurpose.com). These trends are confirmed by other scholars using other means of analysis who come to a similar conclusion: that the period of maximum decentralization in American cities was probably over at least by the end of the 1960s and that American urban dwellers are using less land per capita (Mieszkowski and Mills 1993; Vesterby and Heimlich 1991).

Another indication of this trend can be found in residential lot sizes. Although writing by sprawl reformers suggests that residential lot sizes have gotten continuously bigger over the years, the evidence suggests otherwise. Although house sizes have increased substantially since World War II, lot sizes have remained more or less steady or have declined slightly (National Association of Homebuilders 1998). It also appears that the amount of land used per capita by city dwellers has declined slightly. This can also be confirmed by visual evidence. A trip to the outermost middle- and working-class suburbs of almost any American city today reveals a surprising number of multi-family residences, attached single-family residences, and detached houses on lots that are very small by postwar standards. One reason for this appears to be the fact that more often than in the past a less affluent population is seeking housing at the edge. Another reason might be the smaller size of American households and increasing unwillingness to spend the time taking care of large lots. This hypothesis is consistent with the trend toward condominium ownership and contracted care for outdoor spaces. A final reason for the current trend toward increasing density at the urban periphery of many cities might be the upward pressure on land prices due to the large collection of environmental and other restrictions increasingly in place in most American metropolitan areas, particularly those put in place during the last round of growth control in the 1960s and 1970s.

Whatever the causes, it is clear from even a casual glance at new development on the periphery of cities around the country that it is often much denser than it was in the immediate postwar years. In southern Orange County, for example, something like half of all new units in the 1990s were attached and were often in the range of 12 to 20 units per acre (Hotchkiss 1996). Even in the Midwest and Northeast, which have lower land prices and lower average densities at the edge, this trend is unmistakable. Chicago real estate analysts have predicted that something like 35 percent of housing starts in the Chicago region in the year

2000 will be attached dwellings. These attached dwellings are found both in the inner city and the far periphery, representing sharply decreased densities at the center and increased densities at the edge. In this convergence the city is becoming more like the suburbs and the suburbs more like the city.

In the case of both American and the European cities, then, two different things seem to have been happening in urban structure over the last 100 years. One is the rapid flattening of the residential density gradient. The other has been a rapid overall lowering of densities throughout the metropolitan area. Although it appeared for many years that these two things were inextricably related, it now appears as though they are not necessarily tied to one another. In American cities, at least, overall densities may be rising while the gradient continues to fall. However, in recent years even to talk about a density gradient from central core to outer edge is misleading. With the decentralization of employment and particularly with the development of effectively multinucleated cities, all the previous models for describing the city have become suspect. In a place like Phoenix, with one of the flattest density curves ever seen in a large metropolitan area, residential land densities and land prices hardly vary with distance from the center. In fact it is difficult to speak of a center here at all since the highest commercial land values are actually not downtown but in one of the outlying business centers. It is interesting to note about Phoenix that this remarkable decentralized pattern was largely accomplished without either much public transit or many freeways. Phoenix was very late in developing its freeway system, relying instead on low density and a wide arterial street grid (Gammage 1999).

In some ways the multi-nucleated American urban model is not dissimilar to one seen in a number of large urbanized areas in Europe, such as the Dutch Randstad and the German Rhein-Ruhr region. In both cases, clusters of cities, which because of their proximity and commercial interdependence have long operated as a kind of urban system, are now clearly part of a single, fused urban region. In recent years in the United States, these kinds of settlements are often even more widely dispersed and sometimes lack the large, traditional cities seen in the European examples. A good example of this very dispersed settlement can be seen in the Piedmont area of North Carolina. In this region, although Charlotte does function as a kind of urban center, it is really only one of a number of subcenters (Clay and Orr 1972; Hayes 1976). This very dispersed urban area houses a population at low overall densities with ridges of density extending for miles out along transportation lines. The most spectacular example of this highly dispersed urban system can be found on all sides of New York City. In western Connecticut, for example, clusters of small, formerly agricultural and industrial villages with varying degrees of independence from the surrounding business centers of New York, New Haven, Bridgeport, and Hartford have gentrified and developed into their own loose and very low-density urban system. In the process the last vestiges of traditional distinctions between urban, rural, and suburban have been lost, making it extremely difficult to talk about density in any of the old ways. Scenic areas over a hundred miles from New York City can look as though they are still agricultural landscapes with cultivated fields and small agricultural villages, but the farming may be done entirely on contract, and the actual economy as well as many of the social and cultural functions of the villages and their reason for being are connected with the distant urban center.

CAUSES OF DECENTRALIZATION

As I hope I have suggested, one of the chief reasons that the literature about sprawl has been so unsatisfactory has to do with the fact that the definition has been so vague and has changed so much over time. Even more problematic is the literature about the causes of sprawl. In conventional literature about decentralization two basic hypotheses have been put forward. The first is that this outward expansion was basically a matter of economic and technological determinism. Faster and cheaper modes of transportation led to expanded access to developable land. This in turn led to more development. The other explanation has explored the push rather than the pull factors in decentralization. According to this view the primary causes of outward growth have been social, economic, and environmental problems in the city. Not surprisingly, the first explanation has been most often cited by urban economists and the second by social scientists, planners, and others. Neither, as they are usually formulated, is satisfactory.

No one would deny that transportation played a major role in the decentralization of cities and the flattening of the density gradient. The kind of simple cause-and-effect relationship that is often described, however, is wholly inadequate. As we have already observed, a single means of transportation like the railroad could concentrate vast numbers of people and a great deal of commercial and industrial activity at one point, such as an American central business district or an apartment district near a train station, but it was also capable of dispersing both economic activity and population to quite distant points. This fact explains why central business interests supported both the railroad and the urban freeway. They felt that each of these modes of transportation would enhance their interests by concentrating the transportation web on the central business district. There is no doubt that each of these modes of transportation did that. However, there is also no doubt that they allowed the opposite to happen as well.

The same logic applies to the automobile. The usual assumption is that the automobile has been a major factor, even the primary factor, in decentralization. While there is obviously some truth to this, and American cities did, indeed, empty out at a fast pace during the period that stretches from the 1920s through the 1960s when automobile ownership rates were climbing rapidly, there is much evidence that the automobile, like the railroad, can be a centralizing as well as decentralizing force. So, for example, in the case of Los Angeles, it is conspicuous that the extremely dispersed city of the period 1880-1920 was created when the railroad and streetcar were the chief modes of urban transportation, and the increasingly dense city of the period since World War II has been accompanied by a near total abandonment of rail transportation and reliance on road-based transportation, especially the private automobile. It is even possible that more and better roads, including freeways, might well lead to higher urban densities in some cases because many people move further out in part to escape congestion.

Related to the transportation argument is another, essentially economic thesis, that decentralization is the logical, even inevitable, result of increasing affluence. According to this theory, as urban dwellers are able, they secure for themselves more and more land. Obviously there is some truth to this idea. In general, the large cities of the affluent developed world are far less congested than the cities of the developing world and, at least until recently, as cities in the developed world have become more affluent they have tended to become less dense (Sen, et al. 1998). However, this notion fails to account for much of what is readily visible on the ground in urban areas. It is not true, for example, that levels of density are uniformly lower with increasing levels of wealth among American cities. It is also obvious that a great many extremely affluent parts of most large cities are very high in density and conversely, many very low-income areas are low in density. The Upper East Side of New York counts among the highest densities of any city in the developed world yet it is also one of the wealthiest districts. On the other hand vast areas of many American inner cities and poor first-ring suburbs are currently at very low densities. If there was any simple equation between affluence and a desire to own more land, the last two decades would have produced massive increases in land consumed and this, as already discussed, simply has not happened.

It appears that it is not the amount of land that is crucial but a degree of control over the immediate environment that is important. The resident of a highrise coop apartment might be perfectly happy in a relatively small unit in a very high-density neighborhood if there are compensating social and cultural factors and a considerable degree of control over the immediate residential environment. A sweeping view across a park; a doorman to provide superior security; a chauffeur-driven car or taxi to get to work, to restaurants, or the theater; and a car parked within the building that can be used to get to a weekend house at the shore all go a long way to compensating for any perceived inconveniences of living at high densities. One of the reasons that the single-family house in the suburbs has been such a successful formula has been that it has allowed a large segment of the population to enjoy a similar kind of security, privacy, and control of immediate surroundings at a much lower cost. It might be said that space has been substituted for personnel. If this is true, it might be that substantial increases in affluence among urban dwellers could reduce the demand for low-density urban living and greatly increase the demand for luxury high-density living. It is possible that the modest but rising level of conversions of loft and office buildings into residential units in American downtowns today might be a precursor of large-scale future trends.

The second argument about the causes of sprawl, essentially a sociological one, is that decentralization and sprawl can be attributed primarily to flight from the problems of the central cities. This explanation by itself is just as problematic as the economic explanations. While it is true that many American urban dwellers did flee from pollution and congestion, poverty, racial tensions, and other problems, it is conspicuous that the rate of decentralization does not mirror in any straightforward way any of these variables. Although a great deal of attention has been paid to urban crime, poor schools, and the urban and racial unrest starting in the late 1960s, the highest rates of decentralization in most American cities occurred before these factors came to be perceived as national crises. Also, as Wendell Cox has demonstrated, the vast majority of suburban growth since World War II is largely fueled by simple natural growth and immigration and cannot be attributed to flight from the city (www.demographia.com). A particularly powerful argument against any simple correlation between central city flight and suburban growth would be the case of cities that have had relatively few of the classic American postwar central-city urban problems. In places like Minneapolis the population has spilled out from the central city to the periphery in a way very similar to that seen in Boston or Pittsburgh, suggesting that the push factor is not necessarily a pre-eminent force in decentralization. The same argument can be made by observing that patterns like those seen in American cities are appearing elsewhere around the world (Mills and Price 1984). Even some of the most important critics of recent development trends have admitted that there does not appear to be any straightforward connection between inner-city problems and urban sprawl (Downs 1999).

One final explanation of decentralization that requires some examination is the notion that government policies have contributed to the move of people from the city to the edge and the tendency to build at the edge at lower densities than they might otherwise have done. Among the policies commonly cited at the federal level are FHA housing standards; federal interest tax deductions for homeowners; funding for the extension of highways, sewers, and other infrastructure; and general federal spending patterns. Again there is probably some truth to some of these assertions. The problem is that they, like almost all the other factors usually cited to explain urban decentralization, are almost always double-edged swords. The mortgage interest deduction, for example, started life in the early part of the century as a simple deduction on personal interest. It was clearly not originally intended as a specific subsidy for single-family houses in any location and was not an important factor in housing in any case until the rising federal tax burden and inflation of the postwar years. Its effects have probably been greatly overestimated, moreover, since some portion, quite possibly a substantial portion, of any given individual's theoretical savings from the deduction would likely have been capitalized into the price of the housing (Voith 1999, 7; Hendershott and Abraham 1993). Any savings realized by a given individual would be further eroded by the higher property taxes owed local authorities because of this increase in house price.

More importantly, the mere observation that the majority of the subsidy historically went to suburban dwellers rather than to inhabitants of the central city does not justify the conclusion that the subsidy was necessarily place-specific. There is no reason the mortgage interest deduction could not have benefited the central city over the suburbs. Because the interest deduction was extended to owner-occupied units of all kinds by the 1960s, at just the time when it became an important incentive in residential real estate, housing units, whether in the city or in the suburbs, whether single-family homes or condominiums in multi-family buildings, were eligible. There is no reason that the federal income tax interest deduction could not have been used primarily within the city and have spurred an enormous boom in residential construction there if there had been a demand comparable to that for single-family houses in the suburbs. In that period there was a great deal of vacant land in virtually every central city in America, and even where vacant land was scarce, the very low density of most American cities and zoning permitting much higher levels would have made it possible to redevelop at greatly increased densities if there had been demand. It was the lack of demand rather than a bias in the subsidy that caused it to be used primarily in the suburbs.

The highways and freeways running from the center of American cities, likewise, were not conceived of by most government planners or elected officials primarily as a way to decentralize the city. In fact, as we have seen, they were often conceived of as measures to bolster the old downtowns. The same is true for virtually all federal governmental policies now thought to promote decentralization. With very few exceptions one could have predicted a decentralizing effect or one could have predicted effects that were entirely different. Close analysis of total federal expenditures, moreover, shows that even today they go more heavily to central cities than to peripheral communities (Parker 1995). If the expenditures by the federal government over the life of the cities are taken into account, it is likely that the subsidy of central areas of American cities, if not on the scale of European capitals, has dwarfed any subsidies given to the suburbs. There is certainly little to suggest any direct causal link between federal policies and sprawl (U.S. General Accounting Office 1999).

It also has been argued that the policies of local governments have contributed to decentralization and to sprawl. Claims have been made that zoning regulations and building codes, which often have been used to segregate land use and mandate large minimum lot sizes, accelerate the pace of decentralization. There is certainly some truth to these assertions. However, the fact that these exclusionary regulations in most American cities are of fairly recent date and that decentralization was clearly visible before they became important elements in urban development, tends to suggest that they have not been critical factors. Like so many other aspects of suburban development, it might be considered a symptom of the desire for lower density rather than a cause of it. If densities are starting to edge up at the edge of many cities, moreover, this fact would suggest that zoning is again following, rather than causing, land use trends.

If virtually every factor thought to cause sprawl is a double-edged sword, it follows that there is no reason that those same factors might not also cause a recentralization, as, in fact, has happened in many cities in the south and west of the United States. It also suggests that deliberate efforts to recentralize might not be necessary or might even be harmful if those efforts accelerate the process too much. On the other hand, given the complexity of urban systems, the severe limits in our understanding of how they work, and the record of large-scale reform movements of the past, those efforts could cause results that are the opposite of what is intended. For example, new rail systems, widely advocated as a means of recentralizing sprawling cities, could, in fact, have the primary effect of making it easier for people and jobs to move more easily outward from existing centers. Likewise, stopping new freeways, rather than limiting outward sprawl, might easily lead to more congestion that would push people farther out.

There is certainly some reason to believe that growth boundaries or tight restrictions around any given city, such as Portland, Oregon, or Boulder, Colorado, would just push growth out farther than it would have otherwise and to other cities, sharply raising land prices and hurting affordability in the city that instituted the growth measures, in the process.

THE FIGHT AGAINST LOW DENSITY

In a paper of this scale I cannot adequately detail the various charges leveled against sprawl: that it is inefficient, inequitable, environmentally damaging, socially irresponsible, and aesthetically ugly. What I would like to do instead is to look for a moment at the campaign to raise densities. This process has been called consolidation, and the opposite of sprawl has often been described as the "compact city." Critics of this approach in Britain have used the descriptive but derogatory term *town cramming* to describe the process.

One of the most paradoxical aspects of consolidation or compaction is the degree to which this campaign is heir to the efforts clearly visible at least up until World War II to spread the city out at lower densities. In fact, the single greatest concern of city planning at the time it became a consciously constituted practice in the late nineteenth century was to reduce excessive densities. For most planning reformers the chief goal was to redevelop high-density central areas and to disperse their population to much lower density settlements on the periphery (Bruegmann, forthcoming b).

From garden cities at the turn of the century to urban renewal after World War II, professional planners were preoccupied with reducing densities. The evils of urban "blight" permeated much of the literature up through the postwar years. That densities fell, often very dramatically, is clear. What is unclear is how much conscious planning caused the massive decentralization, which was already underway by the time most of the reformers discovered the evils of high density. The lowering of densities, moreover, was more striking in America without centralized planning than in Europe with a good deal of it. The way this decentralization occurred and the resulting landscape was deeply troubling for many of the very reformers who had so ardently advocated it. So, starting in the interwar years in Britain there was a parallel literature. The majority of what was published still inveighed against overly high densities, but there was a rising tide of commentary about the evils of unplanned, low-density development out into the countryside. With this campaign came the term *sprawl* as a noun used in something like its present sense (Bruegmann, forthcoming a). Curiously enough, the solutions to low-density sprawl were the same solutions as had been advocated for high-density blight. Growth boundaries, greenbelts, new towns were all part of the package. It might be argued that these tools, which were clearly influenced by specific class-based aesthetic preferences, were a set of solutions searching for problems.

The first wave of anti-sprawl writing between the two world wars resulted in the British postwar planning scheme. This set of regulations put enormous powers into the hands of the central government, which used it to enforce the ideas of the interwar reformers. Attempts to contain London did, in fact, stop much of the development from continuing into the greenbelt around the city. However, it did so at the price of driving up land costs sharply and perhaps accelerating the trend of decentralization beyond the belt, probably causing longer commuting times and lower density development than if nothing had been done (Hall 1973). The second great wave of anti-sprawl writing came in the 1950s and 1960s, particularly in the United States, in response to the very rapid growth and decentralization of the postwar years. This resulted in the second anti-sprawl campaign, the so-called slow-growth and no-growth movements of the 1960s and 1970s. In Petaluma, California, in Ramapo, New York, and elsewhere, municipalities used building moratoria, growth boundaries, large-lot zoning, and impact fees to discourage growth. Not surprisingly, as in the case of London, these had the effect of driving up prices and pushing development beyond the boundaries (Garvin 1996, pp. 381–383). One result of this process was that the present anti-sprawl reformers often blame the last round of growth control measures as one of the principal causes of today's problems.

Another legacy of the postwar campaign against growth and sprawl is a widespread anti-highway sentiment. Arguing that it was impossible to "build our way out of congestion" because new road building just induces travel, reformers managed to convince many urban dwellers that it was a good idea to curb the urban road-building program. Of course, it was possible to "build our way out of congestion," as the very success of the early freeways conclusively proved. They dramatically reduced travel times and congestion all over urban America. If they had not, there would never have been the subsequent literature that placed the blame for massive decentralization squarely on these very freeways. A number of cities have also proved that building roads can substantially relieve congestion (Dunphy 1997). Nevertheless, despite the very dubious assumptions, the anti-highway lobby was successful in stopping a number of key urban freeways. Some of these halted projects were eventually completed. Some are still a subject of acrimonious debates. But some were just stopped, and all subsequent urban highway building became much more difficult. Not surprisingly, the fact that road building has not kept up with vehicle use has led to increased traffic problems. Given the nearly insignificant role that public transportation plays in this country, except to deliver people to the cores of a few large cities, even in metropolitan areas that have devoted billions of dollars to new rail systems, it could not have been otherwise.

In short, the complaints about sprawl and proposed remedies have resurfaced every few decades since the 1920s. Every generation has seen an increase in the vehemence of these complaints and a call for a return to the better-planned, more compact settlement patterns seen in the prior era. In this process, there has occurred an astonishing shift in expectations. In the interwar years planners like Thomas Sharp railed against the then-current British planning efforts, based on Garden City principles, to create what he considered excessively low densities of 12 housing units per acre (Sharp 1932, p. 220). At four persons per household at the time this would have yielded 48 people per acre or over 30,720 people per square mile. At the upper end of the spectrum Patrick Abercrombie held that central urban densities should be reduced to no higher than

136 per acre or over 87,000 people per square mile. As late as 1957 the well-known planner Hans Blumenfeld stated that ideal densities should be between 20 to 100 persons per square acre or 12,000 to 60,000 persons per square mile (Blumenfeld 1967, p. 172). By the time Anthony Downs wrote his influential book *New Visions for Metropolitan America* in 1994, his proposal for what he called "very high" density housing in American cities would have averaged 12.5 dwelling units per acre or 10,000 people per square mile. Of course, even Down's proposed dramatic rise in new residential development could happen only very slowly because of the great weight of existing building stock in American urbanized areas, which by 1990 averaged well under 5,000 people per square mile (Downs 1994). So, the desired urban density according to urban reformers has been on a rapidly descending trajectory for decades, constantly lagging behind the realities on the ground by a generation. This, in turn, suggests that many reformers take as normal the conditions they observed in their youth and argue for policies to bring the world back to that point. It also suggests that it might be more useful for urban reformers to speed up the process of adjusting their expectations about the city rather than trying to remake it to conform to these expectations at any given moment.

I think that the history we have been discussing indicates that the driving force in the anti-sprawl movement has never been anything as objective as density itself. It comes as no surprise that not one anti-sprawl reformer has ever advocated Los Angeles as a model despite the fact that it has the highest density of any urbanized area in the country. The reason is that it is not really the density itself but the appearance of urban areas and their symbolic social function that is most important to reformers. Likewise, the problem with the single-family house on an acre of land was rarely low density per se. It was that this arrangement was considered by certain reformers, particularly urban professionals living in apartment buildings, as antithetical to their own personal view of the way cities should work. They disliked neighborhoods of detached, single-family houses because these neighborhoods, unlike the ones in central cities with dense apartment buildings, crowded sidewalks, and bustling parks, were not places that fostered traditional high culture and did not provide visual evidence of traditional social interactions. Riding in private vehicles was likewise unacceptable because it did not conform to a view of transit-riding as a desirable, communal activity. They further objected on aesthetic grounds to what they saw as the monotony of places like Los Angeles that have relatively similar densities spread out over large areas. They preferred the appearance of traditional European cities with their dense historic centers, even if the physical fabric of some of these centers had an extremely negative effect on the health and well-being of their inhabitants.

To obtain what they consider a more urban pattern, reformers have advocated measures that attempt to shape the appearance of the city by reinforcing density in some places and creating open space in others. Well-known efforts to control the shape of cities include the green belts around British cities starting in the 1930s; the axes of development and new towns planned around Paris and the high-density radial spokes prescribed in plans for the Washington DC area, both in the 1960s; and the urban growth boundaries around Portland, Oregon, instituted in the 1970s. The result in each case was directed toward the same end: to impose specific aesthetic norms on metropolitan areas and to preserve visual and symbolic distinctions between city and country. Each was also, at one scale or another, an explicit move to try to reverse the trend of flattening in the density gradient. Like almost any other remedy that is trying to impose specific aesthetic ideas and to buck strong and deeply rooted market forces, these efforts were necessarily based on top-down governmental planning. Finally, each represented an attempt to turn the clock back to re-establish some very specific and highly subjective notions about what proper city form should be.

By now the record of large-scale urban reforms of this kind ought to suggest that the measures propounded by a professional elite of one generation are likely to be blamed by that same elite a generation later either for compounding the problems or for producing other, unintended consequences. Consider for a moment the shifts of opinion on electrical power generation that have led successively to the damming of Western rivers, to the building of nuclear power plants, and then to the subsequent fall from favor of both. Or the way old row houses were swept away to create new public housing blocks that are now being removed in favor of row houses similar to those originally occupying the sites. Similar shifts in opinion have been registered on zoning, urban renewal, freeway building, pedestrian malls, and many other planning initiatives of recent decades. Although a balanced historical treatment of these campaigns will probably show that they were neither as beneficial as initial proponents predicted nor as damaging as later critics have claimed, there is no doubt that elite opinion can oscillate from one pole to the other in rapid succession. There is, at very least, little evidence to justify the optimism of the current anti-sprawl crusaders. Our contemporary urban areas are so complicated that they defy description, let alone silver-bullet solutions like the compact city. In many ways, the anti-sprawl crusade seems to be a classic example of the problems that arise when social scientists, planners, and others rush into complicated human systems filled with nineteenth-century zeal that they can transform the world by replanning its physical structure. A little more research into the history and current state of our metropolitan areas and a great deal more modesty in goals would probably be in everyone's best interest. It is fascinating to speculate on what urban densities will be like in fifty years precisely because we are so likely to be completely wrong.

Chapter 10

Property Rights in a Complex World

ROGER E. MEINERS AND ANDREW P. MORRISS

The Smart Growth movement is presumed to be a well-intended effort to produce a higher quality of life and to protect environmental assets. However, Smart Growth requires significant land-use controls imposed by governments at various levels. Because controls, by definition, restrict personal freedom, they should not be imposed lightly. As other chapters in this book demonstrate, land-use planning has not been the glorious success its proponents had hoped for when the controls and programs were advocated and implemented. Before we enter into further expansion of government restrictions on land use, it is useful to reflect on the legal system that generated freedom, wealth, and environmental quality. We start by returning to first principles.[1]

The law of real property in the United States traces its roots to the Norman Conquest of England in 1066 (Simpson 1986). Like most central authorities around the world, the new king of England, William, asserted all land was under his control. He granted varying rights to land to key supporters in exchange for continued military services. It was William's intent that his lords only be tenants and that land would revert to the crown on the death of a lord or in case military services were not rendered. But the lords, or tenants-in-chief, had other ideas. They wished for their heirs to have the land rather than for it to revert to the crown, and that soon became the common practice. Over the centuries, the law evolved into the common law of property we know today.

The basic components of American property law thus originated in legal conflicts between England's aristocracy and monarchs. Covenants and servitudes, easements and profits, the "fee simple absolute," and the tenancy in common—the elements of property law today—all grew out of English common law centuries ago. How can legal rules devised by such a system be other than archaic and obsolete? In a world in which e-commerce and intellectual property issues are widely seen as demanding immediate changes in the law, is it not time to break with the past in property law? How do these rules of property apply to land development, land-use planning, and the current Smart Growth movement?

The rules of Anglo-American property law offer a resilient mechanism that has not only formed the foundation for our current prosperity but which promises to adapt to our future better than any planned alternative. However technically demanding particular rules of property law may be, common law property rules as a whole compose what Richard Epstein labeled "simple rules for a complex world" (Epstein 1995).

Property law offers a set of legal tools to solve land-use problems. Teaching law students about property is, in large part, equipping them with these tools: estates in land, future interests, covenants, easements, servitudes, and nuisance suits all precede planning tools like zoning in most lawyers' educations. These legal concepts provide a rich set of alternative solutions to problems planners have traditionally approached through command and control mechanisms like zoning. In this chapter we suggest some of the reasons why property rights solutions are superior to the more traditional planning approaches.

The working of the market economy, and the long-term success of the economy, is intertwined in the rights and responsibilities generated by the common law of property. This chapter focuses on the need for strong private property rights to maintain freedom and prosperity. In so doing, it raises important concerns about the costs of compromising property rights in the wake of recent attempts to impose top-down planning through growth management. The complexity of the modern world does not diminish the need for private property; indeed, it strengthens its imperative.

THE NATURE AND SOURCE OF PROPERTY RIGHTS

Modern "rights talk" often centers around sloppy definitions of the term *rights*. For example, the Montana Constitution drafted in 1972 includes a "right to a clear and healthful environment" among its guarantees. Similarly, Soviet-era eastern bloc constitutions contained laundry lists of rights to housing, education, and the like. Closer to home, political debate in the United States often features discourse on rights to benefits defined by political fiat, such as the right to subsidized medical care.

Property rights are quite different from such political rights. Property rights are negative rights; that is, they define the ability to exclude others from participating in decisions about how resources are used. Thus our property rights in our homes allow us to prevent you from moving in with either of us but say nothing about whether our houses are adequate or whether you have to contribute to paying for renovations that will make them so. Rights to medical care, by contrast, require us to contribute to paying your doctors' bills, something that may conflict with our rights to adequate housing.

Property rights differ from politically-granted rights in another important way—property rights predate the state. School children are taught a story that goes something as follows: After the Revolution, the founding fathers wrote the Constitution to establish the Republic and to provide rights to citizens. This modern myth, that the Constitution is "the supreme law of the land," was certainly not what was understood at the time the document was written. When the nation was founded, English common law, and the rights and duties it provides for all citizens, was left in place. The writers of the Constitution presumed inalienable rights that we hold simply by virtue of being a free people in a free nation. As one British legal scholar noted over a century ago, "personal freedom does not really depend upon or originate in any general proposition contained in any written document" (Dicey 1982, p. 123).

The Constitution created the framework for government, expressly limited the powers of government, and provided safeguards against invasions of certain rights. The Constitution did not grant us the rights we have as citizens. Citizens were presumed to have a host of individual rights, often referred to in those days as based on natural law. Some of the natural law was expressed in the common law, but the founders presumed that there were fundamental and inalienable rights with which the government may not interfere. Unlike most countries in the world, a free people chose to establish the government of the United States, which had circumscribed powers.

Property rights' independence of centralized government authority can be seen in the experience of nineteenth-century gold miners in the American West (Morriss 1998; Umbeck 1981). Finding themselves in areas with no government authority, Gold Rush miners, drawn from virtually every corner of the globe, immediately set about creating private systems to allocate and protect property rights. That experience was not unique.

Which is why the debate over private property rights is a key issue of constitutional significance. If traditional property rights are lost in favor of legislated controls over private property, a major cornerstone of liberty has been lost. We then become closer to being like most peoples of the world—having only the "rights" granted to us by governing bodies. In the case of property, with respect to our legal heritage, we are being thrown back a millennium—limited rights to use property are granted to favored citizens by those who control the government, be it a monarch or an elected body. While we tend to regard feudalism as a backward, anti-democratic form of organization, public policy in the United States is moving land control in that direction. No one would call it feudalism, but in practice it looks much like it, under the guise of environmental protection and to prevent alleged evils such as so-called urban sprawl. Under the new feudalism, citizens are allowed to own land, and be taxed on it, but its use is increasingly subject to a vast array of legislated controls that effectively make assorted governments the decisionmaker about how the land may be used. Thus ownership becomes only as meaningful as the sovereign allows it to be.

Common law property rights also differ from rights created by government fiat in another crucial dimension. The common law is an evolutionary process, one which gradually sharpens definitions over time in response to the facts of disputes. Fiat rights, on the other hand, are shaped by the political process and subject to sharp discontinuities in content. Thus the "right" to welfare benefits, championed by various legal scholars and adopted by the courts, underwent major changes over the decades before its demise in the 1990s welfare reform.

The dominant metaphor for property rights—a bundle of sticks—suggests a crucial difference between property rights and fiat rights. As the world changes, people discover new opportunities and problems that require reallocation of existing property rights. By allowing parties to combine and recombine individual sticks from the bundle in response to their evaluation of their needs, property law adapts to the modern world. Indeed, it is its remarkable ability to evolve that has enabled a set of legal rules and concepts originating in the Norman Conquest of England to remain useful and relevant almost one-thousand years later. Property rights, therefore, are negative, evolutionary, and not the result of political fiat.

The astonishing thing about property rights is that a system built on arbitrary rules created out of conflicts between long-dead English aristocrats and kings has proven so durable and flexible that it has enabled us to have a flourishing society today. Property rights, and property rules, are able to do this because they form part of a spontaneous order. A spontaneous order is not planned or constructed, it is not the result of human intention. It is nonetheless an order, as people sort out how to use their property and largely avoid harming others while doing so.

This is not to say that there are not many problems created by individual actions, problems that demand attention. The question is not, therefore, whether we should leave an ideal world of perfect markets or attempt to create such a world but rather how to cope with the problems that exist in society today. Two fundamental kits of tools are available: those based on human design and those based on spontaneous order. Planners have a choice between these two types of tools and have traditionally opted for the former.[2]

What do the methods that rely on spontaneous order look like? Spontaneous orders arise out of individuals' pursuit of their private interests through decentralized market mechanisms. For such solutions to arise there must be, therefore, well-defined and alienable property rights and dispute resolution mechanisms. It also requires that governments act through stable and well-defined rules that enable private actors to make choices. Randall Holcombe's suggestion (see Chapter 8) that planners can contribute by making road-building decisions far enough in advance to allow private actors to respond is thus an excellent example of this approach.

How do planners affect property rights? Thinking of the problem in terms of the metaphor of the bundle of sticks can be helpful here. When governments add discretionary steps to decision-making processes—often in an effort to shift from seemingly harsh rule-based systems to "common sense" approaches—the result is to blur the definition of the sticks in the bundle. When governments restrict land use, they remove sticks from the bundle. Both these steps hinder individuals from engaging in voluntary transactions that increase social welfare by making those transactions more costly. The lack of clarity about rights' content and the lack of transferable rights thus impede solutions. The next section describes an all-too-typical example of how this can occur.

A Modern Property Law Saga

As noted earlier, this conception of property rights that has served well for centuries is under siege and the "pure" version of property rights is increasingly "polluted" by statutory and regulatory intrusions. Consider the case of Lloyd Good's property, which was recently concluded at the U.S. Court of Appeals (*Good v. U.S.* 1999). Good purchased property on Lower Sugarloaf Key, Florida, in 1973, a part of Monroe County. In 1980, he took steps to develop about 10 acres of his property for residential lots on canals that would allow direct boat access. After hiring a firm to begin the process of obtaining permits from various agencies, Good received a permit from the Army Corps of Engineers in 1983 that would allow some dredging and filling of wetlands. The county government objected to the permit, however, so the construction plans were amended and a new Army Corps permit, valid for five years, was issued in 1984, subject to further Corps amendments. The Corps insisted Good wait for further review, which resulted in a third permit being issued in 1988, one that further reduced the construction area.

During the eight years that the Army Corps was evaluating matters, Monroe County had instituted new restrictions that required development to be "in harmony with natural ecology" (*Good v. U.S.* 1997, 87). When Good sought a building permit, the county rejected his request, saying it had a moratorium on all major developments. Good appealed to the Monroe Country Board of Adjustment and was rejected; his appeal to the Monroe County Commission was successful, however, and Good was issued a dredge and fill permit in 1984. A state agency, the Florida Department of Community Affairs (DCA), then appealed the county's approval of Good's permits to another state agency the Florida Land and Water Adjudicatory Commission (FLAWAC), which, in 1986, rejected the building plans. In the meantime, the County had issued new construction rules that posed further barriers for Good. Good sued FLAWAC in state court. Although the state court held in 1987 that the permit rejection was improper, it nonetheless required Good to comply with the new Monroe County rules that had gone into effect after the improper permit rejection.

Good prepared new development plans, which were filed in 1989. Five months later, the county granted preliminary approval, subject to approval also being granted by a third state agency, the South Florida Water Management District (SFWMD). Good dutifully applied to SFWMD. Six months later, in 1990, the application was rejected. In the meantime, the preliminary approval from the county expired since it has a one-year limit on its validity, thereby requiring Good to begin a new application to the county. Good informed the Army Corps of his problems with state agencies and scaled back his development proposal to the Corps in an application filed in 1990.

During the years Good spent in this regulatory labyrinth, three species that live on Sugarloaf Key were added to the endangered species list: a turtle, a rabbit, and a rat. The listing now obligated the Army Corps and the Fish and Wildlife Service (FWS) to take this wildlife into account in evaluating Good's 1990 permit application. The Corps and the FWS tussled over the matter, the Corps allowing its permit to stand; the FWS recommending it be revoked until further biological studies had been done. In 1991 the FWS released a new biological study, which urged further restrictions on construction. Good responded in 1992 with an opinion by an environmental consultant he hired, who opined that the development would not impact the endangered species.

In 1994, the Corps denied Good's 1990 application on grounds of habitat loss for endangered species and notified Good that his 1988 permit had expired and would not be reapproved. Good sued the federal government later in 1994, contending it had taken his property for habitat protection. Although in 1995 the FWS issued a report that it would approve scaled-back development (8 lots versus the 54 originally planned), Good's Army Corps permits had all expired and he proceeded with his suit. The Court of Federal Claims then denied Good's claim because habitat protection did not destroy all economic value. Good appealed to the Federal Court of Appeals, which, in 1999, also held against him.

Twenty-six years after the purchase of the land, and nineteen years after beginning the permit approval process, the appeals court held that Good had no suit for compensation, essentially because not all economic value in the property had been destroyed. While none of the relevant statutes or regulations blocking his development had been in place when Good bought the property, the court found that at that time (1973) the Army Corps "had been considering environmental criteria in its permitting decisions" (*Good v. U.S.* 1999, 1361). Good thus had to know that "rising environmental awareness translated into ever-tightening land use regulations" (*Good v. U.S.* 1999, 1362).

No doubt Good was aware that the rules regarding development were ever tightening, although given that the delays in his development all stemmed from the government agencies it is hard to know what he could have done to speed things up. Nor do we doubt that the decision of the court is correct; the Supreme Court has held that unless a regulation destroys nearly all economic value of land, there is no taking. Hence, the odds of compensation being required when "only" 85 percent of the building plans are eliminated is very unlikely. Land developers can repeat many administrative horror stories. Good's case is unique only in that he devoted large resources to the legal process rather than throwing in the towel or allowing government agents to dictate every aspect of his land development—if the agents from conflicting agencies could have ever agreed on what, if any, development they thought was appropriate.

Administrative Property

Property owners must know that as they enter into the nearly endless permit procuring processes, rules could tighten ever more, so one could well get caught in an endless loop of federal and state regulatory agencies offering conflicting rules. There is no redress for landowners who incur massive bills for lawyers, environmental consultants, permit specialists, and so on, all with no certainty in outcome. The permit givers are the parties who have the most legal ability to determine land use. Lloyd Good is like a feudal serf, allowed to use a piece of a federal-state estate for very limited purposes that may change at the whim of one of the many representatives of the crowns.

If Good's story were unique, it could be dismissed as an aberration; an unfortunate soul lost in the bowels of the normally well-meaning bureaucracy. But this story is no aberration. Remember the horror of biologist Bill Ellen, sent to federal prison for the crime of reclaiming land to become a wildlife sanctuary in Maryland. Ellen failed to get a permit to help a wealthy landowner restore duck ponds and other habitat that had been destroyed by years of cattle pasturing (Yandle 1995). The case drew substantial attention. Attention is the purpose of such prosecutions. Propertyholders are on notice that if they do not jump through all hoops required by various emissaries of the state, which may change at any time, it may be off to jail. Cross the line, fixed or not, regardless of your purpose, and the value of your property may be destroyed and your life left in shambles.

In a nutshell, the general rule regarding current governmental regulation of private property is that, so long as there is a statutory basis for a regulation and regulators have jumped through the appropriate procedural hoops in writing and enforcing regulations under the statutory authority granted to them by the federal or a state legislature, nearly any control may be imposed on any property. Only if there is near total destruction of the value of the property by a change in regulation need there be compensation under the Takings Clause of the Fifth Amendment.[3] If the government wants title to property, it must pay fair market value. Short of taking title to property or destroying its economic value, agencies may, under a variety of statutes, destroy most of the value of property or effectively force it to be used for purposes favored by the agencies. The threat of such action is enough to force many landowners to cooperate in an effort to salvage some of their property. Planners have discovered this and are enjoying great success in persuading property owners to "donate" bike paths and development rights in return for permit approval. Such a course of action destroys the essential element of property rights, converting them from a decentralized mechanism built around negative rights to a centralized, fiat-right. If planners could be relied on to get it right this might not be as catastrophic a development as it is. The nature of planning, however, means that such an approach is doomed to failure.

Consider the private law alternatives. Among the mechanisms available to individuals are such land-use tools as easements, real covenants, servitudes, and nuisance suits. If Monroe County had used these tools it could easily have purchased legal interests from Lloyd Good that would have both accomplished its purpose of wetlands protection and allowed Good to make use of his property. For example, the County could have purchased easements and covenants to protect the wetland area from development. That these solutions would have cost the county money is not a flaw in the solution but a crucial feature. By making the county face opportunity costs, the price of the various solutions would force the county to make explicitly the tradeoffs among its various goals.

Politics or Planning?

Political pressure can be expected to play a major role in the structure of statutes that affect property values, just as politics determines most legislative outcomes. Special interests may seek to enhance the value of their property by providing special benefits to it, by imposing restrictions on competitors' property that makes it less desirable, or by simply seeking to avoid bearing costs that are threatened by new rules—that is, be grandfathered in so the new rules do not impinge on what exists now. The special interest nature of the statutory process cannot be avoided, so those who seek to have controls on property for scientific planning purposes have a massive hurdle to overcome—to get legislators to ignore the interests that are a part of the legislative process. This is, we believe, a utopian dream, but poses a serious problem that advocates of scientific planning of property by government must address.

Further, for those who believe there can be a world in which legislators are immune to special interest pressures, so that efficient central planning is feasible, they have the so-far impossible chore of showing that central planners can make effective or fair use of property. One of the great lessons of the last century was that socialist planning of resources produces ecological and economic disasters. Central planning of land use cannot produce wheat efficiently. The notion that government planners can design how people in complex societies should organize their physical arrangements on land and in houses better than people can decide for themselves as they interact with each other freely is improbable. Further, unless one believes that the ruling elite deserve to exploit the masses, there is nothing fair about the results of central control wherever it has been used. It is also worth noting that the federal government is, by almost any measure, a dreadful keeper of environmental assets.[4]

What, then, is the alternative to state planning and control of property use? Our argument is that it is the traditional common law process that has largely been abrogated by modern regulatory regimes. Private property rights, backed by a state that supports enforcement of such rights, provides for the greatest degree of personal responsibility and opportunity for ordinary people to enjoy their lives in manners most pleasing to them. This is a legal regime in which there is little role for federal government activity with respect to the regulation of private property. While the title of this chapter concerns property rules in a complex world, it is not at all clear that modern complexities mean that traditional common law rules of property are less able to handle challenges posed by bad behavior or new difficulties than was the case in years past. The world may be more complex than a century ago, but the added knowledge and technology mean that we can now address problems that previously could not be understood or solved.

Moreover, we can address those problems using a flexible set of land management tools developed by the private sector. Real covenants, easements, servitudes, and defeasible estates make it possible to creatively solve a wide range of problems yet retain the flexibility of the private property rights system. A local government or nonprofit organization can purchase specific rights in land to address density or environmental concerns at a cost far less than purchasing the land itself. If conditions change, however, making a different use more valuable in one hundred years, the gains from trade can be exploited and the rights recombined into a new configuration at far lower cost than changing a statutory scheme or comprehensive plan. Because these rights transfers must be negotiated only among the affected individuals, the transactions costs are far lower than those associated with state-wide (or even county-wide) planning processes.

Let Me Be, Let Me Be (The Turtles)

Those who decry urban sprawl are, at base, asserting that private parties, left to their own devices, dealing in real property with each other by contract under traditional property law, cannot produce an acceptable ordering of people in their physical locations. People will choose inappropriate locations that are inefficient and ecologically destructive. This is simply the standard market failure argument with a green tint. Because of this failure, government planners at one or more levels must be trusted, with appropriate citizen input, to force people, in their homes and businesses, to favor certain locations and building designs over locations and designs they might otherwise prefer to choose. This is accomplished by taxes, subsidies, and regulations that force people to locate in certain places chosen by regulators or forbid certain uses of property.[5]

Zoning and building regulations have long done much of this, but those who believe urban sprawl should be prevented know there must be more than traditional building controls; more comprehensive planning of land utilization is being advocated. Without considering the inevitable role of politics in such planning, that is, presuming that planners can do their job without special interest intervention, we contend that the planners—no matter how well intentioned, how well informed, or how intelligent—cannot do a better job than people will without such direction. Planners could not produce something as simple as bread in the Soviet Union; they certainly cannot plan something as complex as an extended urban area that will produce results superior to largely unregulated development.

Central planning of land use is conceptually no different than central planning of the communications industry or of food production. The justification for land planning must be that planners can produce a more efficient, less environmentally destructive, and desirable use of land than can a huge decentralized network of people dealing with each other through the market. Centralized planning of land use is incredibly complex, just as it is complex for people to decide to grow wheat—to obtain all the supplies needed to do so, to produce and sell the output, which eventually is turned into bread that appears on store shelves. It happens; but the fact that it happens is so difficult for our minds to comprehend, because of the incredibly complex interactions that occur, that it has long been common for people to assert that there must be central oversight of such processes or they cannot possibly work.

Uncoordinated Markets

To value things, whether it be land preservation or home construction, does not require direct or conscious valuation (pricing) by all persons who benefit from such goods. The incentive structure we call the market weaves uncountable decentralized individual exchange relationships into an extensive web. Explicit valuations only occur at the many events when an actual voluntary exchange occurs. The results of these many revealed valuations are communicated through what we know as the market, across time and space, as signals to other market participants about what is most desired. These signals serve as inputs into the decisions made by current and potential market participants who may know nothing about the details of particular transactions or the parties involved.

Market values are the unintended and undesigned results of decentralized market activity that reflect the preferences and wealth of the persons involved. Market participants confront prices of goods and services in which they are potentially interested in offering or buying. When a person values a good, he does not determine the market price of a good. Instead, as a supplier or a buyer, a person chooses how much he will sell or buy, if any, given what others have determined they are willing to sell or buy. Hence, determination of market values is not in any one party's hands and is typically spread over such a large number of persons that no one person has more than a trivial effect on market values.

While each person at each exchange intentionally chooses the offer or acceptance price, in light of knowledge transmitted from other market participants, it is not correct to say that market values are consciously chosen (Hayek 1948). Consumers do not individually determine market outcomes; those are the result of uncoordinated individual determinations. Economic valuation is possible because no one person (or committee) is responsible for determining the market value of any good or service on the market.

If economic efficiency required consumers to value not only their homes but all of the inputs that go into their homes, it would be impossible for consumers to compute economically meaningful values for these items. No consumer could know enough to value all the inputs that go into the production of a single home. All each consumer knows, and reveals by action, is how much he values a particular home relative to all other choices that might have been made.

Consumers rely on suppliers because of the tremendous wealth-creating advantages of the division of labor so well explained by Adam Smith two centuries ago. While the advantages of specialization and the division of labor are well understood, less appreciated is Hayek's point about the division of knowledge. The competitive market process relies on individual valuations, many of which are done by specialists who focus on a part of the market, such as home construction or habitat preservation. Each valuation specialist enjoys access to "knowledge of the particular circumstances of time and place" (Hayek 1948, p. 84) as they learn about the values that others in the market possess.

What economists call market prices cannot be derived by a process other than by competition in a decentralized and competitive market. Values or prices arrived at by any other means are not comparable to the prices and values generated by persons interacting freely. Most advocates of urban planning probably do not deny that private provision of homes is efficient; there seem to be few advocates of government production of housing. The concern usually expressed is that the market will not provide enough environmental amenities such as green space because the market does not know how to provide such amenities, and that, in any event, less green space will be available because of the large number of people who appear to prefer to have their home on a parcel of private real estate that consumes more space than some planning advocates would prefer. Numerous arguments to this effect have been made to justify public provision of green space; in essence they all boil down to a claim that the market does not properly value the existence of environmental amenities.

The twentieth century has seen the spectacular failure of the central planning model as applied to economies as a whole. The collapse of the Soviet Union and its satellites leaves no question that central planners are incapable of organizing entire economies, whether through Five Year Plans (the Soviet Union), Great Leaps Forward (China), or National Socialism (Nazi Germany). The impossibility of the central planning model demonstrated by market theorists during the "Socialist Calculation Debate" of the first part of the twentieth century was confirmed by experience. Central planning is better thought of as an administrative state. Producers would submit production plans to the relevant central bureaucracies and be given permission to go forward with their plans after revisions were made by administrators. This is not unlike land development in many cities today and could become even more pervasive with Smart Growth plans. Land-use planning is not central planning of the economy, but can involve administrative controls over significant economic resources. Because controls are inherently in conflict with freedom and efficiency, they could not be implemented without clear rationales, goals, rules that can be followed, and limits on planner authority, so that Lloyd Good and Bill Ellen stories do not occur.

Land planners might offer one or both of the following arguments to justify applying central planning to land use. First, they may argue that using planning for a relatively small section of the economy will not have the disastrous consequences of applying it to the entire economy or that, even if such consequences exist, the costs imposed by such planning will at least be exceeded by planning's benefits. Second, they may argue that the environment differs from the production of bread in some fashion that allows planning to perform better with the respect to the environment than it does with respect to bread. Note that it is not sufficient merely to argue that market failures with respect to the environment are more severe than those that may exist with respect to bread. It is the relative performance of institutions that matters, not the absolute performance of one possible institution. In light of the century's disastrous experience with central planning, we suggest that the burden of persuasion must be against planning and in favor of markets.

Is There Not Enough?

How do we know if there is enough green space, territory for habitat protection, or some other environmental goal? Unless we are willing to cede the decision to an autocrat it comes down to popular preferences. The problem, then, is how to determine those preferences.

Markets operate by revealed preference—your actions in the marketplace reveal your preferences through your purchases. If people are offered small, efficient, low emission electric cars and large, gas-guzzling SUVs, we can tell by what they purchase which package of transportation services and environmental protection they prefer. Similarly, if people have a choice between high-density urban housing and large-lot homes in the suburbs, the relative prices of the two types of housing will reflect the relative demand. Planners, however, by definition must rely on non-market signals. How much are people willing to pay for various amenities that planners can force to have happen, such as greenbelts? Further, even if a majority support the provision of costly amenities, they should recognize that the overall consequence is higher-priced housing, a significant burden for lower-income people. Polls indicate that a large majority of people would like to see more environmental amenities. These polls may be accurate, but still not reflect real values (Boudreaux, Meiners, and Zywicki 1999).

Suppose a large number of people truthfully assert that they would be willing to devote some small sum to assist in the preservation of the Florida panther. Respondents to such questions answer based on the assumption that the panther is the only environmental amenity they will be asked to pay for, which is very different than when people have to calculate simultaneously (and know they must actually pay for) the values they place on all other possible environmental amenities, such as green space, national monuments, manatee habitat, tree frogs in Costa Rica, and endangered monkeys in Indonesia. To have more accurate information about personal valuation of environmental amenities, respondents must simultaneously evaluate all relevant amenities, so they could calculate how much they would be willing to pay for panther habitat, knowing that they also wish to donate their personal resources to other desired environmental goods. Further, such a schedule of values must also include how much each person will spend on housing, taxes, food, clothing, transportation, and other existing and future goods and services already under consideration. This is a terribly complex calculation, yet it is one we all make every day as we allocate our resources to multiple purposes.

Valuing environmental amenities is no more difficult than valuing green beans, movies, or church donations we choose, or choose not, to devote resources to. Those who happen to have strong preferences for certain environmental amenities simply do not like the fact that other people choose not to devote as much of their resources to their favored amenity as they would like. But this is no different than some other person's distress at the "failure" of the market to provide a Somalian-food restaurant near where they live. The fact that many people do not share our desire for particular goods or public policies does not mean there is market failure or government failure.

Not only are market valuations the result of uncountable numbers of valuations of participants, but values are constantly changing so that a snapshot of values today is not reflective of values tomorrow. The essence of market activity is its entrepreneurial dynamics and creativity. Prices change constantly to reflect changed facts, values, and new opportunities. Unless resource owners are allowed to react to changing values, market results can not reflect the desires of market participants. If market reflection of personal valuations are restricted, the allocation of resources grows further and further out of kilter and individual freedom has been reduced.

Is It a Public Good?

Another issue that must be considered is if, accuracy of valuation aside, the market will not provide environmental amenities, public intervention may be justified. Public provision of certain services, such as national defense, have long been assumed necessary because there is no other way to be protected from invaders. The military may be an inefficient provider of national defense, so the argument goes, but Microsoft and General Motors are not going to produce national defense because people will not volunteer to pay for enough defense. People (usually "other" people) must be compelled to pay for national defense or we will not have enough and may suffer a catastrophe. The same justification may be posed for public provision of environmental amenities. The government may be a bumbler in the production and provision of services, but it is the only alternative; the consequences would be very few environmental amenities and little environmental protection.

Planning proponents often assert that environmental amenities such as green spaces are public goods; that is, goods that the private sector will under produce because buyers cannot capture the value of their expenditures and because people will free ride on purchases made by others rather than pay for the good. Assertions that there is an under-provision of environmental amenities are value judgments, however. These judgments may be based on expert evaluations, but they are still subjective assertions about how other people should be forced to dedicate their resources via the public sector.

We now know that scare stories about the USSR led to what can be criticized as over-spending on the military for several decades. Military leaders had strong incentives to overstate the Russian threat. Larger budgets are preferred by heads of bureaucracies, such as the military, but aside from their preference for larger budgets, they would prefer overinvestment so that, in the event of a conflict, they could not be blamed for underestimating the enemy. Citizens are in a difficult position. Unlike private providers, who compete with each other to sell us their goods or services and, thereby allow us the benefit of multiple sources of information, governments are often monopoly providers. Not only is the U.S. military the only supplier of national defense to U.S. citizens, it has, via Congress, the power to force us to buy certain levels of military provisions. Even if we are sure we have all the military we need, we cannot refuse the order of Congress to pay for even more.

The providers of environmental amenities such as green spaces are not unlike military leaders in this respect. They will assert there is not enough of the service they favor and that there are critical reasons, environmental in this case, why we must allow ourselves to be taxed or regulated more to pay for more public provision of such goods. While there can be critics of such propositions, once the legislature has spoken, all must pay, like it or not. Public agencies pleading for more resources for environmental amenities are no different than the postal service or highway department or any other public monopoly provider with the power, via the legislature, to coerce.

Suspicion of the motives of public sector providers aside, is it true that without public provision there will not be environmental protection, such as green space preservation? The evidence does not indicate that environmental amenities will not be provided. Around the world there are for-profit and private nonprofit programs that take in huge amounts of land to protect species and other resources that humans believe are worth protecting (Anderson and Leal 1997). People specifically dedicate billions of dollars worth of resources each year to what we call environmental protection (Anderson 1998). Just as measures of gross domestic product (GDP) fail to include the value of housework and time devoted to charitable activities, measures of formal environmental activities do not take into account the value of environmental protection provided by millions of property owners. That is, ordinary home owners have strong incentives to enhance their property and its environment, because prospective property buyers value such amenities and because people simply like to devote resources to such activities. Central planners do not need to instruct property owners to protect their own environments.

No Barriers

The existing legal system, based on traditional property law, does not restrict people from devoting resources to the provision of environmental amenities. At law, there is no limit to the kind of arrangements that people devise to protect and enhance property, in any quantity, so long as there is no violation of public policy or of the rights of other property holders. Conservation easements and covenants, and other legal devices, most of which have existed for centuries, are being used to ensure environmental protection (Korngold 1984). The lack of legal barriers, which allows people to effect their desires to protect property for habitat or other purposes, means the market for environmental protection operates quite freely and is subject to strong legal protection.

Traditional common law provides strong protection for property. In recent decades, popular discussion about matters that affect the environment, including urban sprawl, have unfortunately come to center on public policy. The common law is still there, however, and is active in allowing people to construct the environment in which they prefer to live, and offers strong protection against damages inflicted on that environment by others.

Nuisance law provides the backbone of common law environmental protection. It is a common sense notion that holds it to be an actionable violation of the law for one party to invade another's interest in the use and enjoyment of land (Meiners and Yandle 1999). Such interferences must be substantial and unreasonable or sufficiently noxious to give rise to such an action, so that every trifle that bothers us does not rise to the level of an action at law. When there is an actionable nuisance, there may be damages to compensate for loss of use of the land, or loss of enjoyment of the lawn, as well as injuries to one's health or loss of family member services. Courts know nuisances when they see them; there is no fixed definition. They are, as Justice Sutherland said in a famous bit of dictum, "a right thing in the wrong place, like a pig in the parlor instead of the barnyard" (*Village of Euclid* 1926, 388).

While most nuisance actions are brought by private parties seeking to protect their property, public attorneys may also bring nuisance actions on behalf of a large class of persons similarly affected by a public nuisance. Private land is protected by actions against trespassers, which includes a broad array of offenses that invade one's property without permission. Juries hearing nuisance and trespass cases tend to be harsh against invaders of private property; each year some of the largest tort judgments in the nation are against invaders of private property. The point of this short discussion is that owners of private property know that strong protection exists for their interests. That does not mean there will not be catastrophes or invasions of interests, but there is a strong standard of protection available, which encourages people to invest in land and its protection.

Thousands of land conservation easements have been formally established to prevent property from being developed or to limit its use so that the habitat of certain species will be protected. Numerous foundations, such as the Nature Conservancy, assist in such matters, although many of these foundations have become purchasing agents for the federal government and do not keep the property in private hands. Besides such well-known foundations, there are hundreds of local groups and thousands of private persons who have taken such action without central coordination. The notion that all private land is being plowed up for cookie-cutter housing development simply does not square with what is happening, or has been happening for many years.

Moreover, the experience of private environmental protection efforts underscores the importance of the evolutionary nature of common law property rights. By creatively identifying only those aspects of property that are necessary to accomplish their environmental protection goods, private groups are able to reduce the cost of acquiring the necessary protection. In other words, by carefully selecting the sticks from the bundle which they wish to purchase, private conservation organizations and individuals can lower the price of environmental protection while simultaneously allowing landowners to make economic use of the remaining "sticks" in the bundle. Private entities acting in the marketplace have a powerful incentive to so economize because it enables them to use their scarce resources to acquire "sticks" from other bundles as well.

Compare this to the incentive for a government agency. Unless it purchases land outright or totally destroys the land's economic value, the agency pays nothing for the sticks it removes from the landowners' bundles. Indeed, the only real constraint on planners in such a situation is that they avoid depleting their political capital by issuing too many unpopular regulations. Given the natural ignorance of most voters about the content of statutes and administrative regulations, this is a loose constraint indeed. Planners thus have little incentive to narrowly tailor their regulations.

FREE MARKET ENVIRONMENTALISM

As the Montana Land Reliance (MLR), one of many private land trusts hot linked to the Land Trust Alliance web site (www.ltr.org), explains, a "conservation easement is the legal glue that binds a property owner's good intentions to the land in perpetuity" (www.mtlandreliance.com/introca.htm). The MLR holds hundreds of easements on more than 300,000 acres of "ecologically important land." It notes that in conservation easements, which are individually tailored to meet the needs and desires of each property involved, agriculture and silviculture may be allowed to continue, subject to the terms of the enforceable agreement between the landowner and the MLR, which gives the MLR the right to enter easement areas to monitor activities. Activities that the MLR specifically prohibits are subdivisions for residential or commercial activity, construction of nonagricultural buildings, nonagricultural commercial activity, strip mining, or dumping of toxic or noncompostable waste. When property is dedicated to certain environmental uses, it usually results in an income tax write-off for the property owner or donor and a reduction of estate and gift tax duties, thereby further encouraging such action. The MLR is a part of a substantial private movement. More than 1,200 land trusts protect more than 15 million acres in 48 states (Staley 2000a, pp. 10–12).

The MLR is a successful land trust, although not nearly as large or well known as many environmental groups. Its board of directors includes a senior vice president from Lehman Brothers, a director of Goldman Sachs, and others we might classify as high rollers. Many people of substantial means have dedicated their wealth and property to give the MLR enough assets to have offices in three towns in Montana and to write an average of 40 new easements each year. But for every high roller land trust, there are numerous community efforts that bring together people usually of modest means who wish to help preserve their slice of the environment.

The Green Horizon Land Trust has been operating out of Lake Wales, Florida, since 1991 (www.greenhorizon.org). It focuses on preservation in Polk, Osceola, and Citrus counties. It has easements on about 900 acres. Its sites include the Cowpen Slough Preserve, thirteen acres in Polk County that is habitat for many wetland plant species and numerous birds. Another site in Polk is the Scrub Plum Preserve of six acres, which is used as an outdoor classroom for the students of Babson Park Elementary School. The Van Fleet Trail site of eighteen acres was donated to Polk City to use as a public park.

The experience of the Green Horizon Land Trust is not unusual. They oversee some of the land primarily for species habitat preservation, some managed as private parks and some has been deeded over to various state or local agencies for their management. The lands were obtained by purchase at market price, bargain sales, donations, easements, or other arrangements. There is no limit to the ingenuity that people may use in constructing property transfers or restrictive agreements to meet environmental objectives by the parties involved. No governmental oversight is required for such activities to occur. Indeed, as with all market activities, we posit that there will be more creative and diverse environmental protection when it is left to private parties than if it is directed by government.

Government-run environmentalism is no different than government-run military. While a centralized military may be justified because of the nature of national defense, that is not the case when it comes to habitat protection in Polk County, Florida. The people at the Green Horizon Land Trust probably know more about, and care more about, the environment where they live than EPA employees in Washington, D.C., Atlanta, or Florida, or State of Florida employees in Tallahassee, or even Polk County employees. It is not that the employees of the various governments are ignorant or uncaring; the problem is the one recounted before. Government employees work for legislators, who have imperfect knowledge and who must respond to a host of special interests. Even if special interests could be put aside, which they cannot, no government agency can direct matters better than people on the ground can direct it for themselves. Central planning consistently produces a one-size-fits-all result. If you prefer size 42 suits, black only, you are in luck.

Now and the Future

Every generation acts as if it possesses the wisdom of the ages. When we decide how to allocate our resources, we do it with a host of constraints, including what we think to be correct information. So long as it is only our own resources we command, we cannot do much damage to others. But when, through the governmental process, we command everyone today and in the future to dedicate the resources of many to follow one set of rules, we are playing the role of environmental gods, sure that our wisdom is best for today and tomorrow. Let us consider two examples, one small and one big, of environmental action, that indicate that what the majority thinks is right may not always be so.

A century ago, hawks were considered vermin because they preyed on other birds. Not only did farmers hate "chicken hawks" because they kill chickens, free range or not, even the Audubon Society promoted the eradication of eagles, hawks, falcons, and other such birds because they kill song birds. Governments paid bounties for the killing of hawks because wise public policy dictated that these pests be eliminated.

Raptor killing reached hundreds, even thousands, on a single fall day at Hawk Mountain in Pennsylvania. A conservation-minded woman, Rosalie Edge, differed from prevailing opinion. She wanted to save the vermin. Not wealthy, she scraped together a few hundred dollars, leased hundreds of acres on Hawk Mountain, which was prime raptor grounds, and barred hunting from the area. She eventually purchased the mountainside and created a sanctuary to save them. Located in the Appalachian Mountains of eastern Pennsylvania, hundreds of thousands of hawks migrate past Hawk Mountain each autumn. Once a killing field, Hawk Mountain Sanctuary has become an internationally known conservation, education, and research organization.

Rosalie Edge was considered a nut in her day. The woman was devoted to protecting vermin! Imagine her reception if she attempted to persuade the "Raptor Eradication Board" to save the hawks. Yet, her efforts—one person going against prevailing wisdom and public policy—created the Hawk Mountain Sanctuary and Association. It is funded from membership dues, visitor fees, and private contributions. Today Rosalie Edge is hailed as a wise person. We are not judging if she was wise or not. She was simply doing what she thought was right. She provides us one example of how land ownership can conserve landscapes and protect wildlife if even one individual is committed to preservation (Anderson and Leal 1997, pp. 44–46).

A second, larger-scale example illustrates the danger of putting the power of the government behind an environmental objective. Today we know the Florida Everglades to support a rich and unique array of plant and animal life. It existed, largely undisturbed, for thousands of years until a century of wise public policy attempted to destroy it. Before state and federal policy devoted substantial sums to attempt to drain the Everglades, there were various private efforts, but none were successful because the value of the Everglades, drained, was too low to cover the cost of the enterprise.

Beginning with the Swamp and Overflowed Lands Act of 1850, the federal government authorized the state of Florida push for drainage of swamps. By complying with the act, the state gained title to more than 20 million acres of land (otherwise Florida would today look like a Western state, largely under Bureau of Land Management control). The state encouraged swamp drainage through the Internal Improvement Fund (IIF), which provided state bonds and taxing power to subsidize Everglade development. The IIF saga, which lasted for decades, was one that brought financial ruin to the state and private developers who were lured by the subsidies (Landry 2000).

Years of effort drained less than a million acres prior to the New Deal, which ordered the Army Corps of Engineers to assault the Everglades. During the middle of the twentieth century, federal money poured in to build dams, canals, and other projects that produced what we see today; about 10 million acres were affected. The Nixon administration began to slow the flow of federal dollars as environmentalists began to complain of the damage to the environment. Compounding the environmental problem in the Everglades are the various federal sugar subsidies, which artificially increase the price of sugar grown in the United States so that all consumers can contribute to the sugarcane operations that might not otherwise exist in central Florida.

Today we know that the swamp drainage policies were destructive. A multibillion dollar federal plan is on the table to rework canals and levees to try to undo some of the damage to what we now call precious wetlands, not fetid swamps. Going against public policy that dominated for over a century was the Florida Federation of Women's Clubs. They convinced the Model Land Company to set aside Paradise Key, a hammock fifteen miles from Homestead, that was popular with birders and other tourists. It led to the creation of Royal Palm State Park, which was privately run and operated until destroyed by hurricanes in the late 1920s, at which time the land was turned over to the tender mercies of the federal government.

Why has this state of affairs persisted so long? Are members of Congress and various administrations not aware of this environmental mess? Of course they are, but they face a host of special interests, such as the sugar growers who have been generous campaign supporters over the years. Such powerful special interests, and their employees, are not to be lightly discarded. There is nothing evil with any of this, it is just the political process at work. The story is just one of the many conflicting forces that come together when resources are commanded by edict from Washington, not by people on the ground who must pay for their decisions.

People make mistakes. They destroy resources in futile efforts to make an enterprise succeed that fails. But the costs of these mistakes, from which many learn, is small compared to the costs of having resources controlled by central planners which tend to engage in massive, lumbering projects, such as Everglades drainage, that are harder to stop. Public policy rarely allows different values to be expressed; one set of values is imposed on all and all taxpayers get to share in the costs, whether they like it or not. Even worse may be the loss of information that occurs when resources are centrally commanded. Diversity allows not only freedom of expression of values, but allows others to learn from the choices, good and bad, that people make. In a planned regime, all pay for and get the same results, and we know little of what might have been.

Modern planners may insist that they are different, that they are attempting to preserve, not to destroy the environment. And if proven wrong, reversing the mistakes will not require undoing development but merely opening protected areas up. It may be that humanity has finally unraveled the secrets of the environment sufficiently that we, unlike our parents and grandparents, will not make such costly mistakes as draining the Everglades or hunting hawks to the verge of extinction. Perhaps we are that smart. History suggests otherwise (Pipes 1999). Biology may also yet show that decentralized systems are natural and optimal. "It is the hardest thing for human beings to get used to, but the world is full of intricate, cleverly designed and interconnected systems that do not have control centres" (Ridley 1999, p. 151).

ENVIRONMENTAL CREATIVITY

For the environment to be protected and for people to have spaces to enjoy, there must be experimentation so that we learn more about the environment, what works, and what people prefer. This is will not happen with command-and-control of the environment. The EPA or any other agency, no matter how well intended, cannot possibly be as creative as can people living on the ground and working in their environments. The lack of creativity in public land management stands in stark contrast to developments in the private sector, which gives us clues about the wide array of environment enhancing developments we can expect to see more of, so long as people are willing to pay for it and environmental entrepreneurs are not stymied by reams of government regulations.

The U.S. Fish and Wildlife Service, charged with assisting species preservation, has spent large sums of money reintroducing wolves into the greater Yellowstone area. (The wolves, of course, had been eradicated by a previous generation's government policies of bounties and government hunters.) The plan, and the many public hearings that preceded it, generated controversy and ill will in the area. In short, many ranchers believed they would be forced to subsidize the predators, who would kill lambs and calves. Environmental activists (and Eastern newspaper editorial writers) sneered at the selfishness of the ranchers.

While that controversy was swirling, the Defenders of Wildlife took another tack (Anderson and Leal 1997, pp. 267–74). They sold prints of wolves howling in Yellowstone and raised about $100,000. They then announced that they would pay ranchers who lost livestock to wolves. When a rancher suspected a kill, the Montana Department of Livestock was called. If its inspector said the kill was due to a wolf, Defenders would accept that judgment and pay the rancher the market value of the lost livestock. In effect, Defenders accepted liability for the cost of the wolves. While they do not own the wolves, their liability for costs inflicted by wolves reduced the opposition of ranchers to their presence. The ranchers were not forced to feed the wolves for free.

The program did not turn out to cost very much; after a decade less than half the money collected from the sale of prints had been paid to ranchers. So Defenders announced that it would pay bounties to property owners who identified (verified) wolf dens on their property; thereby encouraging ranchers to let wolves breed in peace. These payments allow those concerned about wolf habitat to effectively provide the habitat, at their expense, across a huge area involving many landowners. Individual contracts with each property owner would be very costly, but the simple act of volunteering to accept cost imposed by the predators significantly reduced traditional hostility toward wolves. Even more importantly, the Defenders' program allows continued use of the ranchers' land—as would not be the case if it had been seized to be added to Yellowstone Park.

The multi-million dollar federal program, on the other hand, offers no solace to ranchers whose livestock feed federal wolves. Since shooting a wolf is a federal offense, the best policy is "shoot, shovel, and shut up." Property owners are put at war with the environment, especially with endangered species, the presence of which could lead to federal mandates to curtail economic use of private property. The Defenders' program revealed that when private actors, faced with real costs to their actions, creatively approach a problem, the cost of habitat protection may not be nearly as high, or as highly charged with emotions.

Will people pay to protect ducks they are likely to never see? Many would say such ducks are classic public goods: nearly anyone (with a gun and a state hunting license) can shoot the ducks, which range over huge areas, migrating from Mexico to Canada. Yet Ducks Unlimited and the Delta Waterfowl Foundation raise tens of millions of dollars a year in contributions from people who like to duck hunt. A donor in Texas may be paying for pothole preservation in Manitoba that will benefit some ducks the donor/hunter never sees, but the result of this private action is that the waterfowl population of North America may be higher now than ever. Side benefits of the private efforts to increase ducks to shoot has been wetlands conservation and restoration, which benefits many species besides ducks (Anderson and Leal 1997, pp. 268–269). Private groups have managed to provide significant amounts of a public good because they have figured out how to do so cheaply, through the creative use of property rights. Just as importantly, private organizations like Ducks Unlimited are able to convince donors their donations will be put to good use, a promise governments find hard to keep.

The evidence is clear that if people have reason to want animals to live, they will thrive and prosper; if people see the animals as a deadly pest, not an asset, no amount of well-intended intervention, by government or by private groups, will do anything to actually help the animals. Private initiatives work because they give all parties the incentive for preservation, whereas government regulation tries to force people to act in ways contrary to their own interests.

CONCLUSION

What should planners concerned about preserving spontaneous orders do? We suggest that planners ask themselves three questions about each action they are considering taking.

1. Will the action I am considering make the *content* of a property right *clearer*?
2. Will the action I am considering make the *content* of the overall bundle of rights held by property owners *more secure*?
3. Will the action I am considering make the *transferability* of individual property rights *cheaper*?

If a planner cannot answer yes to at least one of these three questions, then the action will be destructive of the development of spontaneous order.

Environmentalism is serious business. People are willing to pay for habitat and green spaces when offered credible means of doing so. The real work of environmentalism means on-the-ground work preserving habitat for species, including human usage. It means inventing new methods of improving habitat and providing multiple uses. The evidence is that central planning of environments, as we have in national parks and forests, produces dreadful environmental results. There is no reason to suspect that city planners can make any better use of habitat for humans than the humans living in those cities will sort out for themselves.

An even more powerful point has to do with the critical nature of private property rights. As Harvard historian Richard Pipes discusses in his recent book, *Property and Freedom,* the history of the world, over many nations and centuries, indicates that without strong private property rights, it is unlikely that there will be either personal freedom or economic advancement. The alternative to freedom, of course, is government control. The last century witnessed "disturbing developments . . . that have enabled governments, in the name of social justice and the 'common good,' to abolish or infringe on property rights and, by so doing, sometimes abolish and often restrict individual freedoms" (Pipes 1999, p. 322). We are no different than other peoples in other times. Americans are not blessed with a superior intellect that will allow us to avoid the tragedies of central control that follow from the dreamy promises that help bring it to fruition. As we work to ensure a better quality of life for our children, the best we can do is leave them more freedom and wealth to develop their world. Secure property rights and freedom of exchange creates a system that can best take advantage of the knowledge and preferences of everyone, and avoids the arrogant presumption that some people know best how to design the world for the rest of us.

NOTES

1. An expanded version of this chapter appears as "The Destructive Role of Land-Use Planning." *Tulane Environmental Law Journal* 14, no. 1 (Winter 2000): 95-137.

2.   Note that market mechanisms can be used in either type. Creating a fixed stock of tradeable development rights, for example, would be a more efficient way to allocate artificially limited development but it would not lead to a spontaneous order because the limit would still be politically created.

3.   The most noteworthy case is *Lucas v. U.S.* There, a reclassification of beach-front property formerly zoned residential construction was changed to beach preservation, thereby prohibiting all construction; the Supreme Court held that the state of South Carolina had the right to change the classification of the property but, by doing so, knew it was taking all the value of the property and so must provide compensation for the loss Lucas suffered.

4. See numerous studies reported at www.perc.org that chronicle the failure of assorted federal agencies to protect land under federal control.

5. See, e.g., the Clinton-Gore "Livababile Communities Initiative—Better America Bonds," at www.epa.gov/bonds/.

Chapter 11

Markets, Smart Growth, and the Limits of Policy

SAMUEL R. STALEY

An important value of the Smart Growth movement is to ensure the widest scope possible for citizen participation in the land development process through collective decisionmaking. Through collective decisionmaking, proponents of Smart Growth argue that citizens can determine their own future and design their own communities to enhance livability and their quality of life. Moreover, the Smart Growth movement takes planning as a first principle, and the absence of planning is de facto evidence of poor, uncoordinated development which leads to a declining quality of life.

Whether planning *per se* can achieve these goals is debatable. Chapters 1 and 10 of this book provide brief overviews of the limits of planning versus markets. As a theoretical and practical matter, central planning's success rate (whether in land use or economic production) is marginal at best. Indeed, central economic planning is widely regarded as a failure. Meiners and Morriss question whether centralized land-use planning is more likely to succeed. Their argument, grounded in a property rights view of markets and economic behavior, points out that the fragmented and subjective nature of knowledge provides markets with an inherent superiority in coordinating resources and fulfilling the desires of consumers and households, even in the land market. One of their key points was that systems that rely on central planning cannot incorporate the preferences or desires of consumers and households as efficiently or effectively as the market.

This chapter builds on that analysis by more clearly laying out the hurdles growth management faces given the dynamic nature of land markets, the inherent limitations of a democratic policy-making process, and institutional restraints that preclude effective regional land-use planning even if it were possible in principle. In essence, this chapter hopes to illuminate some of the practical difficulties imbedded in land-use planning that relies on centralized coordination of land development and, in the process, more clearly demonstrate the comparative advantage markets have over traditional planning in the realm of land development, housing choice, and city building.

Indeed, few among market economists or planners have attempted to assess whether the goals of the Smart Growth movement (or other nonmarket policy initiatives) are achievable given the complexity of the land development and urban development process in the United States. Most policy discussions do not even consider the role politics play as a fundamental constraint on political and economic behavior. This question is analyzed more fully by comparing the conditions under which different governance systems are most likely to be successful, given the nature and institutional context for land development in the United States. A *governance system* is defined as a set of rules and other constraints that bind decisionmaking.

More directly, this chapter explores the necessary (but not sufficient) conditions under which different decisionmaking or governance systems can be successful. The governance structures that dominate land development are: (1) legislative, where elected officials determine land development outcomes in a bounded democratic system; (2) bureaucratic, where planners and other professionals use rule-based approaches for land development; and (3) market, where buyers and sellers determine land development outcomes as a product of trade and commerce in the private market.

THE POLITICS OF SMART GROWTH
AND GROWTH MANAGEMENT

While many European and Asian countries have long experience with local policy issues in a national context, the decentralized, federalist structure of U.S. government has prevented local issues from dominating the national public agenda. Urban policy provides a relatively recent exception to the rule (see Chapter 13). Urban renewal programs were launched in the 1940s and 1950s to help revitalize cities, and in the 1960s, as part of the larger social agenda of the War on Poverty, urban development became a formal federal policy issue. Federal initiatives helped create new towns through the Model Cities Program during the late 1960s and early 1970s and represented ambitious attempts to leverage earlier incremental intrusions in the land market (e.g., zoning, public housing, urban renewal, public housing programs) to more comprehensively address urban development and redevelopment problems.

The outcomes of these initiatives fell substantially below expectations. Urban renewal cleared vast tracks of land and housing, particularly low-income and minority housing, while providing little new investment (Anderson 1964). The Model Cities and economic development programs quickly degenerated into political gamesmanship that provided few, if any, meaningful results for cities and their residents (Pressman and Wildavsky 1979). As a result, federal policy retreated from grand schemes of comprehensive neighborhood (and town) redevelopment to programs that were more individually oriented with goals of expanding housing choice and mobility for low-income households (e.g., rental housing vouchers and certificates, job training). Moreover, these programs focused primarily on supporting local municipal economic development strategies (Clarke and Gaile 1999). More recently, empowerment zones are providing federal funding to targeted communities, but these programs are in their infancy and the early results do not suggest they will reverse economic (or social) decline in these areas and are typically not comprehensive or citywide in their coverage.

Growth concerns have spawned a new era of development regulation at both the state and local levels. This new focus differs from previous efforts which had widespread support on the national level and focused on regulating growing areas. Previous urban policy focused primarily on urban redevelopment or stemming urban decline. Not surprisingly, as populations have surged in suburban and exurban cities and towns, national politicians have also begun to focus on suburban environmental and urban development issues (see chapter 2). Increasingly, suburban interests and concerns are dominating the national political agenda (Thomas 1998).

The most recent incarnation of national urban policy is the rise of the Smart Growth movement, which is receiving widespread, bipartisan political support at the grass roots and state levels. Unfortunately, defining Smart Growth is problematic. Proposals and policies are diverse, running from comprehensive, top-down planning such as that in Portland, Oregon, to more incentive-based systems like that in Maryland, to calls for deregulating local land markets to allow the private sector more freedom to develop at higher densities with greater intermingling of land uses. Local governments also engage in Smart Growth policies, although often on a more limited and focused level. For example, rather than pursing comprehensive approaches to land-use planning, local governments may expand park and recreation areas, or preserve open space through conservation easements or agricultural zoning. Most Smart Growth proposals, however, increase the level and scope of government involvement in the land development process, either through wider public participation and collective decision-making or enhanced roles for planners and the planning bureaucracy in guiding and directing development.

The Portland Model

Portland is often projected as the model community for the contemporary Smart Growth movement (see Chapter 7). The State of Oregon laid the groundwork with passage of its landmark statewide growth management act in 1973 (Howe 1993), which required all cities and metropolitan areas to establish urban-growth boundaries and adopt comprehensive planning. Moreover, the state identified explicit goals to which local comprehensive plans and regional plans needed to conform. These goals ranged from protecting farmland and wildlife habitat to ensuring affordable housing and containing suburbanization.

In Portland, the metropolitan planning organization (Metro) is implementing a regional plan covering three counties and 24 local governments that embodies many of the principles of New Urbanism, an urban-design movement that emphasizes higher densities, small lots, mixed commercial and residential uses, and mass transit. The region's growth plan lays out preferred development patterns on a regional level through 2040, and Metro has identified cities and towns as target areas for higher density and employment centers. A key tool of the Smart Growth plan is a regional urban limit line, or growth boundary. The growth boundary has already helped reduce lot sizes from close to 10,000 square feet to less than 9,000 square feet while boosting the amount of multifamily and townhouse development (Staley, Edgens, and Mildner 1999). Growth boundaries have become a key feature of Smart Growth proposals, and similar growth boundaries are being created by legislative fiat in Washington and Tennessee. Growth boundaries have also become staples of statewide growth management policies in Maine and Florida.

In addition to the growth boundary, the Portland region is funding an extensive light-rail mass transit system with the expectation that these investments will promote more compact and dense development patterns and relieve congestion. In fact, about half of the MPO's transportation spending is directed toward light rail and mass transit. (Even with these investments, however, congestion is expected to increase by 2040.) To date, the opening of the East Side rail line has had relatively little impact on congestion or land development patterns. The West Side line appears to be impacting the type of development near transit stops (and rail ridership is higher than some projections by Metro), but has had little practical impact on congestion and traffic flow.

Nevertheless, Portland is often viewed as a model of growth management and planning. In part, this is a result of the process Oregon, and the Portland region specifically, created to manage growth. The Portland area has the unique feature of having an elected regional planning agency (Metro). Thus, citizen participation has always played an important role in the region's growth management decision-making process. Indeed, in a plebiscite in the early 1990s, Portland residents validated Metro's land-use planning authority and authorized the 2040 strategic planning process. The outcome was the 2040 plan, currently in the implementation stage, which emphasizes centralized land-use planning, transit-oriented development, compact land development, and higher densities.

Metro officials are quick to point out that they have not forced local government to adopt its regional planning policies. However, Metro has the authority to mandate the implementation of its policies, including density targets and zoning recommendations. For example, Metro has created a formula for allocating projected population growth among the metropolitan area's cities and towns. Population and density targets are submitted to local cities and towns for approval, but local officials also recognize that Metro has the ability to impose the targets. Cities and towns cannot opt out of the regional planning process; rather, they negotiate with Metro to mitigate the impacts of these density and population targets. One of the early mandates imposed by Metro was a partial deregulation of local land markets by eliminating maximum density limitations and allowing for "granny flats" (extra rooms above the principal structure) in existing single-family residential districts. (Recently, Metro has also approved minimum density mandates for individual cities and towns.)

Maryland

In contrast, Maryland's efforts to manage growth at the state level have been more incentive based. Maryland's efforts may have done more than any other to promote the term Smart Growth, because many officials view the Maryland model as more replicable. Rather than impose central land-use planning directly, Maryland takes a softer approach by providing incentives for people to live closer together, encouraging countywide planning, and purchasing vacant land open space and farmland with public funds to prevent development and preserve open space. The program consists of three broad components: directing infrastructure investment into urban areas, protecting farmland and open space, and encouraging investment in inner-city areas.

The first leg of the program establishes priority funding areas, or PFAs. PFAs are designated by local counties through a comprehensive planning process. The primary purpose is to direct investment in land that is considered prime development or urbanization territory. The state, for example, will not provide funding for infrastructure development outside the PFAs. Therefore, the state can, by simply withholding funding, discourage subsidization of new development, because in reality few local governments will be willing or able to opt out of the program. Moreover, the PFA concept includes an explicit attempt to impose a particular land-use form on development in Maryland by limiting lot sizes and imposing state density standards for urban and rural uses.

The second prong of Maryland's Smart Growth program is to protect open space through an aggressive purchase of development rights (PDR) program and severely curtailing the development potential of farmland. This approach to open space has become popular in more than a dozen states. By using state funding, local officials and Smart Growth proponents hope to permanently remove land from the land market. The most ambitious local program may be in Lancaster County, Pennsylvania, where more than 30,000 acres (7 percent of farmland) has been purchased. New Jersey may have the most ambitious state program. The state anticipates spending as much as $10 billion to remove almost one-half of the remaining developable land from the market (one million acres), designating it as permanent open space.

The third strategy is to provide incentives to redevelop central and inner cities. One policy tool will be a reinvigorated brownfields program that encourages site clean up. Another major policy tool will be job creation tax credits for qualifying firms as long as they locate in urban and poor areas of Maryland's cities. The third policy tool is a program called "Live Near Your Work," where families and households receive subsidized mortgages by locating near their employment, presumably with the expectation that this would reduce automobile use and commuting costs.

KEY FEATURES OF SMART GROWTH PLANS

Portland and Maryland provide a glimpse at the range of growth management strategies and plans that have been implemented. Both strategies have provided key elements of the contemporary Smart Growth movement. Despite their diversity, Smart Growth plans have one overarching principle: they attempt to supplant market-based development mechanisms with top-down, government-driven development control and broader citizen participation. While Portland's strategy does not eliminate the private market from land development, the private sector is relegated to a clearly subordinate position. The regional planning agency determines future land uses and the appropriate mix of uses, using zoning, density requirements, and other tools, while the private sector is expected to build according to the specifications of Metro's 2040 plan. The success of Smart Growth proposals, however, depends crucially on their ability to achieve planning objectives within the existing system of local government policymaking. Embedded in the Smart Growth movement are several overarching assumptions and principles.

First, Smart Growth proposals require cities and communities to be proactive, presuming that urban development is a process that can be planned through a central authority. This is most clearly evident in the Portland case. The urban growth boundaries were intended to include a 20-year supply of developable land, implicitly creating a growth management process that must identify, estimate, and project future land development needs. Moreover, the goal was to create more contiguous, compact development to avoid the leapfrog nature of much low-density, residential development. This type of forward planning became strikingly similar to end-state central planning with the implementation of the 2040 regional planning process in the 1990s. Portland is not alone. Florida's growth management act has similar features and presumptions (see Chapter 8). Of course, this proactive approach presumes an ability to know with reasonable certainty the key features of "appropriate development" and the preferences of current and future residents. This approach also presumes that the development process itself is well understood and known so that growth management plans can identify and manipulate the relevant variables to achieve the desired outcome.

Second, Smart Growth plans rely on urban growth boundaries (or some hybrid combination of an urban service area and strict growth controls) and other growth controls to contain development and encourage higher densities and mixed uses. Many of these techniques are explicitly antimarket, using the political process to impose a politically determined order on land development. Thus, growth boundaries are intended to promote more compactness than would exist in a free market. They also intend to create a distinct separation of rural and urban uses (a "line in the land"). An important underlying value of the Smart Growth movement is the importance of using political institutions (either legislative or bureaucratic public decisionmaking) to allocate resources in the land market in order to achieve an end-state vision of the community. Rarely are these tools compared to more efficient, market-based approaches, such as deregulating the land market to achieve consumer-driven densities. Proposed growth management strategies such as the growth boundary are almost always politically oriented, presuming political markets can more harmoniously coordinate the myriad of housing, neighborhood, work, and commuting desires of local residents. These political strategies, unlike markets, almost always systematically neglect the preferences of future residents; decisions about growth boundary expansion are made by existing residents who are politically active, irrespective of the needs of future residents.

A third characteristic of these plans is the presumption that the legislative process works smoothly, so that adjustments will be spontaneous, with zero or near zero transaction costs, and clearly revealed collective preferences will guide the policy process. The political process is presumed to be an efficient mechanism for revealing the true preferences of local citizens (although not future residents), while local land markets (by definition) represent distortions from the private sector. An underlying theme of many growth management proposals is the belief that developers, acting in their own self-interest, will not be concerned about quality of life issues (which are considered public goods), as if the neighborhood benefits of a high-quality neighborhood will not be an incentive to provide value-enhancing urban design elements. Yet, as the discussion that follows more fully explains, the political process often works inefficiently and ineffectively when addressing issues as complex as housing and neighborhood choice.

In addition, Smart Growth proposals presume that collective action captures all the relevant information about consumer and citizen preferences, and that the political process itself (through public hearings, planning charettes, and public debate) will reveal and articulate all important and relevant concerns. This approach implicitly assumes that any changes in citizen preferences and values will be revealed and addressed in the political process so that changes can be made to the comprehensive plan spontaneously and without significant or distortionary lags.

Fourth, Smart Growth plans presume that an end-state vision of what a community will look like can be identified and achieved through development control and land-use planning. The planning process itself reduces uncertainty about future outcomes and, using land-use controls and other development regulations, can direct investment in the proper directions. Virtually all Smart Growth proposals justify growth management and restrictions on land development based on the importance of local citizen input in determining what their community will look like 20, 30, or even 50 years into the future and an articulated expectation about how it will function. Implicitly, Smart Growth proposals presume that the primary determinant of the pace and pattern of development is land use, and that, because governments have extensive influence over land use through regulation, urban planning allows a community to shape itself, independently of market forces. Thus, through a "visioning process," citizens, planners, and elected officials can determine an optimal urban form and structure and achieve it through the implementation of a comprehensive plan. This approach creates daunting challenges. Cary, North Carolina, for example, had a population of just 21,763 people in 1980. By 1997, Cary's population had ballooned to 82,700, in large part because of the extraordinary growth of hi-tech businesses in the Raleigh-Durham area and Research Triangle Park. By 2015, local planners are projecting Cary's population to grow to 234,784. Few, however, could have predicted the extraordinary growth of this city in 1980 even though it would have required a shorter time horizon than many current planning processes envision.

Demographics are not the only trends difficult to predict. Two decades ago, MS-DOS and compact disks did not exist. The Sony Walkman was on the cutting edge of consumer electronics. As recently as the 1960s, planners and others failed to predict the impact of women in the workforce. Few have a firm grasp of how current changes in Internet technology will impact the workplace, commuting, and home location. Already, more people telecommute than use public transportation (Buckeye Institute 1999).

Fifth, virtually all Smart Growth approaches envision an expanded role for citizen participation in the urban development process. Thus, increasing politicization of the development process is a beneficial aspect of Smart Growth (because of the collective decision-making benefits already discussed). A critical justification for growth management is broadening the role of citizens in informing public policy and impacting the shape of their community. Plans are expected to be "living plans" that reflect the aspirations, hopes, and expectations of the local community concerning what they believe a livable community will look like. Yet, expanded citizen participation also entails trade-offs. Ballot-box zoning, for example, could dampen growth (Staley, 2001). Increased citizen participation could lengthen planning and approval times and dampen innovation and flexibility in the housing market.

The obvious contradiction between long-range, goal-oriented planning and the dynamic nature of citizen-driven collective decisionmaking is hardly ever discussed in any depth or in a meaningful way. In fact, few people have really examined the conditions under which Smart Growth proposals will be (or will likely be) successful (see Chapter 10). Several of the underlying elements of Smart Growth proposals are contradictory, and virtually none of them consider the political, economic, and social institutional environment in which growth management policies are implemented. Indeed, the very structure of democratic decisionmaking makes achieving many growth management objectives rooted in centralized land-use planning at the state, regional, or local level problematic, if not impossible. The following sections investigate these issues in more detail by examining the three primary decision-making processes that influence the pace and pattern of land development in the United States: legislative decisionmaking, bureaucratic decisionmaking (traditional planning), and market decisionmaking.

LEGISLATIVE DECISIONMAKING

Virtually all significant development projects are subjected to a legislative review at some level in the United States. A typical development proposal will usually go through two stages of review: the first considers land use (or preliminary site plan) and often involves the decision to rezone land to accommodate particular types of land development. These are usually (but not exclusively) property owner or developer initiated. The second stage involves review of the site plan (or final site plan), the physical design of the buildings, and the infrastructure needed to develop the property. Each stage of the review process is also subjected to at least two levels of approval: one by the planning board, which typically consists of local citizens appointed by an elected legislative body such as a town council, and the second by elected officials at the town or city council level. Some states have imposed a third tier of review at a regional (e.g., special district such as a coastal commission) or state level.

Legislative review or decisionmaking is characterized, in U.S. governance, by bounded majority rule. Most decisions require a simple majority or super majority to carry at the local level, and local government decisions are bound by state laws and constitutional limits on government action. Most city councils are run by officials elected every four years, so substantial lags exist for transmitting information and signals about important policy issues to elected representatives through the election cycle. Not surprisingly, elected and appointed officials have come to rely on alternative forms of participation, from personal visits in their offices to public hearings, to solicit citizen input and feedback on political issues.

Local planning boards are *not* the final decisionmakers with respect to development regulation and urban planning. Town and city councils ultimately approve or reject rezoning or site-plan decisions (although some cities have adopted supermajority requirements for overriding planning board decisions). Local planning and zoning boards consist mainly of appointed officials that serve at the discretion of elected officials. These boards are the work horses of the American system of development regulation, making recommendations (with input from staff planners) to elected officials who either accept or reject their decisions.

But, effective democratic governance requires a number of important conditions to exist for public policy to be successful. First, a consensus on goals is necessary, as well as general agreement that the problem requires collective action to achieve the final results. Political gridlock occurs when significant disagreement exists over policy goals and options. Because local governments require a majority to approve a request, the lack of consensus, or the presence of dissent, often results in inaction. Thus, actions subjected to collective decision-making tend to be more deliberate than in markets where entrepreneurs and suppliers focus on consumers on the margin.

Unlike private markets, legislative decision-making criteria are based on democratic decision rules that focus on the average consumer (e.g., costs and benefits of a decision are averaged over the entire community). Because consumer preferences in political markets are not revealed in a continuous market (only during election cycles of two or four years), democratic decisionmaking engages in a process of discovery of constituent values and concerns. Because city councils and planning boards are expected to represent the community at large (the average citizen), and information about citizen preferences is largely unknown, the pubic hearing process serves as the primary mechanism for collecting and synthesizing citizen concerns and preferences. The presumption is against rezonings or development projects (they need approval from a public body before they can proceed), creating an inherently conservative collective decision-making process. Officials need to have a convincing and persuasive reason to approve the change to the local zoning map or comprehensive plan. Inaction is the default position for most elected officials since it represents the least political risk.

The planning process (and hence growth management) is complicated by the fact that public goals change. Policy is determined by elected representatives. Thus, the process is subject to changing demographics. For example, as many communities become older, their priorities shift. As new families move in to a community, with different expectations and experiences, community goals change. Thus, a blue-collar suburb may have different priorities than a white-collar suburb; a city with large concentrations of poor will have different concerns than a more affluent city; and young farming communities that rely on leased land to generate income will have different aspirations and expectations for local government than older farming families where land ownership is a core component of family wealth. These shifts and changes do not necessarily respect planning and decision-making cycles.

Some of these attitudinal shifts may already be evident in Portland, Oregon. While many outsiders tend to few the Portland growth management plan as a static end-state vision, Portland planners are more inclined to view the plan as a work in progress, shifting and changing as the community has more experience with the plan's tools and strategies. Of course, this approach is partly pragmatic: comprehensive regional planning cannot control (let alone identify) all the variables in the growth process. While regional planning can (in principle) direct growth, it cannot limit overall growth, directly regulate migration into or within the state, control business formation and expansion, or regulate the birth rate. In fact, most factors that influence regional growth are beyond the control of local governments, in large part because constitutional protections of civil liberties and property rights place them off limits to direct government control and manipulation.

The failure in 1998 to approve funding for Portland's light-rail extensions may be an indicator of shifting priorities among the public with respect to trade-offs in transportation infrastructure. In the same year, a recall in the suburban city of Milwaukie of local elected officials who supported Metro's regional growth management plan was another rare if dramatic reminder that the plan may be imposing significant costs on some residents and groups (Staley, Edgens, and Mildner 1999). Similarly, as housing prices continue to escalate, the citizens may pressure Metro to expand the growth boundary to mitigate the impacts of land shortage. For many communities, public preferences will be a moving target, revealed through the relatively slow and cumbersome process of representative democracy.

A second key to effective legislative decisionmaking is having a clearly defined problem. Often, local officials attempt to develop consensus among their constituents in order to define the problems in ways that can be addressed through public policy with a stable majority coalition. Given the importance of consensus building in democratic governance, Smart Growth becomes problematic. A clear definition of *sprawl* does not appear to exist among the general public, creating important obstacles to designing effective policy solutions because a consensus on policy solutions becomes difficult to achieve. While planners may define sprawl as low-density residential and commercial development, leapfrog or noncontiguous in nature, and automobile dependent, this definition is not universally accepted. When farmers and farm organizations are asked to define sprawl, they often cite the fragmentation of farmland as the key characteristic. When an editorial board of a major urban newspaper (that had been editorializing against sprawl) was asked by the author to define sprawl, the consensus definition was when "commercial development follows residential development out to the periphery." Often, newspaper headlines depict sprawl as any kind of growth outside of existing cities. Many local citizens think of sprawl as any development of open space in their community. Without a generally accepted definition of the problem, identifying policy strategies and solutions with popular support will be difficult if not impossible. Thus, an important component of effective policymaking in legislative decisionmaking—clear goals and consensus—is missing.

The information requirements of the legislative decision-making process are also significant. In an uncertain environment, public hearings serve as a crucial element of the legislative deliberative process. Yet public hearings require public notification, often to potentially affected property owners, to ensure widespread participation, and delays can be lengthy. When planning boards (and town councils) approve development proposals, they often include numerous conditions restricting all manner of site characteristics, from landscaping to building materials to hours of operation, to allay citizen concerns (often unfounded). In other cases, planning boards significantly alter the character of development by further restricting uses and densities (See Seigan 1990).

A third ingredient to effective collective action in a legislative environment is providing a focused, narrow set of issues. Legislative processes rarely can handle multiple issues effectively because decisions are sequential and hierarchical, and democratic governance is part-time. Elected officials respond first to issues with high political visibility. Nonvisible issues become secondary and are given a lower priority. Given American preferences for citizen legislators, few elected officials have professional experience in the field, and the often parttime nature of their positions mean town councils (and planning boards) meet occasionally. Thus complicated projects and debates over development approvals must be narrowed down to essential elements. Complex issues often get overly simplified in an attempt to create clarity.

Not surprisingly, legislative processes are better at addressing broad concerns than micromanaging problems. Broad concerns about policy give way to detailed deliberations of the content, look, and structure of individual site plans and development projects. Again, the Portland experience is worth exploring. The regional plan calls for "balancing" development and growth by allocating population among the metropolitan area's major cities and towns. In addition, the plan calls for increasing density to minimize the pressure to expand the growth boundary and promote "efficiency" in land use (re: use less land). Metro and the city, however, are engaged in micromanaging the local land market to achieve these goals. In addition to actively encouraging higher density through encouraging town house and multifamily housing development—multifamily housing accounts for half the building permits in the Portland region—Metro has recently banned the further construction of "snout" homes (homes with garages facing the street). All garages must be built behind the principal structure.

Portland is not unique, except in its scale and comprehensiveness. Planning boards and city councils are more effective in identifying general concerns about development, such as declining open space or the general character of new development, than determining where parks should go in particular subdivisions, or choosing housing and architectural styles. Yet many Smart Growth proposals require detailed review of development proposals to conform to specific design, density, and engineering criteria. Because planning boards and city councils work as committees, extensive time and resources can be devoted to discussing minor aspects of a proposal or project. Moreover, few of these part-time citizen decisionmakers have the expertise or knowledge of the consumer market to make informed decisions beyond their own direct experience (although the review process is set up to invite attention to every detail of a proposal). Planning boards (and city councils) are legally entitled to examine every aspect of a rezoning request or development proposal, and will often add conditions to zoning and development plan approvals that dictate times of operation, exterior materials, landscaping, lot size and configuration, and architectural style. Thus, micromanagement is institutionally encouraged, further adding to delays, uncertainties, and the transaction costs associated with obtaining development project approval.

Given the political nature of the approval process, and the institutionalized ability to scrutinize all aspects, the pace of decisionmaking is slow, deliberate, and static. This is implicit in the institutional framework of public decisionmaking. Because political markets are "lumpy" (characterized by sporadic periods of activity and inactivity), development issues are often peripheral to larger political questions, and elections occur intermittently (often long after important decisions have been made), the legislative decision-making process becomes a cumbersome mechanism for managing economic growth and regulating land development.

Of course, these general characteristics say little about the quality of the information and input into the decision-making process. In many cases, the information is poor and results in outcomes that are politically expeditious but economically inefficient. For example, at one rezoning hearing for a new subdivision, a developer was required to connect to a city sewer system when a septic system was both cheaper and environmentally sound. Unsubstantiated citizen concerns about the water table and potential groundwater contamination led the zoning board to require the connection to the city sewer system. In other cases, the impact is smaller, but important. A local planning board, for example, haggled over whether to allow a developer to put parking spaces in an island in a cul-de-sac for two hours. Finally, the developer dropped the feature to avoid further delays in the project and site plan approval.

In sum, the legislative decision-making process is both cumbersome and inefficient from the perspective of land development. By subjecting land-use and development decisions to the legislative process, issues that are primarily economic in nature become politicized. Without a clear consensus on goals, high political visibility, and good information, Smart Growth is unlikely to achieve its expected benefits. In fact, its lack of transparency as a policy issue implies that implementing Smart Growth proposals will be problematic at best.

BUREAUCRATIC DECISIONMAKING

An expanded role for politics in land development is one of two strong underlying themes of the Smart Growth movement. The second theme is that planning should play a more prominent role in directing and guiding land development. More specifically, planners, because of their interdisciplinary focus on urban design, architecture, and infrastructure, should play a central role in determining what neighborhoods should look like and, by implication, how they should function. In the extreme case, many New Urbanists propose a general paradigm for neighborhood design that should be universally applied. Planners, with their technical expertise and aesthetic sensibilities, are in the best position to ensure neighborhoods and communities are designed in the public interest.

While most planners argue that citizen input and participation are important elements of any planning process, inherent tensions exist between conventional planning and participation in a democratic political system. Planning, in its purest sense, is the process of identifying goals and implementing the strategies and processes necessary to achieve those goals. The very essence of planning requires having an identifiable goal that is stable; in essence, planning presumes a static environment where preferences and values do not change significantly over time. (Thus, strategies and mechanisms for achieving these goals can be identified and implemented.)

This condition, of course, is impossible to maintain in a democratic society that protects private property rights and values markets as the primary institutional mechanism for allocating resources. In terms of land development and city building, this political and economic system is dynamic and evolutionary. Communities and planners cannot prevent interjurisdictional migration since free housing choice is implicit in these political arrangements. Moreover, while communities can regulate land development, and influence the character and quality of development, they cannot prevent the sale of land or its development without the act becoming a Fifth Amendment taking that requires compensation to landowners.

More importantly, the process of land development and the conversion of land uses implies change; community development is a dynamic process. While a degree of sorting takes place through the Tiebout effect (see chapter 7, p. 123), individuals bring different values, experiences, and preferences to their communities. Old rural farming villages are transformed into blue-collar industrial towns, which are then transformed into larger, more diverse communities with professionals. Thus, community goals are often a moving target.

Even if migration could be tightly controlled or regulated, community values change with experience. Thus, while Portland's urban growth boundary was initially very popular, its impact on housing prices may undermine its political support. As housing prices increase in the city and its suburbs, residents may re-evaluate their goals and desires for their community. If one of those goals is affordable housing, then the political climate could easily shift to one supportive of relaxing (or eliminating) the growth boundary. Cites in Boulder County, Colorado, for example, have mitigated the price impacts of growth boundaries by expanding them through annexation (Staley, Edgens, and Mildner 1999).

In addition, adequate and relevant information about the effects of sprawl is difficult to find. Despite almost universal condemnation of urban sprawl in the professional and academic planning community, a survey of more than 475 studies of urban sprawl has found limited consensus among scholars on its impacts (Burchell et al. 1998). Forty-three costs and benefits of sprawl were identified, but general agreement on the impacts could be discerned for only six: sprawl increased vehicle miles traveled, increased the number of automobile trips, lessened congestion, encouraged the automobile as a more efficient mode of transportation, and reduced agricultural land and the amount of fragile lands (Burchell et al. 1998, table 15, pp. 130-131). Some agreement existed for sixteen (37.2 percent) of sprawl's impacts while no clear outcome could be found for another nineteen (33.2 percent). Among the costs and benefits in this category were whether sprawl created greater fiscal burdens on local governments, whether it made transit less cost effective, whether sprawl reduced farmland viability, and whether it reduced the sense of community. Thus, the academic research provides little support for changing land-use patterns as a mechanism for solving larger urban issues and problems.

These uncertainties and the evolutionary nature of urban development make rule-based decisionmaking of the kind necessary for planning problematic. To be successful, planners and other bureaucratic decisionmakers need to operate in an environment with several important attributes, which include the following:

- *Clear goals*, so that strategies and resources can be marshaled to achieve certain outcomes. For example, the community and/or local government can set a goal of ensuring all new development is transit-oriented (developed with access to mass transit as the dominant design concept). Planners can then evaluate new projects based on whether proposals meet this goal. Few communities have developed a consensus around the definition of urban sprawl let alone whether specific Smart Growth proposals are preferable.
- *Specific tasks*, to ensure accountability since government officials do not face a bottom line in the same way housing developers do.
- *Centralized and specialized information and knowledge* so that planners can understand the complexities and inter-relationships among alternative development scenarios. Many communities have significantly over- and underzoned for particular types of land uses. Planners must know, for instance, what type of housing is preferred by local residents to ensure adequate land is zoned for that purpose. Access to this information gives planners technical expertise that enables them to make competent decisions about appropriate land development and urban design. Some experts note that zoning has created a shortage of industrial land and affordable housing.
- *Consensus on goals* is necessary to give planners the kind of direction and guidance they need to achieve the communities' goals. This is particularly important in a de-

mocratic system where elected officials have the primary authority for setting policy goals.

- *Static environment* to provide the stability necessary to achieve these goals.

Of course, few political environments have these characteristics and this discussion suggests the housing market is much too complex to be handled through rule-based decision-making processes. Communities are not static, and information about housing and neighborhoods are dispersed and fragmented. The economics literature has discovered a myriad of factors that determine housing choice for individual households and families, including the quality of local schools, tax rates, access to jobs, quality of the housing stock, crime, and so forth. While these provide general guidelines for understanding the factors that lead to residential choice, each household assigns different weights to each of these variables when they decide to when to move, buy a house, change neighborhoods, or even stay in their current house and neighborhood. Planners cannot possibly make these decisions explicit in the planning process.

MARKET DECISIONMAKING

Markets, in contrast, are more effective at coordinating the decision of individuals because they function as part of a dynamic institutional environment. Indeed, one function of market prices is to provide information as quickly as possible to producers and consumers about the relative costs and benefits of goods and services to facilitate evolution, change, and innovation. Markets, by focusing on the marginal calculations of individual households and consumers, incorporate diffused and fragmented pieces of knowledge into a market process that minimizes the amount of information each participant needs to make the most appropriate decisions about buying products, and thus expands the capacity of the system to operate. Unlike legislative or bureaucratic decision-making processes, decisionmakers do not need complete information about all aspects of the market. Household preferences and values do not have to be explicit and articulable. On the contrary, they merely need to be revealed through tangible decisions to buy and sell products and services in the housing market. The market works as an iterative process, revealing new information with each transaction. Land developers use the market process of trial and error to discover new information about what consumers want and how preferences for housing and neighborhoods change (e.g., see Hayek 1948; Kirzner 1973). This discovery process is spontaneous; it does not occur through deliberative planning process or legislative fiat. On the contrary, the incentives within the market encourage developers to seek out this information because their livelihood depends on it. In fact, of the groups and interested parties most involved in the land-development process, only the land developers risk direct personal and financial ruin if they fail to gauge household preferences accurately.

An example of the market process in action occurred when a developer recognized that lots for his new subdivision were not selling. He reconfigured the development to appeal to another market: empty nesters. Part of the development included a pond that was added for purely aesthetic reasons. The developer substituted a small park for the pond after he realized the fastest selling lots were farthest from the proposed water area: grandparents didn't want to locate near a pond that was a potential hazard for grandchildren. Because the developer focused on the needs of the marginal consumer, and he had the flexibility (and incentive) to adapt his product quickly and efficiently, he was able to redesign his site to more effectively meet the needs of potential residents. This discretionary behavior is unique to the private market.

This knowledge was dispersed and fragmented in the market, and only became available through the revealed preferences of households buying lots and building homes. Because participation in the market depends on providing goods and services that consumers are willing to buy (most households have the option of not moving), markets provide the direct accountability necessary to make corrections when producers fail to provide the goods and services people want. In general, the conditions under which markets work effectively include the following:

- *Diffuse goals* where little consensus exists for particular outcomes.
- *Many objectives* so that choosing specific strategies or directing inputs to meet particular goals is difficult to identify and coordinate. Moreover, markets are superior when diffuse goals and objectives require experimentation and the concurrent design and implementation of many different strategies and products.
- *Significant uncertainty* about people's values and preferences for certain products.
- *Dispersed information and knowledge,* much of which is inarticulate knowledge that can only be revealed through the decisions of consumers and producers in the market when they are faced with the real opportunity costs of the decision.

The U.S. housing market is strikingly diverse and resilient. The private sector has generated an extraordinary array of housing choices. The growth of suburban cities in the post-World War II period, combined with their maturation and increasingly urban character, has significantly added to this diversity. Moreover, as traditional bedroom communities evolve, higher density and more mixed-use developments emerge providing a broadening array of choices to households along all ranges of income and class. This presents a tremendous calculation and coordination problem that the modern growth management tools, particularly those proposed as part of the Smart Growth agenda, are unable to resolve or negotiate. In fact, under these conditions, the most appropriate institutional mechanism for providing goods and services is the market.

These complexities have been magnified by dramatic reductions in transportation and telecommunications costs. New technology has dramatically reduced the need for workers to be physically located in centralized office environments, freeing them to make housing and neighborhood choices based increasingly on personal quality of life considerations. In this environment, knowledge is becoming even more fragmented, decentralized, and personal, reducing the effectiveness of decision-making processes that rely on the articulation of explicit knowledge and consensus to achieve goals and objectives.

POLICY IMPLICATIONS

The Smart Growth movement has gained popularity among citizens and policymakers because it appears to address specific growth-related problems: traffic congestion, loss of open space, and increasing public sector costs. The tools Smart Growth proponents have promoted—regional land-use planning, regional governance, and tighter controls over development—presume certain conditions exist that allow planners to achieve their goals. Among these conditions are a stable political environment with clear goals and widespread consensus on achieving those goals; centralized and complete information about housing preferences and public service cost impacts; and zero transaction costs to collective decisionmaking. These are necessary but not sufficient conditions for success. These conditions do not exist in the contemporary housing market and in land development. Moreover, these decision-making processes rely on the ability to articulate and interpret accurately information that is inherently inarticulate and subjective.

The market for housing and land is complex, dynamic, uncertain, and sophisticated. Choices about what land to develop and what types of housing to provide depend on a vast, dynamic, interconnected network of suppliers and providers sensitive to consumer behavior. The institutional limitations of legislative and bureaucratic decision-making processes prevent them from adequately addressing the wide variety of preferences and values addressed in the market on a daily basis. The market institutionalizes behavior that focuses on the needs and preferences of the marginal consumers, and allows subjective value and inarticulate knowledge to be integrated into the process for determining what goods and services should be provided and at what level. These dynamic and subjective characteristics of the housing market are enhanced by recent changes in transportation and technology. Neither the legislative nor bureaucratic decision-making processes are capable of meeting these needs due to the inherent, institutional limitations of each system.

Chapter 12

Infrastructure Provision in a Market-Oriented Framework

WENDELL COX

Recently, the U.S. Census Bureau projected that the national population would double by 2100. While this is a considerably slower rate of growth than has occurred in the last 100 years, the addition of more than 250 million new citizens will have a significant impact on land use and the economy. Wherever the new people live or work, there will be a need for new infrastructure, such as schools, roads, electricity, telecommunications, gas, water and wastewater systems.

WHERE SHOULD INFRASTRUCTURE BE PROVIDED?

Proponents of Smart Growth often contend that the costs of infrastructure are higher in the suburbs, as opposed to the more dense central cities. At first glance this might seem to be reasonable, because all things being equal, more pipe and wire costs more to lay than less. One of the principal reasons that the Smart Growth movement seeks more compact, higher density developments is to reduce infrastructure costs (e.g., Burchell et al. 1998). But the reality is not so simple—there is more to infrastructure costs than just the cost of a foot of pipe.

Research by Helen Ladd (1992) indicates that the higher density patterns that the Smart Growth movement would like to implement exhibit higher infrastructure costs than lower density patterns. Per capita infrastructure capital costs were found to be as much as 71 percent higher in the highest density areas with populations of 24,000 people per square mile or more. This directly contradicts the claims of Smart Growth proponents who argue that costs should be lowest in the highest density areas.

The finding that infrastructure costs are higher in more dense areas is not entirely surprising. While some money may be saved because less material is used, other factors increase costs, such as higher right-of-way and property acquisition costs, development costs complicated by an already dense infrastructure environment (sewers, water lines, electric lines, etc.), and higher labor and administrative costs. Since 1950, only 15 percent of the suburban population growth rate can be explained by flight from the central cities in large urbanized areas.[1] The other 85 percent occurred due to the natural rate of increase and the movement of people from rural to suburban areas. As a result, if suburban growth had been more limited, infrastructure systems in urban areas would have had to expand greatly simply to accommodate the new household growth. Moreover, central cities have generally higher-cost building environments. Existing infrastructure is usually inadequate and needs upgrading, and regulatory burdens are often higher than their suburban competitors. Given the complexity and costs of central city infrastructure development, it is not at all clear that the suburban infrastructure system would cost more to develop than in a more dense development pattern.

Moreover, while infrastructure is costly, its burden on public budgets is comparatively small. In 1995, construction costs represented less than 15 percent of state and local government spending.[2] By far the largest portion of state and local government spending is for labor—wages, salaries, and employer paid fringe benefits make up nearly one-half of state and local government spending.[3] Thus, even if infrastructure costs were less in more compact urban developments, differentials in other costs, which consume nearly seven times as much of state and local government budgets, could easily negate any density-based advantages. The evidence suggests exactly that. The overall unit costs of government tend to be higher in the larger central cities, where densities tend to be higher. Ladd found current (operating) spending to be up to 43 percent higher per capita in the highest density areas.

Similar findings apply to municipal governments. U.S. cities of more than 300,000 population spend 60 percent more per capita than the cities of 100,000 and under, while cities from 100,000 to 300,000 spend 31 percent more than cities below 100,000 (see Figure 12.1).[4] Similarly, the largest U.S. public transit agencies exhibited unit costs more than 40 percent above smaller agencies in 1997.[5]

Larger local governments generally have higher unit costs than smaller governments. According to the Advisory Commission on Intergovernmental Relations (1987), "Average costs are generally understood to have a u-shaped relationship to scale of production. As production increases from zero, average costs initially decline, then level off, and finally after a point begin to increase."

Figure 12.1
US City Current Spending Per Capita by Population (1990–91)

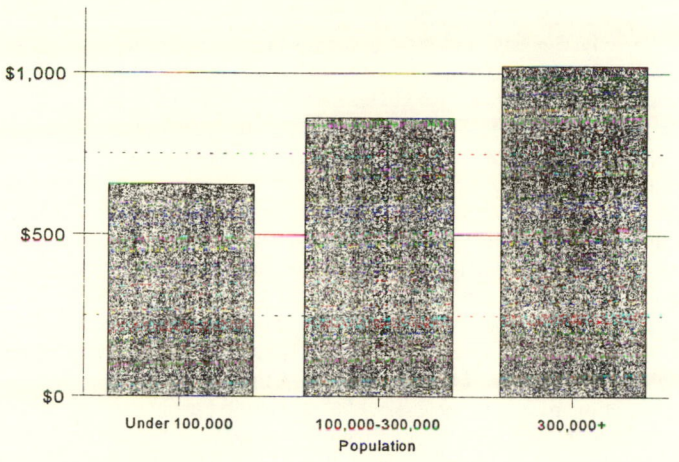

Source: Calculated from US Department of Commerce data.

The view is also expressed that central cities are subsidizing infrastructure in the suburbs. While this might be found to occur in fringe areas of cities that have aggressively annexed otherwise suburban territory (examples of cities with aggressive annexation policies are Phoenix, Austin, Oklahoma City, Nashville and others), it generally does not occur where suburban areas are separate municipal jurisdictions. Typically, suburban jurisdictions fully pay for their own infrastructure. Indeed, it is more likely that suburban jurisdictions subsidize central cities, through programs such as regional taxation supporting public transit[6] or state urban aid programs that often provide more funding per capita to central cities (Husock and Cox 1999).

A similar pattern is exhibited in public transit. Using 1997 data, a survey of the ten metropolitan areas[7] with transit agencies principally or exclusively serving the dense central city found bus costs per hour to be 32 percent higher than for suburban transit agencies in the same metropolitan areas.[8] Among the more dense central cities, the cost differential was higher, at 38 percent (six cases in which central city density exceeded 6,000 per square mile).

One of the most often cited reasons for people choosing to live in the suburbs rather than in the central city is that taxes are generally lower. Taxes are generally lower because the cost of providing services is generally lower. The higher costs associated with the larger, more dense central city jurisdictions is the result of a number of factors.

- *Diseconomies of Management Scale* As governments increase in size they require additional layers of management and support personnel, further increasing costs. For example, the Advisory Commission on Intergovernmental Relations (1987) observes, "One important variant of economies of scale is diseconomies of scale in management. As the size of a provision unit increases, beyond some point, scale economies attained as a technical matter of production may be offset by management difficulties that multiply as the provision unit attempts to organize more production in house."

- *Greater Resistance to Innovation* Smaller governments tend to experiment more than larger governments, and they are more innovative. A healthy competition develops among local governments as the media and citizens take note of comparative efficiency and effectiveness. As government increases in size, there are fewer comparable governments against which to compare their performance. In addition, the larger bureaucracy and stronger public employee unions tend to more successfully resist innovation.

- *Smaller Governments are More Accountable* Smaller governments tend to be more accountable and responsive to their citizenry. They are more accountable to citizens because the individual citizen has more voice in a smaller governmental unit. For example, a voter's voice in a city of 100,000 population carries 10 times as much weight as a vote in a city of 1,000,000. Bigger government is more remote from the electorate and is, by definition, less financially accountable and less responsive.

- *Smaller Governments are More Responsive* As governments increase in size, processes and communications necessarily become more bureaucratized (more rigid). As government processes become more rigid, they become less understandable to the individual citizen. This discourages people from addressing issues with their government. Less efficient and ineffective feedback often causes smaller problems to escalate into crises, as it is only when circumstances become unbearable that citizens have sufficient impetus to deal with the overly complex processes typical of more remote governments. With a less efficient and effective feedback system, the quality of government services is likely to decline.

- *Larger Governments are More Susceptible to Special Interests* This is so for three reasons. First, special interests have the financial resources to hire professional advocates (such as lobbyists) to learn, understand, and manipulate the rigid processes of larger governments. Conversely, individual citizens and neighborhood groups rarely have the financial resources to hire professional advocates. Second, there are economies of scale with respect to political advocacy; it is simpler and less expensive for special interests to influence a larger government than multiple smaller governments. Third, the more diffuse voice of the electorate makes larger government more susceptible to special interest influence. A particularly relevant current example is the adoption of prevailing wage ordinances, which are most frequently adopted in central cities, that artificially raise the costs of public service provision.

- *Smaller Local Governments are More Attuned to Communities and Neighborhoods* Regional governments are necessarily more sensitive to broader geographic issues than local, community, or neighborhood issues. This is because regional governments include a larger number of communities, which diminishes the voice of each such community in the political process. Individual, neighborhood, and community issues are likely to be less effectively addressed by larger, rather than smaller governments. As a result, regional governments are not appropriate for local governance.

- *Large Governments are Less Controllable* Larger governments tend to be more difficult for policymakers to control. As governments become larger, elected officials must rely to a greater degree on their staffs and are less well positioned to effectively exercise their oversight function.

- *Larger Governments Exhibit Lower Degrees of Cost Consciousness* Partially because of the more important role of special interests, larger governments tend to have less of a cost consciousness than smaller governments. This is illustrated by the current trend toward adoption of prevailing wage ordinances which increase the cost of labor on public and some private projects. This higher cost results in lower levels of service, higher unit costs, and lower rates of return on tax and user fee funding.

If cost minimization was a paramount objective in local government, then greater efforts would have been undertaken to implement readily available cost controlling strategies. The most important of these, use of the competitive market, tends to yield cost savings that are greater than the percentage of municipal spending represented by infrastructure.

IMPROVING EFFICIENCY AND EFFECTIVENESS: COMPETITIVE SERVICE PROVISION

Around the world there is an increasing awareness that economic growth is fostered by competitive markets, and that the market induces the most efficient use of scarce resources. For some time, this awareness has led governments to implement competitive methods for delivering public services, especially competitive contracting. The same dynamic operates with respect to the provision of public infrastructure, though progress in the United States has been less rapid than in other nations. Public infrastructure projects can be effectively and efficiently provided through the competitive market. In some cases, private companies compete for the responsibility for developing and operating infrastructure projects on a long-term basis. In other cases, governments grant franchises (concessions) for private companies to build facilities, operate them for a time, then transfer ownership to government at a time predetermined by contract.

Competitive infrastructure development works because it is consistent with the incentives of the market. Participating companies have an ownership interest in efficient development, because they pay—not the government—if there are cost overruns. As a result, costs tend to be lower, as the companies try to avoid overly expensive features that increase costs without providing a market rate return on investment. Projects are developed in such a manner that they have the requisite life cycle, because if they do not, the private developer pays, not government.

There is great potential to improve public infrastructure through competitive mechanisms. Achieving the potential requires enactment of enabling legislation, relaxation of unduly restrictive regulations, delineation of the principles by which genuine public purposes can be best served, and development of programs to select the most efficient and effective providers of public infrastructure projects. The most fundamental advantages of competitive infrastructure development and operation are lower costs, better service quality, and higher tax revenues.

- *Lower Costs* Competitive infrastructure can produce the same services and facilities at lower costs than public agencies. Public agencies can apply the savings to higher public service levels, or tax relief. Lower costs result because of the influence of the competitive market, in which firms pay no more than necessary for the factors of production—they pay the market price. They minimize their costs both by purchasing at the lowest possible price and by productively using the goods and services they have purchased.

- *Better Service Quality* Effectively administered, competitive infrastructure can result in improved quality of service. The public agency can have greater control over service quality, because it can exercise more effective corrective options. For example, many competitive infrastructure contracts provide for fines against contractors in the event of substandard performance. Because fines result in a financial loss (that cannot be passed on to the taxpayers), contractors have a strong interest in achieving quality standards. This type of incentive—imposition of financial loss as a penalty for sub-standard performance—is not duplicable in the public sector.
- *Higher Tax Revenues* Private providers of infrastructure may pay taxes equaling up to 15 percent of the annual contract value (Savas 1987). Generally, publicly operated infrastructure is exempt from taxation and often makes no payments in lieu of taxes.
- *Alignment of Revenues and Costs* Use of the competitive market can provide a mechanism for transparent alignment of infrastructure costs and revenues, so that there are no cross-subsidies.

COMPETITIVE INFRASTRUCTURE DEVELOPMENT

Competitive infrastructure development means that government uses a competitive procurement process to develop or improve publicly sponsored facilities. The process permits competitors wide latitude in designing the project, which is based on broad performance guidelines established by government (capacities, safety standards, etc.). The company that wins the contract takes the risk for obtaining necessary permits, complying with environmental requirements, and delivering the project within the agreed cost. If operations are included under the terms of the contract, the contractor operates the facility. The contractor is responsible for ensuring that the facility is operated in accordance with the performance requirements in the contract and applicable environmental regulations. Competitive infrastructure development offers guaranteed project costs, more advanced technology, and more timely completion of the facility. Two examples show the potential of competitive infrastructure development. The city of Seattle is using competitive development to build and operate a water filtration plant. The savings are expected to be 40 percent over 25 years compared to government development and operation (Reason Public Policy Institute 1997). In Edgewater, New Jersey, the city used competitive infrastructure development for a new wastewater treatment plant. A 20-year contract was signed, with savings estimated at 25 percent (U.S. Environmental Protection Agency 1990).

There are four major forms of infrastructure development.

1. *Competitive Development.* Involves the development and operation of facilities under public sponsorship with private ownership and operation. Contract terms are long (up to 20 years).
2. *Build-Operate-Transfer (BOT).* Involves private development and operation of a facility with ownership transferred to government at the end of the contract. The contractor operates the facility during the period of the contract. Contract terms tend

to be long (up to 20 years). At the end of the contract, new proposals for continued operation can be solicited from the competitive sector.

3. *Design-Build.* Involves, at a minimum, competitive development of detailed design plans and construction, consistent with the general performance specifications outlined in the public agency's call for competition. Ownership is ultimately public from the initiation of the project or upon acceptance by the public agency when operations commence. Operation of the facility may be included in the contract.

4. *Wrap Around Development.* Can be used to apply competitive development to the expansion or upgrade of existing facilities. Government can solicit proposals from the competitive sector to undertake the improvements, while assuming control of the currently operating facility.

COMPETITIVE SERVICE DELIVERY (COMPETITIVE CONTRACTING)

Competitive service delivery occurs when government uses a competitive procurement process to purchase publicly sponsored services from one or more contractors. Competitive service delivery is under the full public policy control of the public agency, which specifies the service to be competitively contracted and determines the quantity and quality of services; ownership of facilities and equipment may be public or private. Competitive service delivery does not necessarily result in private operation of public services. If the public agency demonstrates its ability to provide the same level and quality of public service or facility for less, it is awarded the contract. Competitive service delivery can result in improved longer term cost control by creating competitive pressures on the costs of services remaining under direct public provision.

Several examples illustrate the possibilities for competitive service delivery. The city of Indianapolis is saving 40 percent of its costs over five years as a result of competitive service delivery with respect to its wastewater treatment system (Goldsmith 1997). The city of Bridgeport, Connecticut, has reduced its costs of wastewater operation by 20 percent through competitive service delivery (Reason Public Policy Institute 1997). And Jersey City has reduced its wastewater treatment costs by 35 percent as a result of competitive service delivery (Reason Public Policy Institute 1997). A number of U.S. urban areas have used competitive service delivery to reduce the cost of bus and paratransit (dial a ride) services. Cost savings have been one-third or more in major projects in Denver, Las Vegas, and San Diego (Cox 1999). This trend has been more pronounced in Europe, Australia, and New Zealand, where entire public transport systems have been converted to competitive contracting, including subway, light rail and commuter rail systems (Cox, Love, and Newton 1997). Public policy directives have required or will require competitive contracting for virtually all bus systems in Australia, New Zealand, Europe, South Africa, and Hong Kong.

A SPECIAL CASE: ROADWAYS

To some extent, roadways have been placed in the competitive market through private toll roads that have been built in California and Virginia. However, the larger function of providing and maintaining the roadway system, including freeways, major arterials, and local streets, remains a government monopoly virtually throughout the nation. And, like wastewater and water systems in growing areas that rely on government development and provision, roadway systems are in crisis. Polls indicate that suburban residents are very concerned about traffic congestion, which arises from less than optimal roadway capacity and management. In many suburban communities governments have not provided sufficient roadway capacity to support the development that has occurred. This is not simply a matter of freeway construction, but also includes the provision of primary and secondary signalized arteries. The well-publicized traffic problems of Atlanta are a prime example of this problem. There, reliance on a radial freeway pattern designed for the centrally oriented city of the 1950s and a primitively developed surface arterial system has produced some of the nation's worst traffic congestion.

Do Roadways Create Traffic?

Public officials have been led to believe that building new roadways does not reduce traffic congestion, but rather that it substantially increases automobile use. Two studies are often cited that purport to demonstrate the futility of accommodating traffic by building more roadways. A study by Mark Hansen and Yuanlin Huang (1997) found that the percentage increase in freeway traffic is 90 percent of the percentage increase in freeway lane mileage. This is, effectively, a finding that the mere provision of additional capacity causes people to drive more. This is referred to as induced demand. This type of conclusion has led to the view that it is impossible to build our way out of congestion. A report by the Surface Transportation Policy Project (STPP) (1998) analyzed the 70 urbanized areas in the 1996 Texas Transportation Institute Roadway Congestion Index (RCI)[9] survey. STPP found that the one-half of the urbanized areas that built fewer new roadway miles from 1982 to 1996 had approximately the same RCI as the one-half that built more miles.

The Hanson-Huang study, however, was limited to freeways and did not quantify the impact of freeways expansion on adjacent arterials and other surface streets. When faster roadways, such as freeways, are opened, drivers will switch from slower arterials, which implies that a large percentage of the induced demand found by Hanson and Huang was likely to be demand transferred from other roadways.[10] The STPP report failed to note that the RCI in urbanized areas that built less roadway increased one-third more than in the urbanized areas where more roadway was built. Moreover, STPP failed to account for differences in population growth. The urbanized areas that built more roadway grew 13 percent more than the areas that built less. In the one-half of urbanized areas that built more roadways, the population adjusted Roadway Congestion Index rose 8.9 percent, less than one-third of the 30.5 percent rate of change in the urban areas that built less roadway (see Figure 12.2). These studies purporting to show that additional roadway construction does not alleviate traffic congestion have obvious and serious flaws.

If the mere provision of additional highway capacity were a primary generator of additional traffic, then one would expect that per capita street and highway

Figure 12.2
Change in Roadway Congestion Index Adjusted for Population Change: 1982–1996

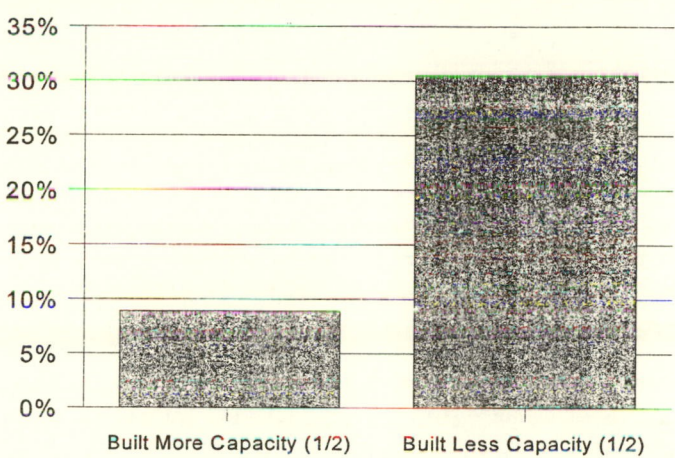

Source: Calculated from Texas Transportation Institute Roadway Congestion Index data (1982 and 1996).

travel would increase significantly more in urbanized areas that expand their highway systems the fastest. This, however, is not the case. From 1982 to 1996, urban areas that expanded highways the most (the top quintile) did so 240 percent more than the urban areas that expanded highways the least (the bottom quintile). The high expansion urban areas experienced street and highway travel per capita increases of 24 percent more than the low expansion urban areas— about one-tenth the rate of roadway expansion[11] (see Figure 12.3).

Figure 12.3
Change in Lane Miles and Miles per Capita: 1982–1996: Urbanized Areas

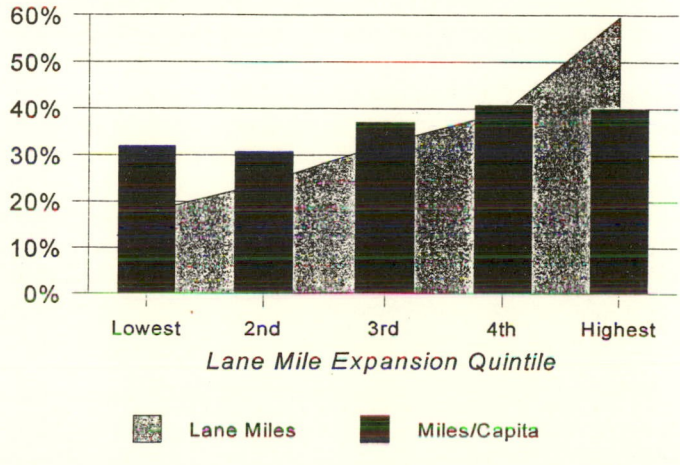

Source: 40 Largest Urban Areas Calculated from Texas Transportation Institute data.

A similar conclusion was recently reached by a University of North Carolina-Charlotte study, which found that the building of Beltways around urban areas was not a material factor in increasing traffic volumes, and may have actually contributed to lower overall traffic levels (Hartgen and Curley 1999). There is no statistically significant relationship between roadway expansion and the increase in vehicle miles traveled per capita.[12] This is not to suggest that there may be a small increase in total miles traveled as a result of new roadways. Faster roadways make it possible for people to gain access to more distant locations without increasing their travel time, which could encourage longer trips. But the actual time traveling is not likely to increase. This is illustrated by the fact that the average commuting time has changed little in recent years. As traffic congestion becomes worse, people make adjustments so that their travel times do not materially increase (see also Chapter 3).

Finally, in the 1970s, planned freeways were canceled in a number of communities, such as Los Angeles, Chicago, and Washington, DC. Not surprisingly, these three urbanized areas have the greatest traffic congestion. Such cancellations were conscious choices made in a policy environment that did not anticipate the obvious consequence of traffic congestion that would become much worse. The intervening quarter century has proven just that. Meanwhile, some urban areas have demonstrated that expanding highways can lead to reduced traffic congestion. For example, expansion of highways lead to an 11 percent reduction in traffic congestion in Houston from 1984 to 1996. And, after adjusting for population, the urban areas that have expanded roadways more have had smaller increases in traffic congestion.

The Problem: Insufficient Supply

While it may not be a popular contention, the fundamental cause of traffic congestion in U.S. urbanized areas is *insufficient road space.* Generally, the most congested urbanized areas have lower ratios of lane miles to population. Thus, it is not surprising that the most dense urban areas have the most significant traffic congestion (Figure 12.4).

The failings of modern roadway systems represent a highly visible government failure. Because of regulatory and financial constraints, governments have simply not supplied enough road infrastructure. Often, user fees (largely gasoline taxes) have been levied at the state level, which has created an obligation to widely distribute revenues for building or expanding roads in both growing and nongrowing areas. But, in most states, growth is concentrated in the largest urban areas. At the local level, major surface arterials are under the jurisdiction of individual municipalities, which have been less than successful in developing an integrated system that moves traffic not only within, but through such communities. This is a particular problem in suburbs, where surface arterial roadway improvements have often lagged far, if not irreparably behind development.

Figure 12.4
Traffic Congestion by Density: 1996

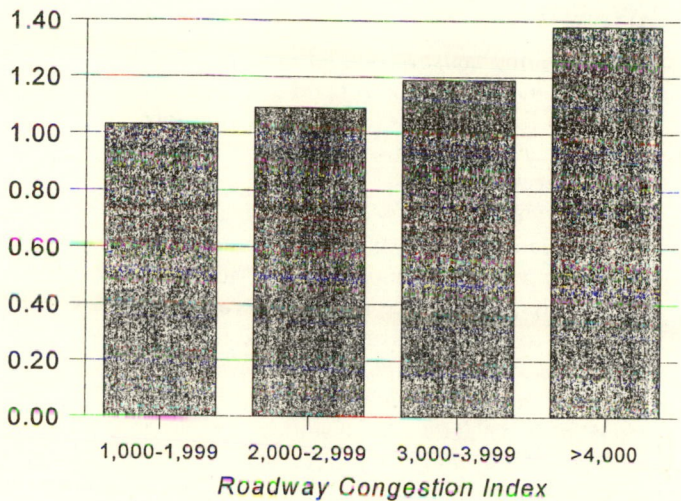

Source: Calculated from Texas Transportation Institute 1996 Roadway Congestion Index data.

Competitive Franchising

Recent technological advances, however, have made competitive roadway provision feasible (see Poole, Chapter 4). In Singapore, road-pricing programs automatically collect tolls from drivers, using overhead gantries, while Toronto's new Route 407 automatically collects tolls as drivers pass at freeway speeds. As a result, it is now possible for communities to franchise their roadway systems, thereby using the competitive market. This could be accomplished by a competitive procurement in which a community specifies various standards, such as average speeds, levels of service, safety considerations, and capacities. Competitive franchising of roadways would reduce or eliminate political interference that might otherwise lead to less than optimal roadway investments. An important consideration would be to keep the conversion to competitive road franchising revenue neutral, so that users do not pay both road user fees and fuel taxes.

At the same time, roadway authorities should develop plans to improve roadway systems that are able to accommodate the demand for travel. Such a course of action would not be without difficulty. In congested suburban areas, it would be necessary to build and expand roadways through developed areas. However, the mistakes of the 1960s and 1970s, when government failed to level with the public with respect to the consequences of canceled freeways, should not be repeated. The public deserves to be made aware of the choices. It could be that there will be insufficient political will to take the actions necessary in such areas to accommodate the demand, but at least a choice will have been made based on complete and reliable data. With respect to developing areas, both development and implementation of plans to accommodate traffic volumes will be more simple.

Who Pays and How

Regardless of the mechanisms used for infrastructure development and provision, infrastructure must be paid for. Until comparatively recently, infrastructure has tended to be financed in several ways. Some infrastructure is provided by the private sector, and financed wholly by users. Major electricity and telecommunications infrastructure tends to be paid for by allocation to the entire rate base, while individual electricity consumption is paid for by individual residential and business consumers. Virtually all electricity in the nation is produced by private companies or government enterprises that are organized in a manner similar to private corporations. The situation is similar with respect to natural gas. Wastewater and roadway infrastructure is largely provided by government. Generally, these forms of infrastructure have been financed by government-imposed user fees or taxes. Schools are provided by government, with support through general taxation. Under this historical approach, the on-site costs of infrastructure development ultimately were paid for by consumers who purchased developed property.[13] This remains the case today. What is changing is the manner of financing off-site infrastructure, such as wastewater treatment plants, roadways, and power plants. Until recently, these facilities had been financed by the entire rate or tax base.

As pressure on public budgets has mounted over the last quarter century, governments have begun to change the way they finance infrastructure, by imposing impact fees. Rather than having the rate or tax base pay for off-site infrastructure expansion, impact fees have been assessed on new developments. Generally, impact fees have been charged only with respect to government-provided infrastructure. Infrastructure provided by the private sector continues to be wholly financed by the rate base. For example, while government have imposed impact fees for waste water and transportation, it has not imposed electricity or natural gas impact fees.

Impact fees represent a form of double taxation with respect to the properties on which they are assessed. In addition to paying the impact fees, owners must pay the full rate or tax that has been assessed to pay for the infrastructure system as it existed before the new development. The use of impact fees represents a fundamental shift in the way that infrastructure is financed in the United States. Before the Second World War and for decades following it, the community paid for infrastructure improvements. Purchasers of new homes and those who occupied or purchased older homes would pay for both the pre-existing infrastructure system and any expansions or improvements that were necessitated by growth. The cost was high, because population growth was substantial after World War II. The cost was intensified by another factor—the movement of millions of people from the dense central cities to the suburbs. As had historically been the case, the generation following World War II provided and paid for the infrastructure required for itself and the next generation. Under the newer impact fee approach, those who move into new housing in a community pay a disproportionate share of infrastructure costs.

The financing of infrastructure through impact fees is inequitable, for several reasons. For example, impact fees are imposed on some home buyers and not others. Impact fees are paid only by new home buyers. Buyers who purchase homes that are not new do not pay. Buyers who purchased new or older homes before the imposition of impact fees do not pay. If impact fees are used to offset the costs of upgrading and maintaining infrastructure, new residents buying existing homes are subsidized by new residents buying new homes. Impact fees raise the price of new housing, which is especially burdensome to buyers of lower cost housing. For example, $10,000 in impact fees represents a much higher percentage of the price of a $100,000 house than a $500,000 house. Impact fees may be $50,000 or higher. By raising the price of housing, impact fees make it more difficult for first time and low income buyers to qualify for mortgages.

DE-POLITICIZING INFRASTRUCTURE

To the extent that there is an infrastructure crisis in urban or suburban America, it is a government infrastructure crisis. No crises exists with respect to the infrastructure provided by the private sector. The traditional commercial user-pay system of financing the building and operation of infrastructure continues today with such private sector services as water service, telecommunications, electricity, and natural gas. Companies in these businesses have the advantage of operating with little or no political interference in their commercial decisions. As a result, the financing crises that typically plague governments have little impact on privately provided infrastructure. The situation is similar to other private commercial sectors, where companies price and provide services and products largely in response to the market. As a result, in both private infrastructure and the remainder of the private sector, there is normally no shortage of goods or services and no cost crisis.

The private or competitive model needs to be applied in the provision of public infrastructure and infrastructure services. As already noted, a number of ways exist for governments to harness the competitive market to control costs and ensure effective supply of infrastructure services. The competitive procurement process minimizes the political manipulations that can make it difficult for government to provide what is essentially a commercial service (e.g., political pressure to keep prices below levels needed to cover maintenance and capital costs). The efficiency and effectiveness of infrastructure can be best improved by de-politicizing it, subjecting infrastructure instead to the market. The first priority for governments should be to permit the competitive market system to develop infrastructure where feasible. This is already occurring in telecommunications and significant advances are pending in electricity. The second priority for governments should be to use the regulated competitive market, where unregulated competition is not feasible. This may be accomplished through franchises that authorize competitive operation or utilize competitive infrastructure development and competitive contracting.

CONCLUSIONS

Governments and urban planners must take into account the reality of consumer preferences. People generally prefer to live in kinds of detached housing that suburban settings provide.[14] They tend to prefer the direct and comparatively quick access of personal mobility that only the automobile is capable of providing for the overwhelming majority of urban trips.[15] These market-driven factors work against the Smart Growth goals of increased population densities and reduced reliance on personal automobile travel.

As if this were not enough, lower quality educational systems and higher crime rates are associated with the more dense central cities. These two factors in and of themselves are likely to deter any significant movement of people into the central cities. As a result, governments need to be prepared to facilitate the infrastructure development that will be necessary to accommodate the living patterns that will continue to emerge. At the same time that suburbanizing trends are transforming the urban form in Europe and Japan, Americans are not likely to be herded into more dense commercial and residential development. And finally, the more that governments rely on market mechanisms for the provision of infrastructure, the less will be the tax burden on their citizens.

NOTES

1.   Urbanized areas with a population of more than one million in 1990 (www.demographia\db-urb-sub50.htm).

2.   Capital costs as a percentage of direct expenditures. Both state and local expenditures are included because infrastructure is provided and financed by both state and local governments. Calculated from U.S. Census Bureau information. Includes all construction (new facilities expansion and refurbishment of existing facilities).

3.   Calculated from U.S. Department of Commerce National Income and Product Account Information (1995).

4.   Calculated from 1990-91 U.S. Census Bureau data. Education and government enterprise (utility) expenditures excluded (in most cities these functions are performed by other public agencies or privately owned utilities). Data does not include amalgamated city-county governments.

5.   http://www.publicpurpose.com/ut-us97mbecsc.htm.

6.   Typically, the overwhelming portion of public transit benefit is received by the central city, in which service levels are higher than in suburban areas and to which most commuting occurs (to the central city's downtown area).

7.   Metropolitan areas of more than 1,000,000 population. Survey included all 13 central city public transit agencies and 56 suburban transit agencies.

8.   http://www.demographia.com/db-ptcitysub.htm.

9.   A Roadway Congestion Index of more than 1.00 indicates that roadway capacity is less than traffic demand. A Roadway Congestion Index of less than 1.00 means that there is more roadway capacity than traffic demand.

10.   One advantage of building freeways is improved safety. In 1994, fatalities per 100 million passenger miles were 60 percent lower on freeways than on the rest of the roadway system (calculated from Federal Highway Administration data).

11.   Analysis of Texas Transportation Institute RCI data, 1982 to 1996, urban areas of more than one million population.

12. Lane miles per capita is used to factor out the traffic volume increasing impact of larger population. A regression analysis found the relationship between lane miles added and the change in vehicle miles per capita to be not statistically significant in urban areas of more than one million population (R^2 of 0.009, degrees of freedom: 38).

13. Developers generally pay for on-site infrastructure and pass the costs on to buyers.

14. For example, see "Consumer Survey on Growth Issues: April 1999," National Association of Homebuilders, Washington, DC and "Los Angeles Times Poll: Study 429: City of Los Angeles and Suburbs: Suburban Life" July 1999, www.latimes.com.

15. Paul M. Weyrich and Paul Lind (1999) note that transit is not a competitive alternative to the automobile for most trips. They define transit competitive trips as "trips for which high quality transit service is available." They further limit transit competitive trips largely to work and entertainment trips. In fact, transit represents a competitive alternative to the automobile only for work and entertainment trips that are downtown. Most urban travel is not to work or entertainment. With barely 10 percent of metropolitan employment in downtown areas, the practical potential for substituting transit use for auto use is small indeed.

Chapter 13

Fixing the Dysfunctional Central City

STEVEN HAYWARD

Revitalizing the central city has taken its place on the hierarchy of Good and Virtuous Things alongside revitalizing the family. There is a striking similarity between the nature of these two issues, starting with the fact that while everyone agrees that both inner cities and families need to be revitalized, no one quite knows how to do it, which leads to a lot of political platitudes and short-cut gimmicks. In recent years the cause of revitalizing central cities has taken on a new and urgent dimension. In addition to saving the central city for its own sake, many now argue that saving the central city is necessary in order to stop suburban sprawl. In fact, suburban sprawl is now blamed in large measure for the decline in central cities, and restricting suburban growth for the sake of the central city has become an increasingly common theme of Smart Growth (Katz, 1998; Rusk 1993, 1999). Less clear is whether Smart Growth has anything truly new or innovative to offer for the ills of central cities.

A politician looking for applause can seldom go wrong calling for revitalizing families or revitalizing central cities. Like our public discourse about the family, our discourse about "fixing the cities" invariably follows a well-trodden path of ritualistic, therapeutic rhetoric. Usually this rhetoric is a sure sign of what therapists call "denial." In fact, when you hear some of the same ideas advanced for both issues—tax credits for child care and tax credits for downtown development—you begin to suspect that some of the deepest aspects of the problems of both families and cities are being avoided. This has become a standard reflex of American politics—if some condition needs changing, throw a tax credit at it. And if a tax credit can't be passed or afforded, there is a sure-fire standby ready in the wings: the public-private partnership, which always generates soothing nods of approval, especially if it promises a win-win result for everyone. The staleness of conventional thinking about urban problems means that we are mostly repeating new variations of old mistakes. Many central cities have shown signs of improvement over the last decade, often in spite of the efforts of urban leaders. Larger improvements will require new thinking, along with a clear understanding of what we should *stop* doing.

The connection between what we today call dysfunctional families and dysfunctional central cities is not a new theme. The deadbeat dads that afflict broken families find their equivalent in the deadbeat bureaucrats who afflict broken cities. Unruly delinquent kids often think their troubles will be solved with a bigger allowance from mom; delinquent urban politicians often think their problems would be solved with a bigger allowance from Washington. Yet beneath these superficial similarities lies a serious thread.

The relationship of the healthy family to the healthy city was the starting point for the earliest known treatise on civic health, Aristotle's *Politics,* written around 340 b.c. Aristotle's approach to the relationship of the family to the city captures the innermost character of modern urban problems. A well-ordered city requires well-ordered citizens, but each depends on the existence of the other, creating a kind of chicken-and-egg problem: which comes first? This is why Aristotle's teaching in *Politics* cannot be fully appreciated without reference to his teaching in the *Nicomachean Ethics* (342 b.c.).

It stretches the limit of credulity, not to mention comic imagination, to suppose that our big city mayors could become suffused with the outlook of Aristotle or even Immanuel Kant,[1] but the classical approach recommends itself as a starting point for thinking anew about the nature of modern urban problems in America (Arkes 1981). A person who is not part of a city, Aristotle wrote (340BC, 1253a 14), "must therefore be either a beast or a god," because the first purpose of a city is to make possible the self-sufficiency of the household. Self-sufficiency was not possible in antiquity without association with a city of some kind, and typically this meant, up until the early twentieth century, living in or near central cities in very high population densities.

But as modernity gradually expanded the potentiality of self-sufficient living with increasing detachment from the central city, culminating in the Internet and Federal Express age (which has made it possible to live a complete life in "exurbia," remote from any city), suburban living has become the dominant form of life for middle-class people. Because of this, modern cities find themselves in circumstances utterly unimaginable to Aristotle or any other ancient or even early modern theorist of civic life. Until the rise of a large and mobile middle class, and the falling transportation and communication costs that have accompanied the rise of the middle class, cities didn't have any reason to fear for competition from any other form of civic life. The central city dominated and thrived by necessity. Today that necessity is a distant memory. In other words, the troubles of the contemporary central city can be seen as a slow-motion casualty of the Industrial Revolution that ironically fueled the vast growth and consolidation of cities in the late eighteenth and early nineteenth centuries before a succeeding wave of progress and prosperity made the suburban diaspora possible.

More than just technological change and economic growth have driven the rise of suburban living. Concurrent social trends have also transformed city life. The deepest trend of all is the one that is hardest to quantify and attribute to any specific policy or economic factor: the ever-expanding sphere of private life. While it may sound grandiose, it is not inaccurate to say that the history of western civilization, at least since the arrival of liberal individualism, has been the history of the ever-expanding sphere of private life. In the city of antiquity, the public square was the focus of almost all city life because so few amenities or sources of entertainment could be found in private homes (such as they were). Early modern philosophers in the eighteenth century noted that one of the implications of the rise of property rights and liberal individualism was that people would increasingly tend toward the cultivation of their private gardens at the cost of a diminished sense of citizenship. In our own time technology and affluence have allowed for a great advance in the material conditions of private life. The increasingly affluent baby boom generation wants to live in a relaxed-fit house to go with their relaxed-fit blue jeans, which is why the average size of new homes is one-third larger than it was in 1970, while the average household size continues to shrink (see Chapter 2). For a mundane but telling example of the ever-expanding sphere of private life, consider that it is no longer necessary to go downtown to the opera house to hear an aria; a good CD player will deliver almost the same quality in the comfort of your own living room, and DVD players can provide a high-quality image on your big screen TV. All of this with none of the traffic and parking hassles of downtown.

This is exactly what communitarian liberals dislike about suburbia today, but it is short-sighted to attribute it solely to the spatial pattern of low-density suburban development. Our low-density suburbs are an *effect* of the long-term trend of expanding private life, not a cause of it. The expanding sphere of private life is the flip side of the supposed decline of civic engagement by Americans. This concern is not unserious, but the issue of Americans' civic engagement is another aspect of modern life that is hard to quantify and analyze in a rigorous way, despite the ingenious work of social scientists like Harvard's Robert Putnam, who has taken measures such as the decline in bowling leagues as a proxy for civic engagement (the famous "Bowling Alone" thesis) (Putnam 1995). But if bowling leagues and other older forms of communal activity have declined, certain others have proliferated, such as the soccer mom phenomenon. So strong is the anti-suburban bias of the chattering classes that when recent scholarship turned up positive conclusions about suburban life the news rated a front page notice in the *The New York Times* ("Some Perched in Ivory Tower Gain Rosier View of Suburbs") (Peterson 1999.).

The point is, the transformation of the American metropolis from an urban-dominated to a suburban-dominated form is a *fait accompli*. As the late Edward Banfield noted back in 1973 in his essay on "The Logic of Metropolitan Growth," even an all-wise and all-powerful government could not change this pattern except by first changing the conditions that give rise to it [i.e., rising affluence and falling transportation and communication costs]. The argument is not that nothing can be done to improve matters [for central cities]. Rather, it is that only those things can be done which lie within the boundaries—rather narrow ones, to be sure—fixed by the logic of the growth process itself. (Banfield 1973, 26)

The technological and social trends that have fueled the rise of suburbia and exurbia have led some observers such as George Gilder to suggest that cities are obsolete. This judgment seems too hasty and sweeping. There are too many examples of central-city neighborhoods that are thriving by catering to a special niche, which will be discussed later in this chapter. The examples of thriving areas within many major cities leads observers to say that what central cities must do is learn to compete with suburbs. This is a mistaken lesson. As Banfield observed, "it is idle to talk of bringing large numbers of the well-off back into the central city" (1973, 45).

Yet this is exactly what we have been trying to do through our urban revitalization efforts. For most of the postwar era urban policy has unfortunately attempted to fly in the face of the logic of metropolitan growth and has tried to recapture a past golden age that never really was. This is the first of two major fallacies plaguing urban thinking, and can be given the shorthand name, "nostalgia complex." Professors Witold Rybczynski and Peter Linneman of the University of Pennsylvania concisely summarize what the replacement of the old downtown "vertical city" with the suburban "horizontal city" means for planning and revitalization efforts:

The horizontal city has been built for a society with much greater disposable income (as a result of real income growth and two-earner families) and different quality-of-life expectations. It is a city that owns (indeed loves) cars. It is a crude generalization, and *one that the proponents of traditional urbanism resist*, but the horizontal city seems to have provided a kind of life that the overwhelming majority of Americans consciously choose—in spite of their romantic image of the old vertical city. (1999, p. 31; emphasis added.)

This nostalgia for the city of a bygone era has led to a string of misguided and often disastrous public policy initiatives that in many cases have aggravated the practical problems of cities. The 1940s and 1950s were the heyday of urban renewal, which in some cases resulted in tearing down four times as many housing units than were built through the program. Martin Anderson (1964) estimated that "the federal bulldozer" displaced more than a million city dwellers from their neighborhoods. Undaunted and unrepentant from this disaster, the 1960s brought into vogue the Model Cities program, which was urban renewal with the face of a social worker. So confident were the social scientists and government planners in their powers to work the wholesale transformation of urban areas that they boasted that they would show the way to "the rebuilding of cities, not only in the United States but throughout the world" (Davies 1996, p. 44). Billions were appropriated for Model Cities, and years of riots and accelerating urban decay immediately followed. *"The government did not know what it was doing,"* Daniel Patrick Moynihan admitted in 1969 (Moynihan 1969, p. 170; emphasis in original).

In the 1970s and 1980s, with the Washington money spigot slowed though not fully cut off, chastened local civic leaders embraced a second planning fallacy that might be called the "Edifice Complex," or alternatively a "Field of Dreams" strategy—if we build it, they (middle-class suburbanites) will come. The Edifice Complex is based on the assumption that saving the downtown area is the key to saving the entire city, as if, as Professor Heywood Sanders of Trinity University writes, "the economic well-being of a Cleveland or Cincinnati or St. Louis depended upon a central business district attractive to people from somewhere else" (1998, p. 59). Downtown shopping malls, hotel/convention center complexes, and major sports stadiums and arenas (or, in the case of Cleveland, the Rock 'n' Roll Hall of Fame) became the hot ticket for revitalizing old city centers (Frieden and Sagalyn 1989). This strategy has obvious appeal to urban politicians who garner more glory from the easy and visible job of cutting red ribbons than through the hard and unseen job of cutting red tape, let alone cutting taxes. Hence, taxes and per capita spending in large cities remain typically more than twice as high as suburban taxes and spending.

What the Edifice Complex shows is that we tend to think of city problems in terms of design and planning, as if physical changes to housing, transportation, entertainment, and retailing venues will suffice to bring back life to a central city neighborhood. This conception of the problem is not wholly insensible. Preservationists of all stripes are fond of quoting Winston Churchill's remark that "First we shape our buildings, and then our buildings shape us."[2] However, a closer look at the details of current revitalization efforts reveals the weakness in this purely physical approach to the problem.

Here it should be observed that the Edifice Complex can be regarded as the downtown variant of New Urbanism. New Urbanism's embrace of "neo-traditional planning" (i.e., narrower streets, houses with front porches and small setbacks, and greater emphasis on mixed use) shares with the Edifice Complex the premise that the physical design is a vital prerequisite—perhaps *the* vital prerequisite—for revitalization. While this concern for physical structure is not insensible, the emphasis currently placed on it both in the suburbs and in downtowns is out of proportion with the actual results that can be expected.[3]

The first and most important observation to make is the distinction between *downtown* (or central business district—CBD) and *central city*. They are not the same thing. Although the downtown CBD may be the physical nucleus of the city, few people actually live downtown; often the downtown CBD accounts for 2 percent or less of a city's population (Kotkin 1999), and virtually no downtown CBD in the United States is experiencing significant employment growth (see Chapter 3). Hence the focus on big ticket downtown projects such as sports stadiums and convention centers is fundamentally misplaced, because they have little effect on central city neighborhoods and small local business districts that are most in need of physical and economic revitalization.

Having said this, a number of high profile revitalization efforts have proven to be a popular success (for example, Boston's Faneuil Hall Marketplace, Baltimore's Inner Harbor, Seattle's Pike Place Market, or San Diego's Horton Plaza, to name a few). Some of the elements in successful revitalization efforts, including the crucial elements of serendipity and spontaneity, are catalogued in

Roberta Brandes Gratz and Norman Mintz's *Cities Back from the Edge: New Life for Downtown* (1998). Gratz and Mintz point to the example of Mansfield, Ohio, an old, declining industrial town halfway between Cleveland and Columbus, which saw a rebound in its main street following the unlikely step of repairing the town's carousel. But no one would suggest that similarly situated towns should try to copy the Mansfield model, which is why Gratz and Mintz observe that "innovation can't be reduced to a formula."

This kind of serendipity extends to private sector trends that have large neighborhood effects. The proliferation of coffee houses in the 1990s, led principally by Starbucks, is a good example. Virginia Postrel notes that the typical Starbucks coffee franchise that is so ubiquitous today was not the original business model the company set out to follow, but was discovered along the way:

The original idea, writes [Starbucks] CEO Howard Schultz, "was to provide a quick, stand-up, to-go service in downtown office locations." Instead, the fastest-growing Starbucks stores turned out to be those near where people lived—the ones that functioned as neighborhood watering holes. The young adults who had grown up hanging out in shopping malls were looking for safe, friendly places to be with other people, places where, in Schultz's words, "No one is carded and no one is drunk." In focus groups, Los Angeles customers said they went to Starbucks because the place felt social. The company adjusted its strategy accordingly, building more and larger neighborhood stores, with more tables to sit around. It now deliberately seeks to foster a social, European-style café environment. (1998, p. 200)

In other words, it is not planning, but the discovery process of the marketplace, that has led to some of the most successful examples of neighborhood revival. Precisely because the successes of central city revival have depended on serendipity and unanticipated factors, devising a widely replicable model is impossible. For every Faneuil Hall in Boston there is a failure like the K Street pedestrian mall in Sacramento, California. Moreover, this kind of redevelopment typically depends on large public sector subsidies, and there is strong evidence that their economic spillover effect to surrounding neighborhoods, let alone the city at large, is very limited. The evidence about the net economic effects of sports stadium and convention center projects is especially dismal. And because tax law changes in the 1986 round of tax reform requires that bonds for sports stadiums must be tax-exempt general obligation (or "governmental bonds"), using a city's limited bonding capacity for an expensive stadium project means the resources are not available to other public works needs (Baade 1991; Baim 1990; Bernstein 1998; Hunter 1988; Mills 1991; Rosentraub, Pryzbylski, and Mullins 1994).

The results for convention centers is equally unimpressive. Heywood Sanders offers this gloomy assessment of convention center projects: "Indeed, in a number of cases, the expenditure of hundreds of millions of public dollars appears to have had almost no impact on individual communities" (1998, p. 59). Los Angeles, for example, spent $500 million ($150 million over the original budget) to expand its downtown convention center by 350,000 square feet, after which the number of visitors was expected to triple. Yet the number of visitors has remained flat. Washington, DC's new convention center has delivered only a fifth of the projected number of hotel stays. Houston's new convention center was supposed to generate 10,000 new jobs in the hotel and restaurant industry downtown by 1995, but fewer than 500 new jobs were generated. Similar poor results can be found in the convention center experiences in Boston, Philadelphia, Providence, and St. Louis. (For the true believers, the answer to these problems is to spend still more public funds to build more hotels near convention centers.)

A closely related strategy has been tax breaks and subsidies to lure—or retain—the large corporate employer at a downtown location. Downtowns have been losing business to the suburbs for 30 years now. The total amount of suburban commercial office space surpassed central city office space about 1980. New York City is the most extreme case. In 1965 the Big Apple was home to the headquarters of nearly half of the Fortune 500 companies. Today fewer than 50 remain. Other companies are "stripping down" their central city headquarters. Modern technology makes it effective and feasible to send most employees to the suburbs while keeping only a skeleton staff of the most senior executives downtown. Chevron is currently in the process of closing its downtown San Francisco headquarters and moving the bulk of its employees to suburban San Ramon (or San Remote, as the relocated employees call it).

Like major sports franchises with stadium demands, many large businesses use their mobility options to blackmail cities into granting them generous tax abatements to locate or remain in place. Former Indianapolis Mayor Stephen Goldsmith[4] summarizes the defect of this approach: "Using tax dollars to compensate for high taxes, crumbling infrastructure, or overly burdensome regulations is easier than actually addressing the problems themselves. When used in this manner, [tax] abatements are truly unsustainable development—a finger-in-the-dike solution to serious structural barriers to urban investment" (1997, p. 82).

In the 1990s the trend of redeveloping old towns, main streets, and warehouse districts has accelerated. Examples include Old Town Pasadena, California, the Gaslight District in San Diego, the West End in Dallas, the SoMa (South of Market Street) district of San Francisco, the City Hall Square area of Milwaukee, and numerous others. Some of these revivals have employed the same kind of subsidies, tax abatements, and tax increment financing schemes that have been used for downtown malls or to lure employers. Yet in many cases the revival has been more market-driven and accomplished mostly through private efforts (sometimes through Business Improvement Districts, which can be regarded as privatized sub-governments within the city limits), as people recognized the value and competitive advantage that existed in these formerly neglected neighborhoods.

Several observations should be made about the old town/main street revival efforts. First, these areas are only available to be reclaimed if they were lucky enough to have been spared the bulldozer during urban renewal 30 and 40 years ago. Even where old neighborhoods escaped the planners' bulldozer, many older neighborhoods in American cities have been partially disfigured by planning and building codes requiring large street setbacks or other modifications that have reduced the attractiveness of these areas for redevelopment.

Second, the economy of these reclaimed downtown neighborhoods is typically dependent on the presence of national chain restaurants (TGIFridays, Starbucks, etc.), a microbrewery or two, and specialty retail. While this works fine for the particular neighborhoods where redevelopment activity reaches critical mass, it is obviously not replicable on a city-wide basis.

Third, a number of old town/main street redevelopment projects have become a significant magnet for the revival of the housing market in surrounding neighborhoods (Chanen 1998, p. 31), but most of the people who locate in these areas are singles, empty-nesters, or young childless couples who will move to the suburbs when they begin families. In other words, the old town/main street revitalization efforts, as successful as many are proving to be, need to be understood as a niche, and not as a general formula for transforming entire cities. It is an open question in several cases to what extent old town revivals have accomplished even this; in some cases, such as the West End in Dallas, the chief accomplishment seems to have been to offer a more stimulating lunchtime environment for downtown office workers who have commuted in from the suburbs.

What might be called a right-wing version of the Edifice Complex holds that the most significant affliction of cities is high taxes and oppressive regulation. Like the fixation on the physical rehabilitation of city neighborhoods, there is considerable truth in this view, and certainly many cities have little chance of thriving economically unless they adopt more sensible fiscal and regulatory regimes. There are, sadly, few examples one can point to of cities that have made a substantial effort at deregulation and tax relief (Hayward 1998), and the efforts at improving the central city business climate through enterprise zones have been unimpressive. In economic terms, enterprise zones can be thought of as the conservative equivalent of a sports stadium or convention center. (The fact that the idea of enterprise zones has been so easily embraced by liberals under their own nomenclature of "empowerment zones" should be a clue that there is nothing especially bold or distinctive about the approach.)

San Diego Mayor Susan Golding forthrightly notes the defects of enterprise zones, saying that "none has been radical enough. If you want a great enterprise zone, look at Hong Kong." But her own experience shows how difficult it is to scrape away the barnacle-encrusted regulatory code of most cities. Golding started her own reform efforts by imposing a one-year moratorium on new regulations and fees when she became mayor in 1993. Then she initiated periodic "regulatory relief days," when the city council would review and reform existing regulations. She eventually succeeded in getting the city council to agree to slash San Diego's zoning code by 140,000 words—or more than a third—including 48 parking requirements, 78 sets of outdoor storage and signage regulations, and 15 different driveway width rules. But that was not the end of the story, as the zoning changes had to be approved by the recalcitrant California Coastal Commission, an appointed body that has final authority over the zoning codes of all coastal cities in the state. This process is still dragging on (Hayward 1998).

Similar state and federal rules tie the hands of mayors and city councils with regard to brownfield development, sewer and water facilities, road building and repair, and so forth. The Democratic Leadership Council (in a statement written anonymously by urban scholar Fred Siegel) offers the following suggestion: "[A]t the same time we test whether empowerment zones can revive dying districts, let's conduct another experiment. For two years, let's allow a major city to forego all federal aid in return for which it and its citizens will be relieved from federal regulations and taxes. Would such a city be better off? It's worth finding out." Indianapolis Mayor Stephen Goldsmith says, "I know a dozen mayors who would jump at the opportunity to find out" (1997, p. 93).

The various job-killing regulations, fees, occupational licensing requirements, and city-granted monopolies (not to mention onerous housing regulations and rent control) are a well known story. In New York City alone, according to an estimate by economists Steven G. Craig and D. Andrew Austin (1997), regulations have cost 1 million jobs. Civil rights litigation may be a more promising long-term route to reform than waiting for fiefdom-protecting city councils to embrace major change (Bolick; Berliner; Bullock; Matias; Mellor).

While the economic disincentives of doing business in the central city are serious, this point can be pushed too far. Consider, for example, the economic growth prospects of the following urban area: It is located in one of the highest tax states in the country, with the highest housing prices in the nation, the third worst traffic congestion in the nation, a severe labor shortage, and a scarcity of vacant land combined with oppressive land-use regulation making it difficult and costly to build new facilities. In the abstract such an urban area would seem highly uncompetitive for attracting new jobs and capital investment. Yet the urban region just described is Silicon Valley. It remains the creative center for high-technology innovation in spite of all the economic disincentives, chiefly because the returns from the agglomeration of the high-tech industry in Silicon Valley outweigh the economic impediments to profitability.[5] Many cities also find themselves in a condition of relative prosperity amidst the nation's booming economy, in spite of being ill-governed. This is not to suggest that cities can be heedless about their business climate, but neither should we delude ourselves that slashing taxes and regulations in Detroit or Buffalo would immediately make these or other cities competitive with Silicon Valley.

Another old idea for urban revitalization has gained fresh popularity and taken on some new aspects in the late 1990s: Regionalism—especially regional government. From a planning perspective, regional government or regional planning suffer all the same cognitive and information difficulties as any other kind of centralized economic planning: resources are not allocated efficiently, and growth and innovation are stifled. Jane Jacobs captured the essence of the trouble with "regionalism" in *The Death and Life of Great American Cities*:

> There is a widespread belief among many city experts today that city problems already beyond the comprehension and control of planners and other administrators can be solved better if only the territories involved and problem entailed are made larger still and can therefore be attacked more "broadly." This is escapism from intellectual helplessness. "A Region," somebody has wryly said, "is an area safely larger than the last one to whose problems we found no solution." (1961, p. 410)

But in the last decade regionalism has taken on broader dimensions than planning: today regionalism is seen as a means of arresting the socio-economic decline of central cities by capturing the tax base—and the residents—of the suburbs. This kind of regionalism seeks to redistribute the tax revenues of the richer suburbs to the poorer central city. Adding an urban growth boundary, which would prevent additional suburbanization and further exodus from the city, would make the policy more effective (Katz 1998; Katz and Bradley 1999; Rusk 1993, 1999). The tacit theory of this kind of regionalism seems to be: don't let people leave the city, or if they do, don't let them take their tax revenues with them. This can be regarded as an attempt by uncompetitive central cities to assert monopoly power.

Dwelling on the defects of regionalism is not necessary, for its enthusiasts are unlikely to overcome the political resistance of majority suburbanites in most cases. Jacobs again provides a common sense perspective:

The voters sensibly decline to federate into a system where bigness means local helplessness, ruthless, oversimplified planning, and administrative chaos—for that is just what municipal bigness means today. How is helplessness against conquering planners an improvement over no planning? How is bigger administration, with labyrinths nobody can comprehend or navigate, an improvement over crazy-quilt township and suburban governments? (1961, p. 410)

The contrary of the conventional wisdom is how we ought to be thinking: perhaps we ought to *break up* or de-annex parts of big cities. Howard Husock of Harvard's John F. Kennedy School of Government has started to explore the idea of urban secession, while urban scholars Rybcyznski and Linneman say that cities should consider the "drastic" alternative of de-annexation.

For example, they [central cities] could de-annex parts of their territory to private developers. If large tracts, in excess of 100 acres, say, were sold as de-annexed, unincorporated areas with associated suburban cost structures, it is possible that developers would find this an attractive opportunity to create "suburban" municipalities in the central areas of the city. . . . . New municipalities would be legally independent of the city. They would control their own governments, schools, and regulations. (1999, p. 41)

This is an intriguing possibility, but it concentrates the mind on the question of just what should be the object of urban revitalization policy. It is usually assumed without question that the goal of urban revitalization is to attract the middle class back into the city (and/or to slow the suburban exodus), as well as stabilize and restore central business districts. But this is a fool's errand. As Ed Banfield bluntly observed, "it is idle to talk of bringing large numbers of the well-off back into the central city. For the city to compete as a residential area with the suburbs, large districts of it would have to be completely rebuilt at very low densities" (1973, p. 45). De-annexing parts of cities might make lowering the density of central cities possible; indeed, a few eastern cities, such as Philadelphia, are starting to raze obsolete, abandoned high-density row housing and redevelop the areas at suburban densities and in suburban styles. But if it did start to occur on a wide scale, and began attracting significant numbers of suburbanites back into the city, the cry would surely ring out (as it already is in Oakland, California) that this represents "gentrification," i.e., a revival of the city "on the backs of the poor." Again, Banfield provides sobriety on the subject: "[I]t would be hard to give the well-off the space necessary to bring them back from the suburbs and still have room for the large number of the not well-off who would have to be accommodated" (p. 46). This brings us back again to the wisdom of Jane Jacobs, who wrote that "A metropolitan economy, if it is working well, is constantly transforming many poor people into middle class people."

This process is taking place in those cities with high rates of immigration, but it is lagging in cities with stagnant immigration rates. Perhaps, to dance around the edges of a new direction for a moment, what is most needed is not just reformed economic and physical structures, but something else that is usually not much discussed in dialogues about central city problems. Where might we look for this new direction?

Let's back into an answer this way: The foregoing criticisms of the current popular as well as heterodox themes in urban revitalization should not be taken to suggest that no wholesale improvement in central city conditions is possible. Already some large-scale favorable trends can be observed that provide hope and guidance for urban reformers. For example, if you had predicted ten years ago that not only would the 1990s experience a substantial drop in the crime rate, but that New York City would lead the way, most audiences would have looked nervously toward the wings for the men in white coats to come cart you away. But the crime rate in central cities is still fours times as high as it is in the suburbs on average, and more than twice as high as it was 40 years ago, which means our cities still have a ways to go before we can be satisfied that we have done all that can be done. Ten years ago most urban leaders seemed resigned to the crime rate, and did not think much could be done about it.

It is often said that crime is the steepest of all marginal taxes on city dwellers because, quite aside from its considerable cost (perhaps as much as $400 billion a year according to a Justice Department estimate in the mid-1980s), it obviously deters investment and economic activity in high-crime neighborhoods. No one has yet made a serious estimate of the economic benefits that may be underway in urban neighborhoods as a result of the falling crime rate, though the Heritage Foundation is conducting research on this issue (Lehrer, forthcoming). Of more significance for revitalization efforts are the lessons of the crime fight that can be transferred to other areas of urban revitalization. Tougher prison sentencing, changing demographics, and an improving economy have all played a role in the falling crime rate, but the wide variation in the crime rate between cities suggests that the most important variable has been the police practices in the most aggressive cities. Community policing, which can mean something as simple as getting patrol officers out of their cars and back into the neighborhood beat on foot or bicycle, is very much in vogue, but perhaps the most significant factor in the success of community policing has been its embrace of the so-called broken window theory.

James Q. Wilson and George Kelling (1982) promulgated the broken window theory in a widely noted article in *The Atlantic Monthly*. The theory argues that when the physical environment of a neighborhood deteriorates—when broken windows go unrepaired—and when the police ignore relatively minor transgressions of civility and decent public behavior (think of the "squeegee men" in

New York City, who practiced petty extortion of motorists at intersections), not only do these transgressions increase, but more serious crimes do as well.[6]

Community policing and the broken window theory represent a rejection of the older root causes approach to crime that dominated public discourse about the urban crime problem for the last generation. Unless the root causes of crime were treated through some comprehensive (and usually expensive) program, it was thought that crime could never be significantly reduced. "If upon taking office," Nathan Glazer wrote, "Mayor Giuliani had consulted sociologists, few would have predicted that having police simply get rid of the squeegee men would have much impact. But that is what the mayor did—and, strangely enough, the squeegee men did not return; nor was there any discernible increase in some other form of uncivil behavior or street extortion" (1997, p. 23).

The experience with crime may have lessons to offer for the other major deterrent to reviving urban neighborhoods—the public schools. The subject of improving urban schools is presently a bottomless pit of controversy among education reformers. As Milwaukee's Mayor John Norquist notes,

Centralization, decentralization, specialization, mainstreaming, busing, magnet schools, Head Start programs, early education, consolidation, conversion of schools from kindergarten-through-grade-eight facilities to junior high then to middle schools and eventually back again, Goals 2000, multicultural education, bilingual education, and, most recently, School to Work have all been tried. . . . Together, all these reforms have not stopped, and may have accelerated, a general decline in educational quality in big cities over the last thirty years. (1998, pp. 83–84)

This is why Norquist and others have embraced the idea of school choice *as an urban revitalization strategy*. Sociologists have long studied the deleterious neighborhood effects of bars, liquor stores, card rooms, and corner drug dealers. The prospect of dozens of small schools that would emerge spontaneously with widespread school choice suggests that the neighborhood effects of school choice might go a long way toward revitalizing central city neighborhoods. The reason small private schools may have more of an effect than public schools is precisely because they are *small* (and therefore more widely scattered throughout the central city), with more of a tie to the local neighborhood. One reason existing public schools do not have as much positive neighborhood effect is that the typical urban school has simply become too large, and is therefore viewed in the neighborhood as yet another impersonal, bureaucratic public institution. Smaller private schools are more tangibly tied to their local neighborhoods, and exist not by compulsion but because people in the neighborhood want it and use it. This reverses the relationship between neighbors and schools, as the neighborhood has a direct stake in the success of the local school.

"Choice [in education] adds crucial value to our cities," Mayor Norquist argues. There is some survey research to suggest that this effect may be substantial. A Calvert Institute survey of people who had moved out of Baltimore, for example, found that among families with school-age children, 80 percent gave poor quality of schools as the primary reason for their departure. Perhaps most significant is the finding that of those who cited poor schools as a reason for leaving, 51 percent said they might have stayed in the central city if full school choice were available.

Urban scholars David P. Varady and Jeffrey A. Raffel, authors of *Selling Cities: Attracting Homebuyers Through Schools and Housing Programs* (1995), offer corroborating evidence. Varady and Raffel note that Cincinnati has been more successful than other Ohio cities in stemming the exodus of middle-class families because it embraced magnet schools instead of forced busing to achieve desegregation. Even more significant, Varady and Raffel think, has been the role of Catholic parochial schools. "The Catholic schools are important for the city because they serve as 'neighborhood anchors,'" they write. "The [Catholic] schools serve to promote a high quality of life, particularly for parents who are neighborhood-oriented. St. Catherine School and Nativity School are examples of quality schools that are helping to maintain racially integrated neighborhoods." Another study of three Catholic schools in St. Louis concluded that the school had been "catalysts of positive neighborhood change" and had reversed the decline of these neighborhoods. "Without the three Catholic schools . . . the three neighborhoods would almost certainly be lost to urban decay" (Development Strategies, Inc. 1996).

Some of the early experiences of pilot school choice programs in central city neighborhoods are encouraging. On Cleveland's lower income east side, a voucher-supported Hope Academy that opened in 1996 has contributed significantly to the revitalization of the surrounding neighborhood. At the time the school opened, an abandoned building located across the street attracted indigents, drunks, and prostitutes, and a nearby bar operated 20 hours a day. But the Hope Academy, said John Morris, who provides management services to the school, "became an anchor for the local community, leading to a community effort among people who didn't even have children in the school. It pulled the neighborhood together to eradicate the bad stuff that had been going on." First, the neighborhood convinced the bar owner to reduce his hours, which led to an immediate decline in public drunkenness and prostitution. The police, who hadn't been much help at first ("They wanted to see if we'd stick around," said Morris), began patrolling more frequently and making more arrests. In the three years after the Hope Academy opened, there were no auto thefts and only one burglary. There are no longer any bars on the school's windows. "The revival of the neighborhood is a byproduct we hadn't counted upon," said Morris.

A similar story comes from Pacoima, California, where Yvonne Chan, founder of the Vaughn Learning Center (a charter school where the mostly minority student body is required to wear uniforms), repeatedly asked the police to shut down a crack house located adjacent to the school. Frustrated by inaction, Chan ultimately bought the crack house for $8,000—with savings achieved by contracting out certain school services—and held a "bulldozing party." Neighbors cheered as the crack house was demolished and a new learning center was built on the site. Because California's charter school law allows contracting out and exempts charter schools from the Davis-Bacon prevailing wage requirements, Chan was able to give the building contract to a neighborhood contractor and so further support the local area's growth (Hayward 1999.)

The neighborhood effects of school choice and the broken window theory of crime fighting both point to a larger, general theme for transforming city life, based on the idea that what is most needed to improve America's central cities is moral more than physical redevelopment. The toleration of broken windows, graffiti, trash in the street, homelessness, vagrancy, loitering, open drug dealing, not to mention the spread of public vulgarity and decline of any sense of public decorum, has had as much to do with the decline of city life as the physical decay of buildings and neighborhoods. What once would have been called "deviant," or at the very least "anti-social," behavior came not simply to be tolerated, but celebrated, in our city life.

Fred Siegel points to the paradigmatic case of Billie Boggs, a homeless schizophrenic woman who sued for her right to live on the sidewalks of New York (and use them for her toilet) in the 1970s, and who was greeted with celebrity status, feted on TV talk shows, and championed by "public interest" lawyers. The Boggs case represented the apotheosis of "lifestyle liberalism," and found its parallels in hundreds of other aspects of our public life, such as the increased difficulty of enforcing discipline in the public schools. Disruptive students and aggressive panhandlers alike were excused as "high-spirited nonconformists." "An unparalleled set of utopian policies produced the dystopia of day-to-day city life," Siegel wrote (1997, pp. 175–176), reminding us of the contrast between the power blackouts in New York City of 1965 and 1977; the first passed peacefully and quietly, while the second was the occasion of widespread looting.

The slow and partial reversal of the social decay of cities has been responsible for the marked improvement of many urban neighborhoods and public places. Some of the public spaces that vagrants and petty criminals had taken over have been taken back in recent years, while other public squares have reached a seemingly stable equilibrium. The important point here, however, is that there is little, beyond jawboning of the Giuliani "be-polite-and-don't-jaywalk" variety, that urban officials can do to bring about an improved moral climate in our cities, chiefly because aggressive laws against vagrancy, loitering, and other public nuisances have been undermined, perhaps irreversibly, by the appellate courts. A public library, a New Jersey court famously ruled, cannot even exclude from its premises a homeless person who refuses to bathe. New York City's Times' Square has become a poster child of sorts for chasing out pornography outlets and other low-life attractions through the aggressive use of zoning powers, but this example, which may not withstand the legal challenge now underway, shows the essential incoherence and thereby the sharp limits of a public law approach to the demoralized social fabric of city life.

We can regulate massage parlors, pornographic outlets, prostitution, liquor stores, and the like, the Supreme Court has said, only if there are harmful "secondary effects," such as providing an attraction for muggers, rapists, and pickpockets. By this same reasoning, Hadley Arkes has pointed out, the Court would have to allow the absurd prohibition of baseball games at Yankee stadium, or the closing down of Grand Central Station, because of their attraction to pickpockets (1999, p. 98). (What the Court might make of professional wrestling is a matter fit for wry speculation.)

While we wait for a restoration of common sense in the jurisprudence of public order, the task of improving the civic standards of public spaces in our cities should be carried on through private efforts. A better example than the clean-up of Times' Square is Bryant Park on 42nd Street, next to the New York Public Library. Bryant Park was for many years the domain of open drug dealing and a home for the homeless, largely avoided by pedestrians and office workers in the surrounding blocks. Local property owners and businesses formed the Bryant Park Restoration Corporation to give the park a makeover (the case of Bryant Park proved an ideal testing ground for Jane Jacobs' ideas of how to make a public space more functional) that would invite a pedestrian flow during the day. Now Bryant Park receives an estimated 8,000 visitors a day, and the Restoration Corporation sees to every detail, from keeping the restrooms clean to keeping the flowerbeds planted. The homeless and vagrants still come to the park, but they no longer dominate it or intimidate the neighborhood from using it (Gratz and Mintz 1998, pp. 38–42; Siegel 1992).

When the subject of restoring the moral order to our cities comes up, it is commonplace these days to hear great emphasis on the need for "faith-based" institutions (which we used to call, simply, churches) to take a leading role. Although the importance of churches as neighborhood anchors should not be slighted in the least, and while hundreds if not thousands of shining examples can be found of successful church-based efforts at neighborhood redemption, churches should be wary of becoming adjuncts for organized public policy approaches to city problems. The risk is that, as in so many other venues of policy, with the flow of public dollars comes the various strings and conditions that mitigate or undermine the effectiveness of religious institutions, ending in their ultimate secular corruption. This is a difficulty that both conservatives and liberals have pointed out (Kramnick and Moore 1997). Far better to think more broadly about this aspect of city life, and seek a private and secular philosophy.

Harvard's Harvey Mansfield sums up the restoration of a more polite and refined fabric of civic life with what might be called the Aretha Franklin Strategy—"bring back *respectability*" (1996, pp. 67–68). Here we come full circle to our starting point with the classical city, for Aristotle's conception of the city merely *began* with self-sufficiency; this was in fact the least important part of the classical teaching. This is why, of course, the classical Greek term—*polis*—translates very inadequately as "the city" (but also why the other modern derivative—politics—doesn't fully capture its essence either). The ancient *polis* is judged by the degree to which it secures not just self-sufficiency but also the degree of human happiness. This depends on what character types a city produces. It is not necessary, because it is not possible, within the horizon of modern liberal individualism to revive the ancient requirement that cities have a nonpermissive view of the "true" character type must be produced (i.e., Sparta) to entertain seriously the thought that democratic cities can have a decent regard for this aspect of their purpose. Not to see the city in light of the kind of citizens it produces means not to see the city as a political man does. In the end even we moderns can judge the excellence of cities by the excellence of their citizens. Hence, Mansfield on "respectability":

Maintaining appearances does not require wealth—it only requires a desire for respectability, which even the poorest people can afford. This desire must be backed up by effort, but perhaps no more effort than the expression of disapproval for unwanted behavior. . . . Offenders against respectability undermine the democratic principle that each person is competent to manage his own life. In embarrassing us, the trespassers against public appearances embarrass our democracy. (1996, pp. 67–68)

This regard for appearances is of course at the heart of suburban life, and is a large reason why suburban life holds superior attractions to the majority of middle-class Americans. This might prove to be the ultimate form of competitiveness that central cities have to master if they are to be glorious and fulfilling places once again.

NOTES

1.   The thought of any of the great "boss" mayors such as Chicago's Mayor Richard Daley, or New York's John Lindsay and Fiorello LaGuardia, instructing citizens about civic virtue would seemingly challenge the best comic minds. On the other hand, Mayor Rudy Giuliani's exhortations for New Yorkers to stop jaywalking and to adopt more hospitable manners is precisely what classical authors would say is necessary for healthy city life, which suggests the possibilities for recovering urban civility may not be wholly outlandish, the quips and jests of late-night talk show hosts notwithstanding.

2.   Few of the preservationists who cite this remark know its full context. Churchill was arguing against the modernists who wanted to build a new, "contemporary" semicircular House of Commons chamber after the old one had been destroyed by German bombs in 1941. Churchill argued in favor of the old design precisely because of the way the old shape—facing benches, a room too small to hold every member of the House—affected the substance of the political process. It was a modern restatement of the classical dictum that "form follows function."

3.   Peter Gordon and Harry Richardson recently observed of New Urbanist suburban communities: "Their residents are overwhelmingly white and affluent, with average household incomes more than 50 percent above those of surrounding communities, which thwarts the egalitarian goals of the New Urbanism. They typically have rigid design codes governing everything from window treatments to paint colors to parking restrictions, thereby reinforcing the suburban homogeneity that New Urbanists detest. Finally, these households have no more children than the average American household, thereby undermining the New Urbanist goal of building child-friendly communities" (Gordon and Richardson 2000.) The point is: the limits of the social changes that are generated from physical changes are not well-understood, and are probably more confined that the enthusiasts of downtown edifices and the New Urbanism are willing to admit.

4.   Goldsmith's experience as a serious reformer also shows the difficulty in achieving fundamental reform; it took Goldsmith four years to abolish the city's dog license regulations.

5.   This same phenomenal return to scale explains why the investment banking industry has not joined the corporate exodus from New York City. The example of both New York City and Silicon Valley show that good economic times can obscure or override the effects of bad policy.

6.   James Q. Wilson (1982) describes the theory thus: "If a factory or office window is broken, passersby observing it will conclude that no one cares or no one is in charge. In time, a few will begin throwing rocks to break more windows. Soon all the windows will be broken, and now passersby will think that, not only is no one in charge of the building, no one is in charge of the street on which it faces." Wilson concludes: "Small disorders lead to larger and larger ones, and perhaps even to crime."

Chapter 14

Policy Implications

RANDALL G. HOLCOMBE AND SAMUEL R. STALEY

In the last half of the twentieth century the United States saw major changes in land use patterns, primarily as a result of two related factors: rising income and widespread availability of automobile travel. As income has risen, one thing people have wanted to buy for themselves is less crowded living conditions, and population densities in most cities have declined as a result. But until the last half of the twentieth century, people's residential choices were constrained by the necessity of being in close proximity to their jobs, or to mass transit that could take them to their jobs. That constraint was eliminated when automobile ownership became an option for most Americans. Suddenly, a new way of life became feasible for the middle class. They could live in suburbs, in single-family homes, and could transport themselves to work, shopping, and recreational destinations whenever they wanted, without reliance on public transportation. Land-use patterns changed rapidly and substantially as a result. Critics of these new development patterns called them urban sprawl, and have been trying to engineer development patterns to undo the effects of sprawl.

Two primary goals of those who want to reverse the effects of sprawl are to produce higher population densities and to reverse the increasing dependence on automobile travel. More compact urban development, the use of infill rather than sprawling development, and the use of public transportation, walking, and cycling rather than driving, can enhance the quality of life, critics argue. But the authors represented in this volume are less optimistic. Development patterns at the beginning of the twenty-first century are the result of market forces that respond to the demands of citizens, as residents, as workers, and as consumers. If one understands the role that market forces have played in generating sprawling development patterns, several things become more obvious. First, it becomes apparent that regardless of the merits of altering current trends, it will be difficult for public policy to do so, because market forces will work in the opposite direction. Second, it is clear that there will be unintended secondary effects from anti-sprawl policies that may make people worse off. Third, these development patterns, responding to public demand, may not be so undesirable after all. And fourth, the way in which to design and implement land-use policy to further commonly held goals becomes clearer. In some cases, the Smart Growth movement is responding to a misconception about the way in which urban and suburban development takes place, so a good place to start in looking at land-use policy at the nature of urban development in the twentieth century.

URBAN DEVELOPMENT

One of the lessons one gets from studying the actual development of land use patterns is that the impression of dense cities being ringed with suburbs that then draw the city population away is oversimplified and misleading. While it is true that population densities in cities fell throughout the twentieth century, and that low-density suburbs began surrounding cities in the last half of the century, these changes were not occurring because people were fleeing the cities to live in the suburbs. At the beginning of the century, people were forced to live in cities because that is where the jobs were. As Robert Bruegmann notes in Chapter 9, population density in the Lower East Side of New York City peaked at about 350,000 per square mile early in the 1900s. At the beginning of the twenty-first century, population density in New York City is about 24,000 people per square mile. Meanwhile, the suburban population living in single-family detached homes has exploded. The same story is true for big cities throughout the world. One could look at Chicago, or Paris, and see the same phenomenon of lower population densities as cities have spread out.

Some of the population losses—and job losses—that some cities have suffered have been due to shortsighted local government policies. Some cities have raised their taxes but have not used higher tax revenues to provide benefits to the taxpayers, causing them to migrate to lower tax locations. The resulting urban blight and higher crime rates have then contributed further to deteriorating inner cities. Steven Hayward discusses some factors leading to healthy cities in Chapter 13. However, population density in cities would have declined somewhat anyway due to market forces, regardless of government policy.

The cases of two Ohio cities are illustrative. From 1940 to 1950, Cleveland's population density increased from 12,016 people per square mile to its peak of 12,197 people per square mile. After 1950—before significant investments in the interstate highway system or federally funded infrastructure—population densities began to fall. By 1970, Cleveland's population density had fallen to under 10,000 people per square mile. By 1980, it had fallen to 7,264 people per square mile. By 1998, the city's population density had fallen to 6,439, about half of the city's peak. The most significant declines were in the 1950s, 1960s and 1970s, not the 1980s and 1990s. Some neighborhoods underwent revolutionary depopulation. The Hough neighborhood, at 23,592 people per square mile in 1970, was Cleveland's densest. By 1990, the city's densest neighborhood was the Buckeye-Shaker neighborhood at 13,345, slightly more than the citywide peak in 1950. Hough had fallen to tenth among the city's 36 neighborhoods.

Two hours south (by interstate highway), Columbus experienced similar trends. Population densities peaked in 1950 at 9,541 people per square mile and then declined significantly to 4,009 people per square mile in 1970, to 3,123 people per square mile in 1980. In part, these declines were due to an aggressive annexation policy. The city's population, unlike Cleveland's, increased dramatically during this period. Yet, Columbus's population density began to increase steadily, from 3,123 in 1980 to 3,315 in 1990 to 3,511 in 1998, and most neighborhoods are expected to become more dense over the next several decades. What is Columbus's secret? In part, the city is repopulating neighborhoods with the aid of historic districts north and south of the downtown. More importantly, Columbus is starting from a low-density residential and commercial pattern more consistent with contemporary land-use trends. Columbus, in essence, annexed low-density suburbs in the decades of decentralization. Moreover, its redevelopment efforts are more consistent with low-density urban living than the high-density urban living of the industrial era. Columbus is not unique: most housing redevelopment efforts are surprisingly low density in both design and neighborhood impact. Even neotraditional redevelopment projects often include a mix of single-family detached housing, single-family attached (townhouse or duplex) housing, and medium density multifamily housing. These land-use patterns are more consistent with the early suburban development that ringed dense downtowns in the early twentieth century than the high-density neighborhoods of the same period.

Land prices also shape the urban landscape because they impact the opportunity costs of living in different neighborhoods. Cities have high population densities because people want to (or sometimes have to) live near where they work, but high population density increases the demand for land, causing high land prices and housing prices. With the widespread availability of personal automobile travel after World War II, average workers, for the first time in history, had a way to move away from their employment locations. Previously, they had to live near their place of employment or near some type of public transportation that could get them to work. One of the major causes of lower-density living conditions was the ability of people to choose to live in residential locations further away from where they worked.

Away from the central city, land prices are also tend to be lower (per acre), allowing people to buy more housing amenities for the same amount of money. As people get wealthier, this same suburbanization is occurring in cities throughout the world. Other nations are behind the United States partly because of government regulations and taxes that hinder suburban development, but mostly because they are not as wealthy as the United States. But one can see, as Bruegmann notes, that as the rest of the world gets wealthier, their land-use patterns are following those observed in the United States. More importantly, perhaps, U.S. urbanization patterns may well follow historical patterns of urban centralization and decentralization, densification and de-densification (see also Anas, Arnott, and Small 1998).

The increased availability of automobile travel is what has given people the opportunity for suburban living, which has lowered population density and increased people's standards of living. Another important factor, however, is increased income and wealth. One thing that people want to buy with their increased prosperity is more living space, and population density has gone down as people have bought themselves more space. Trying to overcome the market forces that lower population density as people want to buy more space is almost impossible to overcome with land-use policy. Land-use policy can try to dictate housing density, but population density will still fall. When people had to live near their jobs, population density was high, which increased the demand for space and pushed up its price. Under these conditions, extended families often lived together. As people became wealthier, as pensions for retirees became more common, and as a result of government programs such as social security, retirees could live in their own homes rather than with their children, lowering population density. Also, in the past century average family size has declined substantially, further lowering the number of residents per household. Thus, changes in family structure and living arrangements have caused a decline in population density.

With higher incomes, single people do not have to live with as many (or any) roommates. Even more prosperous singles might decide to live in two bedroom apartments without roommates. Although poorer people might share bedrooms (e.g., four people to a two-bedroom apartment), they might use higher incomes to buy more space so each person can have his or her own bedroom. Thus, even though the physical housing units have not changed, the number of people living in them has, just because people can afford to buy more space. People can buy two adjoining condos and knock a hole in the wall between them to double their living space, and in suburbs where lot sizes are restricted, people can buy two adjoining lots but only build on one, leaving the other to enjoy as a yard. All the factors listed in this paragraph and the preceding one result from market forces that lower population density regardless of the types of land use and building regulations in force. Thus, one can see that land-use planners may be unable to overcome market forces to generate higher density living patterns.

Technological developments in entertainment and communications also affect land-use patterns. Wealth and recent technological developments mean that people are utilizing private spaces more, and public spaces less, than they would have a century before. At the beginning of the twentieth century, for example, people who wanted to enjoy musical or dramatic entertainment would attend live concerts or plays. While these forms of entertainment are still popular, one can turn on the radio, listen to recorded music, or download music from the Internet. Similarly, television and recorded movies can substitute for live performances. While some of the enjoyment of the live peformance may be missing, technology allows people anywhere to enjoy the most talented performers in the world, and to choose from far greater variety in entertainment than would have been available a century ago, or even a few decades ago. As Steven Hayward points out in Chapter 13, new technology, coupled with larger homes that allow people to entertain at home rather than go to a neighborhood bar or restaurant, have a significant impact on people's lifestyles and therefore on optimal land-use patterns. Different lifestyles mean different patterns of travel and of land use.

Similarly, the telephone has dramatically scaled back the need for face-to-face personal conversation to convey information. People now use the telephone, fax machines, and the Internet to communicate with their immediate neighbors and people on different continents. Television news allows people to be kept up-to-date on recent happenings without leaving their homes. One can see that optimal land-use patterns are affected by changes in demographic trends (such as changing family sizes), changes in wealth, reductions in personal transportation and communication costs, and other aspects of technology. For many reasons, land-use policy must be forward-looking and attempts to recapture the lifestyles of earlier times will be futile.

ENVIRONMENTAL ISSUES

Environmental preservation is a widely held goal, but there are three different issues related to the environment that need to be separated when applying environmental goals to land use planning. The first issue is whether specific environmental amenities that are worth preserving should be placed off-limits to development. The second is whether sprawling development is consuming the natural environment, resulting in a loss of natural environment and agricultural land. After analysis, the facts show that this second issue is not relevant to the issues of development density or patterns of land use. The third issue is how to minimize the environmental impact of development. This issue is certainly the most complex of the three.

With regard to specific environmental amenities that should be preserved, the solution is to prevent development from encroaching on them. The most straightforward way to do this is by having the government or a private land trust purchase the environmentally sensitive land. Another method would be to compensate the landowner for an easement or other method of preventing development. Often, landowners will choose to preserve their own land, and privately funded organizations, financed by donations, also buy land to preserve it in its natural state. More than 1,200 private trusts already own or otherwise control more than 15 million acres of land in the United States (Staley 2000, pp. 10-12). Sometimes it is worth preserving land within developed areas in its natural state to provide parks and natural recreational areas, but the same solutions apply. Nobody would disagree with the goal of preserving some specific tracts of land to keep them from being developed. As Roger Meiners and Andrew Morriss point out in Chapter 10, there are significant property rights issues that need to be dealt with to preserve environmental amenities, and market mechanisms are applicable to the issue. However, the main points of contention in land-use planning do not involve the preservation of specific environmental amenities, but how development patterns in general affect the environment.

Taking up the second issue, critics of urban sprawl argue that lower density development takes up more land to hold a given amount of population, consuming the natural environment and reducing the nation's farmland. More compact development with higher population densities can minimize this loss. This line of reasoning has several weaknesses. First, as Samuel Staley shows in Chapter 2, development is not a threat to farmland. While acreage devoted to farming is declining, this is due to increases in agricultural productivity, not urban sprawl. Chapter 2 also looks at the nation's land use more generally, and shows that only about 5 percent of the nation's total land area is developed. With so much undeveloped land, development is not a threat to open space in general, and there is no reason to pursue a policy of higher density development in order to preserve open space. Any arguments to the contrary are based on a misunderstanding of the facts.

The third issue concerns what development patterns minimize the impact of development on the environment. While this issue is more complex than the previous two, there are many factors that lean toward lower density development as the more environmentally friendly option. Kenneth Green shows in Chapter 5 that pollution levels are higher in areas with higher population density. This makes sense, because of the pollution caused by human activities. Thus, if the main concern regarding pollution is to minimize its impact on people, lower density development can help achieve that goal. Furthermore, it may be that higher density development produces higher overall pollution levels. Automobiles produce more pollution when they are idling in traffic than when they are moving along at high speed, so the traffic congestion associated with higher density development adds to pollution. The environment can absorb some pollution, but with higher density development there is less natural environment to absorb the pollution, meaning that it will spread elsewhere. With lower density development, there will be more open space to absorb stormwater runoff, whereas stormwater will wash pollutants off of roads and rooftops and down storm drains in high-density areas. Thus, for a number of reasons, it may be that policies to create higher density development may actually be harmful to the environment. At a minimum, one can say that there is no clear environmental argument in favor of high density development.

When one examines the environmental issues related to development, it is apparent, first, that there are some important issues that need to be considered, and second, that many irrelevant issues have become a part of the debate. The consumption of farmland and open space is not relevant, but it is important to protect specific valuable environmental amenities, and it is important to consider how development patterns affect the overall quality of the environment. None of these issues points toward policies to create higher density development, however. One might argue that higher density development could result in an increased use of public transportation rather than automobile travel, but this is questionable.

TRANSPORTATION

For many reasons, transportation issues lie at the heart of the debate on land-use planning. As already noted, the major changes in land-use patterns in the last half of the twentieth century were due largely to the widespread availability of automobile travel. Furthermore, despite other concerns that people have about sprawling development, one of the most immediate concerns affecting people's everyday life is traffic congestion. In addition, one of the major policy goals of the Smart Growth movement is to reduce automobile travel by increasing public transportation use, and by creating development where it is more feasible for people to travel by walking or cycling rather than travelling by motor vehicle. Thus, in many ways, land-use policy and transportation policy are inseparable.

At the risk of some oversimplification, there are two different models used in the debate regarding the way in which the transportation network should be developed. The Smart Growth model is to pursue policies that increase population density, which will make public transportation more of a viable alternative, and which will make it more feasible for people to walk or bike instead of traveling by private automobile. This model envisions reversing the trend toward increasing reliance on private automobiles and moving back toward a transportation network where a substantial share of trips now taken by auto are replaced by trips on public transportation. Population density must be high in order to support mass transit, so urban infill and revitalization of downtown areas, which will need to be major employment destinations, are a part of this Smart Growth strategy. The alternative to this smart growth strategy is guided by market forces, and foresees lower population densities and automobile travel as inevitable characteristics of the twenty-first century, and attempts to accommodate those market forces rather than to counteract them.

As noted, land-use planning has limited possibilities for reversing declining population densities regardless of how that planning is carried out. The same thing is likely to be true for travel by personal automobile. Smart Growth advocates emphasize the connection between changes in land-use development patterns and increased reliance on the automobile. People who live in low-density subdivisions must use their cars to get everywhere because the only thing within walking distance is other houses, and the density of development is too low to support public transportation. Following this line of reasoning, patterns of development are pushing people into private automobile travel. The causation, however, can also go the other way.

Travel by private automobile has many advantages over mass transportation, starting with the fact that it is private. Many people would prefer to travel by themselves, or with others they know, rather than with strangers. Automobile travel also has the advantage that people can come and go when they want rather than have to worry about the mass transit schedule or waiting at the stop. With automobiles, people can go directly to their destinations without having to follow a mass transit route, perhaps changing buses or trains in the process. Automobiles allow people to make side trips without much advance planning, to stop at a store or bank, for example, and allow people to carry packages and other cargo more conveniently.

Compared to mass transit, automobile travel is generally quicker, more comfortable, more flexible, and more convenient. As the nation has become wealthier, people have chosen to spend some of it on the transportation amenities that are offered by auto travel. This transportation freedom has increased access to suburban living, with single-family detached homes and yards. Thus, the desire for people to travel by automobile rather than mass transit is in many ways independent of suburban living, and the desire of people to substitute private automobile travel for public transportation has allowed lower density development. While the argument is sometimes made that increasing suburbanization has been responsible for increased travel by automobile, the causation runs both ways. Private automobile travel would have increased regardless of development patterns because people want to buy more transportation convenience as their wealth increases.

Thus, market forces are inevitably leading away from public transportation and toward automobile travel. Smart Growth policy can try to work against those market forces, but by moving people away from the convenience of automobile travel that they prefer, it may well make them worse off: increasing commute times, reducing trip flexibility, and making transportation less convenient.

The argument by many Smart Growth proponents is that reduced traffic congestion will benefit everybody, hence compensating them for the inconvenience of mass transportation. At the beginning of the twenty-first century, only about 5 percent of commuters use public transportation, so even if Smart Growth policies were successful enough to double the use of public transportation, it would reduce the number of cars on the road by only a small amount. A sober look at the data reveals that except for a few densely populated urban areas, public transportation has little potential to reduce traffic congestion (Semmens 1998; Nivola 1999, pp. 59–60).

Recognizing the realities of modern development, Wendell Cox (Chapter 12) suggests that more money be spent on roads. Public policies to support mass transit have increased congestion and made people worse off, Cox argues, because those policies have inhibited road construction. The trend toward more private automobile travel will be difficult to reverse, and the better policy is to encourage development that accommodates people's desires for the convenience of automobile travel. Cox shows that building roads does not appreciably increase miles driven, and that while newly built roads do tend to fill up quickly, they do so by attracting traffic from existing roads, reducing overall traffic congestion.

Paying for new roads offers additional challenges, and Robert Poole offers an insightful analysis in Chapter 4. User charges work best, because they serve to ration the use of roadways and lessen congestion that way. A motor fuels tax earmarked for roads is at best an imperfect user charge: while it charges drivers to pay for roads, it does not ration their use of any particular road. This is a key characteristic of any price mechanism (which user fees attempt to mimic). Furthermore, automobiles have become much more fuel efficient, and more miles per gallon means fewer cents of gas tax per mile of road. Thus, the fuel tax is becoming an increasingly unreliable source of revenues for road construction and repair. Politicians are understandably reluctant to increase taxes of any kind, and the gas tax just has not kept up. Its future is even more shaky as cars using alternate fuels are being developed. Poole argues persuasively that policymakers should start planning now to replace gas taxes with real user charges to finance roads.

User charges could be applied in many ways. Traditional toll roads are an option, and while newly constructed toll roads seem viable, taxpayers strongly oppose charging tolls on roads that are currently freely accessible. HOT lanes take existing underutilized HOV lanes (and proposed HOV lanes) and make them revenue generators and congestion reducers. HOT lanes, which allow drivers to access less congested lanes by paying a toll, are already used in some locations. Poole suggests that new technologies for charging for road use will have to be developed in some cases, but the technology exists now to make more productive use of existing and proposed highways. Already, some toll roads read bar codes on cars to allow them to drive by toll booths at highway speeds. This technology has been successfully used in the United States and Canada. Radio transponders and charges based on odometer readings are other possibilities.

The market-oriented approach to land use planning suggests that reliance on automobile travel will continue for the foreseeable future, and that growth plans should accommodate automobiles. But, as Poole suggests, there are many unanswered questions about what transportation strategies might work best. In situations like this, attacking problems at the local level works better than central planning for growth, because people can better understand the types of solutions that might apply to their local situations, and because if many different approaches are tried, the most successful approaches can be adopted by others.

LAND-USE POLICY

Patterns of land use are driven by market forces and are directly affected by the transportation network, particularly in the United States where a strong system of property rights and presumption in favor of consumer choice exists. For centuries, the key transportation element was waterways; cities flourished where bays would allow seaports and on navigable rivers. After about 1850, railroads ascended to be the most important aspect of the transportation network. After about 1950, roads became the most important element. With the rapid movement toward automobile travel, there has also been a rapid and substantial change in the nature of land-use patterns. Those changes have brought with them some problems, but problems are easier to see in hindsight than are the most appropriate solutions.

One aspect of land-use planning policy that must be clear is that planning the transportation network is a crucial part of the overall land-use planning process. Smart Growth initiatives focus on mass transit options like light-rail lines, the creation of bike paths, and increased density to allow walking to more destinations (and mass transit stops). An approach that responds to market forces rather than trying to counteract them would emphasize road planning to accommodate automobile travel. No matter which type of solution one favors, without adequate planning of the transportation network, the optimal use of particular parcels of land will be impossible. Land that is near major intersections or heavily traveled thoroughfares provides an ideal location for business and commercial activity, whereas residential users will want to be located conveniently to transportation thoroughfares, but far enough away that the traffic does not create a disturbance. Unless people know where those thoroughfares will be located, it will not be possible for public planners or private landowners to know what uses of the property would be efficient. Thus, it is clear that government needs to plan for its own transportation infrastructure development in order for land-use policy to be successful.

As land-use policy is currently practiced, too often it involves detailed planning regarding how private landowners can use their property, but does not adequately plan for its own future transportation network. When one examines the market incentives involved in land use, it becomes apparent that market forces will do much to efficiently allocate land to various uses once the transportation corridors have been established. This argument points toward land-use planning that is less involved in dictating how private landowners may use their property, and is more involved in planning ahead for future transportation infrastructure. In many areas, this was the primary role of land-use planners in the 1950s and 1960s, when cars were big and gas was cheap—and when roads were less congested. After the energy crisis began in 1973, the orientation went from planning for roads toward trying to reduce dependence on the automobile, and roads started getting more congested as a result.

A market-oriented approach to land use planning suggests that if the government planned for its own infrastructure development, private landowners would utilize their land efficiently without any further government intervention. Market forces would minimize incompatible uses of property without government direction. Following the trends of the twentieth century, this would result in lower population densities and a continued reliance on the private automobile as the primary means of transportation in most areas. Public policy measures that try to work in the other direction must work against market forces, and must try to keep people from buying things they want to have to increase their quality of life. In the debate on land-use planning, there is a consensus that better government planning for its own transportation infrastructure is required. However, a consensus does not exist on whether more emphasis should be put on mass transit or on roads for automobiles, or on the degree to which government should be involved in private land-use decisions.

One argument for the market-oriented approach is that it is based on the American principles of government that emphasize the protection of private property rights and freedom of exchange. Regulations that prohibit certain uses of property, limit lot sizes, and so forth replace the principle of protecting private property rights with the idea that private rights are subject to collective approval. One might argue that this restriction in private property rights is justified to further the common good, but when one recognizes that the changes Smart Growth is trying to reverse are the result of market forces and personal choice, the arguments in favor of policies that fly in the face of these preferences lose their force. Counteracting the market forces behind these trends will be difficult, and even if public policy succeeds, it will do so by preventing Americans from buying things they believe will enhance their quality of life.

POLICY FOR THE UNDERPRIVILEGED, THE POOR, AND MINORITIES

A legitimate concern for any type of land-use policy is how it affects those who are less privileged in a society, and in this regard some serious questions can be raised about Smart Growth initiatives. They work by preventing people from developing their property in ways they might otherwise choose, by using urban growth boundaries, and by other devices to increase density. In so doing, they restrict the supply of developed and developable land, raising its price, while lowering the price of land that is outside the growth boundary. This hurts those who own property outside the growth boundary. By raising the price of land inside the boundary, however, it also hurts renters as housing costs rise. Homeowners benefit from the increase in housing prices. Because renters tend to have lower incomes than those who own their own homes, Smart Growth policies favor the rich over the poor. By raising housing prices, they also work against the goal of affordable housing, and contribute to homelessness among those at the very bottom of the economic ladder (Staley, Edgens, and Mildner 1999).

Low-income people tend to live in smaller residences and want to buy more space. The push toward more compact development and higher density development works against them, but upper-income people can afford single-family detached housing, so they find their lifestyles largely unaffected by such policies. Those who favor more stringent growth and environmental regulations tend to be people who already enjoy a high standard of living, and promote public policies that will prevent those less well-off from attaining the standards of living they already enjoy. Similarly, high-income people are the least likely to give up their cars to take public transportation, so policies to migrate commuters toward public transportation will affect low-income people by causing some of them to shift from driving to taking public transportation, which may create less congested roads for those high-income people who will continue to be able to afford to drive.

Public transportation is necessary for some people who do not have access to cars, or who are unable to drive themselves. It is not a good alternative for most people who today are driving their own cars to work. Thus, it would make sense to reorient public transportation policy to make public transit explicitly a social service that assists those who cannot drive. It would be cheaper to do so, and it would provide greater benefits to the people who really need it. Instead of light-rail projects that cover fixed routes at high cost, jitney services that are flexible and relatively inexpensive would be preferable. Money spent on mass transit to try to lure commuters out of their cars has a limited potential, and mass transit always costs more than it receives back in fares. The transportation subsidy would be better spent by offering door-to-door transportation services to those who have no other transportation alternatives.

One can debate the merits of Smart Growth policies and New Urbanism, but it is clear that whatever the merits, the costs of these policies will hit the poor hardest, and the benefits will fall disproportionately on those who are best off.

CONCLUSION

Public policies are often designed with the idea that the world would be a better place if only certain changes could be made, and the push toward land-use planning geared toward producing higher population densities and less reliance on the automobile for transportation fits in that category. What we must remember when analyzing such policies is that the proposed changes, if they can be made at all, will come at a cost. Market forces have been behind the lowering of population densities and the increased reliance on the automobile, because both of these changes bring benefits to people, and with increased incomes and wealth, people can afford to purchase these benefits. Policymakers who want to reverse these trends will be working against these market forces, and will find them difficult or perhaps impossible to overcome. Meanwhile, they are also working against the desires of consumers for more convenient transportation and more living space.

One can imagine how nice it would be to be able to walk to local shops instead of driving to Wal-Mart, but the reason people drive to Wal-Mart is that the selection is better and the prices are lower. One can imagine how nice it would be to be able to walk to the corner grocery rather than drive to the supermarket, but again, supermarkets put the corner groceries out of business because they have lower prices and a better selection. And in either case, if customers want to buy more than a few things, walking may not be a feasible method of getting purchases home. Bicycles seem like a good alternative to driving, unless the weather is too hot or cold, or if it is raining. People prefer driving their cars because that is the most comfortable and convenient way for them to travel, so it makes sense to pursue public policies that enable people to enhance their quality of life.

Despite the fact that the market economy has provided people with unprecedented prosperity, it is fashionable to look down on the results of the market as materialistic, and to argue in support of other values. However, market forces are merely the embodiment of people's desires, and they provide a signal about how people believe that they can best use their resources to enhance their quality of life. In the middle of the twentieth century, many people doubted that markets could work as well as government planning to produce economic prosperity, but at the beginning of the twenty-first century that debate has been resolved in favor of the market. The chapters in this volume show that those same market forces that so efficiently produce goods and services can be utilized in land-use planning, to create efficient land-use patterns, and in the process, to enhance people's living standards. Government planning is needed because key resources—especially the transportation network—is primarily government-owned. However, one can see that the type of planning done in the name of Smart Growth is often counter-productive. It works against market forces, and too often has unintended consequences that worsen the growth-related problems that people are trying to escape. By understanding the way that market forces work in land markets, and the way they can be harnessed to produce more productive policies, government policies can be reoriented to remedy some of the problems that are apparent as the twenty-first century begins, resulting in even smarter growth policies.

How would a market-oriented approach to land-use planning compare to the approach favored by the contemporary Smart Growth movement? An illustrative example is the emerging tool of choice in the Smart Growth movement: urban growth boundaries. In general, growth boundaries are expected to contain urban sprawl and promote more dense, mixed-use development. A survey of the research on urban growth boundaries found at least five identifiable goals: (1) preserve open space and farmland, (2) revitalize urban areas, (3) increase residential densities, (4) provide cost effective and more efficient infrastructure, and (5) ensure an orderly transition from rural to urban uses. Staley, Edgens, and Mildner (1999) analyzed growth boundaries in California, Portland (OR), Boulder County (CO), and Lancaster County (PA), and found evidence that the growth boundaries preserve open space and farmland and increased residential densities in three of the four case studies. Little evidence existed that the boundaries either revitalized urban areas or helped provide more efficient infrastructure. In all four cases, the growth boundaries failed to provide a more orderly transition for land use. In fact, in many cases, including Portland, the growth boundary was becoming a tool for preventing any further development of land (Staley and Mildner 2000).

Staley, Edgens, and Mildner found that growth boundaries suffered from a number of disadvantages (Table 14.1). First, they tended to be "one size fits all," applying general principles about the appropriateness of land for development to parcels with widely differing characteristics. Second, growth boundaries were a particularly "blunt" instrument: they tried to use a simplistic policy tool to achieve complex policy goals. Revitalizing cities, for example, requires more than preventing people from leaving the city boundaries, particularly in a nation that respects basic freedoms such as where to live and work. Third, effective growth boundaries tended to reduce the supply of housing because they constrained the amount of land available for development and thus pushed up land prices inside the boundary (and hence the cost of developing and redeveloping property). Fourth, the growth boundaries had the potential for significantly reducing the overall quality of the housing stock by artificially restricting housing amenities such as lot size, set backs, the preservation of privately-owned open space, and housing style (e.g., ranch versus multistory, single family detached versus multifamily). Finally, the growth boundaries tended to create new special interest groups with vested interests in using the growth boundar to preserve the status quo.

Market-oriented approaches have the potential to address each of the policy goals without the unintended side effects of growth boundaries and other, similarly blunt policy instruments. Rather than generally restricting land use, for

Table 14.1

Comparison of Urban Growth Boundary with Market-Oriented Approach

Goal	Weakness of Urban-growth Boundary	Market-oriented Solution
Preserve open space and farmland	One-size-fits-all; Restricts property rights	Strategic preservation of open space • Purchase of development rights • Conservation easements
Revitalize urban areas	Cities continue to decline; Housing output falls because development is forced onto higher-cost land through infill and refill.	Increase competitiveness of cities • Improve educational choice and quality • Upgrade housing stock • Competitive fiscal policies • Brownfield development
Increase residential densities	Lower neighborhood amenities such as reduced lot size, less private open space, and other housing characteristics	Relax density restrictions to allow market-determined densities
Efficient infrastructure provision	Uncoordinated development and poorly planned infrastructure investments	Full-cost pricing for on-site, infrastructure to align consumer preferences with actual costs of development without subsidized offsite residents.
Orderly transition from rural to urban use	Land restrictive; Politically reactionary & conservative	Full-cost pricing for on-site infrastructure

Source: Samuel R. Staley, Jefferson G. Edgens, and Gerard C. S. Mildner, *A Line in the Land: Urban-Growth Boundaries, Smart Growth, and Housing Affordability.* Policy Study No. 263. Los Angeles: Reason Public Policy Institute, October 1999.

example, market-oriented approaches favor purchase of development rights and conservation easements to preserve strategic parcels of land. Rather than restrict low-density suburban development, market-oriented approaches would focus on ways to make the city more competitive with neighboring communities by improving service delivery inside the city, expanding education opportunity and choice for all residents (including the middle class), and remediating brownfield sites for new development. Rather than mandating higher residential densities that conform to regional targets, market-oriented approaches focus on deregulating the land market to allow for more diversity within the existing real estate market. Full-cost pricing for infrastructure would also provide better information about the true costs and impacts of new development without running the risk of subsidizing new residents or redistributing wealth from new residents to old residents.

This is just one example of how market-oriented approaches could be used to solve America's growth management problems. Another virtue of the market-oriented approach is that it focuses directly on specific problems. If residents are concerned about congestion, the market-oriented approach allows local and regional polcymakers to focus on congestion directly through variable rate pricing for highways or building new roads using tolls. If residents are concerned that a field will be developed for housing when they would prefer it to remain open space, a private land trust can buy the property without impacting the property rights of neighbors. If local residents are concerned about the cost of infrastructure, full-cost pricing ensures that the local community does not subsidize the infrastructure of new development and also that sufficient revenues will be generated to maintain and upgrade existing facilities.

A final advantage of the market-oriented approach is the ability to pick and choose policy options from a variety of specific tools. Because the policy choices match directly and closely to the problems they address, local policymakers will face fewer unintended consequences than using current strategies. The ability to tailor growth management strategies to the needs of residents and consumers gives them flexibility that other strategies do not, avoiding the broad brush that inevitably creates new conflicts and tensions when problems are oversimplified.

Land-use planning involves a number of complex issues, including environmental protection, planning and financing transportation modes and corridors, creating land-use patterns that enhance the quality of life, and the protection of individual rights, among others. The authors of the chapters in this volume do not claim to have all the answers. Rather than providing definitive answers to these land-use issues, the contributors offer an approach to the problems that differs radically from the approach that has been taken in the late twentieth century. The twentieth-century approach to land-use planning placed increasing amounts of power with the government to make land-use decisions. The specific government mechanisms have varied from state to state, and over time, but the trend has been to centralize power and to give governments increasingly greater powers to dictate development. The authors in this volume have demonstrated that this method of land-use planning is often counterproductive, and have shown that market mechanisms have many advantages over government planning for land use. Markets produce efficient land-use patterns, they respect individual rights, and when there is not agreement on the appropriate course of action, markets are more innovative than government planning and often result in solutions nobody envisioned beforehand. Land-use planning in the twenty-first century would be best served if market mechanisms were relied on more heavily, rather than using the political process.

References

Abbott, Carl, Deborah Howe, and Sy Adler, eds. *Planning the Oregon Way: A Twenty-Year Evaluation*. Corvallis: Oregon State University Press, 1994.

Adler, Johnathan H. *Environmental Performance at the Bench: The EPA's Record in Federal Court*. Policy Study No. 269. Los Angeles: Reason Public Policy Institute.

Adler, Robert W., Jessica C. Landman, and Diane M. Cameron. *The Clean Water Act 20 Years Later*. Washington, D.C.: Natural Resources Defense Council and Island Press, 1993.

Advisory Commission on Intergovernmental Relations. *The Organization of Public Economies*. Washington, D.C.: 1987.

American Assembly. "The Economy: Sustaining Growth with Opportunity" Final Report of the Ninety-fifth American Assembly (Columbia University), June 10-13, 1999, Emory Conference Center, Atlanta, Georgia.

American Lung Association. *Breathless: Air Pollution and Hospital Admissions/Emergency Room Visits in 13 Cities*. Washington D.C., June, 1996.

Anas, Alex, Richard Arnott, and Kenneth A. Small. "Urban Spatial Structure." *Journal of Economic Literature* 36 (September 1998): 1426–64.

Anderson, Martin. *The Federal Bulldozer*. Boston: MIT Press, 1964.

Anderson, Terry. "Viewing Wildlife through Coase-Colored Glasses." In *Who Owns the Environment,* P.J. Hill and Roger Meiners, 259–82. Lanham, Md.: Rowman & Littlefield Press, 1998.

Anderson, Terry and Donald Leal. *Enviro-Capitalists: Doing Good While Doing Well*. Lanham, Md.: Rowman & Littlefield Press, 1997.

Anthony, Robert. *Unlegislated Compulsion: How Federal Agency Guidelines Threaten Your Liberty*. Policy Analysis No. 312. Washington, D.C.: Cato Institute, August 11, 1998.

Antonelli, Angela. "Lessons from the Atlanta Experiment." In Jane Shaw and Ronald Utt, 135–52. *A Guide to Smart Growth*. Washington, D.C. and Bozeman, MT: The Heritage Foundation and the Political Economy Research Center, 2000.

———. "Two Years and 8,600 Rules: Why Congress Needs an Office of Regulatory Analysis." *Heritage Foundation Backgrounder* 1192 (June 26, 1998).

Aristotle. *Nicomachean Ethics*. Indianapolis: Bobbs-Merrill, 1962 [335 BC].

———. *Politics*. Chicago: Henry Regnery, 1961 [340 BC].

Arkes, Hadley. "Liberalism and the Law." In *The Betrayal of Liberalism*. Edited by Hilton Kramer and Roger Kimball. Chicago: Ivan Dee, 1999.

———. *The Philosopher in the City: The Moral Dimensions of Urban Politics*. Princeton, N.J.: Princeton University Press, 1981.

Arnold, Chester L., and James Gibbons. "Impervious Surface Coverage: The Emergence of a Key Environmental Indicator." *Journal of the American Planning Association* 62, no. 2 (1996): 247–58.

Avery, Dennis. "Hypoxia: The Dead Zone Lives." In *Big Government and Bad Science: Ten Case Studies in Regulatory Abuse*. Institute for Policy Innovation and the Lexington Institute, 1999.

Baade, Robert A. *Stadiums, Professional Sports, and Economic Development: Assessing the Reality*. Policy Study No. 62. Chicago: The Heartland Institute, 1991.

Bailey, Ron. *Earth Report 2000*. New York: McGraw-Hill, 2000.

Baim, Dean V. *Sports Stadiums as a "Wise Investment": An Evaluation*. Policy Study No. 32. Chicago: The Heartland Institute, 1990.

Banfield, Edward. *The Unheavenly City Revisited*. Boston: Little, Brown, 1973.

Barrett, John. "Taking TMDLs Out of the Ivory Tower." *Water Resources IMPACT* 1, no. 6 (November 1999): 33-35.

Bastié, Jean. *Croissance de la Banlieue Parisienne*. Paris: PUF, 1964.

Bauer, Gérard, and Jean-Michel Roux. *La Rurbanisation ou la Ville Eparpillée*. Paris: Editions du Seuil, 1976.

Beimborn, Edward. *A Transportation Modeling Primer*. Milwaukee: University of Wisconsin at Milwaukee, May, 1995. http://www.uwm.edu/dept/CUTS/primer.htm

Berliner, Dana. *Running Boston's Bureaucratic Marathon*. Washington, D.C.: Institute for Justice, n.d.

Bernard, Yvonne. *La France au Logis, Etude Sociologique des Pratiques Domestiques*. Liege: P. Mardaga, 1992.

Bernstein, Mark F. "Sports Stadium Boondoggle." *The Public Interest* 132 (Summer 1998): 45–57.

Beyers, William B. "Trends in Producer Service Employment in the U.S.: The 1985-1995 Experience." Presented at the North American Regional Science Association Meetings, Santa Fe, New Mexico, 1998.

Blair, John P., Samuel R. Staley, and Z. Zhang. "The Central City Elasticity Hypothesis: A Critical Appraisal of Rusk's Theory of Urban Development." *Journal of the American Planning Association* 62 (1996): 345–353.

Blumenfeld, Hans. *The Modern Metropolis: Its Origins, Growth Characteristics and Planning*. Cambridge: MIT Press, 1967.

Boarnet, Marlon G. "Road Infrastructure, Economic Productivity, and the Need for Highway Finance Reform." *Public Works Management and Policy* (April 1999): 289–303.

Boettke, Peter. "Towards a History of the Theory of Socialist Planning." In *Socialism vs. the Market: The Socialist Calculation Debate*. Edited by Peter Boettke. New York and London: Routledge, 2000: 1–39.

Bolick, Clint. *Brightening the Beacon: Removing Barriers to Entrepreneurship in San Diego*. Washington, D.C.: Institute for Justice, n.d.

———. *Entrepreneurship in Charlotte: Strong Spirit, Serious Barriers*. Washington, D.C.: Institute for Justice, n.d.

Boudreaux, Donald J. and Randall G. Holcombe. "Contractual Governments in Theory and Practice." In *The Voluntary City*. Edited by David Beito and Peter Gordon. (forthcoming).

Boudreaux, Donald, Roger Meiners, and Todd Zywicki. "Talk Is Cheap: The Existence Value Fallacy." *Environmental Law* 29, no. 4 (1999): 765–809.

Bourne, L. S. "The Myth and Reality of Gentrification: A Commentary on Emerging Urban Forms." *Urban Studies* 30, no. 1 (1993): 183-189.

Boyce, Joseph N. "Nonwhites Wake to 'American Dream.'" *Wall Street Journal,* October 7, 1997: A2, A14.

Boyd, James. "The New Era of the Clean Water Act: A Critical review of EPA's Proposed TMDL Rules." Resources for the Future Discussion Paper 00—12, Washington, DC, March 2000.

Boyne, G.A. "Local Government Structure and Performance: Lessons from America?" *Public Administration* 70 (1992): 333–357.

Brindle, Ray. "Four Titles Touching On 'Sustainable Transport.'" *Road and Transport Research* 4, no. 1 (1995) 126–131.

Brown, Jeffrey, et al., *The Future of California Highway Finance: Detailed Research Findings.* Berkeley: Institute of Transportation Studies, UC Berkeley, UCB-ITS-RR-99-3, August 1999.

Bruegmann, Robert. "Urban Sprawl." In *International Encyclopedia of Social and Behavioral Sciences.* Amsterdam: Pergamon, forthcoming, a.

——. "The Paradoxes of Sprawl Reform." In *Urban Planning in a Changing World* Edited by Rob Freestone. London: Routledge, forthcoming, b.

——. "The American City: Urban Aberration or Glimpse of the Future." In Michael Cohen et al. *Preparing for the Urban Future: Global Pressures and Local Forces.* Baltimore: Johns Hopkins Press, 1996: 336–67.

——. "Schaumburg, Oak Brook, Rosemont and the Recentering of the Chicago Metropolitan Area." In *Chicago Architecture and Design 1923-1993* Edited by John Zukowsky. .Munich: Prestel-Verlag, 1993.

Buckeye Institute. *If You Build It, Will They Ride? The Potential of Rail Transit in Ohio's Major Cities.* Columbus, Ohio, October 1999.

Bullock, Scott. *Baltimore: No Harbor for Entrepreneurs.* Washington, D.C.: Institute for Justice, n.d.

Burchell, Robert W., Nancy Neuman, Alexa Sakrewsky, and Stephanie DiPetrillo. "Eastward Ho! Development Futures: Paths to More Efficient Growth in Southeast Florida." Report prepared for Florida Department of Community Affairs and U.S. Environmental Protection Agency, February 1999.

Burchell, Robert W., et al. *The Costs of Sprawl—Revisited.* Transit Research Program Report No. 39. Washington, D.C.: National Academy Press, 1998.

"Burning 'burbs'" *Economist* (Jan. 27, 1996): 42.

Calthorpe, Peter. *The Next American Metropolis: Ecology, Community, and the American Dream.* New York: The Princeton Architectural Press, 1993.

Carrns, Ann, and James R. Hagerty. "On a Rainy Night in Georgia, What Can You Do But Eat?—There are More Obese People All Over, but Peach State Really Takes the Cake." *The Wall Street Journal* (October 29, 1999): A1.

Cervero, Robert. "Surviving in the Suburbs: Transit's Untapped Frontier." *Access* (Spring 1993): 29–34.

Chanen, Jill Schachner. "Downtown Milwaukee Housing Picks Up." *The New York Times* (June 7, 1998): 31.

City of Olympia, Public Works Department. "Impervious Surface Reduction Study." Olympia, WA, May 1995.

Clark, C. "Urban Population Densities." *Journal of the Royal Statistical Society* 114 (1951): 490–94

Clarke, Susan E. and Gary L. Gaile. "The Next Wave: Postfederal Local Economic Development Strategies." Reprinted in *Appraoches to Economic Development.* Edited by John P. Blair and Laura A. Rees, 165–77. Thousand Oaks, CA: Sage Publications, 1999.

Clay, James W. and Douglas M. Orr, Jr. *Metrolina Atlas*. Chapel Hill: The University of North Carolina Press, 1972.

Clout, Hugh D. "The Growth of Second-Home Ownership: An Example of Seasonal Suburbanization." In *Suburban Growth*. Edited by James H. Johnson. London: Wiley. 1974.

Coastal Programs Division and the Coastal States, Territories and Commonwealths. *Sustaining America's Coastal Communities and Resources: A Strategic Framework for the Coastal Zone Management Program*. Washington, DC: U.S. Department of Commerce.

Colborn, Theo, et al. *Our Stolen Future*. New York: Penguin Books, 1996.

Colburn, David R. and Lance deHaven Smith. *Government in the Sunshine State*. Gainesville: University Press of Florida, 1999.

Cox, Wendell. "Competitive Tendering in the United States: Comprehensive Review." Presented at the 6th International Conference on Competition and Ownership in Public Transport, Cape Town, South Africa, September 1999.

Cox, W. Michael and Richard Alm. *Myths of Rich and Poor: Why We're Better Off Than We Think*. New York: Basic Books, 1999.

Cox, Wendell, Jean Love, and Nick Newton. "Competition in Public Transport: International State of the Art." Presented at the 5th International Conference on Competition and Ownership in Public Transport, Leeds, May 1997.

Cox, Wendell and Ronald Utt. *Flawed Federal Land Use Report Encourages Unnecessary Spending*. Backgrounder No. 1368. Washington, DC: Heritage Foundation, May 2000.

Cox, Wendell, Ronald Utt, and Howard Husock. *How Smart Is "Smart Growth"? Implications for Pennsylvania*. Harrisburg, PA: Commonwealth Foundation, April 2000.

Craig, Steven G. and D. Andrew Austin. "New York's Missing Million Jobs." *The City Journal* (Autumn 1997): 43–51.

Crone, Thomas M. "House Prices and the Quality of Public Schools: What Are We Buying?" *Business Review: Federal Reserve Bank of Philadelphia* (September/October 1998): 3–14.

Cullingworth, Barry. *The Political Culture of Planning: American Land Use Planning in Comparative Perspective*. New York: Routledge, 1993.

Cummings, Jean L. and Denise DiPasquale. "The Low-Income Housing Tax Credit: An Analysis of the First Ten Years." *Housing Policy Debate* 10, no. 2 (1999): 251–308.

Daniels, Tom. *When City and County Collide: Managing Growth in the Metropolitan Fringe*. Washington, DC: Island Press, 1999.

Dantzig, George B. and Thomas L. Saaty. *Compact City: A Plan for a Liveable Urban Environment*. San Francisco: W.H. Freeman and Co., 1973

David Schrank and Tim Lomax. *The 1999 Annual Mobility Report, Information for Urban America*. College Station: Texas Transportation Institute, 1999.

Davies, Gareth. *From Opportunity to Entitlement: The Transformation of Great Society Liberalism*. Lawrence: University Press of Kansas, 1996.

De Lucchi, Mark. "Total Costs of Motor-Vehicle Use." *Access* 8 (Spring 1996): 7–13.

Development Strategies, Inc. *The Impact of Catholic Schools on Selected Neighborhoods in the City of St. Louis*. 1996.

Dézert, Bernard, Alain Metton, and Jean Steinberg. *La Périurbanisation en France*. Paris: Sedes, 1991.

Dicey, A.V. *The Law of the Constitution*. Indianapolis: Liberty Press, 1982 [1885].

DiLorenzo, Thomas J. *Suburban Legends: Why "Smart Growth" Is Not So Smart*. Contemporary Issues Series 97. St. Louis: Center for the Study of American Business, Washington University, November 1999

Dittmar, Hank and Shelley Poticha. "Transportation and the New Urbanism" *Progress* 9, no. 3 (1999).

Doppelt, Bob, Mary Surlock, Chris Fissell, and James Karr. *Entering the Watershed: A New Approach to Save America's River Ecosystems.* Washington, DC: Island Press, 1993.

Downs, Anthony. "Some Realities about Sprawl and Urban Decline." *Housing Policy Debate* 10, no. 4 (1999a): 955–74.

——. Quoted in *Surface Transportation: Moving Into the 21st Century.* Washington, DC: General Accounting Office, GAO/RCED-99-176, 1999b.

——. *New Visions for Metropolitan America.* Washington, DC: Brookings Institution; and Cambridge, Mass: The Lincoln Institute of Land Policy, 1994.

——. *Stuck in Traffic: Coping with Peak-Hour Traffic Congestion.* Washington, DC: Brookings Institution, 1992.

Dunn, James A. Jr. *Driving Forces: The Automobile, Its Enemies and the Politics of Mobility.* Washington, DC: Brookings Institution, 1999.

Dunphy, Robert T. "Passing Gridlock." *Urban Land* 56, no. 7 (November 1997): 58-61, 83.

Dzurik, Andrew A. *Water Resources Planning.* Lanham, MD: Rowman and Littlefield, 1990.

Easterlin, Richard A. "The Worldwide Standard of Living Since 1800." *Journal of Economic Perspectives* 14, no. 1 (2000): 7–26.

Edgens, Jefferson G. "Farmer Challenges EPA's Authority Under Clean Water Act." *Environment News* (January 2000): 6.

——. "EPA's Bad Science Targets Michigan Farmers." *Monroe Evening News* (December 17, 1999a).

——. "TMDLs, Agriculture and EPA's Flawed Science." *Water Resources IMPACT* 1, no. 6 (November 1999b): 30–32.

Edgens, Jefferson G. and Samuel R. Staley. "The Myth of Farmland Loss." *FORUM on Applied Research and Public Policy* 14, no. 3 (Fall 1999): 29-34.

Edmonston, B. *Population Distribution in American Cities.* Lexington, MA: Lexington Books, 1975.

Ehrenhalt, Alan. "New Recruits in the War on Sprawl." *New York Times* (April 13, 1999): A23.

Einsweiler, Robert C. and Deborah A. Miness. *Managing Growth and Change in Urban, Suburban, and Rural Settings.* Cambridge, MA: Lincoln Institute for Land Policy, 1992.

Eppli, Mark J. and Charles C. Tu. *Valuing the New Urbanism: The Impact of the New Urbanism on Prices of Single-Family Homes.* Washington, DC: The Urban Land Institute, 1999.

Epstein, Richard A. *Simple Rules for a Complex World.* Cambridge: Harvard University Press, 1995.

Evans, Alan W. "The Land Market and Government Intervention." In *Handbook of Regional and Urban Economics.* Edited by Paul Cheshire and Edwin S. Mills, vol. 3. Amsterdam: North-Holland, 1999: 1637–1669.

——. "Dr. Pangloss Finds His Profession: Sustainability, Transport, and Land Use Planning in Britain." *Journal of Planning Education and Research* 18 (1998): 137–144.

——. "'Rabbit Hutches on Postage Stamps': Planning, Development, and Political Economy." *Urban Studies* 28, no. 6 (1991): 853–870.

Evenson, Norma. *Paris, A Century of Change 1978-1978.* New Haven: Yale University Press, 1979.

Ewing, Reid. "Is Los Angeles Style Sprawl Desirable?" *Journal of the American Planning Association* 63 (1995): 107–26.

Fielding, Gordon J. and Daniel B. Klein. *High-occupancy/Toll Lanes: Phasing in Congestion Pricing a Lane at a Time.* Policy Study no. 170. Los Angeles: Reason Public Policy Institute, 1993.

Fischel, William A. "Comment on Carl Abbott's 'The Portland Region: Where City and Suburb Talk to Each Other—And Often Agree.'" *Housing Policy Debate* 8, no. 1 (1997): 65–73.

Fisher, Ronald C. *State and Local Public Finance.* 2nd ed. Chicago: Irwin, 1996.

Fitzsimmons, Allan K. *Federal Ecosystem Management: A "Train Wreck" in the Making.* Policy Analysis No. 217. Washington, D.C.: Cato Institute, 1994.

Florida Department of Community Affairs. *Technical Memo.* 4, no. 4 (undated, released in 1989).

Foldvary, Fred. *Public Goods and Private Communities: The Market Provision of Social Services.* London: Edward Elgar, 1995.

Fouchier, Vincent. *Les Densités Urbaines et le Développement Durable, le Cas de l'Ile de France et des Villes Nouvelles.* Paris: Edition du SGVN, 1997.

Francois, Francis B. "TQ Interview." *Transportation Quarterly* 53, no. 2 (Spring 1999): 79.

Freilich, Robert H. and Bruce G. Peschoff. "The Social Costs of Sprawl." *The Urban Lawyer* 29, no. 2 (1997): 183–98.

Fretwell, Holly L. *Paying to Play: The Fee Demonstration Program.* Bozeman, MT Policy Series: PERC (www.perc.org), 1999.

Frieden, Bernard J. "The New Regulation Comes to Suburbia." *The Public Interest* 55 (1979): 15–27.

Frieden, Bernard J., and Lynne B. Sagalyn. *Downtown, Inc., How America Rebuilds Its Cities.* Cambridge, MA: MIT Press, 1989.

Friedlaender, Ludwig. *Darstellungen aus der Sittensgsechichte Roms in der Zeit von August bis zum Ausgang der Antonine.* Leipzig: S. Hirzel, 1910.

Fukuyama, Francis. *The End of History and the Last Man.* New York: Free Press, 1992.

Gammage, Jr., Grady. *Phoenix in Perspective: Reflections on Developing the Desert.* Phoenix: Herberger Center for Design Excellence, 1999.

Gannon, Michael. *Florida: A Short History.* Gainesville: University Press of Florida, 1993.

Garvin, Alexander. *The American City: What Works, What Doesn't.* New York: McGraw Hill, 1996.

Gerondeau, Christian. *Transport in Europe.* Norwood, MA: Artech House, Inc., 1997.

Gilmore, Jim. "Governor Gilmore to Sign Chesapeake Bay 2000 Agreement." Press release, Governor's Office, May 3, 2000.

Giuliano, Genevieve. "Land Use Policy and Transportation: Why We Won't Get There From Here." Transportation Research Board Circular, 1999.

———. "Urban Travel Patterns." In *Modern Transport Geography.* Edited by Brian Hoyle and Richard Knowles, 2nd ed. Chichester: John Wiley & Sons, 1998: 115–134.

Glazer, Nathan. "Unsolved Mysteries." *The New Republic* (June 23, 1997): 23.

Goldsmith, Stephen. *The Twenty-First Century City: Resurrecting Urban America.* Washington, D.C.: Regnery Publishing, 1997.

Gordon, Peter and Harry Richardson. "Are Compact Cities a Desirable Planning Goal?" *Journal of the American Planning Association* 63 (1995): 95–106.

———. "Defending Suburban Sprawl." *The Public Interest* 139 (Spring 2000): 70.

———. "The Destiny of Downtowns: Doom or Dazzle?" *Lusk Review* 3, no. 2 (1997): 63–76.

———. *The Facts About "Gridlock" in Southern California.* Policy Study No. 165. Los Angeles: Reason Foundation, 1993.

———. "You Can't Get There From Here." *Reason* (August/September 1989): 34–37.

Gordon, Peter, Harry W. Richardson, and Gang Yu. "Metropolitan and Non-metropolitan Employment Trends in the U.S.: Recent Evidence and Implications." *Urban Studies* 35, no. 7 (1998): 1037–57.

Gordon, Peter, Yu-chun Liao, and Harry Richardson. "Household Commuting." In *Network Infrastructure and the Urban Environment: Recent Advances in Land Use/Transportation Modeling*. Edited by Lars Lundquist, Lars-Goram Maltson, and Tschagho John Kim. New York: Springer, 1998: 84–95.

Gore, Albert. *Access With Trust*. Washington, D.C.: National Partnership for Reinventing Government, 1998.

Gratz, Roberta Brandes and Norman Mintz. *Cities Back from the Edge: New Life for Downtown*. New York: John Wiley & Sons, 1998.

Green, Kenneth G. *Innovative Approaches for Meeting the Georgia Ozone Challenge*. Atlanta: Georgia Public Policy Foundation, 1999.

Hall, Peter. "Forces Shaping Urban Europe." *Urban Studies* 30, no. 6 (1993): 883–98.

——. *The World Cities*. New York: McGraw-Hill, 1966.

Hall, Peter, H. Gracey, R. Drewett, and R. Thomas. *The Containment of Urban England*. London: PEP, 1973.

Halpern, Richard. "Dirty Pool." *American Outlook* (Winter 2000).

Halstead, Leah S. and Gerard C.S. Mildner. "Gentrification in Multnomah County, Oregon, 1990–96." Working Paper, School of Urban Studies and Planning, Portland State University, November 1998.

Hamilton, Bruce W. "Zoning and Property Taxation in a System of Local Governments." *Urban Studies* 12 (June 1975): 205–211.

Hansen, Mark and Yuanlin Huang. "Road Supply and Traffic in California Urban Areas." *Transportation Research* 31 (1997): 205–18.

Hartgen, David T. and Daniel O. Curley. *Beltways: Boon, Bane or Blip? Factors Influencing Changes in Urbanized Area Traffic, 1990-1997*. Charlotte: University of North Carolina-Charlotte, Center for Interdisciplinary Transportation Studies, 1999.

Hayek, Fredrich A. "The Use of Knowledge in Society." Reprinted in *Individualism and Economic Order* by F.A. Hayek: pp. 71–91. Chicago: University of Chicago Press, 1948.

——. *The Constitution of Liberty*. Chicago: University of Chicago Press, 1961.

Hayward, Steven. "The 'Neighborhood Effects' of School Choice." *Policy Review* (January/February 1999): 47.

——. "Slashing Through the Regulation Thicket." *Policy Review* (November/December 1998): 5–6.

Hendershott, Patric H. and Jesse M. Abraham. "Patterns and Determinants of Metropolitan House Prices, 1977-91." In *Proceedings of the 25th Annual Federal Reserve Bank of Boston Conference*, Boston: Federal Reserve Bank of Boston, 1993: pp. 18–42.

Henke, Cliff. "More Cities Prepare to Join Rail Club." *Metro* (July 1999): 32–36.

Higgins, Neal. "Real Estate Report for Metropolitan Portland, Oregon." Volume 89. Portland: University of Portland, August 1999.

Hines, Lawrence G. "The Long-Run Cost Function of Water Production for Selected Wisconsin Communities." *Land Economics* 45 (1969).

Hise, Greg. "Home Building and Industrial Decentralization in Los Angeles: The Roots of the Postwar Urban Region." *Journal of Urban History* 19, no. 2 (1993): 95–125.

Holcombe, Randall G. *Public Policy and the Quality of Life*. Westport, CT: Greenwood Press, 1995.

——. "Distributional Aspects of Florida's Concurrency Requirement." *Florida Policy Review* 5 (Winter 1990a): 8–14.

——. "Growth Management in Florida: Lessons for the National Economy." *Cato Journal* 10, no. 1 (Spring/Summer 1990b): 109–25.

Hotchkiss, Frank. "Urban Design in Suburbia: Oxymoron or Opportunity." Paper presented to the American Institute of Architects Annual Conference, Minneapolis, 1996.

Howe, Deborah A. "Growth Management in Oregon." In *Growth Management: The Planning Challenge of the 1990's*. Edited by Jay M. Stein. Newbury Park, CA: Sage Publications, 1993: 61–75.

Hoxby, Caroline M. "Does Competition Among Public Schools Benefit Students and Taxpayers?" National Bureau of Economic Research working paper 4979, 1994.

Hunter, William J. *Economic Impact Studies: Inaccurate, Misleading, Unnecessary*. Policy Study No. 21. Chicago: The Heartland Institute, 1988.

Husock, Howard and Wendell Cox. "Keeping Kalamazoo Competitive." Report prepared for the city of Portage, Michigan (www.portagemi.com/report), June 1999.

Ikeda, Sanford. *Dynamics of the Mixed Economy: Toward a Theory of Interventionism*. London: Routledge, 1997.

Immergluck, Daniel. "Job Proximity and the Urban Unemployment Problem: Do Suitable Nearby Jobs Improve Neighborhood Employment Rates?" *Urban Studies* 35, no. 1 (1998): 15–27.

Jackson, Kenneth. *The Crabgrass Frontier: The Suburbanization of the United States*. New York: Oxford University Press, 1985.

Jacobs, Jane. *The Death and Life of Great American Cities*. New York: Random House, 1961.

Jacoby, Tamar and Fred Siegel. "Growing the Inner City?" *The New Republic* (August 23, 1999): 22–27.

Kain, John F. "The Urban Transportation Problem: A Reexamination and Update." In *Essays in Transportation Economics and Policy*. Edited by Jose Gomez-Ibanez, William B. Tye, and Clifford Winston. Washington, DC: Brookings Institution, 1999.

———. "The Use of Straw Men in the Economic Evaluation of Rail Transport Projects." *American Economic Review* 82, no. 2 (1992): 487–493.

Katz, Bruce. *Reviving Cities: Think Metropolitan*. Policy Brief No. 33. Washington, DC: Brookings Institution, 1998.

Katz, Bruce and Jennifer Bradley. "Divided We Sprawl." *The Atlantic Monthly* (December 1999): 26–42.

Katz, Peter. *The New Urbanism: Toward an Architecture of Community*. New York: McGraw-Hill, 1994.

Kirzner, Israel. *Competition and Entrepreneurship*. Chicago: University of Chicago Press, 1973.

Klein, Daniel B., Adrian T. Moore, and Binyam Reja. *Curb Rights: A Foundation for Free Enterprise in Urban Transit*. Washington, D.C.: Brookings Institution, 1997.

Knaap, Gerrit J. "Land Use Politics in Oregon." In *Planning the Oregon Way: A Twenty-Year Evaluation*. Edited by Carl Abbott, Deborah Howe, and Sy Adler. Corvallis, OR: Oregon State University Press, 1994.

———. "The Price Effects of Urban-growth Boundaries in Metropolitan Portland, Oregon." *Land Economics* 61, no. 1 (February 1985): 26–35.

Knaap, Gerrit and Arthur C. Nelson. *The Regulated Landscape: Lessons from Land Use Planning in Oregon*. Cambridge, MA: Lincoln Institute of Land Policy, 1992.

Koenig, J. "Down to the Wire in Florida: Concurrency is the Byword in the Nation's Most Elaborate Statewide Growth Management Scheme." *Planning* 56, no. 10 (1990).

Korngold, Gerald. "Privately Held Conservation Servitudes: A Policy Analysis in the Context of in Gross Real Covenants and Easements." *Texas Law Review* 63, no. 3 (1984): 443–95.

Kotkin, Joel. *The Future of the Center: The Core City in the New Economy*. Policy Study No. 264. Los Angeles, CA: Reason Public Policy Institute, October 1999.

Kramnick, Isaac and R. Lawrence Moore. "Can the Churches Save the Cities?" *The American Prospect* 35 (November-December 1997): 57–53.

Ladd, Helen F. "Population Growth, Density and the Costs of Providing Public Services." *Urban Studies* 2 (1992): 273–295.

Landis, John and Robert Cervero. "Middle Age Sprawl: BART and Urban Development." *Access* 14 (1999): 2–15.

Landry, Clay. "Unplugging the Everglades." Bozeman, MT: PERC Working Paper (www.perc.org) 2000.

Lang, Marvel. "Redefining Urban and Rural for the U. S. Census of Population: Assessing the Need and Alternative Approaches." *Urban Geography* 2 (1986): 118-34.

Lebergott, Stanley. *Pursuing Happiness: American Consumers in the Twentieth Century.* Princeton: Princeton University Press, 1993.

Lehrer, Eli. "The Economic Effects of Falling Crime Rates." Washington, DC: The Heritage Foundation, forthcoming.

Leopold, Luna B. *A View of the River.* Cambridge, MA: Harvard University Press, 1994.

Lessinger, Jack. "The Case for Scatteration." *Journal of the American Institute of Planners* 28, no. 3 (1962): 315–25.

Levine, Jonathan. "Access to Choice." *Access* 14 (1999): 16–19.

Light, Ivan. *Cities in World Perspective.* New York: Macmillan, 1983.

Louchart, Philippe and Jean-Jacques Ronsac. *Atlas des Franciliens: Rencensement de la Population de 1990.* Paris: IAURIF, INSEE, 1991.

Mansfield, Harvey. "Bring Back Respectability." *The American Enterprise.* 7, no. 6 (November-December 1996): 67–68.

Martin, John H. "Implications of C.A.R.E. vs Southview Farms on the U.S. Livestock and Poultry Industry." *Journal of the American Water Resources Association* 33, no. 4 (August 1997): 741–46.

Mastrull, Diana. "U.S. Study on Land Development Was Wrong." *Philadelphia Inquirer* (April 28, 2000).

Matias, Donna. *Entrepreneurship in San Antonio: Much to Celebrate, Much to Fight For.* Washington, DC: Institute for Justice, n.d.

May, Christopher W., et al. "Effects of Urbanization on Small Streams in the Puget Sound Lowland Ecoregion." *Watershed Protection Techniques* 2, no. 4 (June 1997).

McMurrer, Daniel P. and Isabel V. Sawhill. "Economic Mobility in the United States." Urban Institute No. 6722 (1996).

Meiners, Roger and Bruce Yandle. "Common Law and the Conceit of Modern Environmental Policy." *George Mason Law Review* 7, no. 4 (1999): 923–63.

Mellor, William H. *Is New York City Killing Entrepreneurship?* Washington DC: Institute for Justice, n.d.

Metro, Growth Management Services Department. *Housing Needs Analysis: Technical Appendix I.* Portland, OR: Author, May 1997.

——. *Urban Growth Report Addendum.* Portland, OR: Author, August 1998.

——. *Urban Growth Report Discussion Draft.* Portland, OR: Author, May 1996.

Metropolitan Council. "Growing Smart in Minnesota." www.metrocouncil.org/ (February 29, 2000).

Mieszkowski, Peter and Edwin C. Mills. "The Causes of Suburbanization." *Journal of Economic Perspectives* 7, no. 3 (September 1993): 135–47.

Mildner, Gerard C.S. *Growth Management in the Portland Region and the Housing Boom of the 1990s.* Urban Futures Working Paper No. 98–1, Reason Public Policy Institute, 1998.

Mildner, Gerard C.S., Kenneth J. Dueker, and Anthony M. Rufolo. "Impact of the Urban growth Boundary on Metropolitan Housing Markets." Research Project Report No. PR097, Portland State University, Center for Urban Studies, 1996.

Mills, Edwin S. "Truly Smart Growth." *The Illinois Real Estate Letter* 13, no. 3 (Summer 1999).

———. *Should Governments Own Convention Centers?* Policy Study No. 33. Chicago: The Heartland Institute, 1991.

Mills, Edwin S. and Jee Peng Tan. "A Comparison of Urban Population Density Functions in Developed and Developing Countries." *Urban Studies* 17 (1980): 313–321.

Mills, Edwin S. and Luan Sende Lubuele. "Inner Cities." *Journal of Economic Literature* 35 (June 1997): 727–756.

Mills, Edwin S. and Richard Price. "Metropolitan Suburbanization and Central City Problems." *Journal of Urban Economics* 15, no. 1 (January 1984): 1–17

"Mobility in America: Up, Down and Standing Still." *Economist* (February 24, 1996): 30–31.

Monclús, Francisco Javier. "Decentralization, Containment and Green Corridors: Compact City Strategies in Spanish Cities." In conference proceedings, *Twentieth Century Urban Planning Experience.* Sydney: Faculty of the Built Environment, University of New South Wales, 1998a.

———. *La Ciudad Dispersa, Subrubanización y Nuevas Periferias.* Barcelona: Centre de Cultura Contemporania de Barcelona, 1998b.

Moore, Stephen and Julian L. Simon. *The Greatest Century That Ever Was: 25 Miraculous Trends of the Past 100 Years.* Policy Analysis No. 364. Washington, DC: Cato Institute, 1999.

Morley, Neville. *Metropolis and Hinterland: The City of Rome and the Italian Economy 200 B.C. – A. D. 200.* Cambridge: Cambridge University Press, 1996.

Morrill, Richard L. "Myths about Metropolis." In *Our Changing Cities.* Edited by John Fraser Hart. Baltimore: Johns Hopkins University Press, 1991.

Morriss, Andrew P. "Miners, Vigilantes, and Cattlemen: Overcoming Free Rider Problems in the Private Provision of Law." *Land and Water Law Review* 33 (1998): 581–696.

Morriss, Andrew P. and Roger E. Meiners. "The Destructive Role of Land Use Planning." *Tulane Environmental Law Journal* 14, no. 1 (Winter 2000): 95-137.

Moynihan, Daniel Patrick. *Maximum Feasible Misunderstanding.* New York: Basic Books, 1969.

Muller, Peter O. "The Evolution of American Suburbs: A Geographical Interpretation." *Urbanism Past and Present* 4 (Summer 1977): 1-10.

———. "Transportation and Urban Form: Stages in the Spatial Evolution of the American Metropolis." in *The Geography of Urban Transportation.* Edited by Susan Hanson. 24–48. New York: The Guilford Press, 1986.

Muth, Richard F. *Cities and Housing: The Spatial Pattern of Urban Land Use.* Chicago: University of Chicago Press, 1969.

Myers, Dowell. "Demographic Dynamism and Metropolitan Change: Comparing Los Angeles, New York, Chicago and Washington, D.C." *Housing Policy Debate* 10, no. 4 (1999): 919–54.

Myers, Phyllis. "Livability at the Ballot Box: State and Local Referenda on Parks, Conservation, and Smarter Growth, Election Day 1998." Discussion paper prepared for The Brookings Institution, Center on Urban and Metropolitan Policy, January 1999.

Myron, Orfield. *Metropolitics: A Regional Agenda for Community and Stability.* Rev. ed. Washington, DC: Brookings Institution, 1997.

National Association of Homebuilders. "Housing Opportunity Index: Third Quarter 1998." Washington, D.C.: 1998.

Natural Resources Defense Council. *Breathtaking: Premature Mortality Due to Particulate Air Pollution in 239 American Cities.* Washington D.C., May 1996.

Nelson, Arthur C. "Privatizing the Neighborhood: A Proposal to Replace Zoning with Private Collective Property Rights to Existing Neighborhoods." *George Mason Law Review* 7, no. 4 (1999), 827–880.

———. "Characterizing Exurbia." *Journal of the American Planning Association* 6, no. 4 (1992): 350-68.

———. *Evaluating Urban Containment Programs*. Ph.D. dissertation, Portland State University, Portland, Oregon, 1983.

Nelson, Arthur C. and Kathryn A. Foster. "Metropolitan Governance Structure and Income Growth." *Journal of Urban Affairs* 21, no. 3 (1999): 309–324.

Niskanen, William A. "Bureaucrats and Politicians." *Journal of Law & Economics* 18 (December 1975): 617–43.

———. *Bureaucracy and Representative Government*. Chicago: Aldine-Atherton, 1971.

Nivola, Pietro S. *Laws of the Landscape: How Policies Shape Cities in Europe and America*. Washington, DC: Brookings Institution, 1999.

Norquist, John. *The Wealth of Cities: Revitalizing the Centers of American Life*. Reading, MA: Addison-Wesley, 1998.

Nozick, Robert. *Anarchy, State and Utopia*. New York: Basic Books, 1977.

1,000 Friends of Florida. "Concurrency Key to Growth Management." *Foresight* 1 (December 1988): 1.

1,000 Friends of Oregon. "Managing Growth to Promote Affordable Housing: Revisiting Oregon's Goal 10." (September 1991).

O'Flaherty, Brendan. *Making Room: The Economics of Homelessness*. Cambridge: Harvard University Press, 1996.

O'Regan, Katherine and John M. Quigley. "Where Youths Live: Economic Effects of Urban Space and Employment Prospects." *Urban Studies* 35, no. 7 (1998): 1187–1205.

O'Toole, Randal. *ISTEA, A Poisonous Brew for American Cities*. Policy Analysis No. 287. Washington DC: Cato Institute, November 1997.

Oates, Wallace E. "An Essay on Fiscal Federalism" *Journal of Economic Literature* 37, no. 3 (1999): 1120–1149.

Olsen, Donald J. *Town Planning in London: The Eighteenth and Nineteenth Centuries*. New Haven: Yale University Press, 1982.

Olson, William and Alan Woll. *Executive Orders and National Emergencies How Presidents Have Come to "Run the Country" by Usurping Legislative Power*. Policy Analysis No. 358. Washington, DC: Cato Institute, October 1999.

Orfield, Myron. "Portland Metropolitics: A Regional Agenda for Community and Stability." Report to the Coalition for a Livable Future, July 1998.

Orski, C. Kenneth. "In Search of Livability." *Innovation Briefs* 10, no. 5 (Sep/Oct 1999): 1.

O'Sullivan, Arthur. *Urban Economics*. 4th ed. Boston: Irwin McGraw Hill, 2000.

"Our Hopes for 2000" *Los Angeles Times*. (January 2, 2000): M4.

Park, Robert E., Ernest W. Burgess, and Roderick McKenzie. *The City*. Chicago: The University of Chicago Press, 1925.

Parker, R. Andrew. "Patterns of Federal Urban Spending: Central Cities and Their Suburbs, 1983–1992." *Urban Affairs Review* 31, no. 2 (1995): 184–205

Peirce, Neal R. "Littleton's Legacy: Our Suburban Dream Shattered." *Washington Post* (June 6, 1999).

Peterson, Iver. "Some Perched in Ivory Tower Gain Rosier View of Suburbs." *The New York Times* (December 5, 1999): 1.

Pickrell, Don. *Urban Rail Transit Projects: Forecasts Versus Actual Ridership and Cost*. Washington, DC: Office of Grants Management, Urban Mass Transit Administration, U.S. Department of Transportation, 1990.

Pickrell, Don and Paul Schimek. "Trends in Motor Vehicle Ownership and Use: Evidence from the Nationwide Personal Transportation Survey." *Journal of Transportation and Statistics* 2, no. 1 (1999): 1–17.

Pipes, Richard. *Property and Freedom*. New York: Knopf, 1999.

Pisarski, Alan E. *Commuting in America II: The Second National Report on Commuting Patterns and Trends.* Policy Study No. 165. Washington, DC: Eno Transportation Foundation, 1996.

Poole, Robert W., Jr., *Defederalizing Transportation Funding.* Policy Study No. 216. Los Angeles: Reason Public Policy Institute, October 1996.

Poole, Robert W., Jr. and C. Kenneth Orski. *Building a Case for HOT Lanes: A New Approach to Reducing Urban Highway Congestion.* Los Angeles: Policy Study No. #257. Reason Public Policy Institute, 1999.

Postrel, Virginia. *The Future and Its Enemies: The Growing Conflict Over Creativity, Enterprise, and Progress.* New York: Free Press, 1998.

Pozdena, Randall J. *The Modern Economics of Housing.* Westport, CT: Quorum Books, 1998.

——. *Where the Rubber Meets the Road: Reforming California's Roadway System.* Policy Study No. 191. Los Angeles: Reason Public Policy Institute, August 1995.

Pressman, Jeffrey L., and Aaron Wildavsky. *Implementation.* 2nd ed. Berkeley: University of California Press, 1979.

Putnam, Robert. "Bowling Alone: America's Declining Social Capital." *Journal of Democracy* 6, no. 1 (January 1995): 65-78.

Reason Public Policy Institute. *Privatization 1998: 12th Annual Report on Privatization.* Los Angeles: Authors, 1998.

——. *Privatization 1997: 11th Annual Report on Privatization.* Los Angeles: Authors, 1997.

Richardson, Harry W. and Chang-Hee Bae. 1998. "The Equity Impacts of Road Congestion Pricing." In *Road Pricing, Traffic Congestion and the Environment: Issues of Efficiency and Social Feasibility.* Edited by K. J. Button and E.T. Verhoef, 247–62. Aldershot, England: Edward Elgar, 1998.

Richardson, Harry W. and Peter Gordon. "Is Sprawl Inevitable? Lessons from Abroad." Paper presented at the Meetings of the Association of Collegiate Schools of Planning, Chicago, 1999.

Richmond, Jonathan. *New Rail Transit Investments—A Review.* Cambridge: Harvard University, John F. Kennedy School of Government, 1999.

Ridley, Matt. *Genome: The Autobiography of a Species in 23 Chapters.* New York: HarperCollins, 1999.

Romer, Paul M. "Why Indeed in America? Theory, History, and the Origins of Modern Economic Growth." *American Economic Review* 86 (1996): 202–06.

Rosentraub, Mark S., David Swindell, Michael Przybylski, and Daniel R.Mullins. "Sport and Downtown Development Strategy: If You Build It, Will Jobs Come?" *Journal of Urban Affairs* 16, no. 3 (1994): 221–39.

Roth, Gabriel. *Roads in a Market Economy.* Brookfield, VT: Ashgate Publishing Co., 1996.

——. "Should the Federal Highway Trust Fund be Reauthorized?" *Transportation Quarterly* 49 no. 4 (1995): 5–13.

Rubin, Thomas A., James E. Moore II, and Shine Lee. "Ten Myths about U.S. Urban Rail Systems." *Transport Policy* 6: 57–73.

Ruhl, J. B. "Discussion—The (Political) Science of Watershed Management in the Ecosystem Age." *Journal of the American Water Resources Association*, 36, no. 1 (February 2000): 229–31.

——. "The (Political) Science of Watershed Management in the Ecosystem Age." *Journal of the American Water Resources Association* 35, no. 3 (June 1999): 519–26.

Rusk, David. *Inside Game, Outside Game: Winning Strategies for Saving Urban America.* Washington, DC: Brookings Institution, 1999.

——. *Cities Without Suburbs.* 2nd ed. Washington, DC: Woodrow Wilson International Center, 1995 (1st ed. 1993).

Rybczynski, Witold and Peter D. Linneman. "How to Save Our Shrinking Cities." *The Public Interest* 135 (Spring 1999): 30–44.

Salins, Peter D. "America's Permanent Housing Problem." In *Housing America's Poor*. Edited by P. D. Salins. Chapel Hill: University of North Carolina Press, 1987.

Samuel, Peter. "Transport—Technology Change and Its Liberating Impacts." Conference presentation, Advancing Technology and the Changing Context of Public Policy Justification," Santa Clara University, January 2000.

———. *How We Can "Build Our Way Out of Congestion."* Policy Study No. 250. Los Angeles: Reason Public Policy Institute, January 1999.

Samuelson, Paul A. *Economics*. 9th ed. New York: McGraw-Hill, 1973.

Sanchez, Jesus. "Telecom Invasion Rattles Downtown L.A. Boosters." *Los Angeles Times* (November 2, 1999): A1.

Sanders, Heywood T. "Convention Center Follies." *The Public Interest* 132 (Summer 1998): 58–72.

Sato, Koji and Wendy A. Spinks. "Commuter and Work Pattern Changes After the Great Hanshin Earthquake: Policy Implications for Greater Tokyo." Presented at the New International Perspectives on Telework: Telecommuting to the Virtual Organization Workshop, Brunel University, U.K., 1996.

Savas, E.S. *Privatization: The Key to Better Government*. Chatham, NJ: Chatham House Publishers, 1987.

Schmidt, Charles. "The Specter of Sprawl." *Environmental Health Perspective* 106, no. 6 (1998): A274–79.

Schrank, David, and Timothy Lomax. *The 1999 Annual Mobility Report, Information for Urban America*. College Station, TX: Texas Transportation Institute, 1999.

Scott, James C. *Seeing Like a State: How Certain Schemes to Improve the Human Condition Have Failed*. New Haven: Yale University Press, 1998.

Seigan, Bernard H. *Land Use Without Zoning*. Lexington, MA: D.C. Heath, 1972.

———. "Non-Zoning in Houston." *Journal of Law & Economics* 13 (April 1970): 71–147.

———. "Land-Use Regulation Should Preserve Only Vital and Pressing Government Interests." in *Private Property Rights, Land-use Policy and Growth Management,* ed. John W. Cooper. Tallahassee, Florida: Montpelier Books, 1990.

Semmons, John. "Rethinking Transit 'Dollars and Sense': Unearthing the True Cost of Public Transit." Policy Study No. 243. Los Angeles: Reason Public Policy Institute, August 1998.

Sen, Ashish, et al. *Highways and Urban Decentralization*. Chicago: Urban Transportation Center, University of Illinois at Chicago, 1998.

Sharp, Thomas. *Town and Countryside: Some Aspects of Urban and Rural Development*. London: Oxford University Press, 1932.

Shoup, Donald. "Instead of Free Parking." *Access* 15 (1999): 8–13.

Siegel, Fred. "Is Regional Government the Answer?" *The Public Interest* 137 (1999): 85–98.

———. "Reclaiming Our Public Spaces." *The City Journal* 2, no. 2 (Spring 1992): 35–45.

———. *The Future Once Happened Here: New York, D.C., L.A., and the Fate of America's Big Cities*. New York: Free Press, 1997.

Simpson, A.W. Brian. *A History of the Land Law*. 2nd ed. Oxford: Oxford University Press, 1986.

Sivitanidou, Rena. "Are Service Agglomerations Weakening? Evidence from Metropolitan Los Angeles." Paper presented at the Western Regional Science Association, Napa, California, February 1996.

Smeed, Reuben, et al. *Road Pricing: The Economic and Technical Possibilities*. London: Department of Transport, 1964.

Smith, Fred L. "Auto: The Liberating Benefits of a Safer, Cleaner, and More Mobile Society." *Reason* (1990): 22–26.

Staley, Samuel R. "Ballot-box Zoning, Transaction Costs, and Land Development." *Journal of the American Planning Association* 67, no. 1 (Winter 2001).

——. *The "Vanishing Farmland" Myth and the Smart-growth Agenda.* Policy Brief No. 12. Los Angeles: Reason Public Policy Institute, January 2000a.

——. "The Political Economy of Land Conversion on the Urban Fringe." In *Freeing Up Agricultural Land.* Edited by Bruce Yandle and Terry Anderson. Palo Alto, CA: Hoover Institution Press, 2000b.

——. *The Sprawling of America: In Defense of the Dynamic City.* Policy Report No. 251. Los Angeles: Reason Public Policy Institute, January 1999.

——. "Environmental Policy and Urban Revitalization: The Role of Lender Liability." *Capital University Law Review* 25, no. 1 (1996): 51–75.

Staley, Samuel R., and Gerard C.S. Mildner. "The Price of Managing Growth." *Urban Land* (February 2000): 18–23.

——. *Urban-Growth Boundaries and Housing Affordability: Lessons from Portland.* Policy Brief, no. 11. Los Angeles: Reason Public Policy Institute, October, 1999.

Staley, Samuel R., Jefferson G. Edgens, and Gerard C.S. Mildner. *A Line in the Land: Urban-growth Boundaries, Smart Growth, and Housing Affordability.* Policy Study No. 263. Los Angeles: Reason Public Policy Institute, October 1999.

Staley, Samuel R. and John P. Blair. "Institutions, Quality Competition and Public Service Provision: The Case of Public Education." *Constitutional Political Economy* 6 (1995): 21–33.

Sullivan, Edward C. *Evaluating the Impacts of the SR-91 Variable Toll Express Lanes Facility, Final Report.* Sacramento: Caltrans, May 1998.

Surface Transportation Policy Project. *An Analysis of the Relationship Between Highway Expansion and Congestion in Metropolitan Areas: Lessons from the 15-Year Texas Transportation Institute Study.* Washington, DC, November 1998.

Taub, Theodore C. "Florida's Growth Management Concurrency Doctrine—Moratorium or Impetus to Fund Needed Infrastructure." *Environmental and Urban Issues* 15 (Fall 1988): 5–12.

Taylor, Brian and William McCullough. "Lost Riders." *Access* 13 (1998): 19–26.

"Telecom Invasion Rattle Downtown LA Boosters" *Los Angeles Times* (November 2, 1999): p. A1.

Thomas, C. Scott. *The United States of Suburbia.* Amherst, NY: Prometheus Books, 1998.

Thomas, June Manning. "The Forces of Urban Heterogeneity Can Triumph." *American Quarterly* 46, no. 1 (1994): 49–54.

Tiebout, Charles. "The Pure Theory of Local Expenditures." *Journal of Political Economy* 64 (October 1956): 416–24.

Toulan, Nohad A. "Housing as a State Planning Goal." In *Planning the Oregon Way: A Twenty-Year Evaluation.* Edited by Carl Abbott, Deborah Howe, and Sy Adler. Corvallis: Oregon State University Press, 1994.

Tweeten, Luther. "Competing for Scarce Land: Food Security and Farm Preservation." Occasional Paper ESO #2385. Columbus, Ohio: Department of Agricultural, Environmental, and Development Economics, Ohio State University, August 1998.

——. *Farm Policy Analysis.* Boulder, CO: Westview Press, 1989.

Umbeck, John R. *A Theory of Property Rights with Applications to the California Gold Rush.* Ames, IO: Iowa State University Press, 1981.

Umberger, Mary. "Nothing Raises Rancor in the Suburbs like a Townhouse Proposal." *Chicago Tribune* (October 24, 1999).

United States Department of Agriculture. *Summary Report: 1997 National Resources Inventory.* Washington, DC: National Resources Conservation Service and Iowa State University Statistical Laboratory, December 1999a.

———. *Cropland Use and Urbanization*. Washington, DC: Economic Research Service Issues Center, October 1999b.

———. *Census of Agriculture 1997*. Washington, DC: National Agricultural Statistics Service, 1998.

———. *Agricultural Resources and Environmental Indicators, 1996–97*. Washington, DC: Economic Research Service, July 1997.

U.S. Department of Transportation. "G-7 Countries: Transportation Highlights." BTS99-01 Washington, DC: Bureau of Transportation Statistics, November 1999.

———. *Our Nation's Travel: 1995 NPTS Early Results Report*. Washington, DC: Office of Highway Management, Federal Highway Administration, 1997.

U.S. Environmental Protection Agency. *National Air Quality and Emissions Trends Report, 1997*. Washington, D.C.: Author, 1997 (http://www.epa.gov/oar/aqtrnd97).

———. *Public-Private Partnership Case Studies: Profiles of Success in Providing Environmental Services*. Washington, D.C.: September 1990.

U.S. General Accounting Office. *Water Quality: Key EPA and State Decisions Limited by Inconsistent and Incomplete Data*. Report to the Chairman, Subcommittee on Water Resources and Environment, Committee on Transportation and Infrastructure, House of Representatives, GAO/RCED-00-54, March 2000.

———. *Extent of Federal Influence on 'Urban Sprawl' is Unclear*. GAO/RCED-99–97. Washington, DC: 1999.

VanHelmond, Gregg and Angela Antonelli. *Why CARA is Fiscally Irresponsible and a Threat to Local Land Use Decisions*. Backgrounder No. 1370. Washingont, DC: The Heritage Foundation, May 9, 2000.

Varady, David P. and Jeffrey D. Raffel. *Selling Cities: Attracting Home Buyers Through Schools and Housing Programs*. Albany State University of New York Press, 1995.

Vesterby, Marlow and Ralph Heimlich. "Land Use and Demographic Change: Results from the Fast-Growth Counties." *Land Economics* 67, no. 3 (August 1991): 279–91.

Vickery, William S. "Statement on the Pricing of Urban Street Use." Hearings, U.S. Congress, Joint Committee on Metropolitan Washington Problems. Washington, DC: Nov. 11, 1959.

Voith, Richard. "Does the Federal Tax Treatment of Housing Affect the Pattern of Metropolitan Development?" *Business Review of the Federal Reserve Bank of Philadelphia* (March/April 1999): 3–16.

Volokh, Alexander, et al. *Environmental Information: The Toxics Release Inventory, Stakeholder Participation, and the Right to Know, Part 1 of 2: Shortcomings of the Current Right-to-Know Structure*. Policy Study No. 246. Los Angeles: Reason Public Policy Institute, November 1998.

Wachs, Martin. *Ethics in Planning*. New Brunswick, NJ: Center for Urban Policy Research, 1985.

Wachs, Martin, et al. *Curbing Gridlock: Peak-Period Fees to Relieve Traffic Congestion*. Washington, DC: Transportation Research Board (Committee for Study on Urban Transportation Congestion Pricing), National Academy Press, 1994.

Walker, Barrett. *Preserving Surface Waters with a Stormwater Utility*. Policy Report Los Angeles: Reason Public Policy Institute, forthcoming.

Walters, Alan A. "Track Costs and Motor Taxation." *Journal of Industrial Economics* 2 (April 1954): 135–46.

Weyrich, Paul M., and William Lind. *Conservatives and Mass Transit: Is it Time for a New Look?* Available at www.apta.com/info/online/, 1999a.

———. *Does Transit Work? A Conservative Reappraisal*. Study sponsored by business members of the American Public Transit Association, Washington, DC, May 1999b.

Whitney, Craig R. "To Burden of Poverty in France, Add Racism." *The New York Times* (January 16, 1998): A3.

Wilbur Smith Associates. "Technology Requirements for Pricing Options." Technical Memorandum No. 2Ci, prepared for the REACH Task Force, February 20, 1996.

Wildavsky, Aaron. *Searching for Safety.* New Brunswick: Transaction Publishers, 1988.

Wilson, Elisabeth. "The Coming Backlash." *Florida Trend* (January 1989): 54–58.

Wilson, James Q. and George L. Kelling. "Broken Windows: The Police and Neighborhood Safety." *The Atlantic Monthly* (March 1982): 29–38.

Yandle, Bruce. "Property Rights and Regulatory Takings." In *Farmers, Ranchers, and Environmental Law.* Edited by Roger Clegg, 143–670 Washington: National Legal Center for the Public Interest, 1995.

Index

About the Editors and Contributors

RANDALL G. HOLCOMBE is DeVoe Moore Professor of Economics at Florida State University. He taught at Texas A&M University and at Auburn University prior to coming to Florida State in 1988. Dr. Holcombe is also Chairman of the Research Advisory Council of the James Madison Institute for Public Policy Studies, a Tallahassee-based think tank that specializes in issues facing state governments, and is a member of Governor Jeb Bush's Council of Economic Advisors. He is the author of ten books and more than 100 articles published in academic and professional journals. His primary areas of research are public finance and the economic analysis of public policy issues.

SAMUEL R. STALEY is director of the Urban Futures Program at Reason Public Policy Institute (RPPI), a national think tank based in Los Angeles. Prior to joining RPPI, Dr. Staley was research director for The Buckeye Institute in Columbus, Ohio, an economic development consultant to local government, and full-time economics instructor at Wright State University. Dr. Staley has authored more than 50 articles on urban policy, growth management, and planning issues, including two books. His articles have appeared in the *Journal of the American Planning Association*, *Planning and Markets*, *Planning*, *Urban Land*, and numerous other professional publications. He is the author of the RPPI policy studies *The Sprawling of America: In Defense of the Dynamic City; A Line in the Land: Urban-Growth Boundaries, Smart Growth, and Housing Affordability* (coauthored with Jefferson G. Edgens and Gerard C.S. Mildner), and *The "Vanishing Farmland" Myth and the Smart Growth Agenda*. He is also a member of his local planning board and former chair of his city's Charter Review Commission.

ROBERT BRUEGMANN is an historian of architecture, landscape, and the built environment. He is currently Professor of Art History with appointments in the School of Architecture and the Program in Urban Planning and Policy at the University of Illinois at Chicago. Among his books are a 3-volume catalog titled *Holabird & Roche/Holabird & Root, An Illustrated Catalog of Works* (1991), *The Architects and the City: Holabird & Roche of Chicago 1880–1918* (1997), *Benicia, Portrait of an Early California Town* (1981) and *Modernism at Mid-Century: the Architecture of the United States Military Academy* (1994), which he edited. He has published widely in the history of architecture, urban development, landscape, and planning and historic preservation, and is currently at work on a book on urban sprawl.

WENDELL COX is Principal of Wendell Cox Consultancy, a firm specializing in demographics, transportation, and economic analysis founded in 1985. He has completed dozens of projects for a variety of clients in North America, Europe, Australia, Asia, and Africa. Mr. Cox is a member of the Amtrak Reform Council, having been appointed by the Speaker of the United States House of Representatives in 1999. He also served from 1977 to 1985 on the Los Angeles County Transportation Commission, having been appointed by Mayor Tom Bradley, and served as chair of the commission's service coordination committee. In addition, Mr. Cox has held positions with the National Academy of Science's Transportation Research Board, the Urban Mass Transportation Administration, and the American Public Transit Association. The firm maintains two Internet websites: www.publicpurpose.com and www.demographia.com.

JEFFERSON G. EDGENS is Assistant Professor and Natural Resources Specialist with the Department of Forestry at the University of Kentucky. His main research interests include land use (farmland loss, forestry), watershed management, and water quality. Dr. Edgens is an adjunct scholar with the Georgia Public Policy Foundation and the Mackinac Center for Public Policy in Michigan. His work has appeared in *FORUM for Applied Research and Public Policy, Water Resources IMPACT* (the magazine of the American Water Resources Association), and *Michigan Forward* (the publication of the Michigan Chamber of Commerce). He is co-author (with Samuel R. Staley and Gerard C.S. Mildner) of *A Line in the Land: Urban Growth Boundaries, Smart Growth, and Housing Affordability* (1999) and author of *Managing Suburban Development: Is More Government the Answer?* (1999). His popular articles have appeared in the *Detroit News, The Atlanta Journal, Macon Telegraph, Augusta Chronicle,* and other newspapers. Dr. Edgens is a frequent contributor to *Environment and Climate News*, a monthly publication of the Heartland Institute.

PETER GORDON is a Professor in the University of Southern California's School of Policy, Planning and Development, and in its Department of Economics. He is also currently director of USC's Master of Real Estate Development program. Dr. Gordon's research has been published in most major urban, planning, and transportation research journals, and he is coeditor of *Planning and Markets*, a referred electronic journal. His article "Is LA Style Development a

Desirable Planning Goal?" co-authored with Harry W. Richardson in the *Journal of the American Planning Association* has emerged as one of the most influential essays on metropolitan development patterns during the debate on urban sprawl and Smart Growth. Gordon and his colleagues have developed the Southern California Planning Model which they are now using to calculate the economic costs of major earthquakes and other natural disasters. He has consulted for local, state, and federal agencies; the World Bank; the United Nations; and many private groups.

KENNETH GREEN is Chief Scientist and Director of the Environmental Program at Reason Public Policy Institute (RPPI), a nonprofit, nonpartisan policy research institution headquartered in Los Angeles. Dr. Green's policy research focuses on air quality and environmental risk management. Through his research and writing, Dr. Green seeks to promote environmental risk management strategies that maximize effectiveness and efficiency while preserving the powerful risk-reducing attributes of an open, economically robust society in which waste is minimized, while personal responsibility is closely tied to individual choice.

STEVEN HAYWARD is Senior Fellow and Director of the Center for Environmental and Regulatory Reform at the Pacific Research Institute for Public Policy in San Francisco, where he co-authors *The Index of Leading Environmental Indicators*, released each year on Earth Day. During 1997-98, he was also a visiting fellow at the Heritage Foundation in Washington DC, where he studied urban issues. He has testified about urban sprawl issues before the U.S. Senate Environment and Public Works Committee and the Pennsylvania State Legislature; he has been interviewed on this subject by PBS TV documentary and by "The News Hour with Jim Lehrer." Dr. Hayward writes frequently on a wide range of current topics, including environmentalism, law, economics, and public policy. He has written for *National Review, Reason,* and *Policy Review,* and his newspaper articles have appeared in *The New York Times,* the *Wall Street Journal,* the *Baltimore Sun,* the *San Francisco Chronicle,* the *Chicago Tribune,* and dozens of other daily newspapers. The paperback edition of his business book, *Churchill on Leadership: Executive Success in the Face of Adversity* was released in October 1998. He is currently working on a major book, *The Age of Reagan: A Chronicle of the Closing Decades of the American Century.*

ROGER E. MEINERS is Professor of Law and Economics at the University of Texas at Arlington and a Senior Associate of the Political Economy Research Center in Bozeman, Montana. Meiners has also been a professor at Texas A&M University, Emory University, and Clemson University, and was Atlanta Regional Director for the Federal Trade Commission. He has been a visiting professor at universities in France, Guatemala, and Italy. His research focuses on common law and market solutions to environmental issues and on the economics of higher education. Meiners serves on the board of the Roe Foundation and Consumer Alert and has published several books, including *Taking the Envi-*

ronment Seriously (with Bruce Yandle) and *Who Owns the Environment?* (with P.J. Hill), and has published in various popular and scholarly journals.

GERARD C.S. MILDNER is Assistant Professor of Urban Studies and Planning at Portland State University in Oregon and an academic advisor to the Cascade Policy Institute, an independent public policy think tank based in Portland. His work has been published in journals such as *Transportation Quarterly* and *Land Economics*, and he is the co-author of *Scarcity by Design: The Legacy of New York's Housing Policies* (1992). In addition, Dr. Mildner has published policy studies on the efficiency of light rail, taxicab regulation in the United States, growth boundaries, and the role of stadium owners on sports franchise mobility. His research focuses on the economics of local government, including land-use planning, growth management, housing policy, transportation, and professional sports and public policy.

ANDREW P. MORRISS is Associate Dean for Academic Affairs and Professor of Law at Case Western Reserve University, Cleveland, Ohio, and Senior Associate at the Political Economy Research Center in Bozeman, Montana. Professor Morriss has published widely on topics including property rights, environmental issues, employment law, law and economics, and empirical analysis of the legal system. His recent publications have appeared in the *New York University Law Review*, the *Ecology Law Quarterly*, *Environmental Law*, and the *Land & Water Law Review*. He teaches property, environmental economics, and administrative law at Case Western Reserve University.

ROBERT W. POOLE, JR. is founder of the Reason Foundation and Director of Transportation Studies at its Reason Public Policy Institute. Prior to founding the Reason Foundation, Mr. Poole was editor and publisher of *Reason* magazine and an aerospace engineer. His book, *Cutting Back City Hall* (1980), is widely acknowledged as a seminal work in privatizing public service provision, effectively launching the contemporary privatization trend. His 1988 Reason Foundation policy paper on private toll roads as congestion relievers directly inspired California's 1989 private tollway law, subsequently emulated in 14 other states. He has advised both the federal and California departments of transportation during the 1990s. He served on the Caltrans Privatization Advisory Steering Committee in 1990 and was a member of California's Commission on Transportation Investment in 1995-96. His work on transportation policy has included airport privatization, commercialization of air traffic control, congestion pricing, and public-private partnership models for highway development.

HARRY W. RICHARDSON is the Irvine Chair of Urban and Regional Planning in the School of Policy, Planning, and Development at the University of Southern California. His research fields include metropolitan spatial structure, travel behavior, land-use controls, economic impact models, natural disasters, and international urban development. He is the author of more than 20 books and more than 150 research papers. He has consulted for the World Bank, the United Nations, U.S. AID, and other international, national, and local agencies.